Worthy and Unworthy

How the Media Reports on Friends and Foes

Worthy and Unworthy

How the Media Reports on
Friends and Foes

Devan Hawkins

IFF
BOOKS

London, UK
Washington, DC, USA

CollectiveInk

First published by iff Books, 2024
iff Books is an imprint of Collective Ink Ltd.,
Unit 11, Shepperton House, 89 Shepperton Road, London, N1 3DF
office@collectiveinkbooks.com
www.collectiveinkbooks.com
www.iff-books.com

For distributor details and how to order please visit the 'Ordering' section on our website.

ISBN: 978 1 80341 543 7
978 1 80341 605 2 (ebook)
Library of Congress Control Number: 2023940545

A CIP catalogue record for this book is available from the British Library.

Design: Lapiz Digital Services

UK: Printed and bound by CPI Group (UK) Ltd, Croydon, CR0 4YY
Printed in North America by CPI GPS partners

We operate a distinctive and ethical publishing philosophy in all areas of our business, from our global network of authors to production and worldwide distribution.

Contents

Introduction

In the predawn hours of April 3, 1948, rebels assembled on the slopes of Mount Hallasan, a volcano that is located at the center of Jeju Island. On that highest peak in South Korea, the rebels lit fires that were meant to signal the start of armed resistance against both the occupation of South Korea by the United States and in support of the reunification of Korea, which had been divided in half since the end of the World War II. This uprising was preceded by previous incidents in which police fatally fired on protesters.[1]

In a letter sent to residents of the island, the rebels wrote:

Fellow citizens! Respectable parents and siblings! Today, on this day of April 3, your sons, daughters, and little brothers and sisters rose up in arms for the reunification and independence of our homeland, and for the complete liberation of the people. We must risk our lives for the opposition to the betrayal of the country and the unilateral election and government. We rose up in arms against the brutal slaughter done by American cannibals that force you into hardship and unhappiness. To vent your deep-rooted rancor we rouse up in arms. You should defend us who fight for the victory of our country and should rise up along with us, responding to the call of the country and its people.

Over the course of the next day, these rebels would launch attacks on police outposts and on other locations thought to contribute to repression on the island.

This was the beginning of the Jeju Uprising. Following failed negotiations with police, additional troops would be sent to the island to crush the rebellion. During the next several months, periodic fighting would continue between rebels on the island

and Korean forces. Following an incident where members of the South Korean military sent to the island mutinied and killed many of their commanders, dictator Syngman Rhee declared martial law. As part of the military's efforts to end the rebellion, horrific incidents including the destruction of entire villages, mass rape, and the massacre of thousands of civilians occurred. Reports of the number of dead vary significantly from a low of 15,000 to a high of 65,000. The vast majority of civilian deaths were the responsibility of South Korean security forces. Tens of thousands fled from Jeju to Japan to escape the violence. Three hundred villages and tens of thousands of houses were destroyed.

If you were a dedicated reader of *The New York Times*—the paper which declares on its front page that it publishes "All the News That's Fit to Print"—during the Jeju Uprising you would know very little about the horrors that transpired on Jeju Island in 1948 and 1949. Using the *Times* search database, I only identified eight articles that discussed Jeju (then rendered as Cheju) for the entirety of 1948 and 1949. All of these articles were fairly short reports, appearing in the newspaper's back pages. Many of them focused on the activities of the rebels:

Communists on Cheju Attack Villages—Demand Police Surrender, No Election
Constabulary Chief on Cheju Shot While Sleeping
Snipers Fire at U.S. Plane At Airport in South Korea

As well as alleged involvement by the Soviet Union:

Soviet Submarines Said To Help Reds in Korea

In the last article identified about Jeju, on April 1949, the *Times* devoted less than 50 words to publishing a United Press report about "1,193 Koreans Slain on Cheju" and the thousands more left homeless. The report makes no mention of responsibility for those dead, despite the fact that the vast majority of civilians were killed by the South Korean military. The number reported as being killed is an underestimate, at least by a factor of ten.

On the same day that last report about Jeju was published by the *Times*, a story appeared in the *Times* about the Berlin Airlift, an operation led by the United States and United Kingdom to supply West Berlin (an exclave of the United States-allied West Germany) with supplies after it had been blockaded by the Soviet-allied East Germany, which surrounded it. The period of the blockade and the airlift that followed almost perfectly matched with the period of the Jeju Uprising. During this period, there were over a hundred articles describing the blockade and the airlift that followed, many featured on the front page of the *Times*.

There are numerous reasons why the Berlin Airlift likely received more attention than the uprising and massacre on Jeju Island. Berlin is located in the center of Europe, while Jeju is a relatively remote island in East Asia. However, a year after the Jeju Uprising when the Chinese Communists captured Hainan, another remote island in East Asia, from the Chinese Nationalists, the *Times* published dozens of articles about the operation, suggesting that remoteness does not make significant reporting impossible.

Berlin was also seen as the frontline of the Cold War, while in the years before the Korean War, the Korean Peninsula was often treated as a periphery issue. However, during the period of the Jeju Uprising, the *Times* published hundreds of stories about Korea, many of which focused on infiltration of communists from the north into the south. Furthermore, the United States was already heavily invested in Korea, having occupied the southern half of the peninsula since the end of

World War II. At the time of the uprising, there were thousands of US troops in Korea. Indeed, a report from the South Korean government published decades after the uprising found that the United States shared responsibility for the military operations on Jeju Island.[2]

The role that disregard for non-Europeans might play in the dearth of coverage should also be considered. Jeju Islanders, unlike Berliners, were East Asians and, therefore, potentially less sympathetic in the minds of some readers of the *Times*. To compare Jeju Island to another contemporaneous issue in Europe, the final operation of the Greek Civil War, which occurred a few months after the conclusion of the Jeju Uprising, received more coverage in one month than the Jeju Uprising received in a whole year. The fact that the Greek Civil War involved Europeans may have been a factor in this higher level of coverage.

There is another possible cause for the general lack of coverage of the Jeju Uprising: geopolitics. Berliners were a sympathetic population who were being oppressed by the new official enemy of the United States—the Soviet Union. In contrast, the people of Jeju Island were the victims of a regime that had been put into place and supported by the United States with the goal of preventing the spread of Soviet-aligned communism.

Stated another way, the people of Berlin were worthy victims and the people of Jeju Island were unworthy victims.

This formulation of Worthy and Unworthy victims was first developed by Edward Herman and Noam Chomsky in their seminal book *Manufacturing Consent*. As they wrote:

Our prediction is that the victims of enemy states will be found "worthy" and will be subject to more intense and indignant coverage than those victimized by the United States or its

4

clients, who are implicitly "unworthy." Put another way, the media will be more likely to portray the victims of actions of official-state enemies in unfavorable terms, while portraying the victims of allies in more favorable terms.

In the book Herman and Chomsky go on to show how crimes committed in client states of the Soviet Union received far more attention than crimes in client states of the United States. For example, the murder of Catholic Polish priest Jerzy Popieluszko "not only received far more coverage than Archbishop Oscar Romero, murdered in the U.S. client-state El Salvador in 1980; he was given more coverage than the aggregate of one hundred religious victims killed in U.S. client states, although eight of those victims were U.S. citizens."[3] Herman and Chomsky's book has been influential in how the US media and Western media are viewed more broadly, with writers like Robert McChesney, John Nicholas, and Alan MacLeod expanding on the work.

This formulation of "Worthy and Unworthy victims" is part of Herman and Chomsky's larger Propaganda Model, which postulates that "the media serve, and propagandize on behalf of, the powerful societal interests that control and finance them. The representatives of these interests have important agendas and principles that they want to advance, and they are well positioned to shape and constrain media policy. This is normally not accomplished by crude intervention, but by the selection of right-thinking personnel and by the editors' and working journalists' internalization of priorities and definitions of newsworthiness that conform to the institution's policy."[4]

Herman and Chomsky's argument is compelling and provocative because it argues that despite the fact that media in the United States is not state-run and press freedom is generally protected in the country, the media still serves a similar purpose as it did in the Soviet Union and other countries where media is predominately state-run and where journalists do not have the same press freedom protections.

To explain their Propaganda Model, Herman and Chomsky proposed that there are five filters that tend to restrict media coverage in Western countries, particularly the United States. These filters are:

Ownership: Media companies are mostly large corporations with the fundamental imperative to make a profit. These companies are disincentivized from covering topics that may threaten their profit.

Advertising: In a similar way, almost all media companies are dependent on advertising for their revenue. Therefore, media companies are also disincentivized from covering topics that may lose them advertisers.

Sourcing: Media outlets frequently use official, government sources for their information. These sources will tend to reflect the biases of the government.

Flak: Individuals who provide dissenting viewpoints will often face concerted campaigns to discredit them. These campaigns will make journalists less likely to decide to cover stories that may result in such flak, including those that may portray allies of the United States in a negative light.

Anti-Communism/Fear: Reporting will often play into the fears of official enemies (Communists during the Cold War, Islamic Terrorism during the War on Terror, etc.). Playing into these fears will often mean that official state enemies will receive more coverage.

Together, these filters create a situation where even in a country, like the United States, with relatively few state controls on the media, reporting will tend to reflect the official standpoint of the government.

This tendency for reporting to reflect the standard positions of the government is seen most powerfully in foreign affairs.

Unlike domestic issues, where there is at least some daylight between the two major parties, with respect to foreign policy there is much less difference in foreign affairs. While the language used and the particular issues emphasized will often be different, the fundamental positions of both Democrats and Republicans do not tend to differ substantially. For example, if you compare each party's platforms[5,6] before the 2016 election (in 2020 the Republicans did not adopt a new platform, not allowing for a direct comparison) with respect to Venezuela, Iran, Israel, China, and Russia, you generally see only minor differences. This book will try to make the argument that this same general uniformity in political perspectives about foreign affairs is reflected in media coverage in the United States.

Methods of the Book

In the pages that follow, I present case studies in how media coverage in the United States differs according to whether the country is a geopolitical ally of the United States or not. While designing these cases studies, I endeavored to carefully select comparable cases. Of course, the world is not a controlled experiment in a laboratory. So there will be differences in the cases that are chosen. In each case, I discuss these differences and their likely contribution to different coverage.

The comparisons have both a quantitative and qualitative component. For all of the events considered, I will first compare the amount of coverage received, meaning the number of pieces (reporting, opinions, videos, etc.) published. The qualitative component will focus on the nature of that coverage such as the framing of the stories and the sources for the stories. Based on Herman and Chomsky's model, it would be predicted that more coverage would be given to events occurring in state enemies compared to similar events in countries that are not state enemies or are allies and that the coverage of state enemies will be more negative and, as Herman and Chomsky write, "more intense and indignant."

While the quantitative component is an objective fact with the numeric comparison only being limited by the fact that I may not capture all of the relevant pieces in my review, the qualitative component is subjective. I will try to make my argument about the qualitative nature of the coverage as clear as possible with direct references and quotes from the pieces. However, I encourage all readers to review at least some of the coverage on their own and see if their assessment is similar to mine.

My analysis focuses specifically on reporting from *The New York Times*. I have chosen to focus on the *Times* for several reasons. First, the *Times* is frequently considered the "newspaper of record" in the United States. Meaning that its accounts of events will be an important part of documentary history of those events. Second, despite cutbacks that have occurred in foreign reporting in the newspaper industry, the *Times* still has substantial reporters stationed overseas and therefore would be expected to provide more coverage of stories in other countries compared to other outlets regardless of whether the events fall into the worthy or unworthy categories. Third, despite the fact that traditional media outlets have seemingly declined in their importance, *Times* reporting is still an important part of the national conversation about current events. The website of the *Times* is the most visited news website.[7] It is also among the most engaged with news sites on social media, such as Facebook.[8] Finally, the *Times* is often portrayed as a liberal (or even left-wing) media outlet. In such outlets you would expect criticism of US foreign policy and skepticism about criticism of US state enemies to be higher. Therefore, using the *Times* coverage as opposed to an outlet that is perceived as more right leaning (such as *The Wall Street Journal*) would mean that you would expect the *Times* to be more critical of US allies and therefore their coverage would be less likely to conform to the worthy/unworthy hypothesis or, at least, not conform to the hypothesis as much other outlets.

However, focus on a single newspaper does have limitations. Media engagement is higher for other non-newspaper media outlets (such as *CNN* and *Fox News*), so the *Times* is not the most important driver of news conversations. In the appendix, I provide a summary of the coverage in quantitative terms given by other notable news organizations to the events discussed in this book.

I do not presume to know what the correct amount of media coverage is. I am not a journalist. I have never worked for a media company. I am a news consumer. There are a lot of factors that will impact coverage given to an individual topic. However, when coverage is different between two similar stories, it is important to investigate why there is that difference. In a similar way, I do not seek to argue that any story should have received less coverage. Even if the media does tend to focus on the crimes of official state enemies more than those of allies, that does not mean that the crimes of enemies should not receive coverage or are not important. While I will argue that often the coverage of crimes of state enemies tends to be used for harmful purposes that does not mean that the stories should be ignored. Instead it means that we should critically examine how the stories are being used. Encouraging such critical thinking about medica coverage is one of the goals of this book.

I also do not intend to suggest that the media is lying or covering stories up. Journalism, especially foreign affairs journalism, is hard work. I respect the reporters doing this work. Although in some instances I will critique aspects of reporting of certain stories, I do not intend this as a blanket attack on the reporting itself.

It may be tempting to view the Herman and Chomsky Propaganda Model and the formulation of Worthy and Unworthy victims as an anachronism. When Herman and Chomsky were writing in the 1980s the media landscape was very different. The Internet was still unheard of by most people. There was no cable news. No social media existed. However, even in this modern age of Facebook, YouTube, and Twitter, much of what is shared on these platforms is still traditional reporting and therefore the perspectives offered in these other media outlets will be impacted by the traditional reporting.

For better or worse, our views about the world, even those among us who try to think as independently as possible, are at least partially products of the media that we consume. This impact will be especially seen in foreign policy because most of us will not have intimate personal experiences with the countries covered. This effect of media on public sentiments has consequences. Public favorability of foreign countries in the United States will often track with coverage given to particular stories.[9] These shifts in public opinion can then make it easier for politicians to push for actions against these countries be it increased military spending, embargos, or war. In a similar way, when the crimes of allies receive less attention, it can make it less likely for the United States to stop supporting those crimes. By critically examining this coverage, hopefully we can begin to understand how this coverage is used for political purposes.

Chapter 1

Worthy and Unworthy Memories

Even among the long list of atrocities in the twentieth century, the near total destruction of the Jewish people of Europe during World War II stands out for its brutality. The Nazi Holocaust has become a yardstick against which other atrocities are often compared. It is a reminder of the capabilities of humans for evil and for others to ignore that evil. It is, fortunately, something that is taught throughout schools in the United States. Thousands of books have been written about it. It has been the topic of Oscar winning films.

For many, it would be hard to believe that this was not always the case. While the horrors of the Nazis' actions during the war were rumored and the true scale of those atrocities became clear as Soviet, American, and other Allied troops liberated the camps, discussion of the Holocaust was not always the most welcome topic in the years after the war ended. In his memoir, Raul Hilberg, the author of one of the earliest comprehensive histories of the Holocaust, *The Destruction of the European Jews*, describes the prevailing view of the Holocaust when he began his research in the 1950s:

on the whole I was engaged in a lone endeavor. In the prevailing atmosphere, which drew attention of American Jews to Israel and the Arabs, and which directed thinking of Americans as a whole to the cold war with the Soviet Union, my subject was relegated to the past. This was the time when those—like survivors—who were plagued by memories, were told to forget what had happened, and when the Nuremberg trials were conducted not so much to understand

Germany's history as to conclude unfinished business in order that Germany might be reconstituted with a clean slate in the North Atlantic community of nations confronted with the threat of communism. Under these circumstances I was reluctant to mention my preoccupation in conversations with strangers.[1]

If the memory of an atrocity as destructive as the Holocaust can be ignored for political reasons, it is not hard to imagine that memories of more recent events can be ignored in much the same way and how past events that occurred in geopolitical enemies may be emphasized. In this chapter, we will examine how the *Times* has focused on the memory of one particular tragedy—the Tiananmen Square Protests and crackdown in Beijing in 1989—and has mostly ignored the memories of other comparable tragedies—the Gwangju Uprising in South Korea in 1980, the Caracazo protest and crackdown in Venezuela in 1989, and the Gujarat riots in India in 2002. In particular, I will focus on discussing how these events were covered on their anniversaries one, two, five, ten, 20, and 30 years after the events occurred. The hypothesis of this chapter is that the events in Tiananmen Square—a "worthy memory"—will receive more coverage compared to these other events—"unworthy memories." To cast as wide of a net as possible, an anniversary is defined broadly to include a two month period, with the anniversary of the events themselves falling roughly in the middle.

Background

Tiananmen Square, 1989
There was a very long lead-up to the protests in Tiananmen Square. They were launched after the April 15th death of former Communist Party General Secretary Hu Yaobang, who was

seen by many in China as a reformer who had been wrongfully forced out of his position by party leadership, including Paramount Leader Deng Xiaoping. The commemoration of Hu quickly grew and eventually morphed into a call for greater liberalization of the country. Motivated by discontent, especially as it related to inflation brought about by recent market reforms and party corruption, the protests grew. Protesters felt spurned by the Chinese Premier Li Peng's refusal to meet with them and an editorial in the April 26th edition of the *People's Daily*, which labelled the protests as being antigovernment. The protests became more serious as a number of students began hunger strikes. The situation was exacerbated by a visit from then General Secretary of the Soviet Union's Communist Party Mikhail Gorbachev as part of a thawing in Sino-Soviet relations following the decades' long split between the two communist powers. The protests were so severe that Gorbachev could not be welcomed in Tiananmen Square as planned. Many members of the international press came to cover the meeting, but soon turned their attention to the ongoing protests in the Chinese capital.

While the representatives from the central government did meet with protests and provided food and other support to try to soften relations, the protests grew as they gained support from students from other parts of the country, some labor unions, and many citizens in the capital. Seeing dim prospects for a resolution to the protests, the Chinese government declared martial law on May 20th, with People's Liberation Army (PLA) troops, most of whom were unarmed, entering the city. After orders were given to clear the protesters from Beijing, the troops began to clash with protesters. Eventually live ammunition was used. The estimated number of fatalities, the vast majority of which were protesters, has varied but is generally believed to be between the low hundreds and low thousands. Contrary to popular perception, there were few to no deaths in Tiananmen Square itself with most deaths occurring in surrounding areas of the city. Following a negotiation between the PLA troops, any weapons held by protesters in the square were surrendered and most left the square.

Gwangju, 1980

Although it has sometimes been referred to as "Korea's Tiananmen Square," the protest and subsequent deadly crackdown that occurred in Gwangju in southwest South Korea occurred nearly a decade before. The protests that preceded the Gwangju uprising started following the 1979 assassination of South Korean dictator Park Chung-Hee who had been ruling the country for the previous 18 years. These protests extended across the whole country, but they were particularly fierce in the South Jeolla Province where Gwangju is located.

In late May the protests began to grow in size. South Korean soldiers were sent to Gwangju to end the uprising. These soldiers have been accused of starting the violence when they beat and possibly bayonetted protesters. The use of live fire began on May 20th, when some protesters were shot near Gwangju station. Protesters began to fight back more forcefully against soldiers. Some protesters were able to secure arms for their resistance. The city was then blockaded. Several committees were established to negotiate with the military for an end to the fighting. These committees unsuccessfully tried to encourage the protesters to disarm. After these negotiations failed, the military fully retook the city on May 27th.

As with the events in Beijing, estimates for the number that were killed during the protests and crackdown vary. The government at the time estimated that fewer than 200 civilians were killed. Other estimates have suggested that the full death toll was between 1000 and 2000. Twenty-two soldiers were killed, many by friendly fire.

Caracazo, 1989

The Caracazo protests and crackdown occurred between February and March 1989, a few months before the event in Beijing the same year. The name for the protest itself is meant to reflect the fact the events took place in the Venezuelan capital of Caracas. The protests were sparked by the policies of then President Carlos Andrés Pérez, from the center-left Democratic Action party. During his first term, Pérez had a reputation for maintaining social spending, despite falling oil prices, Venezuela's main source of revenue, in the late 1980s. He was reelected in 1988 on the promise of maintaining these policies.

However, after this election Pérez launched a period of economic liberalization of the Venezuelan economy based on recommendations from the International Monetary Fund. These reforms followed a standard neoliberal line and included privatization of state enterprises and tax reform. One of the most controversial policies was the reduction in fuel subsidies leading to increases in the cost of transportation, including public transportation.

Protests about these policies quickly spread around Venezuela, but were particularly intense in the capital of Caracas and surrounding cities and towns. In many cases, these protests led to rioting in which businesses were destroyed. A state of emergency was soon declared and the military began acting to suppress the protest. In some cases, protesters fired on soldiers. Officially it was declared that 276 had died during the crackdown, but it has been estimated that the true number killed may be as high as 2000.

Gujarat, 2002

The most recent event considered in this chapter is the Gujarat riots of 2002. The Gujarat riots were sparked by a burning of a train carrying Hindu pilgrims returning from Ayodhya, an important pilgrimage site in India. In response to the train burning, which was blamed on Muslims, weeks of targeted violence started throughout the province of Gujarat, especially in the capital city of Ahmedabad. This violence included violent attacks, rapes, and house burnings. Future Indian Prime Minister Narendra Modi of the Hindu nationalist Bharatiya Janata Party (BJP), who was then Chief Minister of Gujarat, faced accusations of facilitating the violence both through instructing police not to intervene and through providing the addresses of Muslim residences. There were also cases of Muslims killing Hindus. Official numbers have reported hundreds killed during the riots, most of whom were Muslims. Other sources estimate that over 2000 may have been killed during the riots. Multiple sources have referred to the riots as an example of state ethnic cleansings.

The Numbers

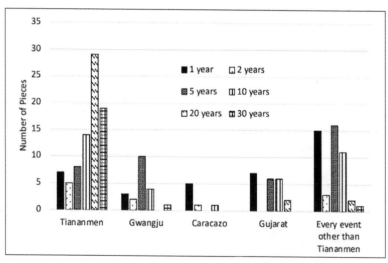

Figure 1. Coverage of the anniversaries of selected historical events by anniversary number (first, second, fifth, tenth, twentieth, and thirtieth)

Figure 1 shows the coverage of the four events discussed in this chapter on the first, second, fifth, tenth, twentieth, and thirtieth anniversaries of their occurrence. The anniversary of Tiananmen Square almost universally gets more coverage than other events. When making comparisons based on the number of years since the event occurred, there is only one exception to this pattern: Gwangju had two more articles that discussed the protests and crackdown on the fifth anniversary compared to the fifth anniversary of Tiananmen. Additionally, Gujarat had the same number of articles on its first anniversary as Tiananmen and only one fewer article on its fifth anniversary. It should be noted that in the case of the Gwangju articles, I included articles that made any reference to the events. In most cases, the articles were about other issues and made brief references to the protests and crackdown.

In all cases, except for Tiananmen, coverage declined after the fifth anniversary of the event. In contrast, coverage of Tiananmen's anniversary increased, doubling between the tenth and twentieth anniversaries, and remained higher than the first from the tenth to thirtieth. In the case of Caracazo there was no mention on the twentieth and thirtieth anniversaries. Gwangju was not mentioned at all on its twentieth anniversary and mentioned only once on its thirtieth anniversary.

Based purely on the numbers, it is clear that the memory of Tiananmen, especially in more recent years, has been emphasized by the *Times*. In the next sections, we will discuss the specific differences in this coverage and factors that might account for more attention being given to Tiananmen.

The Coverage

Tiananmen Square, 1989

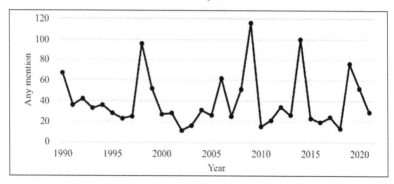

Figure 2. Any mention of "Tiananmen" in The New York Times *between May 1ˢᵗ and June 30ᵗʰ, 1990 and 2021*

Figure 2 shows any mention of the word Tiananmen between May 1ˢᵗ and June 30ᵗʰ by year between 1990 and 2021. These results do not filter out references to Tiananmen that were not related to the event of 1989, but are rather presented to give an overall impression of the rhythm of coverage. As can be seen, references to Tiananmen have not reduced much as the events of 1989 have left the realm of current events and entered the realm of history as happened with the other events covered in this chapter, but there is a rhythm to this coverage. While coverage did decline through the 1990s, it spiked in 1998, which was then followed by spikes on the twentieth (2009), twenty-fifth (2014), and thirtieth (2019) anniversaries.

On the first anniversary of the 1989 protests in 1990, there were seven pieces published discussing them. An opinion article appearing in early May castigated the George H.W. Bush administration perceived unwillingness to challenge the government in Beijing. Despite setbacks following the events in Tiananmen Square, this was still the period of "opening up" where US administrations were enticed with the potential of the Chinese market.[2] This follows a pattern in that the volume of coverage (if not necessarily their tone) would increase as China evolved from a potential economic partner to a competitor in the minds of politicians over the next thirty years. Another piece connected the liberal democracy movement in China to similar movements that had succeeded in Hungary and other Soviet-aligned republics in the months following the events in Tiananmen.[3]

The first piece of reporting from Nicholas Kristof who was in Beijing during the protests and crackdown, published on the exact date of the anniversary of the crackdown (June 3rd), focused on the identity of the infamous "Tank Man" who is shown in a well-known picture standing in front of a line of tanks exiting Tiananmen Square on June 5th. In the article, Kristof casts doubt on some of the higher estimates of the numbers killed. For example, about the claim of 2700 dead Kristof writes:

The problem with these higher estimates is that they are difficult to reconcile with specific figures from hospitals, obtained from doctors who in many cases were appalled by the killings and had no reason to cover up the scale of what happened. Over the last 12 months, various doctors, in disclosures not authorized by the authorities, provided figures for 11 hospitals, including most hospitals in the area where the worst killing took place. Those figures suggest a lower total of perhaps 400 to 800 people killed, with perhaps 5,000 injured.[4]

Subsequent reports focused on commemorations of the events in Hong Kong,[5] a late night/early morning protest in Beijing,[6] and statements about human rights in China from officials in the US, including President Bush.[7]

Coverage reached its lowest level on the second anniversary of the Tiananmen Crackdown in 1991. The first piece published that year was a long article by Kristof describing the escape of a protester Liu Xiang from Beijing to Hong Kong and then New York after being imprisoned for his role in the protests.[8] Two other articles detailed Beijing students spreading leaflets to encourage commemoration of the protests and small scale protests on the actual anniversary date.[9,10] Echoing themes from the previous year, a letter to the editor criticized President Bush for not being critical enough of the Chinese government.[11]

On the fifth anniversary of the protests in 1994, the first two articles published in May discussed the release of dissident Chen Ziming, a participant in the 1989 protests, on medical parole.[12] This move and a similar move to allow another dissident Yu Haocheng a passport to leave the country was portrayed in light of the Chinese government's effort to improve financial ties with the United States:

> Even if releasing Wang Juntao and Chen Ziming involves a great risk for the Chinese government, today's action shows that the Chinese Government is willing to take this risk in order to win renewal of its low tariff privileges in the American market.[13]

Another article dealt with the efforts of the wife of Bao Tong to get him released from prison. Bao was a close associate of former General Secretary of the Communist Party Zhao Ziyang, who lost his position and spent the rest of his life under house arrest due the perception that he had acted too sympathetically to the protest movement.[14] Bao would only be released in the late nineties. A similar article detailed efforts of student protesters to reverse the labelling of the 1989 protests as "riot and counter-revolutionary rebellion." Reflecting the sentiment at the time that perspective about the protests may have been changing, the article quotes then Paramount Leader Jiang Zemin as saying that the protests were "a bad thing that has been turned into a good thing ... As a result, our reform and opening-up program has forged ahead with steadier, better and even quicker steps, and our advantages have been brought into fuller play."[15]

Much like during the Bush administration, articles were written criticizing President Clinton as being too subservient to the Chinese government and ignoring human rights in the country.[16] Another article detailed the unveiling of a replica of the "Goddess of Democracy" statue, a famous symbol of the protests, in San Francisco. The article quotes Nancy Pelosi, a then seven year congressperson and a consistent critic of China, as saying:

The world witnessed the brutal suppression of individual freedom and liberty in Tiananmen Square. The brave men and women who demonstrated did so in the spirit of our forefathers. They quoted Thomas Jefferson, and built a Goddess of Democracy fashioned after our own Statue of Liberty.[17]

In the final coverage in 1994, an article described the Chinese government's efforts to prevent commemoration of the events of 1989. The article reflects a seeming sentiment of the time that memories of the events and their political relevance were seeming to fade:

Gladdened by President Clinton's decision last week to stop linking China's human rights performance to its $30 billion in exports to America, Communist Party leaders are hoping to pass the anniversary weekend without incident.

Today the national flags of China and Cambodia lined the Avenue of Eternal Peace, which crosses Tiananmen Square, in honor of a state visit by King Norodom Sihanouk of

Cambodia. In a gesture underlining China's goal to convey a determined normalcy, President Jiang Zemin ceremoniously greeted the King on the square on Friday.[18]

Coverage increased on the tenth anniversary of the protests in 1999. The first article from June 1, 1999 focused on the efforts of activists in China and outside of the country to have Chinese leaders, particularly former Premier Li Peng, held responsible for what happened in June 1989.[19] On June 3, the *Times* published an opinion article by Jonathan Mirsky describing his firsthand experience of the violence during the protests.[20] The *Times* also reported on more openness to discussing the events of 1989 in Chinese official state organs, reporting on an editorial that was published the *People's Daily* that declared that the government's actions in 1989 ensured "national independence, dignity, security and stability and insured the sustained, healthy development of economic reforms and opening to the outside world." The article also detailed state efforts to prevent wide discussion of Tiananmen Square.[21] The *Times* also produced teaching material about the protests as part of an effort titled "The Learning Network." The module—"Riot, Revolution and Reform"—includes reading and sample questions about the protests for students from grades 6 to 12.[22]

Coverage from 1999 also discussed how memories from 1989 seemed to be fading including the general lack of commemoration in Beijing and other parts of China, lack of public discussion of the events, and reflections from exiled protest leaders and dissidents.[23,24,25,26] The reporting also reflected the seeming recession of the events of 1989 from an important political question to a historical one. One article covered the perennial question of exactly how many people died in June 1989.[27] The *Times* also reported about how large-scale protests persisted in Hong Kong, which came under Chinese control in 1997.[28]

In some of this reporting the prospect that China was changing not only economically but also politically was described:

> The taboo regarding June 4 sits uncomfortably in a country whose opinionated citizens now debate environmental pollution, corruption and foreign trade. China today is richer, less ideological and more pluralistic, and it offers many more opportunities to its citizens.

Some suggested that the tendency to move on may not be entirely bad: "I think that June 4 is an event that should be left to history to judge," said a 34-year-old man who uses the English name Andy. "There are disagreements here that will be unresolved for 10 or 20 years. And until then we should do what we can do in the present circumstances and not provoke a crisis."[29] During Bill Clinton's commemoration of the tenth anniversary he was quoted as arguing that expanded trade with China would be a "force for change."[30]

However, some pieces lamented the fact that politicians seemed more interested in securing further business ties with China rather than challenging their human rights record. One article in particular seemed to regret that politicians were not more bellicose in their rhetoric: "Senator John McCain, a Republican candidate for President, wants troops used to achieve military victory against Serbia, but does not seem interested in even partial political victory in China—no bombs, no troops needed, just democratic conviction."[31] This article appeared less than one month after US bombs had killed three Chinese journalists in Belgrade, Serbia during NATO's fierce bombing campaign in Yugoslavia.

The 20th anniversary in 2009 corresponded to the year with the most coverage (figures 1 and 2). As with previous years, much of this coverage focused on reporting about the experience of players in the events of 1989 including the arrest of a former student protest leader, Zhou Yongjun, who was accused of entering China on a false travel document[32] and the publication of excerpts from former Premier Zhao Ziyang's memoir where he discussed the events of 1989.[33,34,35] The coverage of Zhou's arrest was notable for revealing how the number of imprisoned Tiananmen protesters had dwindled in recent years:

> The [Dui Hua] foundation ... said it believed that about 30 people remained in jail, down from the 50 to 60 prisoners it had previously reported. The group lowered its estimate after Chinese officials notified it of the early release of several former protesters, and other researchers documented the status of 104 demonstrators who had been jailed in Beijing No. 2 Prison after the June 4 crackdown. All but six of those prisoners have been released.[36]

As with past anniversaries, the *Times* covered the fading of memories of the protests. One particularly well-reported article focused on students and faculty at Peking University. The article summarized the sentiments at the university in this way:

> disinclined to protest, but also lacking the economic grievances that helped ignite protests in 1989; proud of China's achievements and flocking to the Communist Party, but seldom driven by ideology.[37]

On May 30th, this theme of fading memories was made explicitly with the publication of four reminiscences from people about the events of 1989. These articles are complemented with four consecutive images of the famous Tank Man photo slowly fading away.[38,39,40,41] Later an over 2500 word report would discuss the history of the photo.[42]

Closer to the actual date of the crackdown, coverage was given to discussion of the events of 1989 in the Chinese government-funded, English language paper *Global Times*,[43] protests held in Hong Kong[44,45] and India,[46] and censorship efforts by the Chinese government,[47] including blocking access to the then new Twitter.[48] A video was posted showing the actual security measures in the square.[49]

There were many reminiscences of the events published including from a solider who reported that he was in the square and later became an artist,[50] a photographer,[51] and a man who left China before Mao became leader and watched the protests on TV.[52] Contemporary Chinese dissidents also reflected on the current political situation in the country.[53] One reflection about the legacy of the 1989 protests where the writer lamented the fact that he "can no longer watch funny video clips on YouTube" because of the site being blocked included a surprising optimistic conclusion:

So I part company with romantics who say Tiananmen was a noble failure. China may be decades from Westminster-style democracy, and the Communist Party would sooner jump off the top of the new Shanghai World Financial Center (world's tallest building, by some measures) than give up its monopoly on power. But you need only observe the absurd lengths to which official China is going to un-celebrate this anniversary — and suppress all mention of its genesis — to grasp the real verdict of history: The pro-democracy demonstrators may have lost the battle of June 4, but they have won the war for China's future.[54]

Such sentiments likely reflect the odd period of 2009 when Chinese-US relations were generally good, especially in light of China's role in easing the financial impact of the then ongoing recession. Such sentiment was further reflected in a statement issued by then Secretary of State Hillary Clinton published by the *Times* in an article about unsuccessful efforts by protest leader Wu'er Kaixi to turn himself in. The statement, while calling on the Chinese government to "examine openly the darker events of its past and provide a public accounting of those killed, detained or missing, both to learn and to heal," also acknowledged, "a China that has made enormous progress economically, and that is emerging to take its rightful place in global leadership."[55] Such statements from US government officials are hard to imagine now.

Similarly, Kristof, who provides another reminiscence about the protests, noted before discussing challenges in the country:

> many of those rickshaw drivers and bus drivers and others in 1989 were demanding not precisely a parliamentary democracy, but a better life and they got it. The Communist Party has done an extraordinarily good job of managing China's economy and of elevating economically the same people it oppresses politically. Living standards have soared, and people in Beijing may not have the vote, but they do have an infant mortality rate that is 27 percent lower than New York City's.[56]

Much had changed by the 30th anniversary in 2019. In the ten years since 2009, relations between the United States and China had worsened. These difficult relations were reflected in the *Times* coverage. Among the remembrances published in 2019 were a recounting of the events of 1989 by a former People's Liberation Army Lieutenant Jiang Lin,[57] writer Paul Theroux,[58] new photos of the protests,[59,60] a report from a United States student who was studying in Chengdu during the protests,[61] and another piece from Kristof.[62] In an opinion piece from a former imprisoned, now exiled student leader Wang Dan, he described how he had left the square shortly before soldiers arrived after his "proposal to retreat from the square had been overruled by other student leaders," and also discussed the contemporary relevance of the protests:

In a perverse way, President Trump's tough stance against Beijing, despite its unpredictability, is proving effective. Through this trade war, I hope Washington will show the Chinese leadership that the West will not tolerate the use of technology for spying and controlling ordinary citizens.[63]

In another article describing the release of new alleged documents of government discussions during the protests, suddenly China had not changed much from the China of 1989:

The newly published documents lay bare how after the massacre, party leaders quickly set about reinforcing a worldview that casts the party and China as menaced by malign and secretive forces. It is an outlook that continues to shape Chinese politics under Xi Jinping, the party leader facing off with President Trump in a trade war ... Since coming to power in 2012, Mr. Xi has redoubled demands for obedience to himself as the top leader, and entrenched his power in 2018 by abolishing a term limit on the presidency, meaning that he can hold power indefinitely.[64]

A report was published detailing the publication of documents relevant to 1989. The publisher of the documents, Bao Pu, the son of Zhao Ziyang associate, Bao Tong, conformed with the tenor of much of the coverage in 2019.[65] The report described the fear of the publisher about the possibility of being extradited to China following the passage of an extradition law in Hong Kong.

While Tiananmen was mentioned in many instances in the *Times* in June of 2019 (figure 2), especially post June 4th much of this coverage is not described here, because it was primarily focused on the 2019 Hong Kong Protests (see Chapter 2).

Conclusion

Coverage of the anniversary of the Tiananmen Square Protests continues to be extensive. Even twenty and thirty years after they occurred, the *Times* was publishing editorials about the events. In 2019, the coverage was so extensive that the *Times* published a guide to this coverage.[66] Over the six anniversaries covered in this chapter, the *Times* published at least 19 opinion pieces and editorials, in addition to many letters from readers. While coverage was the highest during the 2009 anniversary, it has remained persistently high.

Gwangju, 1980

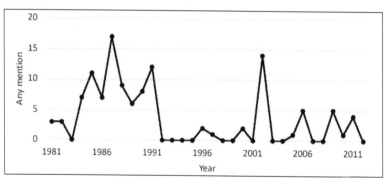

Figure 3. Any mention of "Gwangju" or "Kwangju" in The New York Times *between May 1ˢᵗ and June 30ᵗʰ, 1981 to 2011*

As shown in figure 1, there were three pieces about Gwangju during the first anniversary of the protest and crackdown and two during the second. The highest amount of coverage for the anniversaries considered here was on the fifth anniversary in 1985 when there were ten pieces. In subsequent years the numbers were much lower, with no mentions identified during the 20th in 2000. As shown in figure 3, any mention of Gwangju (whether related to the protest and crackdown or not) followed a similar trend with very few references after the early 1990s. The spike in 2002 is driven by the World Cup that year, which featured matches played in Gwangju.

Among the three pieces published on the first anniversary of the Gwangju protests and crackdown, the first was a three paragraph report about 30 Roman Catholic priests who had gone on a hunger strike to protest the imprisonment of Koreans who had been jailed for their involvement in the events of the previous year. Notably, the article refers only to "last year's violent Kwangju uprising" keeping it ambiguous who was responsible for the most violence—the protesters or the government.[67] A similarly short three paragraph article described protests commemorating the anniversary of the event in which several protesters were arrested.[68]

The second article focused on President Chun Doo-hwan who came to power amidst the protests that led to the events in Gwangju. The article frames its discussion of Chun around the stability that had followed the events of the previous year. The article quotes an unnamed diplomat who is satisfied with this stability and is only concerned about the economy:

"The only sector they have to worry about now is the economy," a Western diplomat said, adding that political opponents, religious dissidents and student militants, "are having trouble getting people to do much." They would "need a Kent State-type situation" in order to stimulate activity, he said, referring to the 1970 incident in which Ohio National Guardsmen killed four persons at an antiwar protest at Kent State University. "Several Days of Riots."[69]

On the second anniversary of the protest and crackdown there were two articles that referenced the events. Both of these references were only tangential. The first described the views of a South Korean dissident—Kim Young-sam—who predicted that the regime of President Chun would soon fall and listed an investigation into the crackdown in Gwangju as a precondition for a transition to democracy.[70] The second article discussed the trial of several South Koreans in the city of Busan who were accused of burning down a United States cultural center. Part of their justification for the arson was to protest the silence of the United States "during the Kwangju uprising when Chun used brute force to solidify his power."[71]

The fifth anniversary had the most coverage of all of the years analyzed in this chapter with a total of ten articles, equal to all of the other years combined. Two of the pieces were letters to the editor commenting on President Chun's recent announcement that he would relinquish power in 1988, three years later. Both articles list the government's crackdown in Gwangju as evidence of the repression of the current Korean government, but the protests are not the focus of the letters.[72,73]

The rest of the discussion of Kwangju in 1985 dealt with a student protest to commemorate the protests. This coverage included initial reporting about a student led demonstration throughout the country, which involved clashes with police and vandalism.[74,75] Later the protest evolved into the occupation of a US government office building in Seoul.[76] The students were motivated by a demand that "the United States apologizes for what they view as American complicity in the suppression of the May 1980 Kwangju uprising" claiming that "the United States commanding officer of the American armed forces, who also serves as operational commander of the South Korean armed forces, authorized South Korean troops to move against demonstrators," a claim which was rejected by a US representative in South Korea.[77] The students later left the office and were arrested along with other students protesting in solidarity with them.[78,79,80,81]

Discussion of Gwangju on the tenth anniversary of the protest and crackdown also focused on protests in the country. These protests included calls for "the ouster of President Roh Tae-woo, a general who helped Chun Doo-hwan, the former President, establish a military rule in 1980." One protester was quoted as saying, "America is all behind this and they're still trying to colonize us."[82] Protests in Gwangju that year escalated to the point that there were 10,000 South Koreans in the street, who the *Times* characterized as having "rampaged" in the city. The protests escalated to the point that police fired warning shots at the crowd.[83] Commentary about the protests that year focused on the "Communist-enforced division" of the country and uneven development experienced in South Korea, with South Cholla province, the location of Gwangju, not developing as rapidly as other parts of the country as reasons for the protests.[84] The final article dealing with Gwangju that year discussed another attack on a symbol of US presence, this time a "newly reopened American Cultural Center" at which "[r]adical students threw hundreds of homemade firebombs."[85]

No coverage was identified on the twentieth anniversary of the protests. On the thirtieth anniversary in 2010, one opinion piece titled "South Korea's Collective Shrug" was published. The piece, which primarily focused on the changing nature of South Korean's relationship with the North, had one paragraph that briefly referenced commemoration of the events of 1980:

Sympathy for Pyongyang is especially widespread in the peninsula's chronically disgruntled southwest, and not just because this farming region profits whenever food aid is sent to the North. Gwangju, the largest city in the region, just commemorated the 30th anniversary of a brutal government massacre of civilian demonstrators, many of whom were defamed in the official news media of the time as North Korean agents.[86]

Conclusion

The Gwangju protests and crackdown received the most coverage during their first five anniversaries. Coverage was limited in later periods. Most of this coverage, especially in the later years, was not focused on the events in Gwangju, but rather mentioned them in the context of other stories from the Korean Peninsula.

Caracazo, 1989

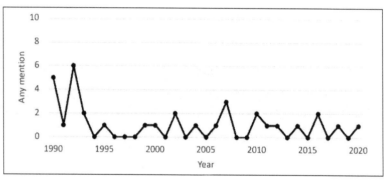

Figure 4. Any mention of "Venezuela," "Riots" and "1990" in The New York Times *between February 1st and March 31st, 1990 and 2021*

As shown in figure 1, Caracazo was mentioned most frequently on its first anniversary in 1990 with a total of five articles. This coverage quickly declined on subsequent anniversaries with only one mention identified on the second and tenth anniversaries and none on the fifth, twentieth, and thirtieth. This pattern is reflected in a search that was done to identify references to the Caracazo in subsequent years (figure 4).

On the one year anniversary of the protests, there were a total of five articles that discussed the protests and crackdown. In most cases, this coverage did not focus on the events, but rather mentioned them in the context of other events, particularly the economic crisis in the country. The first mention was in an article that provided an overview of the economic situation throughout different Latin American countries. In the article, the *Times* framed the protests as being caused by the austerity policies of President Pérez:

> President Carlos Andres Perez largely created the recession with a drive to reshape the state-dominated economy along free-market lines. He has cut subsidies and tariffs, encouraged foreign investment, put state companies up for sale and started talks on debt relief with foreign bankers. One goal is to lure back an estimated $60 billion in capital that has been sent abroad. The austerity required to carry out the changes set off riots in Caracas a year ago in which about 300 people died. An inflation rate of 80 percent also contributed to a poor showing of Mr. Perez's party in 1989 elections. Mr. Perez has sought to soften the blow by creating public works programs and unemployment insurance. A recent rise in oil prices has provided some relief.[87]

A similar perspective was offered in an article about the Pérez government agreeing to a plan to restructure their debt with the Bush administration and a discussion of Venezuela's plan to boost oil production.[88,89,90] In all of this coverage, the events of 1989 were referred to as riots.

The next year during the second anniversary there was only one mention of the protests and crackdown. In contrast to coverage from the previous year, in 1991, when the Venezuelan economy was starting to improve, the riots were used to contrast the present situation with the situation in the past:

The gross national product, which grew 5 percent in 1990, expanded by an annualized rate of 10 percent during the first half of this year, according to figures released here in late August. Memories are now fading of 1989, the rough first year of President Carlos Andres Perez. That year, the economy shrank by 8 percent and a reduction of food and gas subsidies set off riots that killed 300 people.[91]

No discussion of Caracazo was found on the fifth anniversary in 1994, the twentieth in 2009 or the thirtieth in 2019. The last mention on the anniversaries covered here was during reporting about the inauguration of Venezuela's then new president Hugo Chávez in 1999:

> The turning point of his life occurred in 1989, when food riots here led him and other young officers to start the coup three years later against President Carlos Andres Perez.[92]

None of the coverage on the anniversaries considered here was about commemorating the actual protests and crackdown. Even when searching for discussions of the events of 1989 during other anniversaries, no articles were found that were primarily about commemorating the events. Frequently during the coverage of the Presidency of Chávez and his successor Maduro, the memory of the protests was brought up as a shadow haunting the government:

> The killings at the anti-Chávez demonstration rocked the country, reviving memories of the violent events in 1989, known as the Caracazo, in which hundreds were killed by government forces. Venezuelans across the political spectrum swore that such violence would never take place again.[93]

An attempt by a previous government to raise gasoline prices in 1989 left hundreds of dead in riots, making the current, highly unpopular president, Nicolás Maduro reluctant to reduce subsidies.[94]

Conclusion

There was very little historical reporting about the Caracazo protests, riots, and crackdown identified in the *Times*. In most cases, coverage was just passing references to the fear of similar events occurring or the relevance of the events in the careers of contemporary politicians.

Gujarat, 2002

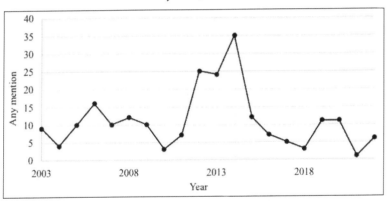

Figure 5. Any mention of "Gujarat" in The New York Times *between February 1st and March 30th between 2003 and 2022*

As shown in figure 1, on the first anniversary of the Gujarat riots there were seven pieces published, none on the second, six on the fifth and tenth, two on the twentieth. Figure 5 shows any reference to Gujarat remained relatively low during the first ten years after the 2002 events but began to pick up in the early 2010s. Many of these references were not to the riots, but rather to Narendra Modi, Chief Minister of Gujarat during the riots, who became a more prominent politician and was elected Prime Minister during that time period.

There were seven articles dealing with the events in Gujarat on the first anniversary in 2003. In a detailed analysis of the role that Hindu Nationalism played in Indian politics, the contribution that both the organization the Rashtriya Swayamsevak Sangh (RSS) and the political party Bharatiya Janata Party (BJP) made to the Gujarat riots was discussed:

> After the massacres in Gujarat last year, the Hindu nationalist response was shockingly blunt. "Let Muslims understand," an official R.S.S. resolution said in March, "that their safety lies in the goodwill of the majority." Speaking at a public rally in April, Prime Minister Vajpayee seemed to blame Muslims for the recent violence. "Wherever Muslims live," he said, "they don't want to live in peace." Replying to international criticism of the killings in Gujarat, he said, "No one should teach us about secularism."[95]

In an opinion piece discussing the complexities of secularism in India, the role that the BJP—in particular Modi—played in exploiting the riots for votes was discussed:

> Capitalizing on riots that left 2,000 Muslims dead, Gujarat's BJP chief minister, Narendra Modi, called new elections, campaigned on an anti-Muslim platform and was reelected in a landslide. One analyst called the gruesome strategy: "Kill Muslims and win the Hindu vote." Hindu fanatics speak of making Gujarat a laboratory for the entire nation. But reports of the death of Indian secularism are greatly exaggerated. Gujarat was an aberration, not a harbinger of India's future.[96]

A one paragraph article reported the arrest of a Muslim cleric—Maulana Hussain Umarji—who was blamed for planning the train burning that preceded the riots.[97] The riots were also mentioned in the context of orders from an Indian court to begin excavation at a holy site in Ayodhya, which is disputed between Muslims and Hindus[98] and the murder of a former minister in Gujarat, who had been blamed for the riots.[99,100,101] The minister who was killed, Haren Pandya, had testified in a tribunal investigating the events in Gujarat in 2002. He was a rival of Modi, whose testimony had implicated Modi in the riots.[102]

On the fifth anniversary, memory of the riots was discussed in a story about how some states in India had banned the showing of a film about them—*Parzania*.[103] There was a brief reference to the riots in a book review of *In Spite of the Gods* by Edward Luce[104] and reports about the bombing of a train going from India to Pakistan.[105,106,107]

On the tenth anniversary in 2012, an article dealing with the increased prominence of Modi in Indian politics described his role in the riots:

In the days that followed the burning of the coach, riots broke out in Gujarat that left hundreds dead, most of them Muslims. As the massacre continued, journalists, activists and several senior police officers in Gujarat who spoke to the news media on the condition of anonymity said that Mr. Modi's government was complicit in the violence. Mr. Modi, for his part, asserted that the violence was "a spontaneous reaction of the Hindus."[108]

On a blog hosted by the *Times*, a retrospective about the riots, including the original reporting, was published.[109] In another retrospective report about the riots, a survivor whose son went missing during the riots was quoted as saying: "I will fight until my dying day to see that Modi and his band of rogues are nailed."[110]

On the twentieth anniversary of the riots in 2022, there were two brief mentions of the events in Gujarat. One appeared in an article about the construction of a township because one of the officials involved in its construction had served with Modi in Gujarat,[111] and the other in a report on the rise of anti-Muslim hate speech in India.[112]

While not one of the anniversaries were included in figure 1, the fifteenth anniversary also coincided with an election victory for Modi, who was now Prime Minister of India. The only mention of the riots briefly described Modi's role in them: "While Mr. Modi has largely steered clear of divisive language on religion as prime minister, his party has a Hindu nationalist philosophy, and he was accused of complicity in anti-Muslim violence as the leader of his home state of Gujarat."[113]

Conclusion

While coverage of the Gujarat riots was the highest during the first anniversary of the events, a number of articles discussing them were identified through the tenth anniversary. However, in many instances the events in Gujarat were not the main focus of the articles, but were discussed in the context of other contemporary issues in Indian politics. The events were always described in a negative light. Coverage of the events had declined, even as Modi has become a more prominent politician in India.

Gawkadal, 1990

I also intended to compare coverage of another event in India — the Gawkadal bridge protest and crackdown in 1990 — with coverage of Tiananmen. In the late 1980s, there had been an increase in tensions in India controlled Kashmir brought on by a number of factors including accusations of vote rigging in Kashmir elections. The government began to crackdown more forcefully on protests in the region following the kidnapping of a government minister. After the arrest of hundreds of Kashmiris, a mass protest began. During the protests, Indian troops fired on protesters. It is estimated that at least 50 protesters were killed from either gunshots or jumping to the river that the bridge went over to escape the gunfire. In the succeeding weeks hundreds more would be killed in Kashmir.

While the initial reports about the killing were published in the *Times*[114,115,116] I was not able to identify any substantial discussions in subsequent anniversaries. Even the term Gawkadal did not appear in my searches of the *Times*'s archives. For years following the protest, I identified a total of 54 articles that mentioned "Srinagar" (the city where the Gawkadal Bridge is located) and "1990" (the year the killings took place), but none of them were found to refer to this specific incident. Another search for "Srinagar" and "Bridge" did not lead to any references to the events of 1990.

I did identify other references to the memories of other historic killings of protesters in Kashmir. Including references to another government killing in 1990:

On May 21, 1990, as thousands of people wound through Srinagar's streets carrying the body of Maulvi Mohammad Farooq—the valley's senior cleric and the most influential public opponent of Indian rule in the valley, assassinated earlier in the day—troops fired on the procession, killing at least 47 people and wounding 150.[117]

Indian paramilitary forces rampaged through a town in the Vale of Kashmir today, killing at least 40 people and setting houses and markets ablaze, according to reports from Kashmir. More than 100 people were reported wounded in what was described as indiscriminate firing by Indian forces. If confirmed, the death toll would be the worst in Kashmir since May 1990, when security forces opened fire on a funeral procession for the region's leading Islamic cleric, killing 67 people.[118]

In April 1990, after a series of massacres by Government troops, described in compelling detail by *The Daily Aftab*, Kashmir's Governor ordered the paper closed. But 10 days later, a judge in the Srinagar High Court reversed the Governor and Mr. Bhat was back in business.[119]

Are the Events Comparable?

None of the events discussed in this chapter are perfectly comparable. They are all unique situations that emerged from the distinct social, political, and economic situations in very different countries during different time periods. However, the questions to consider are (1) whether the events are comparable enough to compare them in terms of the coverage that they received, and (2) to the extent that they are different, do those differences warrant the increased attention that the event in Beijing in 1989 received? In this section, I will discuss several aspects of the events in order to assess how comparable the Gwangju, Caracazo, and Gujarat events are to the Tiananmen Square event.

Size

It has been estimated that at its height, there were one million protesters participating in the Tiananmen Square Protests.[120] These numbers fluctuated substantially from early May, when the protests began, to early June when the crackdown began.

In the early days of the protests, those participating were mostly residents of Beijing, especially university students; as they continued many students came from around the country and joined the protests. In Beijing, there were about 6,200,000 residents in 1989.[121] Although all of the protesters were not residents, this would mean that the equivalent of about 16% of the city participated in the protests at their height. There were also protests of varying sizes that took place throughout China in solidarity with the protests in Beijing including in large cities like Shanghai and Chengdu.

In Gwangju, it has been estimated that over 200,000 residents participated in some form in the protests.[122] In 1989 the population of Gwangju was about 700,000,[123] so this number would represent about 28% of the population of the city. As with Tiananmen, there were solidarity protests in South Korea, including in the capital of Seoul where as many as 100,000 protesters may have participated.[124,125]

I did not identify records of the size of the Caracazo protests and riots, so it is difficult to make a direct comparison with Tiananmen. The protests affected large swathes of urban sections of Venezuela and resulted in hundreds to 2000 deaths,[126] and required a substantial military and police response so it is likely that the protests were in the tens of thousands, if not higher.[127]

Because the Gujarat riots were not a protest, but rather a case of communal violence comparing the numbers of participants directly to Tiananmen is not fitting. However, looking at the number of Muslims in Gujarat that were made homeless as a result of the events of 2002 can give a sense of their scale. In one report, it was estimated that as many as 70,000 Muslims were displaced from the Gujarat region following the violence.[128] Other have suggested that as many as 150,000 refugees were in these internally displaced camps following the riots.[129]

In terms of absolute numbers, the events in Tiananmen Square may have been the largest of the events considered here. However, this is partially explained by the fact that Beijing has a larger population than Gwangju and Caracas. Especially in the case of Gwangju, the proportion of the population who participated is comparable to, if not greater than, Tiananmen. In all the cases being compared to Tiananmen, the number of participants was likely not on a different scale from Tiananmen.

Reasons for Event

All of the events considered here had very different causes. Tiananmen was motivated by a desire for democratization and liberalization. Under the surface, there were also economic causes with China having recently experienced a period of intense inflation following the first attempt at relaxing price controls.[130] The Gwangju protests had similar motivations with students seizing on a period of instability following the assassination of President Park to push for democratization. There was also a wide sense of alienation among residents of Gwangju, who often felt disconnected from the country's government in Seoul. With respect to Caracazo, the motivations were primarily economic with Venezuela going through a destabilizing period following the introduction of market reforms promoted by Western financial organizations. The protesters were expressing dissatisfaction with the government's acquiescence to these reforms. Finally, the Gujarat riots were an event of intercommunal violence primarily of Hindus in the region against Muslims in response to accusations of Muslims killing Hindus. There is strong evidence that the regional government allowed and may have facilitated much of this violence.

While the motivations and the circumstances for all of the events covered were different, it is not clear that these differences in reasons should mean that they are less worthy of recalling.

The Gwangju protests were a similar call for democratization. With respect to Caracazo, the protests reflected serious economic concerns with a changing economy, which were frequently felt throughout the late 1980s and early 1990s, and similar to the feelings of economic dislocation in China associated with periods of reform and opening up. The Gujarat violence, although part of a long history of inter-communal violence, was probably the largest such event in recent Indian history, making it particularly noteworthy.

Actions of Protesters

Another difference between the events is the actions taken by the protesters or other participants in the events. For example, it may be that a government crackdown against a violent rebellion is more understandable and, therefore, less newsworthy than a crackdown on completely peaceful protesters. I do not necessarily find such an argument convincing. Is it not at least as notable when people of a country take up arms against their government as when protests use nonviolent means? However, this is an argument that could be made. It could also be argued that by taking up arms, deaths of protesters who may be using violent tactics are less notable. These related arguments could be a major objection to why the memory of Tiananmen has garnered more attention than the memory of Gwangju. Gwangju is often referred to as the "Gwangju Uprising" because there was an armed response from many in Gwangju to the initial crackdown against protest in the city.[131] However, the number of soldiers actually killed (fewer than 30, many by friendly fire) and wounded was many times lower than even the conservative, government estimates of the civilians killed in the uprising.[132]

Although it is not well known, there was also a violent response by a minority of protesters in Beijing in 1989 to the presence of soldiers. When troops first entered Beijing, many were unarmed.[133] Some incidents of violent resistance coming after the declaration of martial law, but some preceding the military crackdown are described in *The Power of Tiananmen* by Dingxin Zhao:

> on the evening of May 22, soldiers from the 113th Division of the 38th Army were starting to withdraw, as had been agreed upon by troop and student negotiators, when a few people in the crowd shouted: "Beat them, beat these soldiers to death!" "Do not let them enter the city!" Bricks were cast at the soldiers. Early the next morning similar conflicts occurred, again in the same region. According to government sources, a total of 116 soldiers were wounded in these conflicts, and 29 were seriously injured.... The soldiers did not fight back, but they were very angry as a result. After two days of stalemate, the government had to order the troops to withdraw on the morning of May 22. The popular resistance went on successfully.[134]

On the evening of June 2, the government broadcast was criticizing the Statue of the Goddess of Democracy. We were curious and went to see it ... When we were close to Tiananmen Square, we saw some military trucks being stopped. Many workers were trying to break tires and smash the trucks. They also cast bricks at soldiers and pulled them out to beat them. It was around midnight at the Xidan intersection. At that time, the soldiers did not fight back ... I felt that this was not right, so I asked a male classmate to stop them. However, several people came over and asked who he was. They suspected him of being a secret policeman. To avoid further conflicts, I had to rush forward and tell them that we were students. Then they let us go. My classmate still wanted to argue with them. I saw the situation was quite tense, so I pulled him away.[135]

Residents and students also started to find weapons. Rumors said that the troops were deliberately sending weapons to the street to let civilians seize them, in order to create excuses for a repression. From what I have reconstructed, the martial law troops did send many weapons into Beijing in civilian vehicles. However, they did so mainly because their soldiers had infiltrated Beijing in plainclothes and unarmed. Therefore, they had to ship the weapons separately. After June 2, residents and students were on the alert for suspicious civilian vehicles. As a result, they caught several such vehicles with military equipment. For instance, on the morning of June 3 students and Beijing residents stopped three tourist buses carrying military equipment at the Liubukou Intersection. In a rage, some people in the crowd took out guns, machine guns, grenades, bullets, helmets, and gas masks, and displayed them on the street to show that the government was going to use live ammunition against the people. The Martial Law Headquarters had to send about five hundred riot policemen and soldiers to recover the weapons. Conflict immediately broke out. In the process, the riot police used clubs and tear gas, and many people were wounded. In the afternoon, soldiers and riot police attacked civilians in other places for similar reasons. Both sides became increasingly hostile.[136]

From a protester describing the negotiations that made it possible for many protesters to leave Tiananmen Square:

At this moment, the four intellectuals who were still fasting at the Square played an important role. To avoid violence, they went from place to place to ask students and local residents to get rid of the rifles and other weapons that they had collected in order to defend the Square.[137]

So while the military response was without any doubt grossly disproportionate as was Gwangju, it would not be accurate to label the protests as being completely nonviolent. Additionally, the events in Venezuela in 1989 also involved violence and looting on the part of the protesters. There were also violent responses to the violence in Gujarat with many Hindus being killed during the rioting,[138] although many fewer than the Muslims killed even according to government estimates.[139]

In all of the events covered, while most protesters were nonviolent, there were cases of violence. This violence does not in any way justify the response of the respective governments, but it does make it difficult to make the case that the action (or lack of actions) of protesters in Tiananmen was more deserving of a reaction than in the other events considered.

Death Toll

Probably the most controversial aspect of all of the events described here are the death tolls caused by them. Governments and protesters have incentives to both underestimate and overestimate death tolls. For all the events a clear and objective rendering of the number killed is not available. The death toll is important for consideration because one would expect, all else being equal, more deadly events to illicit more attention. My intention in this section is not assess the most accurate number of the death toll, but rather to give a sense for the ranges suggested and to determine whether these ranges are substantially different from each other.

The range generally given for deaths in Beijing in 1989 range between 300 (government figures)[140] and 2700 (from an initial estimate from the Chinese Red Cross and a Swiss Ambassador).[141] A number which Nicholas Kristof in the *Times* cast doubt on (see above).[142] However, most estimates are in the hundreds to one thousand range. For example, a US government cable estimated 180 to 500,[143] while Amnesty International estimates about 1000.[144] With respect to Gwangju, the South Korean government shortly after the events stated that 144 civilians were killed.[145] Other estimates have put the numbers killed between one to two thousand. It has been suggested that these higher estimates would be consistent with the fact that the number of deaths in Gwangju during the month of the protests was over 2000 higher than the monthly average.[146] The official figures for the number dead during Caracazo is 277.[147] However, some have estimated that thousands may have been killed.[148] Finally, with respect to Gujarat, official figures estimate that 790 Muslims and 254 Hindus were killed.[149] However, estimates from other agencies put the total number killed closer to 2000.[150,151]

While there is a wide range of possible deaths during all of the events discussed in this chapter, the uncertainty and the low and high ends of these estimates are comparable. The scale of death is not different enough to consider any of these events as not being comparable based on the metric of deaths.

Conclusion

None of these events are perfectly comparable to each other. However, all events represented massive protests and/or government approved or facilitated crackdowns that resulted in hundreds to thousands of deaths. With the exception of Gujarat, the protests were motivated by social, economic, and political dissatisfaction with the governments. In the case of Gujarat, the riots were motivated by sectarian hatred against Muslims and made possible by government inaction and, possibly, facilitation.

Reasons for Differences

We now turn to potential reasons why the anniversaries of Tiananmen may have received so much more media attention than the other events considered. All of these reasons are speculation.

Initial Coverage

While this chapter is only concerned with the memory of historical events, in the course of research for it, I also reviewed the initial coverage of the events. The events in Beijing in 1989 received multiple times more coverage than the next closest event—Gwangju, 1980—with nearly 200 articles published about what happened in Beijing in 1989 compared to a little more than 20 for Gwangju and less than 20 for all of the others. Some of the differences in the coverage of the anniversaries of subsequent events may be tied to this initial coverage. As discussed while reviewing the *Times*'s reporting of the anniversaries of Tiananmen, some of the articles were from reporters, like Nicholas Kristof, who had been present during the protests and crackdown.

It should be noted that this disproportionate initial coverage does not mean that the events in Beijing were more worthy of coverage than the other events. This initial coverage very well may be further evidence of the "Worthy/Unworthy" paradigm with the media tending to focus more on the crimes of enemies than on geopolitical friends. The best ways to assess the worthiness of attention the events considered in this chapter received were covered in the section dealing with the comparability of the events, such as the justification for the protests and the government's response. Furthermore, one of the reasons why there was so much coverage of Tiananmen in 1989 was because there was already a focus on Beijing at the time due to the visit of Gorbachev to the city amid thaws in the Sino-Soviet split—a major historical event.

Relevance

It could also be argued that perhaps Tiananmen Square has received more coverage because it is more relevant to the present geopolitical realities during the anniversaries. China is still ruled by their Communist Party, while South Korea and Venezuela have gone through different administrations since the Gwangju protests and Caracazo. In the case of Gwangju, this chapter considered several anniversaries where the country was still ruled by the regime responsible for the crackdown. On the first, second, and fifth anniversaries in 1981, 1982, and 1985 Chun Doo-hwan, who led the country during the crackdown (although not yet formally president), was still the leader of the country. Despite this fact, only on the fifth anniversary did Gwangju receive more attention than Tiananmen on its fifth anniversary. Additionally, although the Communist Party of China was still in power during those subsequent anniversaries the country's paramount leader was Jiang Zemin, who had replaced Deng Xiaoping, the leader during the crackdown. One of the main reasons why Jiang had been elevated to the position of paramount leader was because as a leader in Shanghai during the protests, he was not associated with the crackdown. Furthermore, by meeting with solidarity protesters in Shanghai, he had shown himself to be more adapt at dealing with protests.[152] However, some leaders responsible for the crackdown, like Premier Li Peng, remained in powerful positions for a decade after the crackdown.

The Gujarat riots are a stronger counterexample for this claim. Since the Gujarat riots, the party and in fact the very leader perhaps most implicated in them—the BJP and Narendra Modi—have, in fact, gained power. While Modi's exact role in the riots is debated, with some suggesting he just failed to stop them and others claiming complicity in a pogrom or even ethnic cleansing, Modi was certainly a central player in the events. The

US government was convinced enough of his complicity to ban him from travelling to its territories until he began to rise in Indian politics at the national level.[153]

Since 2002, Modi has gone from being the Chief Minister of Gujarat, to the Prime Minister of all of India, a position he took in 2014. In contrast, Xi Jinping, the paramount leader of China since 2012, had no involvement in the events in Tiananmen Square, serving faraway in Fujian province when they occurred. In fact, coverage in the *Times* even suggested that Xi's father may have been sympathetic to the protests:

> [Xi's] father, Xi Zhongxun, a veteran Communist turned supporter of economic reform, had been a friend of Hu Yaobang, the Communist Party leader demoted in 1987 for his liberal tendencies and whose death in 1989 sent thousands swarming into Tiananmen Square to voice their grief and demand steps toward democracy. There are some indications that the elder Mr. Xi obliquely signaled opposition to martial law but stepped into line after June 4, said Warren Sun, a historian at Monash University in Australia.[154]

Despite the seeming relevance of the events in Gujarat given Modi's new power and concerns about increased persecutions of Muslims in India including in Kashmir in 2019 (see Chapter 2), coverage and discussion of its anniversary have remained sparse.

Punishment for Those Responsible

Since the events covered in this chapter have occurred, there have been differences in government responses to punish those responsible. It may be the case that the *Times* and other media outlets feel more compelled to cover stories for which there is a perception that those who were responsible never faced punishment or that adequate responsibility has not been taken. In the case of Tiananmen, I have not identified any punishments for anyone responsible whether troops on the ground or leaders responsible for issuing the orders. The government has maintained that the crackdown was the correct response in the face of a potential revolution. The closest the government has come to acknowledge fault has been through offering payments to some family members of those killed[155] and former Premier Wen Jiabao's alleged advocacy for reassessing the government's stance about the events in Beijing.[156]

With respect to Gwangju, for roughly the first decade after the events of 1980 the government persisted in asserting it was the correct action to suppress the protest, and prosecuted those who were involved. In the late 1980s after the end of the presidency of Chun Doo-hwan a reevaluation of the events began. In 1996, several political leaders, including President Chun, were tried for their role in the events in Gwangju. Although they were convicted, they were pardoned. Beginning in the late 2010s, several reports and commissions were established to study the events.

I could not identify any punishments for those who ordered or were involved in the suppression and killings during the Caracazo protests. There was a government commission shortly after the protests, which established the lower end of the estimate for the number who were killed.

Following the events in Gujarat there were hundreds of arrests and prosecutions of those on the ground who carried out the killings and other crimes. These cases were transferred to the Bombay High Court, because of fears about bias in the courts in Gujarat. As of writing, there have been fewer than 300 convictions.[157] There have also been several inquiries into the events in Gujarat, both by entities in the Indian government and foreign NGOs. These reports have generally found strong evidence for compliancy of the Gujarat government. I have not been able to identify any members of the Gujarati government who received punishment for the events in 2002 or any official apologies. It is also worth noting that with respect to the Gawakdal protests and crackdown, whose memory received little to no coverage in the *Times*, I could not identify instances of punishment of those responsible.

Geopolitics

The final potential factor that I will consider is the "Worthy/ Unworthy" hypothesis. The argument for this hypothesis is that one of the main reasons why anniversaries of the Tiananmen Square Protests and crackdown have received a disproportionate share of the coverage is because Tiananmen in 1989 is an example of a "worthy memory," a memory that serves the interests of the United States geopolitically to remind the public of the evils of a regime viewed as unfriendly. China, especially over the past decade, has grown in prominence as a geopolitical rival of the United States. South Korea has remained an ally. India has had a more complicated position vis-à-vis the United States, but relations between the countries have grown closer since the "War on Terror" and since the United States has begun to see India as a potential counterbalance to China in Asia. These closer ties are seen most clearly in India's participation in the "Quad," a security arrangement with the United States, Japan, and Australia. Venezuela, while a geopolitical enemy (see Chapter 3), was not an enemy during the Caracazo protests and, in fact, received financial support from the United States shortly after. Hugo Chávez, the man most responsible for Venezuela's political realignment with respect to the United States, was an officer in the military during the crackdown, but reported being too sick to work during it. One wonders whether the events in Venezuela in 1989 would have received more coverage on its anniversary had Chávez had a more prominent role.

Support for the fact that memory of Tiananmen is useful for geopolitical purposes is also suggested by much of the coverage, which focuses on tying the events in 1989 to current political realities in the country. Similar discussions are not present to the same extent in discussions of the other events. Although arguably not as relevant as in South Korea, many of the same divisions made evident in Gwangju in 1980 are still present. For example, protests against the impeachment of Park Geun-hye, the daughter of the president whose assassination triggered the events that that led to the Gwangju uprising, almost resulted in a declaration of martial law.[158,159] The Muslim-Hindu divide and violence made evident in Gujarat in 2002 has, if anything, grown in recent years, especially under the Modi presidency. The 2019 crackdown in Kashmir (see Chapter 2) and the Assam Detention Centers (see Chapter 7) are just two examples. In all instances, historical parallels between the past and the present exist, but they are drawn most consistently in the case of China and Tiananmen Square.

Conclusion

The anniversaries of events in China's Tiananmen Square in May and June of 1989 have received far more attention than similar historical events in Gwangju, South Korea in 1980, Venezuela in 1989, and Gujarat, India in 2002. Coverage of the anniversaries of these other events has diminished and in some cases disappeared, while the coverage of Tiananmen has grown in some years. On the later anniversaries (the tenth, twentieth, and thirtieth) Tiananmen has received more coverage than the sum of the coverage of all the other events considered (figure 1). Although none of these events are perfectly comparable, I believe that they are comparable enough that if coverage about the events was based solely on the events themselves they would be similar. In some cases, you could make arguments that the anniversaries deserve more attention given present relevance, especially in the case of the anniversaries of the Gujarat riots. Although other explanations for the difference in coverage may explain some of the increased focus on Tiananmen (such as the likely larger number of participants in the protests in Beijing and the lack of punishment for those responsible), I believe that the best explanation for this increased coverage is the geopolitical position of China. Namely, because China is increasingly a geopolitical adversary of the US coverage of historical protests in that country fall into the category of "worthy memories" while events in the other countries considered are treated as unworthy.

Chapter 2

Worthy and Unworthy Protests in Asia: Hong Kong and Kashmir, 2019

Anti-Communism defined the foreign policy of the United States through the second half of the twentieth century. From Cold War diplomatic standoffs with the Soviet Union, to dropping millions of tons of bombs in Southeast Asia, to supporting right-wing dictators in Latin America, anti-Communism was a core motivator of some of the worst aspects of the United States' foreign policy. Due to the centrality of anti-Communism to political discourse in the United States during the Cold War, the fifth filter of the Herman-Chomsky Propaganda Model when *Manufacturing Consent* was first published was anti-Communism. The filter of anti-Communism meant that coverage of foreign issues involving communist or even countries that could be linked to communism in any way would be filtered in such a way that destructive actions against those countries committed by the United States or its allies would generally be portrayed in a less negative light than would seem to be warranted. In a similar way, anti-Communist allies in other countries, even when committing atrocities or grossly violating human rights, would not receive the criticism that they may seem to warrant. In contrast, the crimes of communist and communist-aligned countries would be emphasized.

Since the publication of *Manufacturing Consent* and the end of the Cold War, Herman and Chomsky suggested a wider definition of this filter:

Anti-communism has receded as an ideological factor in the Western media, but it is not dead and is still used when needed to denigrate individuals who can be tied to Stalin or Mao or Soviet Russia more broadly (e.g. Milosevic), and the crimes of Stalin or Mao and the Black Book of Communism can be featured periodically to warn against socialism and wrong-headed state intervention. The "war on terror" has provided a useful substitute for the Soviet Menace. Also, the antithesis of communism, the "free market," has been elevated to more prominent ideological status, and has proven to be a strong co-replacement for anti-communism and the basis for the new world order of neoliberalism now in some disarray but without an ideological rival resting on any kind of power base.[1]

However, as the US has begun to pull back from the Middle East (while still maintaining a significant presence in the region) and as discussions of a new Cold War with China grows, it may be worth considering how anti-Communism, now primarily represented by opposition to the People's Republic of China as opposed to the USSR, serves as a filter in present media coverage. In particular, this chapter will consider whether media coverage of state actions in China and protests against those actions differ from coverage given to similar state actions and protests against those actions in a country more geopolitically aligned with the US—India. In the summer of 2019, we were provided with an opportunity to make such a comparison when protests broke out in regions of China and India, namely Hong Kong and Kashmir.

Background

Hong Kong Protests, 2019[2]
On a trip from Hong Kong to Taiwan in 2018, Chan Tong-kai brutally murdered his girlfriend Poon Hiu-wing. Because of

the controversial territorial jurisdictions between the People's Republic of China that controls mainland China and Hong Kong and the Republic of China that controls Taiwan, the accused murderer, Chan, could not be charged with murder in Hong Kong, but instead needed to be extradited to Taiwan to face those charges. However, Hong Kong did not have an extradition treaty with mainland China, which meant that there was no legal mechanism to have Chan extradited to the mainland, to then be sent to Taiwan. Poon's mother asked for an arrangement to be made as soon as possible, fearing that as more time passed the possibility that her daughter's murderer would not face prosecution became more likely.[3]

In response, the Hong Kong government drafted the "Fugitive Offenders and Mutual Legal Assistance in Criminal Matters Legislation Bill 2019" frequently referred to as the Extradition Bill. The bill, like most other extradition treaties, provides for a process by which a person can be extradited to face punishment for crimes in another jurisdiction where they are accused of committing a crime. The mainland China government had long wanted an extradition agreement with the Hong Kong government because of concerns about mainland Chinese officials and financiers hiding money in Hong Kong and in some cases fleeing to Hong Kong to avoid corruption charges.[4]

However, many in Hong Kong were concerned that the law would be used for political purposes to arrest opponents of the mainland government. The law itself would likely not lead to the arrest for political crimes because the law stipulated that extradition would only be possible in cases when the accused crime would be "punishable with imprisonment for more than three years and triable on indictment in Hong Kong."[5] Meaning that only acts that were already illegal in Hong Kong could result in extradition to mainland China. Indeed, nine offenses that were crimes in Hong Kong were actually excluded from those that could result in extradition.[6]

Some Hong Kong legal scholars criticized the law because of concerns about human rights and the fundamentally different legal systems between mainland China and Hong Kong, which inherited its legal system from its former colonizer—the United Kingdom.[7] This legal system is unique in that it includes judges from foreign countries. It should be noted that despite these fundamental differences, the law stipulated that final decisions about whether extradition will proceed are in the hands of the Hong Kong courts. Indeed, many countries with very different legal systems from China have extradition treaties with them, including at least ten European Union countries.[8]

Kashmir Protests, 2019

Controversy over the status of Kashmir extends back to the partition of British India in the late 1940s. During that time, British colonial officials sought to divide the colony into a predominantly Muslim country, which would become Pakistan (the eastern part of which would eventually gain independence, following a bloody war, as Bangladesh), and a predominantly Hindu country, the modern state of India. During this time, Jammu and Kashmir was a princely state ruled by a Hindu Maharaja, but with a population that was at least three-quarters Muslim.

After initially deciding to keep the state independent, when the Maharaja dismissed his pro-independence Prime Minister, which was interpreted as indicating that he may decide to join India, Pakistan sponsored insurgents were sent into the region to try to take control of it. Following this excursion, with pressure from the Governor-General of India Lord Mountbatten, the Maharaja agreed to have the territory join with India. The region was the center of fighting during the Indo-Pakistani War of 1947. By the end of the war, Pakistan controlled territory became the provinces of Azad Kashmir and Gilgit-Baltistan, while the larger Indian controlled portions of the territory became the state of Jammu-Kashmir. In the Indian controlled portion of the region, the Muslim population of the territory is heavily concentrated in the Kashmir Valley region to the north, while the Jammu territory to the south is about two-thirds Hindu and one-third Muslim. Until the passage of the Jammu and Kashmir Reorganization Act in 2019, Jammu and Kashmir also contained the territory of Ladakh, which is about 46% Muslim, 40% Buddhist, and 12% Hindu.[9]

After the conclusion of the Indo-Pakistani War, the United Nations Security Council passed Resolution 47, which called for (1) the withdrawal of Pakistani troops from the region, (2) India to minimize the number of troops in the region, and (3) a plebiscite to determine the final status of Kashmir. Article 370 of the Indian Constitution granted limited autonomy to the region of Jammu and Kashmir. Since Partition, Kashmir has remained a tense part of the Indian subcontinent with frequent protests, insurgent attacks, and massacres such as the Gawkadal Massacre (see chapter 1).

On August 5, 2019, the Parliament of India officially revoked the special status of Jammu and Kashmir afforded by Article 370 through the Jammu and Kashmir Reorganization Act. Such revocation had been a longtime goal of the nationalist Bharatiya Janata Party, which had come to power under Prime Minister Narendra Modi. The act had a number of provisions. Notably, it separated Ladakh from the rest of Jammu and Kashmir and it provided for a Lieutenant Governor, appointed by the President, to have executive power in the territory. In anticipation of protests against the revocation, the Indian government instituted a lockdown in Kashmir starting on August 5, 2019. The lockdown banned foreign journalists from the territory, enacted a curfew, and blocked out Internet and mobile phone systems in the region. Tourism to the region was ended and schools were closed. Despite these controls, protests launched across the region.

The purpose of this chapter is not to discuss the relative merits of the Hong Kong and Indian governments' actions or the merits of the protests in reaction to those actions, but rather to compare the media attention given to them in quantitative and qualitative terms and to discuss and evaluate potential reasons for differences in coverage. I look specifically at articles about Hong Kong and Kashmir published in the *Times* in the first three months following the beginning of the protest against the Hong Kong Extradition Bill (June 2019 through August 2019), and the revocation of Jammu and Kashmir's special status (August 2019 through October 2019).

The Numbers

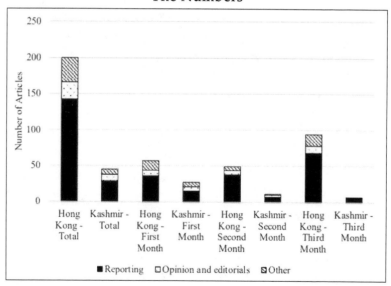

Figure 6. Coverage of 2019 Hong Kong (June 1, 2019 to August 31, 2019) and Kashmir Protests (August 1, 2019 to October 31, 2019) by month and type of coverage

A total of 200 pieces dealing with the Hong Kong protests were identified during the three months after the protest began. This represents an average of over two pieces per day. Fifty-seven pieces appeared in June, 49 in July, and 94 in August. Focusing on the 170 articles, there were a total of 142 pieces of reporting, 20 opinion articles, four letter collections, and four editorials.

With respect to Kashmir, a total of 45 articles/videos/photos were identified. This represents an average of less than one piece per day. Only 18 of these pieces appeared after August, the month that the revocation occurred, and protests started. Among the 41 articles, there were a total of 29 pieces of reporting, seven opinion articles, three letter collections, and two editorials.

From these numbers it is clear that quantitatively Hong Kong received much more attention than Kashmir, but numbers certainly do not tell the whole story. It is important to also consider the nature of the coverage that was received.

The Coverage

Hong Kong Anti-Extradition Protests

The First Month

Large-scale protests against the extradition bill began in June 2019, following smaller scale protests since the March introduction of the bill. On June 4, an opinion piece titled "The Death of Hong Kong as We Know It?" was published. The article was written by Ray Wong Toi-yeung, a veteran activist from the Umbrella Movement, a 2014 protest campaign against changes to election laws in Hong Kong. In the piece, he laid out many of the central arguments from the anti-Extradition Bill protesters including concerns about the Chinese legal system being "corrupt and ... a tool of repression" and fears that the law "would apply to anyone—a Hong Kong citizen, a mainlander, even foreigners traveling through the city—accused by the Chinese authorities of having broken Chinese law." Toi-yeung's party "Hong Kong Indigenous" represents the fairly fringe localist movement that believes in Hong Kong self-rule. One poll showed that only about 17% of the Hong Kong population support independence for Hong Kong.[10]

The first piece of reporting about the protests in June came five days later.[11] The article contains many of the same topics that would appear in future pieces including concerns about the law and questions about the size of the protests (240,000 as estimated by police, higher numbers suggested by protesters). The article also had predictions about the consequences of the protests:

> Despite the size of the protests, the government was unlikely to be swayed, said Ivan Choy, a senior lecturer in the department of government and public administration at the Chinese University of Hong Kong.
>
> "The major problem is that Xi Jinping holds power in China, and he is a strongman," Mr. Choy said, referring to China's top leader. "He will back up Carrie Lam's decision to push forward."

This reporting was complemented with a video from the protests.[12]

After the June 9th article, reporting about the Hong Kong protests continued at a fast clip. Between June 10th and June 14th, the day before the Extradition Bill was rescinded, there were a total of 21 pieces about the Hong Kong protests, about four per day. These pieces included two more opinion pieces and an editorial written in opposition to the bill. One opinion article by Bret Stephens mischaracterized the nature of the bill:

Imagine if in 2018 the Trump administration had proposed legislation that would allow the government, on nearly any pretext, to detain, try and imprison Americans accused of wrongdoing at secretive black sites scattered across the country ... Finally, imagine that there was no effective judiciary ready to stop the bill and uphold the Constitution. That, approximately, is what's happening this week in Hong Kong.[13]

The "approximately" is doing a lot of work here. As already noted, the bill only applied to a narrow set of laws, and any crime for which someone in Hong Kong might be extradited to mainland China would need to be illegal in Hong Kong a well. The Editorial Board engaged in similar speculation:

But to the democracy-minded people of Hong Kong, this was only cover for a portion of the bill that would also allow extradition to mainland China, which would enable Chinese authorities to pry political foes from Hong Kong by leveling false accusations and demanding their extradition. That, in effect, would extend China's reach into Hong Kong and strip its residents of the protection of the law.[14]

The nature of violence at the protests, especially the parties that played instigating roles in instances of violence, was a common topic during this period. On June 11th, an article described an attempt by some protesters to overrun the Legislative Council building where debate about the Extradition Bill was supposed to take place. This earlier article portrayed the protesters as contributing to the initial clashes: "Riot police officers turned downtown Hong Kong into a tear-gas-filled battlefield on Wednesday as they pushed back against protesters who tried to storm Hong Kong's Legislative Council."[15] By the next day, this narrative had been flipped with coverage almost exclusively focusing on the role that Hong Kong Police played in violence during clashes.[16,17] Headlines would often portray the police as the instigators, while reporting in the article would suggest that the protesters may have been the main instigators. One article was titled "Police Violence Puts Hong Kong Government on Defensive," but in the text it was reported that, "When some protesters charged the police in an attempt to enter the building, riot control officers opened fire with rubber bullets and more than 150 canisters of tear gas."[18]

The size of the protests was also a frequent topic in the articles published during this period. Articles early in the protest reported that estimates of one million participants in the marches came from protest organizers and reported lower estimates of 240,000 provided by police.[19,20] Later reporting on these high estimates were without the caveat about who was making the claims.[21,22,23,24,25] Estimates based on crowd density and the size of the streets with protests have tended to be close to the police estimates.[26,27] These estimates were generated after the articles reporting the higher numbers were published. I did not identify any corrections about protest sizes issued by the *Times*.

The articles during the four day period between the June 9th and the eventual repeal of the law on June 15th are also filled with predictions that the passage of the Extradition Bill was likely to happen:

The measure is likely to pass, with pro-Beijing lawmakers holding 43 of 70 seats.[28]

But the bill is likely to pass soon, possibly next week, because pro-Beijing lawmakers hold 43 of 70 seats in the Legislative Council.[29]

Mr. Tien predicted that the legislature would pass the law next week, and said that he and other business leaders now just want to prevent it from being abused.[30]

The bill is widely expected to eventually pass because a pro-Beijing political faction controls the Legislative Council.[31]

Despite these predictions, the bill was suspended on June 15. As the *Times* reported, following the suspension Lam said, "We will adopt the most sincere and humble attitude to accept criticisms and make improvements."[32]

The article describing the suspension of the bill reported that many of the protesters were not satisfied with a suspension and wanted, instead, an outright withdrawal. Indeed, the very day that the bill was suspended the *Times* printed an opinion piece titled "Why Hong Kong Is Still Marching" arguing for why the protests should continue.[33]

The *Times* coverage bore this out. There was just as much coverage of the Hong Kong protests in the days after the bill's suspension as during the period between the beginning of large-scale protests and the suspension. Despite the (at least) partial success of the protests, the coverage in the periods following the suspension of the bill became darker. For example, one article published two days after the repeal was titled "For Hong Kong's Youth, Protests Are 'a Matter of Life and Death'" and quoted a protester as saying, "The extradition law is a danger to our lives." It was only in one of the final paragraphs that the article mentions that the bill was suspended days earlier.[34]

Storming of the Legislative Council Building
One of the most well-known events of the protests occurred on July 1st, when protesters broke into the Legislative Council building, the Hong Kong equivalent of the Capitol Building.

During the storming, a few hundred protesters from a larger group outside the building entered and vandalized it. In the *Times* coverage of the breach, reporting was careful to accurately report that it was only a small minority of protesters who had breached the building. While noting that many in the protest tried to deter those seeking to storm the building, the *Times* still provided quotes from those outside providing justification for why the storming was taking place:

> "I don't support violence, no matter what, but I understand why people would do it," said Emily Lau, a former lawmaker. "They are very frustrated because they say they have protested so much … We have been too peaceful for the past few times, so the police think we are easily bullied," said Natalie Fung, 28, who supported protesters with food and drinks outside the legislature. "The younger people are risking their safety and their futures for us."[35]

While previous coverage had focused on the excessive use of force by the Hong Kong Police, coverage of the legislative council building storming portrayed the police as being too passive in response to the protesters:

> For hours, the police, who had been accused of excessive force in earlier protests, largely stood by, and they made a surprise retreat once the protesters began to breach an inner door. Some questioned why Mrs. Lam did not urge the police to step in sooner. "Why did she let the people get into the Legislative Council?" said Jean-Pierre Cabestan, a political scientist at Hong Kong Baptist University. "In what country is the Parliament not protected by the police?"[36]

This seeming disappointment with the police not using harsher measures to deter the storming may be consistent with a strategy employed by protesters. The *Times* published a piece just a day before the storming, titled "A Hong Kong Protester's Tactic: Get the Police to Hit You," subtitled, "Using aggressive nonviolence to provoke the authorities and win over the public." In the piece, protester Fred Chan Ho-fai, wrote

> The protesters should thoughtfully escalate nonviolence, maybe even resort to mild force, to push the government to the edge. That was the goal of many people who surrounded and barricaded police headquarters for hours on June 21.

The piece was edited after publication to explicitly state that the storming of the Legislative building was consistent with these tactics.[37]

Coverage also noted that it tended to only be "pro-Beijing" lawmakers who criticized the protest, while opposition lawmakers tended to be more equivocal.[38] In comparison, when pro-Trump rioters stormed the US Capitol Building in a similar way, lack of condemnations was often seen as tacit endorsement of the actions.

An opinion piece published by the *Times* offered a wide variety of justifications for the storming:

> To the young activists, the storming of the Legislative Council was an act of desperation. Three times in the past month, tremendous numbers of Hong Kong residents—at one point estimated to be more than two million—marched peacefully to protest against a controversial extradition bill with China, which they fear would undermine Hong Kong's judiciary and its freedom. The government suspended but did not

withdraw the law. It did not even meet representatives of those who marched.[39]

Locust: The Role of Anti-Mainland Chinese Prejudice in the Protests

Following the suspension of the Extradition Bill, the contours and the justification for the protest shifted as well. One particular issue was sentiments directed against mainland Chinese in Hong Kong. There have been elements of anti-Mainland sentiments in Hong Kong protests going at least back to 2012. That year the Hong Kong newspaper *Apple Daily* printed an advertisement depicting mainland visitors and immigrants to Hong Kong as locusts with the message "Hong Kong people have had enough!" Elaborating on these complaints, the ad called attention to mainland visitors' spending increasing prices in the city, crowding caused by mainlanders, and the fact that some mainland mothers gave birth in the city.[40]

Such sentiments were reflected at some points during the protests. In one particularly ugly instance during protests at the Hong Kong airport, which resulted in over 200 flight cancellations,[41] two mainland Chinese men (one of whom, Fu Guohao, was a reporter for a mainland China newspaper) were tied up and beaten by protesters.[42] In another instance, a Mandarin-speaking mainland Chinese banker was punched in the face and told to go back to the mainland, after declaring that, "We are all Chinese," during an argument with protesters.[43] On another occasion, a shop owner was reported to have shouted at a child after he asked to buy a toy while speaking Mandarin.[44] It was speculated that this violence may have contributed to declines in tourism from the mainland.[45]

While the binding and beating of Fu Guohao were briefly mentioned in two of the seven articles identified that dealt directly with the airport protests, there was a general lack of coverage of the incidents targeting mainland Chinese in most of the articles about the protests. One could read all of the *Times* coverage of the Hong Kong protests and have very little sense of this element of the protest movement.

The Military Takeover That Wasn't

The prospect of the Chinese military entering Hong Kong with the goal of crushing the protests also frequently appeared throughout the *Times* coverage. The prospect of such a reaction was not only a concern because it might lead to a brutal crackdown on protesters, but also because the Hong Kong Basic Law bans interference of the People's Liberation Army in Hong Kong's local affairs.[46] Such fears were encouraged by President Trump Tweeting, "Our Intelligence has informed us that the Chinese Government is moving troops to the Border with Hong Kong. Everyone should be calm and safe!" during the protests.

The *Times* coverage frequently referred to the possibility of China using its military to end the protests in Hong Kong. In one article discussing the buildup of forces in Shenzhen on the border with Hong Kong, Professor Minxin Pei was quoted saying, "It's a credible threat ... The Chinese government does not want to leave any doubt that, if necessary, it will act."[47] The Chinese government did not do much to end this speculation with an editorial in the *Global Times*, a state newspaper, noting: "The assembly of the Chinese Armed Police Forces in Shenzhen has issued a clear warning to the Hong Kong rioters that if Hong Kong cannot restore the rule of law and order through its own power, and the riots in Hong Kong become intensified, it will be inevitable that the central government will take direct measures in accordance with the Basic Law."[48] Speculations about intervention were amplified by an opinion piece titled, "Is a Crackdown Coming in Hong Kong?", which concluded with "For someone seen as an all-powerful leader—the 'chairman of everything,' as he is called—that might be a bridge too far. Without seduction in his arsenal, Mr. Xi may have to resort to force."[49]

Ultimately military intervention never took place. Indeed, the only time that the People's Liberation Army made an appearance in the streets of Hong Kong (months after the period of the protests examined here) was to remove bricks that had been left in the streets by protesters to impede traffic.[50]

Opinion Pieces

During the protest the *Times* published a total of 20 opinion pieces and four editorials dealing with the protests working out to more than one piece every four days. Most of these pieces provided a similar perspective about the protests in Hong Kong. In total, only two of the opinion pieces provided a perspective that could be considered as not completely endorsing the protests. A thoughtful piece by the economist Eswar Prasad argued that the mainland government felt more comfortable challenging Hong Kong institutions because the mainland economy now dwarfs Hong Kong's economy, which was not the case after the handover. However, even this piece concluded critically:

> But there is no mistaking Beijing's plans for Hong Kong, which do not include preserving what its people and international investors once cherished—the value placed on free enterprise along with democracy, freedom of expression and the rule of law. The protesters are right to fear what's coming.[51]

Regina Ip, a "pro-Beijing" legislator in Hong Kong Legislative Council, wrote an opinion piece in which she argued for continually working for the implementation of the "One

Country, Two Systems" style of governance on Hong Kong. In the piece, which is often critical of the protests, Ip offers some sympathy, writing:

> Nothing justifies violence, but given these divisions, the young of Hong Kong can be forgiven for feeling frustrated, helpless and even angry at the lack of direction and of a common vision for Hong Kong's future. They also face a growing wealth gap, an acute land and housing crisis and shrinking opportunities for upward mobility given rising competition from elites and entrepreneurs from mainland China. Successive Hong Kong leaders have failed to convince them that Hong Kong's future will be brighter than were its days before reunification.[52]

The remainder of the opinion pieces were supportive of the protest movement. In some cases, these pieces seemed to even support more militant tactics. In one piece provocatively titled "The People's War Is Coming in Hong Kong," Yi-Zheng Lian seemed to endorse Maoist-style tactics against the Hong Kong government:

> Back in 1938, Mao called for a "people's war" against the imperialists—for the broad and, if needed, protracted mobilization of the people in the countryside, with whatever makeshift means, to support his ragtag collection of Communist soldiers. Today the protesters in Hong Kong are using the same idea and trying to garner strength in preparation for Oct. 1, the 70th anniversary of the founding of the Communist regime in China.
>
> So in the weeks ahead, expect the peaceful-rational wing of the protest movement to keep up the pressure on the Hong Kong authorities with low-attrition activities—such as

industry-specific rallies or strikes and international lobbying—while the courageous militant wing takes a break to strategize and organize. The people's war is coming again, with a surreal, postmodern twist: this time, in one of the world's leading financial centers and against a Communist juggernaut.[53]

Conclusion

The *Times* coverage of the Hong Kong protests during their first three months was substantial and could be described as overwhelming. For example, on June 13th, two oil tankers were attacked in the Gulf of Oman. The attack was blamed on Iran and heightened tensions in the volatile part of the world to the extent that the United States deployed 1000 additional troops to the region. In the week after the attack, the volume of coverage of the incident was equal to that given to the Hong Kong protests. This extensive coverage continued into future months as well. Through the remainder of 2019 there were dozens more articles dealing with the Hong Kong protests. In general terms, the coverage was sympathetic to the protests. This sympathy could be seen in the portrayal of violence at the protests as well as the general lack of coverage of less savory aspects of the protest movement, such as anti-Mainland sentiment. The coverage also tended to be hyperbolic about the risk of mainland military intervention in the protests. Finally, the opinion pieces published about the protests were overwhelmingly sympathetic. In some cases, this sympathy was such that even potentially violent resistance was justified.

2019 Kashmir Lockdown Protests

August

The first article about the Kashmir status revocation and lockdown was published on August 5, the same day as the revocation, and provided a factual account of the revocation and the fears of protest that would follow it.[54] The next day an editorial was published, that labelled the decision to revoke Kashmir's special status as a folly.[55] Later coverage also reported on critics of the move within India[56] and Pakistan's reaction.[57]

Detailed coverage of the response of Kashmiris to the revocation was not seen until August 10th, five days after the revocation. In this coverage, it was reported how Indian security forces had beaten up people for shopping in violation of the curfew imposed after the revocation and how these same security forces opened fire on protesters marching in opposition to the revocation. This reporting also covered how many young Kashmiris were joining the insurgency against Indian rule, motivated by the change in the region's status.[58] Following the *Times*'s reporting of this fairly serious, violent repression, the next story two days later reported on how journalists in Kashmir had to use a variety of methods to print stories about the clampdown due to the fact that communications systems in the territory were shut down.[59] In both of these early pieces, violence by protesters is described:

> "At any point day or night," said Ravi Kant, a soldier based in the town of Baramulla, "whenever they get a chance, mobs of a dozen, two dozen, even more, sometimes with a lot of women, come out, pelt stones at us and run away."[60]

> Protests continued to erupt, and residents said packs of young men attacked security officers, hurling stones.[61]

On August 16, the *Times* coverage focused on an indication from Indian officials that the lockdown in the region would soon be eased. It was only at the end of the article that skepticism of the potential for the restrictions to be lifted was offered:

Usman Rashid, 22, a Kashmiri shop owner visiting New Delhi, said he was skeptical that the Indian government would lift the restrictions in Kashmir quickly, considering how upset people there were. Mr. Rashid said he expected mass protests once communications were restored.

"Whatever harm the Indian government has done to Kashmiris, do you think they will not come out to seek revenge and vent out their anger?" he asked. "The situation will worsen."[62]

Rashid was correct to be skeptical of the announcement. Restrictions were not fully lifted until February 2021, with some of the elements of the restrictions eased before then, such as the introduction of limited 2G Internet service with the government only allowing access to 301 "white-listed" websites in January 2020.[63] The *Times* did release a video essay that contradicted many of the claims of the Indian government, especially their claims regarding the lack of protests and an article on the roundup of thousands of Kashmiris without due process.[64,65]

For the first month after the lockdown began, many of the articles dealing with the lockdown did not focus directly on the experience of those in Kashmir, but rather placed the lockdown in the larger geopolitical context of conflict with Pakistan. This reporting included Pakistan's decision to halt bilateral trade between the two countries over the crisis in Kashmir[66] and how the crisis in Kashmir potentially made peace talks in Afghanistan more difficult.[67]

September

Even as the lockdown and protests continued, *Times* coverage dropped off substantially in the months of September and October. There were a total of ten pieces in September and eight in October. This diminishing coverage is surprising given the fact that the coverage that did exist documented a worsening situation in the region. The first piece published in September described an incident where a 16-year-old Kashmir boy — Asrar Ahmed Khan — was killed after being shot with buckshot when Indian security forces fired on a crowd gathered in Srinagar. While the piece itself described several witnesses reporting that the boy was killed by Indian security forces and the Indian authorities' denials of the accusations, the title of the piece itself left responsibility ambiguous: "Teenager Dies in Kashmir Amid Protests After Autonomy Was Revoked."[68]

Eleven days later, the next piece of reporting about Kashmir focused on violence committed by Kashmiri separatists including an incident where these militants shot and seriously injured a five-year-old girl and another incident where militants shot and killed a shopkeeper who refused to follow their demands to keep his shop closed. The piece did discuss violence committed by state security, including the torture of Bashir Ahmed Dar. Dar was beaten with sticks while "his sobbing pleas for mercy" were broadcast over loudspeakers because he did not know the whereabouts of his brother, a suspected separatist. However, the focus of the piece is primarily on separatist violence. It does not mention the death of Khan earlier in the month.[69]

The next piece of reporting about the region switched focus across the Line of Control to Pakistani controlled Azad Jammu and Kashmir. The piece described protests in the region, some of which were claimed to be calling for independence of the region from Pakistani control.[70] For the remainder of the month of September, of the three pieces of reporting dealing with Kashmir, only one reported about developments in the region.[71] The other two focused on how the Kashmiri issue and other abuses by the Modi government were interfering with his scheduled visit to the United States and plans for the Bill & Melinda Gates Foundation to give him an award,[72] and coverage of the Pakistani Prime Minister's speech to the UN where he warned of a potential "blood bath" in Kashmir.[73]

October

The first piece of reporting from October covered the effects that the lockdown had on medical care in Kashmir, including an inability to call ambulances, order medicine, and for doctors to consult with each other.[74] Two pieces focused on the Indian government's plans to restore mobile phone service access to the region after more than a month with no mobile phone communications available and the eventual return of that service.[75,76] Most of one piece focused on Kashmiris being able to contact family and friends from whom they had been cut off. Close to the end of this piece it is revealed that this reprieve was not available to everyone as "service was restored only for those with billing plans with phone companies, not for those using prepaid phones."

On October 15th, the *Times* reported on further militant actions in the region including the fatal shooting of a truck driver. While the piece did discuss the continued India lockdown in the region, it also indicated that militants in the region played a substantial role in life not being able to return to normal:

> But separatist militants are determined to disrupt any resumption of normalcy and maintain the resistance. There are only a few hundred militants in the Kashmir Valley, members of various outlawed groups who are poorly trained and lightly armed compared with the Indian forces they are fighting.
>
> Still, they have managed to keep much of the population in check through fear. The militants have hung posters and passed threats person to person, ordering the population to stay off the streets, or else.

The piece only briefly deals with accusations of human rights abuses against Indian security forces.[77] A piece published at the end of the month would also report on the murder of five construction workers by Kashmir militants.[78] The two other pieces of reporting from October covered India allowing far-right European politicians to visit the region, even as journalists and other politicians were banned from travelling there,[79] and the effects of being kept out of school on Kashmiri children.[80]

Opinion Pieces

Throughout the three month period reviewed here, there were two editorials, seven opinion pieces, and three collections of letters published by the *Times* about the situation in Kashmir. Both editorials focused on the need for the international community to act on the situation.[81,82] With respect to the seven opinion pieces, five provided a negative view of the developments in the region, one provided a positive perspective, and one piece did not address the revocation of the status directly, but rather reflected on the experience of a Hindu Kashmiri, whose family fled the region following violence directed at her community in the nineties.[83]

The positive piece titled "India Is Building a More Prosperous Kashmir" was published in mid-September. The piece argued that the revocation of the special status will make it possible for the Indian government to have an influence on areas of governance that will ensure prosperity in the region. The piece also argued that Pakistan wanted to prevent prosperity from developing in the region:

Pakistan has a vested interest in preventing prosperity in Jammu and Kashmir, and in the Ladakh area of Kashmir, because a weak economy fuels separatist sentiments in some quarters. This fits into Pakistan's larger strategy of using terrorism as a political tool. This is a country whose fingerprints are on terrorist strikes across the world and that was home to Osama bin Laden in his last days. So it also opposes the repeal of Article 370, which legitimized discrimination and hindered economic progress.[84]

This piece was written by then Indian Ambassador to the United States Harsh Vardhan Shringla. While Ambassador, Shringla was reported by the *Intercept* to have worked with a lobbying firm to prevent congress from passing a resolution that condemned the Indian government's revocation of the special status of Jammu and Kashmir.[85]

Conclusion

The *Times* coverage of the revocation of the special status of Jammu and Kashmir and the protests that followed was much less extensive than the coverage of the Hong Kong Extradition Bill protests. The coverage declined substantially in the weeks after the special status was revoked even as the lockdown and other government actions to curtail protests continued. The coverage that did exist tended to be negative, but coverage often reported on government announcements closely. Coverage of the situation in Kashmir continued to decline throughout the remainder of the year with fewer pieces of reporting from the region published in November and December than were published in October. This decline in reporting occurred despite the fact that the lockdown continued (with some of its harsher measures being lifted) through 2021.

Are the Situations Comparable?

Quantitatively, in terms of the amount of coverage received, and qualitatively, in terms of how the protest and government actions were covered, it does appear that the Hong Kong and

Kashmir events were reported differently by the *Times*. Before considering potential reasons for this different coverage, it is important to discuss whether the situations are comparable. If they are not comparable and if this lack of comparability would lead one to expect more coverage of the Hong Kong protests, then we can understand why Hong Kong received more coverage than Kashmir and why this coverage was different.

So what is similar about the situations? Kashmir and Hong Kong are both regions of large Asian countries. The population and size of Kashmir are both larger than Hong Kong. Both regions have local languages spoken (Kashmiri and other Indo-European languages in Kashmir, Cantonese and other Chinese languages in Hong Kong) with English frequently used in both due to both being former colonies of the British Empire.

In both cases, there was a proposal to change some status quo in regions of a country that were governed more autonomously than other parts of the country. In the case of Hong Kong, the Extradition Bill would have made it possible for prisoners to be extradited to the mainland, which had not been possible since the handover of Hong Kong to China in 1997. In the case of Kashmir, the autonomy of the region of Jammu and Kashmir, which was guaranteed by the Indian Constitution, was ended and a large portion of the territory was turned into a new state.

The government actions or proposed actions in the case of Kashmir and Hong Kong were not popular. While it is difficult to find recent polls from Kashmir about their opinions of the status of the territory, one poll from 2010 found that 43% of those surveyed favored independence in a hypothetical poll, the most popular option. In Srinagar, the joint capital of Kashmir and the region's largest city, support for independence was 82%. The next most popular option was to remain joined with India (28%); this option had very little support in the Kashmir region of Jammu and Kashmir, and instead got most of its support from the Jammu and Ladakh areas. The next most popular option was to make the Line of Control permanent. Very few people in the Indian controlled part of Kashmir supported the idea of joining Pakistan.[86] With only a minority of residents of Jammu and Kashmir supporting even being part of India, action to completely revoke the autonomy of the region would likely be very unpopular.

With respect to popular opinion in Hong Kong, a 2019 poll found that 59% of respondents supported the Anti-Extradition Bill protests, while 30% opposed them. 37% of respondents reported that they had participated in the protests.[87] However, Hong Kong residents were less supportive of more radical protest demands. 56.3% of Hong Kong residents opposed independence with 20% indicating support.[88]

These situations are not exactly the same. First, in the case of Kashmir the law revoking Kashmir's special status was actually passed. Indeed, the protests and lockdown occurred after the revocation. In contrast, the Hong Kong protests were in response to the potential for the passage of the Extradition Bill, which was suspended soon after protests started. Additionally, the change that occurred with the revocation of the special status of Jammu and Kashmir was more radical than even the proposed Extradition Bill in Hong Kong. The revocation of Jammu and Kashmir's special status would be more equivalent to China ending Hong Kong's autonomous status and the "One Country, Two Systems" arrangement, which according to Hong Kong's Basic Law is meant to be maintained through 2047. Although Jammu and Kashmir's special status as granted by the Indian Constitution was also intended to be temporary, until a formal decision was made about the region's status through a referendum, court decisions had determined that these provisions, because they had been in place for so long, had taken on the characteristics of permanent elements of the constitution.[89] So while the situations are not the same, with respect to two of the elements that made them different: (1) the fact that Jammu and Kashmir's special status was actually revoked, while the Extradition Bill was suspended, and (2) the revocation of Jammu and Kashmir's special status being a more radical change than the Extradition Bill, one would expect more focus on the situation in Kashmir.

The size of the protests may have contributed to some of the difference in coverage. As discussed above, the protests in Hong Kong were very large. Although the *Times* often reported numbers from protest organizers that were exaggerations, official estimates do suggest that around 240,000 people protested in one of the largest protests, about 4% of the city's residents. One protest in which organizers claimed that two million residents marched was estimated to have had about 338,000 by police.[90] This number would represent closer to 5% of the city's population. Making direct comparisons between the size of protests in Kashmir and Hong Kong is difficult. The total land area of Hong Kong is about 1100 square kilometers with density of over 6700 people per square kilometer. In contrast, Jammu and Kashmir has a total area of over 42,000 square kilometers and only 290 people per square kilometer. It was difficult to find reporting about the size of protests in Kashmir. One report from Reuters described "at least 10,000 people protesting" in Kashmir's summer capital city of Srinagar, which was denied by Indian officials.[91] This number would represent about 0.5% of the city's population. However, there were likely many more protests throughout the region. According to one report, there were at least 500 protest in the weeks following the revocation of Kashmir's special status.[92] These protests were dispersed throughout the large region. Because of there being less reporting coming from Kashmir, it is difficult to make a firm conclusion about the size of protests in other parts of the region.

Factors contributing to potentially lower numbers of people protesting in Kashmir also are worth considering when discussing why the coverage of Kashmir was different from Hong Kong. In Kashmir, a lockdown and curfew was imposed on the population as soon as the special status of the region was revoked. As reported by the *Times* this lockdown included "[cutting] off practically all communication from the area," which meant, as one Kashmir described it, "there is no way even ordinary Kashmiris here can like communicate with each other, and know what exactly is going on. Everybody is in a state of absolute shock and panic."[93] The lockdown was so severe that organizing would be very difficult. As one Indian official was quoted as saying, "the number of protests could be much higher and bigger without the blockade in force."[94] In the case of Hong Kong, no such lockdowns were imposed. While Hong Kong authorities would often deny permits to protests, in an attempt to prevent them,[95] there was never any general curfew imposed on the people of Hong Kong. Communications systems in the city were also never cut.

It is clear that the actions of the authorities in Kashmir were more severe than those imposed on the people of Hong Kong. One might expect that a more severe lockdown would result in more media attention, because it would be an indicator that the situation is more serious. However, that was not the case. It could be the case that the severity of the lockdown resulted in less attention from the *Times* simply because it was more difficult to report from the region, with any journalists still in the region after the lockdown was implemented facing severe limitations on their reporting.[96] This situation could have created a paradoxical situation: because it was easier for journalists to report from Hong Kong, the protests there, and any repression taking place, received more coverage, which could then create the impression among readers that the repression in Hong Kong was worse than that in Kashmir.

The reporting from both Hong Kong and Kashmir did tend to take a negative view of the actions of their governments and security forces; reporting from Kashmir was frequently framed around government announcements. For example, as stated above, there were two pieces that described India's plans to ease the lockdown before any such easement occurred.[97,98] In contrast, just the possibility of the intervention of the People's Liberation Army in Hong Kong received substantial attention. While the *Times* did report about the methods of responding to protesters in both cases, there were many more articles dealing with the violence of Hong Kong Police compared to Indian security forces. This greater focus is surprising given evidence that the Indian security forces' response to protests was likely more violent than that of the Hong Kong Police. In Hong Kong, there were no deaths that occurred in the three month period covered by this review. In later periods of the protest, one protester would die after falling from a parking garage, which was likely an accident.[99] In another instance, a Hong Kong resident was injured in a conflict with protesters after being struck in the head with a brick after trying to remove bricks that the protesters had left in the street.[100] In another case, a Hong Kong protester set a construction worker on fire. The man set on fire by the protesters survived.[101] In contrast, according to a report from the Association of Parents of Disappeared Persons and Jammu Kashmir Coalition of Civil Society, there were at least six deaths caused by Indian security officials in the period covered by this review:[102]

August 5: 17-year-old Usaib Altaf Marazi was beaten by Central Reserve Police Force (CRPF) personnel and fell into a river where he died.

August 9: Fehmida Rafiq died after inhaling "excessive tear smoke and pepper gas fired by police to disperse the protesting youth in the area."

August 17: Mohammad Ayoub Khan (57) choked to death after CRPF personnel fired "teargas and pepper shells on people assembling to protest the CRPF highhandedness in reaction to a minor stone pelting incident in the area."

August 22: Abdul Gaffar Wani (65) "died after he inhaled tear gas when there were clashes going on in the area."

September 4: Asrar Ahmad Khan was killed by teargas shells and pellets fired by CRPF personnel while playing cricket.

September 6: Riyaz Ahmad Tikrey "was brought home dead from a local police station where he was kept for four days, after his arrest by police from his home in connection with a protest post abrogation of Article 370 and 35 A. Police told his family he had committed suicide but lack convincing theory to back their claim. However, the condition of the body speaks itself of torture death."

By the end of December, it was estimated that 19 civilians had been killed by Indian armed forces.[103] On August 26, there was also an incident of a civilian potentially killed by protesters when a truck driver was struck and died after being hit with stones thrown by protesters. During the same period there were multiple killings by militants, many of which were covered the *Times*.

With respect to potential killings by security forces, I only identified mentions of the death of Asrar Ahmad Khan (see above). Following the initial report of Khan's death, I did not identify any further mentions of it in the period reviewed. In contrast, when a Hong Kong protester was alleged to have been shot in the eye resulting in serious injuries, this event was mentioned at least five times.[104,105,106,107,108] In Hong Kong, the case was a source of controversy both regarding the responsibility for the eye injury and the extent of the injury.[109]

With respect to the coverage of the Hong Kong protest, because of the frequent coverage many of the articles provided a detailed perspective on the protests. Consider these headlines:

With Hymns and Prayers, Christians Help Drive Hong Kong's Protests[110]

A Protest Song in Hong Kong[111]

Why Hong Kong's Protesters Are Turning to G-20 Leaders for Help[112]

What Denise Ho, Jackie Chan and Others Think About the Hong Kong Protests[113]

Hong Kong Protesters Take Their Message to Chinese Tourists[114]

Hong Kong Protesters' New Target: A News Station Seen as China's Friend[115]

Hong Kong's Civil Servants Protest Their Own Government[116]

Fueling the Hong Kong Protests: A World of Pop-Culture Memes[117]

Hong Kong Protesters Love Pepe the Frog. No, They're Not Alt-Right[118]

Reporting from Hong Kong also tended to provide detailed overview of the methods used by the protesters. In an article titled, "A Bird's-Eye View of How Protesters Have Flooded Hong Kong Streets," the *Times* created a comprehensive, interactive map showing important locations during one of the protest marches.[119] In another piece—"Protesters in Hong Kong Have Changed Their Playbook. Here's How"—the *Times* provided a full overview of the different methods used by protesters.[120] Another piece discussed the use of artificial intelligence technology to track the size of the protests.[121] In a video report, the *Times* performed a thorough investigation into the use of violence by police.[122] The *Times* frequently published videos from the protests; by my count there were a total of 24 video reports published during the first three months of protests as compared to two such video reports from Kashmir.

The reporting from Kashmir tended to provide much more general overview and updates. Consider these headlines:

Inside Kashmir, Cut Off From the World: "A Living Hell" of Anger and Fear[123]

India Shut Down Kashmir's Internet Access. Now, "We Cannot Do Anything."[124]

India's Move in Kashmir: More Than 2,000 Rounded Up With No Recourse[125]

Abused by Soldiers and Militants, Kashmiris Face Dangers in Daily Life[126]

In Kashmir, Growing Anger and Misery[127]

Finally, another difference between the two regions is that Jammu and Kashmir has among the lowest per capita GDPs of Indian states and union territories, while Hong Kong has the second highest per capital GDP of all Chinese provinces and regions, following only the other Special Administrative Region of Macao. While it is possible that this socioeconomic reality could result in different coverage, it is hard to consider this an acceptable justification for the differences.

Conclusion

In terms of the reasons for the protests, the two situations were fairly similar. The differences between them were related to the action taken by the Indian government actually being implemented and being much more severe than even the proposed Extradition Bill. Additionally, the violence by state forces was more severe in the case of India with actual deaths occurring, which was not the case in Hong Kong. The only factor that could have contributed to more reporting being given to Hong Kong is the larger size of the protests. As discussed, this difference may be due to the more dispersed nature of the Kashmir population and the severe lockdown imposed on Kashmiris, another factor that one would think would justify more coverage of Kashmir.

Reasons for Differences

One argument for differences in the coverage may be that protests in Kashmir have been the norm essentially since the region was partitioned in the late 1940s, whereas wide scale protests in Hong Kong are a new phenomenon. News often tends to emphasize new developments. While it is certainly true that there have been frequent protests and sometimes violent state responses to protests in Kashmir throughout India's history (see, for example, the discussion of the Gawkadal killings and related incidents in Chapter 1), what happened in 2019 was an entirely new development, with the entire region's status being radically changed from the norm that had existed for decades. Additionally, in the case of Hong Kong, while the history of protests against governments in the territory is not as extensive as the history of such protests in Kashmir, they certainly have existed. In particular, there were protests in 2014 (the Umbrella Movement) against electoral law changes, there have been annual protests to mark the anniversary of the Tiananmen Square Protests, and, going back to the 1960s, there were large-scale protests (such as the Leftists Riots) against British Colonial control of Hong Kong, which resulted in dozens of protesters being killed by British security personnel.

Another factor that may have contributed to differential reporting is the nature of violence in Kashmir and Hong Kong.

Security forces' response to the protests was a common topic in coverage of both the Hong Kong and Kashmir protests. A total of at least five pieces, including video reporting, centered on police violence in Hong Kong.[128,129,130,131,132] In contrast, while security force violence in Kashmir was a frequent topic of coverage of the Kashmir protests, especially during the first month of coverage, none of the articles were primarily framed around this state violence. One would expect state violence to have received more attention in the case of Kashmir, because (as described above) there were at least six incidents where deaths may have been caused directly by police response to the protests.

There is an element to violence in Kashmir that was not present in the Hong Kong situation, namely the active insurgency in Kashmir compared to Hong Kong. While as discussed above one opinion piece argued that militancy was a possible path for the Hong Kong protesters to take, and since the period considered in this chapter, some protesters have been arrested, accused of stockpiling weapons.[133] However, Hong Kong did not have and does not have an active militant insurgency. Kashmir does have a longstanding active militant movement seeking to end Indian administration of the region. As discussed, these organizations were active during the period covered in this review, which included attacks targeting both state security forces and civilians in the region. Such an active militant organization would seem to encourage more attention from the *Times* rather than less.

Arrests of protesters and dissidents in the two regions is another factor that could result in different coverage. Through early October, one month past the period considered by this review, there were reported to have been nearly 2400 people arrested in the course of the Hong Kong protests. In contrast, one month after the protests in Kashmir began, it was reported that nearly 3800 people had been taken into custody by Indian authorities and 2600 released. Arrests were frequently due to stone throwing and other actions during the protest.[134] Among those who were arrested were over 200 politicians "including two former chief ministers of the state." Arrests in China included members of banned independence parties and pro-democracy activists like Joshua Wong.[135] In many cases, those arrested were released on bail shortly after their arrest. For example, after Wong was arrested in late August, he was released on bail within hours.[136] Other protesters would frequently be released after being taken into custody.[137] In Kashmir, many of those who were arrested were held under the authority of the Public Safety Act, which allows detention for up to two years.[138] In both Hong Kong and Kashmir there were thousands arrested. However, in the case of Kashmir, many of those arrested, especially prominent figures, were detained for longer periods. Among the two former chief ministers arrested, Mehbooba Mufti, the Chief Minister of Kashmir from 2016 to 2018, was kept in custody for over a year until October 2020. Omar Abdullah was released in March 2020. The number of arrests was likely higher in the case of Kashmir with potentially longer detainment periods and more prominent arrests in Kashmir.

The *Times* also tended to consult human rights and other international organizations more often in the coverage of Hong Kong compared to Kashmir. I identified four references to Amnesty International's perspective[139,140,141,142] and five to Human Rights Watch[143,144,145,146] about the protests and state responses in Hong Kong identified. I did not identify any such references for Kashmir. Both human rights organizations' websites discussed both regions in their official publications during the periods considered.

With respect to this comparison, the "Worthy/Unworthy" hypothesis is a viable explanation. In particular, actions of a country that is often considered a geopolitical enemy of the United States (China) and protests against those actions received substantially more coverage than actions by a government that is often viewed as being more in alignment with the United States (India). While there were differences between the two situations, in most cases those differences would be expected to contribute to more coverage for Kashmir compared to Hong Kong (the more severe state actions, the fact that in Kashmir the state actions actually took place, the fact that India's actions could threaten war with Pakistan).

If you accept this conclusion that one would expect coverage of Kashmir to at least be equal to that of Hong Kong based solely on the facts of the two stories, the question still remains about why Hong Kong received more attention. Considering Herman and Chomsky's five filters, the most relevant are likely sourcing, and anti-Communism. With respect to sourcing, Hong Kong and mainland Chinese sources were frequently quoted in the coverage, but these quotes were often portrayed differently than statements from the Indian government. Coverage in Kashmir was almost always reactive, reporting on new actions by the government. This is most evident by the fact that coverage of the situation in the region did not really begin until after special status was revoked. Before August, I found only two paragraphs mentioning the BJP's plan for Kashmir in the *Times* coverage, both of which occurred following the BJP's election.[147,148] This scant coverage of an important issue occurred despite the fact that challenges associated with the election in Kashmir were mentioned several times and despite the fact that it was on the platform of Modi and the BJP during the 2019 election:

We are committed to annulling Article 35A of the Constitution of India as the provision is discriminatory against non-permanent residents and women of Jammu and Kashmir.

We believe that Article 35A is an obstacle in the development of the state. We will take all steps to ensure a safe and peaceful environment for all residents of the state. We will make all efforts to ensure the safe return of Kashmiri Pandits and we will provide financial assistance for the resettlement of refugees from West Pakistan, Pakistan occupied Jammu and Kashmir (POJK) and Chhamb.

In a similar way, while there was substantial discussion of the potential for China's People's Liberation Army to take action in Hong Kong, the actual deployment of troops to Kashmir did not receive as much attention. Some of this difference may be due to the fact that India already had a military presence in the region because of the insurgency (China also has PLA troops stationed in Hong Kong, but they are not allowed to operate in the city, except in extreme circumstances), but the fact that the Indian military was being deployed because of protesters was significant, especially given the violence against protesters.

It is more difficult to quantify the role that anti-Communist sentiments play in the differing coverage. The fact that journalists as well as readers may be more used to negative coverage of the Chinese government compared to the Indian government may contribute to a different baseline acceptance of negative stories. For example, despite the fairly different situations, there was frequent discussion of Tiananmen Square Protests in the coverage of Hong Kong, while previous massacres of protesters in Kashmir and Muslims in India were not frequently discussed, despite the fact that the Prime Minister of India has been implicated in at least one case of alleged ethnic cleansing directed against Muslims while he was governor of Gujarat (see Chapter 1).

At the same time, US readers and journalists may be more sympathetic to the Indian government's actions, because

India can be portrayed as responding to the threat of Islamic terrorism in the region, just like the US has been portrayed as responding to the threat of Islamic terrorism in the Middle East for decades. Although previous massacres of Kashmiri civilians or Muslims in India were not frequently discussed, there was an opinion article describing the horrible exodus of Kashmir Hindu Pandits from the region that occurred in the nineties in response to militancy.[149] Such coverage can contribute to this sympathy.

Conclusion

In 2019, coverage of Hong Kong's proposed Extradition Bill received substantially more media attention than coverage of the revocation of Jammu and Kashmir's special status by the Indian government. This increased attention occurred despite the fact that the Hong Kong bill was suspended, while the Kashmir revocation actually occurred. Additionally, while coverage in both instances focused on the severity of state actions and violence, more attention was given to Hong Kong, despite the fact that evidence suggests that the actions of Hong Kong security forces were more severe, possibly resulting in several deaths. In both cases there were thousands of arrests, but in the case of Kashmir, those arrested included more prominent politicians who were often detained for longer periods. Additionally, India instituted a media blackout in Kashmir, which did not occur in Hong Kong. While the protests in Hong Kong were likely larger than those in Kashmir, the size is at least partially due to the different geographic conditions and the fact that the lockdown in Kashmir was so severe.

Both the situations in Hong Kong and Kashmir were important geopolitical events that deserved media attention. However, the fact that Kashmir receives less attention should be concerning. Because of the relationship between the US government and

Kashmir, it is theoretically more possible for the US to have some influence on actions in the region. In contrast, because of the often adversarial relationship between the US and China, the US's role in Hong Kong is often going to have a negative impact. For example, funding of groups associated with protests by the US government's National Endowment for Democracy[150] was sometimes used by the Chinese media as evidence of US meddling in the region and justification for further actions to prevent alleged foreign influence in Hong Kong.[151]

Chapter 3

Worthy and Unworthy Protests in South America: 2019 Venezuelan Protests, 2019–2020 Bolivian Protests, and 2019–2021 Colombian Protests

Latin America has frequently and condescendingly been referred to as the backyard of the United States. In 2022, Joe Biden changed the region's status to the "front yard,"[1] but the fact remains that the countries south of the Rio Grande have been perceived by Washington as a place where the United States has a special strategic interest. This tendency goes back to the Monroe Doctrine when the US, while stating that it would oppose European intervention in the region, also indicated that it would be a region where the US would be free to intervene to protect its own interest. Since that time, and especially since the twentieth century, the United States has intervened in devastating ways throughout the region whether through supporting coups, providing assistance to militias, or direct military intervention.

Throughout the United States' involvement in the region, there have been governments that have been seen as friendly to the United States and those who have been seen as enemies. The friendly regimes will often be propped by any means necessary, while the unfriendly ones will often face the threat of blockades, coups, and invasion. The position of countries in this hierarchy have often fluctuated. In recent years, the main enemies in the region often have been those where leftists leaders have come to power amid the so-called "Pink Tide." In the twenty-first century, the South American countries of Venezuela, ruled first by Hugo Chávez and later by Nicolás Maduro, and Bolivia until recently led by Evo Morales have attracted negative attention. In contrast, Colombia has been one of the United States' most consistent geopolitical allies as made evident by the strong diplomatic and military relations between the two countries. Based on the Unworthy/Worthy hypothesis one would expect that protests against leaders not geopolitically allied with the United States (such as Maduro in Venezuela or Morales in Bolivia) would receive more attention than protests against allied governments (like that in Colombia or the government that succeeded Morales in Bolivia). Additionally, one would also expect that protests against any regimes that succeeded the unfriendly regimes would receive less attention.

In the period between 2019 and 2021, several protests and crises throughout South America provided the opportunity to test the Unworthy/Worthy hypothesis. The specific events considered in this chapter include protests against Maduro following a contested election in 2018, protests against the reelection of Evo Morales and then subsequent protests against the government that succeeded him in 2019 and 2020, and several rounds of protests against the economic policies of the Colombian government between 2019 and 2021.

Background

Venezuelan Protests, 2019

Relations between the United States and Venezuela have been fraught ever since the election of Hugo Chávez as the country's president in 1999. Chávez, while serving as a military leader under President Carlos Andrés Pérez (president during the Caracoza protests—see Chapter 1), secretly began plotting to overthrow his regime, which eventually resulted in a coup in 1992 for which Chávez was imprisoned for leading. After being pardoned, Chávez became a prominent opposition leader in the country before winning election as President in 1998 with over 56% of the vote. During his reelections in 2000 and 2006 he would receive larger shares of the vote. In his final reelection in 2012 he received 55% of the vote. Chávez's political project focused on addressing poverty, and other social and economic problems that had plagued Venezuela. During his time in office, Chávez focused the government on increasing access to housing and healthcare, while also improving literacy. During this time, some Venezuelan industries were nationalized.

Many of the policies of Chávez attracted the negative attention of the United States. In particular, Chávez brought Venezuela into closer relations with left-wing governments including Cuba. Chávez was also accused of ruling Venezuela in an authoritarian manner. In 2002, Chávez was briefly removed from office in a coup by military officers. The United States had advanced knowledge of the coup plot[2] and may have permitted[3] or even assisted in it being carried out.[4,5] In 2013, just a few months after being inaugurated for his fourth presidential term, Chávez died from cancer. He was succeeded by his Vice President Nicolás Maduro. Soon after, Maduro narrowly won an election to the presidency. Alan MacLeod's excellent book *Bad News from Venezuela: Twenty Years of Fake News and Misreporting* provides a comprehensive overview of the often biased coverage many of these events received in the Western media.

In May 2018, Nicolás Maduro was reelected as the president of Venezuela in a disputed election. Even before the election was held, there was controversy because the date of the election was moved back from December to April and then to May. Some organizations identified irregularities in voting results. Before the election, the opposition and many Western governments had accused the Maduro government of being responsible for the economic crisis in the country. The United States as well as many

Latin American and European countries did not recognize the election results. On January 10th, 2019, Maduro was inaugurated for his second term. At the same time, the National Assembly, led by its president Juan Guaidó, with a majority that did not back Maduro, rejected the inauguration and declared a state of emergency. Large-scale protests against Maduro soon followed.

Bolivia, 2019–2020

Like Hugo Chávez, the election of Evo Morales as President of Bolivia in 2005 with over 53% was seen as being emblematic of the "Pink Tide" of leftist leaders coming to power in Latin America. As with Chávez, Morales focused on social and economic policies after being elected and also improved Bolivia's relationship with other left-wing governments in Latin America. Morales was reelected in 2009 and 2014 with greater shares of the vote (over 60% in both instances) than he had received in his initial 2005 election.

In October 2019, Evo Morales was reelected for his third term as President of Bolivia. As with the Venezuelan election, there was controversy in the lead-up to the election, because the Bolivarian constitution limited presidents to two terms. A referendum to change this requirement failed before the Supreme Court of Bolivia rejected the provision limiting presidents to only two terms as a limitation of the human rights of Bolivians. Morales won the election with a margin slightly over 10% (47.08% versus 36.51% for his closest rival). Reaching the 10% bar was necessary to prevent a runoff between the two leading candidates. There was controversy about some of the election results. Protests broke out in the country, especially in the capital of La Paz against Morales. After losing the support of the military Morales left the country for Mexico. A government led by Jeanine Añez, a member of the legislator from a right-wing opposition party, took over the government. Protests were then launched against Añez. These protests would pick up again in 2020 as many in the country called for a new election to be held.

Colombia

Colombia has traditionally been one of the United States' strongest allies in Latin America. This close relationship has persisted among both Democratic and Republic presidents, and has included close coordination in terms of anti-Communism, drug policy, and terrorism. Colombia has consistently received millions of dollars in aid from the United States with much of it going to its military,[6] which has faced credible accusations of severe human rights abuses. Three rounds of protests that occurred in Colombia between 2019 and 2021 are discussed in this chapter.

November 15, 2019 to February 15, 2020

The first round of Colombian protests was launched because of a wide variety of issues that had been challenging Colombia for some time. These issues included government corruption, the imposition of austerity measures, the slow peace process for Colombia's decades long civil war, and inequality.

Colombia, September to November 2020

The second round of protests in Colombia were tied to a very specific event: the police killing of Javier Ordóñez in Bogotá, the Colombian capital. Police were filmed holding Ordóñez on the ground and using a stun gun on him. It was estimated that he was tasered at least twelve times. He was taken to a police station where a friend found him severely injured. After the friend begged for him to be taken to a hospital, Ordóñez died from his injuries.

Colombia, April 15 to July 15, 2021

Like the earlier round of protests, there were many reasons for the third round of protests. They were sparked in particular by proposed reforms to the tax and healthcare system in the country. The health reform proposed included elements of increased privatizations of the healthcare system. At the time, Colombia was also suffering from the effects of the COVID-19 outbreak and many were unhappy with the government's response.

The Numbers

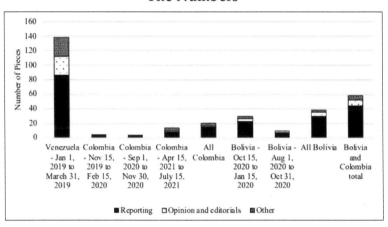

Figure 7. Coverage of 2019 Venezuelan, 2019–2020 Bolivian Protests, and 2019, 2020, 2021 Colombia Protests by type of coverage

The three initial months of the Venezuelan crisis received substantial coverage in the *Times* with 138 pieces published, for an average of about 1.5 pieces per day. There were 86 pieces of reporting and 26 opinion pieces. The initial three months of the first round of Bolivian protests had a total of 29 pieces, while the three months of the second round had a total of 9 pieces. Three months of each of the three Colombian Protests considered had

4, 3, and 13 articles published. The sum of all the coverage for the Bolivian and Colombian Protests was less than one-half of the coverage given to Venezuela.

The Coverage

Venezuelan Protests, 2019

January 2019

While the protests against the Maduro government are generally considered to have begun on January 10, 2019, coverage of stories relevant to the lead-up to the protests began to appear on January 4, when it was reported that representatives from the US and several Latin American and Caribbean countries did not consider the results of the election held the previous year as legitimate.[7] When Maduro was inaugurated several days later, the coverage contrasted the apparently smaller crowds attending with larger crowds present during his first inauguration in 2013. The absence of representatives from the United States, European Union, and some Latin American countries was also reported. In a discussion of the economic situation in the country, international sanctions, which included embargos and the seizure of assets owned by the Venezuelan government, were only mentioned once.[8] Similarly, later in the month, in a brief primer about the economic and political crisis in the country, the focus is put on governance failures of the Maduro and Chávez governments, with no mention of the important role played by falling gas prices in the 2010s and sanctions.[9] Later a UN report indicated that these sanctions contributed to the economic difficulties in Venezuela.[10]

Shortly after Maduro's inauguration, Juan Guaidó, the recently elected president of the National Assembly, declared that he was prepared to take control of the country and hold new elections. Following this declaration, Guaidó was briefly detained by Venezuelan authorities.[11] After his detention, further coverage focused on Guaidó including his plans to declare the presidency vacant with support of the United States, the possibility of the National Assembly declaring him president, and a detailed discussion of his rise to political prominence. This coverage often featured US-based voices praising the young leader:

He's breathed new life into the opposition ... The opposition has finally put forward a fresh face that has courage, new ideas and leadership skills that has started to revive them.[12]

The strength of US support for Guaidó grew throughout the month of January. Vice President Mike Pence released a video where he declared his support for mass protests in the country, which led Maduro to ask, "Who elects the president of Venezuela? Mike Pence?"[13] The coverage of Guaidó culminated in his declaration of himself as the rightful President of Venezuela during a large protest. Then President Donald Trump quickly recognized this declaration.[14] The *Times* published a video of Guaidó's swearing-in ceremony.[15]

While then Secretary of State Mike Pompeo was trying to rally countries, including members of the Organization of American States (OAS) in opposition to Maduro,[16,17] Russia warned the United States against intervening militarily in the country.[18] Trump had kept the possibility of such an intervention open when he said that "all options are on the table" with respect to Venezuela.[19] In response to the possibility of a coup against Maduro, the Venezuelan defense minister declared himself in support of Maduro.[20]

Reports discussed arrests of members of Venezuela's National Guard who declared their support for Guaidó.[21]

Maduro's government may have been particularly sensitive to the possibility of military actions against the government because of an earlier coup attempt against his predecessor Hugo Chávez.

In another primer about the situation in the country, the *Times* offered a blunt description about why it was taking place: "The short version: Venezuela's government has overseen the destruction of its democracy and its economy. Public outrage is coming to a head." The same article described the 2002 attempted coup against Chávez, but failed to mention the allegations of US's support or awareness of the coup before it took place.[22]

Through much of the end of January, coverage focused on contrasting Maduro with Guaidó. One video posted by the *Times* compared addresses given by the two leaders.[23] The impact that Florida Senator Marco Rubio had in encouraging the Trump administration to support Guaidó was also discussed.[24] After the US instituted sanctions against Venezuela's state-owned oil company Petróleos de Venezuela, Guaidó's "nascent government" was reported as "making every effort it could to get control of Venezuela's international assets—and mainly the state oil company." When interventionist neoconservative John Bolton reported on these sanctions, he held a notebook with "5,000 troops to Colombia" written on it.[25] The *Times* published letters supporting and opposing this move.[26] Later reporting covered how the US government gave Guaidó access to frozen Venezuelan bank assets.[27] In reporting about the effects of the sanctions, the *Times* described how the suffering that they would cause was a part of the goal of regime change in Venezuela and the alignment of the opposition with the US Government:

But the opposition contends that for a country suffering from economic free-fall and increasingly authoritarian governance, this could be the path to much-needed change.

Many opposition leaders are sanguine about the turbulence ahead, welcoming Washington's kingmaker role in Venezuela's political standoff as crucial to restoring democracy and starting to rebuild a nation ravaged by mismanagement under Mr. Maduro.[28]

Another article described former military members living in exile in "Peru, Colombia and other countries" plotting to back Guaidó and overthrow Maduro. Some of these leaders were reported to have met with the Trump administration.[29] While reporting on this plotting, the *Times* also covered allegations of Cuban military support for the Maduro government.[30] The military connections between the US and potential rebel military leaders were made more ominous by a declaration from Bolton that, "All Options Are on the Table" with respect to Venezuela, not ruling out a potential military intervention.[31] Maduro responded to these seeming threats of a military intervention, saying:

Let's not allow a Vietnam in Latin America ... If the United States intends to intervene here, they will have a Vietnam worse than what they can imagine. Let's not allow violence.[32]

February

In the beginning of February, the *Times* solicited stories from their readers in English and Spanish, asking them to describe how the Venezuelan crisis had affected them.[33,34] The *Times* then published several vignettes describing the plight of Venezuelans motivated to protest against the government. In one particularly tragic story a mother described her son's struggle with leukemia:

"It is like the world opens in half and you just want to jump into the crack," said Mrs. Cedeño, describing how she felt six years ago when she first found out her son, Miguel, had leukemia. Things were still manageable then. Her son was moved from a private hospital to the public Central Hospital of Venezuela where he was given medical treatment paid for by the state. He went into remission for years, but in 2017, Miguel's cancer returned. That's when, Mrs. Cedeño said, everything changed. It was a race against time to get him proper treatment. "I had to buy everything," she said. "The chemotherapy, the antibiotics, the needles. But now it's even worse. I have to buy gloves, cotton, alcohol, water, even the tubes for the lab if I need to ask for a blood test."

Venezuela's main hospital has become a symbol of the catastrophic unraveling of the country's health care system. It is often without running water, medicine and even doctors. The electricity regularly cuts out, which has resulted in patient deaths, opposition politicians say.[35]

While US sanctions did not directly affect medicine, a report from the Washington Office on Latin America indicated that the loss of oil revenue due to sanctions made it more difficult to buy essential medical supplies.[36] While not acknowledged in the piece that described the mother's experience with her son's leukemia, the fact that the sanctions would have a devastating effect on the Venezuelan economy was at least acknowledged in another profile of Guaidó:

Oil sanctions imposed by the United States last week will soon strangle the country's already-devastated economy, which will most likely cause shortages of fuel and make food and medicine even more scarce. Bracing for the destabilizing effects of the sanctions, Mr. Guaidó and his allies in the international community said they intended to start pumping humanitarian aid into the country this week. Doing so would undermine Mr. Maduro, who recently scoffed at the prospect by saying "we're not a country of beggars."[37]

Further reporting covered the likelihood of the effect of the sanctions falling disproportionately on the poorest Venezuelans: "'I'm not sure the U.S. has a Plan B if this doesn't work in getting rid of Maduro,' said Francisco Rodríguez, a Venezuelan economist at Torino Capital, a brokerage firm. 'I'm afraid that if these sanctions are implemented in their current form, we're looking at starvation.'"[38]

The *Times* reported an uptick in the protest with an estimated 800,000 protesters in the streets.[39] The *Times* also published a video about the personal experiences of a mother whose son died during the protests.[40] At that time, the focus of coverage shifted to the diplomatic complexity of having two ambassadors—one representing Guaidó and the other representing the Maduro government—in Washington.[41] In February, the increasing division of the world between countries that back Maduro and those that back Guaidó was covered,[42] especially after many European countries joined the US and some Latin American countries in recognizing Guaidó.[43] At the UN, the representative of the Maduro government organized a coalition of countries opposed to the US's policies against his government.[44]

The *Times* attempted to adjudicate these differing claims for who is the rightful leader of Venezuela[45] and Pope Francis offered to mediate the situation between the two sides.[46] At this time, it was the opposition who was primarily opposed to such talks:

On Tuesday, Pope Francis said he would be willing to mediate a peaceful resolution if asked by both Mr. Guaidó and Mr. Maduro. He said Mr. Maduro had written him a letter asking for dialogue. "We are always willing," said Francis on the papal plane, but added that both parties needed to be willing. The opposition is suspicious of Mr. Maduro's calls for talks, and hopes that its aid plan will accelerate his ouster.[47]

While many countries were debating which government to back, the *Times* Editorial Board made its position clear that it believed Guaidó was the best choice to lead Venezuela:

> There is no question that President Maduro must go, the sooner the better. Heir to the socialist rule of Hugo Chávez, he has led his oil-rich country into utter ruin. Its currency is useless, basic foods and medicines have disappeared and more than three million people have fled, fomenting refugee crises in Colombia, Brazil and Ecuador. The only solution is an interim government under Mr. Guaidó, who as the head of the National Assembly has a legitimate claim to the presidency under the Venezuelan Constitution.[48]

Later in the month, the Editorial Board again made its recommendations for Venezuela clear, essentially advocating for a military coup: "Yes, the military should abandon Mr. Maduro, who has guided one of Latin America's richest countries to total ruin, and join the opposition leader Juan Guaidó in trying to put Venezuela back on track."[49]

In late February, controversy over the Maduro government's blocking of the opposition's effort to bring humanitarian aid into the country was discussed.[50,51,52,53] During this same period, the US military became involved by flying aid intended for Venezuela to Colombia.[54] This support was bolstered by President Trump threatening that the Venezuelan military would lose everything by supporting Maduro.[55] The *Times* published a video showing the Colombian border town where the aid was being held up, featuring an interview with a Venezuelan military defector.[56] Other such defections were also covered.[57] These conflicts at the border turned violent when it was reported that the Venezuelan government fired on and killed several protesters near the Brazilian border.[58,59,60,61,62] Videos and photos were published showing a concert on the Colombian side of the border organized by billionaire Richard Branson.[63,64]

During this time, the *Times* also covered in more detail Venezuelans moving over the border and out of Venezuela into Colombia. The role of sanctions in the economic plight contributing to this exodus are not mentioned in the article.[65] Similarly, in an article detailing the suffering of Venezuelans in hospitals needing treatment, only the impact of Maduro refusing aid is mentioned, not the sanctions.[66] In late February, Vice President Mike Pence travelled to Colombia to announce even more sanctions and to pressure countries that had not taken a stance in the conflict to recognize the Guaidó government.[67,68]

Debate about the attempts to send aid across the border led to conflict between the United States and Russia at the United Nations Security Council, where the Russian ambassador said that the aid was a tool of the US government to "oust an inconvenient regime."[69] This conflict grew more heated as the United States sought to pass a resolution calling for new elections through the Security Council.[70] Russia along with China would later veto this resolution (with South Africa also voting against it), while an alternative resolution offered by Russia did not pass.[71] There were fears expressed during debate about the motion, that it may be used as a justification for military intervention, which were bolstered when Pence reiterated, while introducing new sanctions, that military intervention was still on the table.[72]

Univision reporter Jorge Ramos was detained by the Venezuelan government while covering the conflict.[73] A few days later, the *Times* published an opinion piece from Ramos about his experience.[74]

March

In another editorial where the board made its suggestions for the situation in the country, they labelled the beliefs of many Venezuelans as "claptrap": "And a dictator who has already destroyed his country—and has the support of Russia and China—is not one who gives a fig for the suffering of his people, a sizable portion of whom still harbor an attachment to the 'Bolivarian socialist' claptrap of his predecessor and mentor, Hugo Chávez."[75]

In early March, Guaidó returned to Venezuela.[76,77] At the same time, an opinion piece seemed to suggest that only a coup would be able to remove the Maduro regime:

> Mr. Guaidó and his international allies may have no option but to entertain an interim civilian-military partnership under some form of international tutelage. They need to continue to reach out to some of the more honest military officers, those interested in the integrity of the institution, to turn against not just Mr. Maduro but also the disparate groups across the military. The mission: Bring the military institution back to order.[78]

At this same time, Venezuela experienced blackouts due to the loss of power at a substation attached to the country's large Guri Dam. Guaidó and the US blamed the Maduro government's mismanagement of the dam for the blackouts, while the Maduro government blamed sabotage.[79,80,81,82] Secretary of State Mike Pompeo pointed to Cuba as being responsible for the blackouts:

> When there is no electricity, thank the marvels of modern Cuban-led engineering ... When there's no water, thank the

excellent hydrologists from Cuba. When there's no food, thank the Cuban communist overlords.[83]

An article from the *Times* aligned with Pompeo's critique of the Cuba-Venezuela relations, when it used reports from some anonymous sources who claimed that medical care (frequently provided by Cuban doctors) was often used to coerce votes and not provided to political opponents.[84] Later articles suggested that Maduro was trying to pin blame for the blackouts on the recently returned Guaidó.[85] At the same time, Pompeo warned Venezuela that any move to arrest Guaidó would result in an "immediate reaction" from the international community.[86] Soon after, Guaidó's Chief of Staff was arrested.[87]

Near the end of March, the *Times* coverage seemed to be more resigned to the fact that Maduro was not likely to fall from power anytime soon with both a video and article discussing how he stayed in power.[88,89] During this time, Russia sent two military planes to the country, which was suggested to be a show of solidarity between the two countries,[90] which led to Trump telling Russia to "get out" of Venezuela while meeting with Juan Guaidó wife, Fabiana Rosales, in the Oval Office.[91,92] The UN also began to encourage cooperation between Maduro and Guaidó to coordinate aid entering the country,[93] shortly after aid began entering the country, facilitated by the Red Cross.[94] The last article discussed how the economic crisis in the country remained a source of hope for many in the opposition that the Maduro government would eventually fall.[95] In one strange phrase in the article, the *Times* seems to obfuscate support for oil sanctions in the country:

Less than half of Venezuelans said they were against President Trump's sanctions against the Venezuelan oil industry, according to a survey by the country's leading pollster, Datanalisis, in early March. It was a surprisingly low share given the direct impact of the sanctions on living standards.

It would have been clearer to report the percentage who supported the sanctions. I was not able to identify the poll, which was not linked in the article to check if support for sanctions was greater than opposition. A later poll mentioned in an opinion piece in the *Times* outside of the period covered here reported that 68% of Venezuelans believed that the sanctions had a negative impact on their quality of life.[96]

Venezuelan and Domestic US Politics

The frequent coverage of the Venezuelan situation also meant that its relevance to domestic politics in the United States was often discussed. Soon after the protests began, the *Times* reported about the almost universally supportive attitude towards the protests of Venezuelans living in the United States.[97] The fact that Republicans could seize on the Trump administration's hardline stance with respect to Venezuela to gain votes among the Venezuelan ex-pat community was also discussed.[98] Trump's attacks on Maduro were interpreted as part of an effort to gain votes for the coming 2020 Presidential Election.[99]

A piece by columnist Bret Stephens suggested that the crisis in Venezuela should be treated as a lesson in the dangers of socialism,[100] which was critiqued by some readers.[101] In a seeming response, economist Paul Krugman wrote an article a few days later saying:

> In fact, whenever you see someone invoking Venezuela as a reason not to consider progressive policy ideas, you know right away that the person in question is uninformed, dishonest, or both. It basically shows that the speaker or writer isn't willing to engage in serious discussion, preferring

to scare people with a boogeyman of which he or she knows nothing.[102]

Opinion Pieces

Throughout the first three months of protests, a number of different opinion pieces were published about the situation in Venezuela. On January 24th, two letters to the editor appeared. One was sympathetic to the protests against Maduro and the second offered caution against US interference in Latin America.[103] Another opinion piece broadly praised Juan Guaidó as a new class of Venezuelan opposition leaders. Much of the piece focused on how a military coup would be required for Guaidó to come to power:

> Unless high-level military officers can be given sufficient guarantees that they will not have to pay for their crimes, Mr. Guaidó's path forward could be blocked. To his credit, he has shown he understands the crucial role of the military. He has appealed to them with non-vindictive messages, including persuading the National Assembly on Jan. 15 to adopt an amnesty law for those who act "in favor of the restitution of democracy in Venezuela."
>
> Winning over the military will require patience and sophisticated and discreet negotiations. The notion of "negotiations" is anathema to much of the opposition, given the failure of previous efforts at "dialogue." But now that the tables have turned—the Maduro government is weaker and the opposition stronger—negotiations might well be more fruitful.[104]

In an editorial that cautioned against the risks associated with US meddling in Venezuela, the Editorial Board offered broad support for the policies of Trump: "The Trump administration

is right to support Mr. Guaidó." The Board also made judgments
as the arbiter of what is best for Venezuela: "That Mr. Maduro
must go has been obvious for some time ... What is indisputable
at this tense moment is that Mr. Maduro's misrule has become
intolerable and that he must go."[105]

The times did publish three opinion pieces that argued
against US interference in Venezuela. One argued that the
United States could not play a constructive role in the crisis:

> But the United States has no constructive role to play in
> Venezuela's political crisis. Regardless of how one feels
> about Mr. Maduro, it's clear that Washington is not a
> trustworthy partner in pushing for regime change. The
> Trump administration's actions—and its personnel—recall
> the long and sordid history of United States intervention in
> Latin America.[106]

The other argued that the US's role in Venezuela was part of a
larger geopolitical strategy:

> As in most proxy conflicts, Venezuela is a spoil in a larger
> prize. For the United States, it represents an opportunity to
> control the agenda in the region, sideline Russian influence
> and ensure that China takes a back seat. In a fight among
> elephants, it's Venezuelans who stand to lose.[107]

The third, while arguing against US intervention, presented a
curious set of options for Venezuela:

> Venezuela will either put this nightmare behind it and join
> its democratic neighbors in Latin American and Western
> community, or become a full-fledged ally and protectorate
> of Russia, Cuba, and to a lesser extent, China. This is the real
> choice Venezuela and its true friends face.[108]

The *Times* opinion pages often provided an opportunity for the voices of people involved in Venezuelan opposition to have their views aired.[109] One Venezuelan opposition protester described the protests:

> But the strangest observation is that I am no longer the opposition. For more than a decade, I have been fighting against a government. Now I am fighting for one. And I am not in the minority, either. Millions of Venezuelans have risen up to show our support for the interim president, and much of the world is on our side. On that Friday afternoon, after Mr. Guaidó left the stage, I locked eyes with perfect strangers who had come from across Caracas to come listen to the interim president, and I realized that we were all smiling uncontrollably, sharing in trying to make sense of this very foreign but very exhilarating experience. Just then, someone next to me in the crowd started complaining about how the news coverage of the recent events had mentioned coups d'état and a military invasion. I can't remember what they said, though. I was too busy enjoying the normalcy of it all.[110]

An opinion piece advocated paying the Venezuelan military to promote political change in the country.[111] The *Times* also published an opinion piece written by Guaidó where he confirmed meeting with the military, as had been reported in the *Times*.[112]

> The transition will require support from key military contingents. We have had clandestine meetings with members of the armed forces and the security forces. We have offered amnesty to all those who are found not guilty of crimes against humanity. The military's withdrawal of support from Mr. Maduro is crucial to enabling a change in

government, and the majority of those in service agree that the country's recent travails are untenable.[113]

Another opinion piece criticized the economic impact of the United States sanctions on the Venezuelan economy and people.[114]

Conclusion

Coverage of the three month crisis in the *Times* was extensive. There were very few days when at least one piece was not published about the situations in the country. On many days, there were multiple stories published, including videos and opinion commentary. The stories tended to portray the Maduro regime in a negative light and were generally sympathetic to the claim that Guaidó was the rightful leader of the country. Calls for the military to remove Maduro from office were often published. In one notable instance, the *Times* published a report that contradicted opposition claims about the Venezuelan army being responsible for the burning of aid at the border.[115,116] Opinion pieces, especially editorials, generally strongly opposed Maduro and supported the US's antagonistic relationship with him, with some exceptions, while still sometimes criticizing the Trump administration's approach to solving the crisis.

Bolivia, 2019–2020

Earlier reporting from the *Times* about the 2019 Bolivian Presidential election described the results and how Morales was close to not receiving the 10% margin of victory to avoid triggering a runoff. Despite winning the highest percentage of votes in the elections, most of the quotes in the article were from Morales critics.[117] As Morales began to increase his lead as more votes were counted, coverage focused on complaints about possible voter manipulation including claims of irregularities from the Organization of American States and anti-Morales demonstrations.[118] Protests against Morales became more intense after Morales declared himself the winner of the election. Among those quoted in an article discussing these protests, many expressed fears of violence, but there was no one quoted who directly supported Morales.[119] In another article, one protester explicitly connected the events in Bolivia to the events in Venezuela earlier in the year:

> We are repeating history, like Venezuela ...What we see is a government that wants to remain in power arbitrarily and that cannot stand.[120]

The Organization of American States began an audit of the election results. However, this move did not placate opponents of Morales:

> As anger against Mr. Morales has swelled, many in the opposition have shifted from calling for a runoff between the president and his main challenger, Carlos Mesa, to demanding the ouster of Mr. Morales, who has been in office since 2006.[121]

The protests continued to escalate. Several protesters were shot and one pro-Morales mayor was attacked.[122] Morales accused opponents of organizing a coup, as members of his government resigned. Protesters took control of the state broadcasts. Some police in the capital of La Paz joined the protests.[123] The push to have Morales removed was further strengthened when the commander of the Bolivian military called for him to step down, even as Morales endorsed calls for a new election.[124] Shortly after Morales and his Vice President, Álvaro García Linera, resigned.[125] The events leading to his resignation were categorized by García and several other Latin American leaders as a coup.[126] After his resignation, Morales accepted an offer of asylum from Mexico. Despite earlier assurances from the military that it would "would not crack down on protesters,"[127] the military began to assist the police in defending parts of La Paz as protesters in support of Morales began to flood into the city.[128]

In an opinion piece that discussed the Bolivia crisis in context of other events in Latin America and defended the "Washington Consensus" in the region, the author discussed protests against neoliberalism and the Washington Consensus in Chile where neoliberal policies were introduced after a violent coup and the deaths of thousands and torture of many more opponents of general Augusto Pinochet who took power during the coup:

> Chile is Latin America's great success story, even if its citizens disbelieve this narrative, or reject it outright.[129]

In a strange editorial, the *Times* simultaneously praised the protest against Morales as an example of popular protests overthrowing a populist, turned tyrannical leader, while at the same time, encouraging Morales to prevent such a popular uprising against any regime that might be put in to power:

> The citizens who went into the streets in Bolivia were not seeking to reverse Mr. Morales's social or economic reforms, from which many of them benefited, but to uphold democratic rules and institutions he tried to subvert...
>
> A leading opposition politician, Jeanine Añez Chávez, the second vice president of the Senate who appears to be next in line for the presidency, went on television offering to lead the country to new elections. The sooner they can be held the better, and if Mr. Morales hopes to salvage any of

his legacy, he would do well to call on his backers to clear the way.[130]

The day after Morales fled Bolivia, Añez did declare herself as President. The *Times* described her path to power:

Minutes after she spoke, Bolivia's highest constitutional court issued a ruling that backed her assumption of power. She was the highest-ranking politician in the line of succession after Mr. Morales and other top officials stepped down.[131]

The legal legitimacy of the move was more complicated with requirements that the resignation of the President of the Senate—Adriana Salvatierra, a member of Morales's party—be accepted before Añez could receive a vote. This process never occurred as Salvatierra and members of Morales's party were barred from entering the Senate.

As Añez consolidated power, the *Times* published a detailed piece about the semantics of considering the events in Bolivia as an uprising or a coup:

Bolivia's crisis, where the stakes of using the right label seem unusually high, also exemplifies why scholars consider the old binaries to be outdated, misleading, even harmful.... Today, coups often come after mass uprisings calling for change, with generals describing their interventions as temporary measures to restore democracy. And few, if any, popular uprisings succeed without military support, if only in the form of generals refusing to come to the government's aid.[132]

Later the *Times* covered Añez's promise to "Reconstruct Democracy," while also reporting on the continued protest against her rule.[133] In an opinion piece published around the same time, the writer authored a reflection on the need for undemocratic or as the quote says "semi-democratic" means to supposedly protect democracy:

> For liberal democrats lamenting the trend toward democratic erosion worldwide, the collapse of Evo Morales's administration in Bolivia on Sunday offers a glimmer of hope. At last checks were effectively placed on a government that tried to do away with all checks. That is the good news. The bad news is that the confrontation that was needed to contain this government was not as clean as one would hope. The process involved civil resistance, but also military bullying; peaceful demonstrations, as well as opportunistic radicals. Perhaps this untidiness shouldn't surprise us. Bolivia is a reminder that the process of stopping semi-democratic leaders is likely to be semi-democratic as well.[134]

With the overthrow of Morales, an indigenous Aymara who was seen as a voice for the country's native populations, and the installation of an ethnic European as the president, many native Bolivians feared that the progress which had been made in terms of the rights of indigenous Bolivians during the Morales Presidency would be lost. Añez had previously expressed discriminatory beliefs towards native Bolivians as reported by the *Times*:

> Añez had published provocative posts on Twitter mocking Indigenous people's culture, branding their religious rites "satanic" and calling Mr. Morales a "poor Indian."[135]

Despite her blatant bigotry, the *Times* blamed Morales for the fraught ethnic situation in the country:

Mr. Morales has fanned the growing cultural and racial tensions from his Mexican exile. In frequent news conferences and Twitter postings, he has called his opponents "racists and coup-mongers."[136]

Sacaba and Senkata Massacres

This ethnic element of the conflict would characterize the most shocking events that occurred during the Bolivian Crisis: the Sacaba and Senkata Massacres. Both massacres occurred after Añez issued a decree that exempted the Armed Forces from criminal responsibility for actions taken when fulfilling constitutional functions. During the Sacaba Massacre, Bolivian coca growers passed through the town of Sacaba, planning to protest the recent overthrow of Morales in the city of Cochabamba. The protesters were stopped and clashed with security personnel who eventually opened fire on the protesters with at least 11 demonstrators being killed and nearly one hundred injured. Arrest and abuse by the security officials soon followed.

Incredibly, I only identified a brief one paragraph long discussion in an article otherwise dealing with Añez's reintroduction of Christianity into the government of Bolivia about this seemingly momentous event. The article underestimates the number killed and incorrectly reports that it occurred in Cochabamba, when it actually occurred outside the city on a bridge in Sacaba:

> The leader, Jeanine Añez, also called on security forces to restore public order and police responded by opening fire Friday on coca farmers protesting against the government in the central city of Cochabamba. The clash left nine protesters dead and dozens injured, the worst violence yet in the country's monthlong political crisis.[137]

A few days later, another massacre occurred in Senkata, a neighborhood of El Alto, a mostly indigenous city outside of Bolivia's Capital, La Paz. The massacre occurred following attempts by protesters opposed to the overthrow of Morales to block a natural gas plant. After clashes between protesters and security forces, some tried to enter the plant and the security opened live fire on the protesters. Eleven protesters were killed.

While ostensibly this massacre received a whole article devoted to it, the article, which also underestimated the number killed, began with a discussion of the current political situation in the country and attempts to hold early elections. Descriptions of the massacre are only returned to in the second half of the article.[138] I did not identify any more extensive discussions of the massacres in later periods.

Later Period

One might expect these seeming escalations in violence and protests to warrant more coverage. However, this was not the case. *Times* reporting about the situations in Bolivia began to precipitously drop off after Añez came to power. In the one month period between October 15th, 2019, shortly before the election, and November 15th, shortly after Añez came to power, 21 articles were published, over 70% of all the articles during the three month period considered. In the remaining two months, I only identified eight more articles dealing with Bolivia. This reduction in coverage occurred despite the continued protest against the fall of Morales and the continued suppression of protests by the Añez administration, questions about the response to the Sacaba and Senkata Massacres, and discussions about when a new election — a promise of the Añez administration — would be called.

During this period, the *Times* published an interview with Morales from exile in Mexico where he said that he was not desperate to be President, but wanted to be able to return to Bolivia.[139] The next day, the *Times* published an article about how Añez came to power, where one of the interviews framed her rise as a means to prevent a military takeover:

> Much was at stake. As looting and violence escalated, Bolivia's civilian leaders became increasingly worried that generals might take control to restore order, returning the country to its dark history of military dictatorships.

While the article itself did not mention the Sacaba massacre, photos accompanying it did display an image of someone wounded in the massacre. However, the responsibility for deaths was not made clear with the victims of state violence being labelled as people "killed in the turmoil."[140]

In a report about the continued resistance of coca farmers to the government, only a brief generic reference is made to "30 pro-Evo protesters killed in clashes with security forces."[141] Another article reported on the Organization of American States' final report where they concluded that there had been interference from Morales supporters in the election. The article briefly acknowledge critics of this report.[142] Researchers from MIT would later indicate that the analysis in this report was flawed.[143] In an editorial, while calling for new elections the *Times* Editorial Board did briefly criticize Añez for issuing "a decree exempting security forces from criminal prosecution when maintaining public order; the following day, eight protesters were killed in a lethal crackdown, and more have been killed since."[144] The final piece about the first part of the crisis in Bolivia during the period considered discussed the interim government expelling diplomats from Mexico and Spain for their alleged role in assisting Morales administration officials who were seeking asylum.[145]

Bolivian Protests, August 2020 to October 2020

The first article covering the renewed protests against the Añez administration that began in August 2020 framed these protests around the impact that they were having: "Six million people have been marooned by 70 roadblocks set up to protest the government's response to the coronavirus and the postponement of the country's general election." The first part of the article focused on the effect that the protest was having on the delivery of medical care with only a secondary focus on why Bolivians were protesting.[146]

Two weeks later, another piece appeared discussing the poor response from the Bolivian government to the pandemic and how this poor response motivated the protests.[147] In September, an opinion piece in support of Luis Arce from Morales's party Movement for Socialism in the upcoming election was published. The piece contrasted Arce with Morales:

> Mr. Arce is not Evo Morales. He is a technocratic, pragmatic and cosmopolitan leader. An economist educated in Britain, he was the principal architect of Bolivia's economic rise under Mr. Morales, led by a nationalized gas industry. According to the International Monetary Fund and the World Bank, the country experienced over 4 percent annual growth in the 13 years that Mr. Morales was in power, a quadrupling of the G.D.P., and more than a 30 percent decrease in extreme poverty. Mr. Arce is simply cut from a different cloth when contrasted to Mr. Morales's populist persona.[148]

In his pitch to voters, the *Times* reported Arce echoing this message: "I have no interest in power," he said. "I want to move the country forward, leave it in the hands of young people, and I'll go."[149] Añez dropped out of the presidential race so that the right-wing vote would not be split.[150] Arce won the election.[151,152]

The victory, despite being a win for Morales's party, was frequently framed as the country moving beyond Morales, such as in an opinion piece:

> As a candidate, Mr. Arce signaled his willingness to turn the page on Mr. Morales, whose controversial tactics and unconstitutional bid for a fourth presidential term ended in his expulsion from the country last year after the military called on him to step down. Mr. Arce committed to a return to the stability and inclusion that defined much of Mr. Morales's government. With the more moderate Mr. Arce on the ballot, the Movement Toward Socialism party, or MAS, actually outperformed expectations increasing its share of the vote by eight percentage points over last year's results.[153]

Conclusion

Initially coverage of the crisis in Bolivia was extensive, especially in the period between the election and Morales's resignation. Most of this coverage focused on questions about the integrity of the elections and the motivations of protests opposed to the continued rule of Morales. Following Morales's resignation, the coverage declined. This decline in coverage occurred despite continued protests and questions about the legitimacy of the new government and its policies towards Bolivia's indigenous population. In particular, two notable massacres of supporters of Morales did not receive extensive coverage. The 2020 election in which a member of Morales's party was elected president was not extensively covered.

Colombia, November 15, 2019 to February 15, 2020

There were only four articles identified about the first round of protests in Colombia. The first article was not published until November 26th, over a week after the protests began. As the title makes clear "Death of Colombian Teenager Drives Protesters Back to Streets," the protests had already been ongoing, but there was no coverage that I could identify of those earlier protests. The article discusses Dilan Cruz who was killed, as the paper puts it, "after being struck by a police projectile." The article presents the wide variety of reasons for the protests: "corruption and the conservative policies of President Iván Duque ... inequality, corruption and possible austerity measures ... rising violence in the countryside, which has been linked to drug traffickers, rebel groups like the National Liberation Army and former members of the Revolutionary Armed Forces of Colombia, or the FARC, who have returned to arms."[154]

Because of the scant coverage of the protests, I allowed articles to meet the inclusion criteria if they mentioned the protests at all, even if the article was primarily about another topic. An additional discussion of the protests would not appear for another month when an opinion piece about Brazil mentioned other protests in Latin America, including Colombia:

> In Colombia, students, workers and indigenous people have been demonstrating since late November against rumored pension cutbacks and changes to labor laws. Protesters accused the center-right president, Iván Duque, of failing to address issues like corruption, economic inequality and the murder of human rights activists.[155]

Another mention of the Colombian protests again appeared in an article discussing corruption in Brazil:

> in Colombia and Argentina, a lack of political will has prevented investigations into Odebrecht's corruption from advancing. Vice President Marta Lucía Ramírez of Colombia called the failure to crack open the Odebrecht case deeply

troubling in a country that has been roiled in recent days by mass protests. "It has very serious consequences, and it's seriously undermining people's trust in institutions, political parties, Congress and the justice system," she said. "That puts the future of democracy in jeopardy."[156]

The final identified mention of the protests during this period came from an article that discussed Russian trolls on Twitter who the State Department accused of seeking "to sow confusion in South American nations that oppose the Moscow-backed government in Venezuela." The Colombian government joined with scapegoating these alleged trolls for encouraging the protests in their country:

> In Colombia, where Secretary of State Mike Pompeo is scheduled to visit this week, hundreds of thousands of protesters demonstrated in November against pension changes, corruption and rising violence. The protests have since ebbed, and in December, Colombia's vice president, Marta Lucía Ramírez, accused Russia and its allies in Venezuela of fomenting protests through social network campaigns.

Colombia, September to November 2020

The first of the three articles about this round of protests described the police killing of Javier Ordóñez:

> The video circulating on social media showed a man pinned to the ground by Colombian police officers, who shocked him repeatedly with a stun gun for more than two minutes. "Please, no more," he begged. The man, Javier Ordóñez, a father of two, died shortly afterward in police custody. Within 24 hours, thousands of Colombians had taken to the streets

of the capital, Bogotá, in protests against police violence that began late Wednesday and continued into Thursday, laying bare months of pent-up tension.[157]

The article also discussed the protests, arrests and further police killings that followed:

Dozens of police stations were set on fire or vandalized. At least eight more people were killed, and nearly 400 were injured, according to the police. At least 66 people had bullet injuries. Nearly all of the people killed in the protests were young, between the ages of 17 and 27. The police said the deaths were under investigation, and declined to say whether officers were involved. The city's mayor, Claudia López, called the protest deaths, "a massacre of our young people."[158]

Despite the widespread protests and the police violence, I did not identify any more articles that dealt directly with the protests. The protests were mentioned in an article dealing with an increase in mass killings related to the decade long civil war in the country:

In recent days, Colombia's capital, Bogotá, erupted in violent protest after a man who was subdued by police and repeatedly shocked with a stun gun died in custody. The images, caught on video, drew thousands to the streets in demonstrations that left at least 10 dead and hundreds of people injured. The cause of those deaths is under investigation. But many say that at the heart of the outpouring is a deeper frustration with the pace of change. "The last government tried to end the war and it didn't work," said Eliana Garzón, 31, whose brother-in-law, Javier

Ordóñez, was the man killed by police. "This is a country that is fed up," she went on. "His death was the perfect excuse to head to the streets."[159]

Finally, an article in October described a separate protest by indigenous people in Bogota against mass killings related to the civil war. The contemporary protests against the killing of Javier Ordóñez were not mentioned.[160]

Colombia, April 15 to July 15, 2021

The first article about the third round of protests in Colombia dealt with the 19 people who were killed and the motivation for the protests:

> The dead include a ninth grader who went out to protest with his brother; an artist shot in the head as cameras rolled; and a teenager whose mother's anguished cries of grief—"son, I want to be with you!"—have been shared thousands of times online. At least 19 people were killed and hundreds more injured during days of protests across Colombia, in which tens of thousands of people have taken to the streets to demonstrate against a tax overhaul meant to fill a pandemic-related fiscal hole.

In response to the protests, the government did withdraw the tax plan that initially sparked the protests, but the protests continued as they "morphed into a national outcry over rising poverty, unemployment and inequality sparked by the arrival of the coronavirus last year."[161] The *Times* published two videos of the protests.[162,163]

State violence continued in response to the protests with the death toll rising to 24.[164] The fact that the Colombian police had a history of fighting in the country's civil war was presented as a factor contributing to their violent and deadly response to the protests.[165] The *Times* used articles about the escalating violence as a teaching tool for high school students.[166] An opinion piece was published encouraging President Biden to take a role in facilitating dialogue to defuse the protests.[167] The *Times* then published an explainer article about the protests.[168] At the end of May, videos were published showing the violence at the protests, describing different methods of violence used by the police including recklessly using live fire and firing "less than lethal" munitions at close range.[169]

Another piece would not appear for nearly a month, when the ongoing protests were mentioned in an article otherwise dealing with the impact of the COVID-19 pandemic in the country.[170] The protests were also mentioned in an article describing unknown assailants firing at the Colombian President's helicopter.[171] The final piece published during this period discussed the unrest throughout Latin America; in contrast to many of the countries discussed, the article discussed how the United States had remained committed to supporting Colombia:

> In an interview in May, President Iván Duque Márquez of Colombia said he did not doubt that the United States would continue to support his country, despite human rights concerns about his government's tactics. "We have to be all honest and put our hands on our hearts for a certain moment," Mr. Duque told reporters for *The New York Times*. "We're living in very complicated times around the world. We have seen high levels of political polarization. You're living it in the United States. And you know that when you combine polarization with social media and opinions that sometimes are not based on thorough understanding, they can also generate violence."[172]

Conclusion

While all three series of Colombian protests were covered by the *Times*, coverage in general was not very extensive. Despite the large amount of state violence, this violence was not a focus of much of the coverage, with the exemption of the third round. There were often large gaps in coverage of the protests, unlike the almost daily coverage of the Venezuelan protest, and in the case of the first round of protests coverage did not start until the protests had been ongoing for several days.

Are the Situations Comparable?

Is the situation in Venezuela really comparable to the events that occurred in Bolivia and Colombia? Starting with the Bolivia comparison there is a strong case that can be made for the comparability of the two events. First, they both involved disputed elections in which a candidate who was in power and officially won the election was from a left-wing movement that the United States is generally antagonistic towards. In both cases there were wide scale protests against the outcome of the elections. In both cases, protests were spread across the country. In the case of Bolivia, there were large protests in the capital of La Paz and nearby El Alto, while in Venezuela there were frequent protests in Caracas as well as the border areas with Colombia where there was the controversy about letting aid into the country.

There was also state violence utilized to suppress the protest and massive arrests. There are not clear estimates of the numbers killed. It is difficult to get exact numbers, especially for the period considered in this chapter. In the case of Venezuela, a study from the UN Human Rights Office "documented 66 deaths during protests between January and May 2019, 52 attributable to Government security forces or colectivos."[173] It should be noted that this estimate includes deaths occurring in two months (April and May) not included in the analysis in this chapter. In the case of Bolivia, as reported by Amnesty International: "According to publicly available information from the Office of the Ombudsperson, 35 people died between 30 October and 28 November, and 832 were wounded between 24 October and 21 November."[174] The number of deaths in Venezuela is greater, but these deaths occurred over a longer time period. The magnitude of state violence in both instances is comparable.

The difference in the scenarios is, of course, their outcomes. In the case of Bolivia for roughly the first month of the coverage considered here, Morales stayed in power, but afterwards, he left Bolivia, and a new regime came to power. Interestingly, this provided a helpful point for internal comparison. Protests did not stop after Morales left, it is just the protesters changed, when Morales supporters, many of whom were indigenous people from rural parts of Bolivia, began protesting against the new regime that they viewed as being hostile to them. During the period between September 15th to October 15th when the protests were against Morales, roughly corresponding to shortly before the election to shortly before Morales's fall, 21 pieces appeared, still less than the 46 articles per month average for the Venezuelan protests, but much greater than the average for all the Colombian protests or the four articles per month average for the final two months of the Bolivian protests (against Morales's removal) or the three per month average for the protests against the Añez government in the summer and fall of 2020.

Turning to the comparison with Colombia, with respect to state violence in the Colombian protests, again exact numbers are hard to determine. During the first round of protests, one report from *Al Jazeera* reported that at least 13 people had been killed.[175] During the protests about the killing of Javier

Ordóñez in 2020, an article from *CNN* in Spanish reported the number of killed as at least 13.[176] The 2021 protests have the most drastic differences with respect to estimates of the number killed. Human Rights Watch reported that they had evidence for 25 police killings,[177] while the Colombian NGO—Temblores and Indepaz—estimated as many as 61 killed.[178] The earlier two rounds of protests had slightly lower estimates than the estimates for the number killed in Venezuela (66). The Venezuelan number is not drastically different from the Colombian estimates and is comparable for the number killed in the third round of protests in Colombia.

One important way that Venezuela's crisis differed from those in Bolivia and Colombia is the migrant crisis that Venezuela experienced, with many people fleeing the country during the protests. There was not a similar large-scale migrant crisis in Bolivia or Colombia. However, it is worth noting that while it is true that Venezuela has had a much higher number of asylum seekers and other migrants (roughly four million more refugees, asylum seekers, and external displaced people came from Venezuela compared to Colombia during the period considered—the numbers of refugees, asylum seekers, and external displaced people from Bolivia are negligible), Colombia has consistently had a very high number of internally displaced people (IDP), with the United Nations reporting that Colombia has the second highest number of IDPs falling only after Syria.[179] This crisis may have contributed to some of the more attention given to Venezuela, but it is likely to explain the multifold more attention that one period of protest in Venezuela received compared to three protests in Colombia.

The size of the protests were also comparable, but estimates tended to vary widely. For the Venezuelan protests, as mentioned, the *Guardian* estimated tens of thousands participating in January 23 protests in the capital of Caracas,[180] while according to the *Economist* at least one million people participated in the same protest.[181] Estimates of the size of the Colombian protests varied as well. The *Guardian* estimated hundreds of thousands participating in the first round.[182] Protest organizers estimated one million, while the government reported around 200,000.[183] The *BBC* estimated that tens of thousands participated in the 2020 Javier Ordóñez protests in Colombia,[184] while *Al Jazeera* estimated tens of thousands participating in the 2021 protests.[185] The number of participants in the Bolivian protests is even less clear. The *Times* would often estimate protests in the thousands,[186] but this was mostly focusing on the capital region; many of the protests occurred in rural parts of the country, where Morales drew much of his support.

Conclusion

The Bolivian, Colombian, and Venezuelan protests were all protests occurring in Latin America around the same period between 2019 and 2021, and dealt with dissatisfaction with the governments in the country. These protests frequently spiraled into violence with dozens killed in all cases. The size of the protests were difficult to estimate, but were likely of a comparable scale, with at least one of the Venezuelan protests likely being larger than the protests in the other countries. The Colombian protests differed from those in Venezuela and Bolivia because they were not related to electoral politics. One factor that makes Venezuela less comparable to the other cases was the migrant crisis in the country. Overall, based on the facts of the protests, it would seem that they all would warrant generally similar levels of coverage. However...

Reasons for Differences

In quantitative terms, it is clear that the Venezuelan crisis and protests received far more coverage than two rounds of protests in Bolivia and three rounds of protests in Colombia, even when the amount of coverage for the Bolivian and Colombian protests are combined. This increased coverage occurred despite the fact that in broad terms a strong case can be made for these events, especially those in Bolivia, being comparable to the events that occurred in Venezuela.

Different justifications may be offered for the differences in coverage. One argument which could be made is that the crisis in Venezuela is more important because Venezuela had been suffering through economic and political crises for close to two decades at the time when the protests began. While these crises picked up pace after Maduro succeeded Hugo Chávez, even before then, the country had faced an attempted coup. Perhaps those protests received more coverage because of this long history. However, this argument would neglect the fact that Colombia had been in crisis for even longer than Venezuela. The crisis in Colombia included a decades long civil war with thousands killed and hundreds of thousands displaced. The government response to the civil war included an incident known as the "False Positives" scandal in which members of the Colombian military murdered innocent Colombians and falsely presented them as guerillas killed in combat. Such an argument may have somewhat more validity in Bolivia, which has not struggled with the same level of de-stability as in Colombia or Venezuela. However, the rule of Morales has consistently been controversial and frequently attracted media attention. The logic behind such an argument is not exactly clear either. Novelty often attracts more media attention.

Some may also have argued that the situation in Venezuela is more relevant to the United States than the situations in Bolivia or Colombia. Venezuela, as a large exporter of crude oil, does indeed have an important role in the global economy.[187] However, Colombia, although not nearly as large an exporter as Venezuela, has seen its crude exports grow in recent years.[188] In a similar way, Bolivia, although not a crude oil exporter, has become increasingly important for the global economy because of its mining operations, especially those related to lithium, an important battery component. When someone on Twitter brought up the potential that the US supported the overthrow of Morales with the goal of getting access to Bolivia's lithium reserves, Elon Musk, the owner of the electric car company Tesla, which uses lithium in its batteries, stated (possibly in jest), "We will coup whoever we want! Deal with it." The mining operations in Bolivia are indeed geopolitically important. For example, the country's decision (during the Presidency of Morales) to partner with a Chinese firm in their over $2 billion mining operation attracted controversy.[189]

Some may also argue that the protests in Venezuela are more deserving of coverage because Venezuela has an authoritarian government in contrast to Colombia and Bolivia. While there can be debates about where Venezuela lies on any democratic/ authoritarian gradient, even if they are at the far authoritarian end, it is not clear why protests in a non-authoritarian country would be less deserving of protests. Additionally, with respect to the comparison to Bolivia, this argument does not really hold water because the government that took power after the fall of Morales came to power without a clear popular mandate and, therefore, if protests against authoritarian regimes receive more coverage, one would have expected protests against the Añez government to have received more coverage.

The final argument and the one that I feel does the best job explaining the differences in coverage is the Worthy/Unworthy hypothesis. The Venezuelan government under Chávez and Maduro has been one of the most unpopular governments in Washington, attracting condemnation from both Democrats and Republicans. The US government has been antagonistic to these governments, imposing sanctions and having, at the very least, advanced knowledge of one coup against the leadership. In 2020, there was another attempted coup that failed early on because of the seeming ineptitude of the coup planners, which included Americans, although it has not been proven that this attempted coup had the sanction of the US government.

The Bolivian government under Morales, although not to the same extent as Venezuela, has also been unpopular in Washington, which likely at least partially explains the wide coverage that was received during the protest immediately after the election questioning whether Morales had really been victorious. However, after an opponent of Morales came to power, this coverage dissipated, even as state violence in the country increased. Later protests against this government, which eventually led to it losing an election, did not receive substantial attention.

With respect to Colombia, the country has traditionally been a staunch ally of the United States. The Colombian military has close ties to the US military, serving as the United States' strongest ally in Latin America. During the "Pink Tide" when many governments in the region turned to left-oriented governments, the Colombian government stayed in the hands of conservative parties. Only the 2022 election of the left-wing presidential candidate Gustavo Petro may potentially impact this tendency. Therefore, using the Worthy/Unworthy paradigm, protests against the Colombian government would fall into the unworthy category and therefore be expected to receive less attention.

Conclusion

Three months of antigovernment protests in Venezuela received more than twice as much coverage as two rounds of similar protests in Venezuela and three rounds of antigovernment protests in Colombia combined. Size and the scale of state violence were comparable in several instances. While the coverage often portrayed the government in a bad light in all three cases, the extent of this negative coverage was stronger in the case of Venezuela, with some calls for regime change in the country published in the *Times*. Violent incidents tended to receive more coverage in the case of Venezuela, while they were often barely mentioned in the cases of Colombia and Bolivia.

It can reasonably be argued that the media focus of an official state enemy of the United States government—Venezuela—will have the impact of reinforcing the antagonistic perspective of the United States with respect to that enemy. It can also contribute to support for policies like sanctions, which often have a negative impact on the people of the country, and even support regime change operations including coups. In a similar way, the dearth of coverage of other protests, in non-enemy countries especially those in Colombia, may encourage the US government to continue to be supportive of governments in that country, even as they commit human rights abuses. If the US media sees Latin America as its backyard or front yard like its government does, it is clear that some parts of the yard are in the sun while others are in the shade.

Chapter 4

Worthy and Unworthy Dissidents: Alexei Navalny, Catalan Independence Politicians, Pussy Riot, and Pablo Hasél

The hope that the end of the Cold War would also bring about the end of the antagonistic relationship between the United States and Russia is clearly no longer tenable. Even before the War in Ukraine, this contentious relationship between the US and Russia has been growing. Whether considering conflicts in the former Yugoslavia, the Middle East, or the Caucasus, where the US and Russia have often on opposite sides, many of the global divisions of the 20th century have returned. This worsening relationship between the United States and Russia has had an impact on popular perception of Russia in the United States. According to Gallup, while in 1989 62% of people in the United States had a favorable opinion of Russia, by 2015 this favorability of the country had dropped to 24%.[1]

Some of this changing perception can likely be attributed to media coverage of Russia. In particular, dissidents within the country have frequently attracted the attention of the US media. The increased attention given to dissidents in countries that are widely viewed as enemies of the United States compared to its allies has been previously described by Herman and Chomsky:

> The torture of political prisoners and the attack on trade unions in Turkey will be pressed on the media only by human rights activists and groups that have little political leverage. The U.S. government supported the Turkish martial-law government from its inception in 1980, and the U.S. business

community has been warm toward regimes that profess fervent anticommunism, encourage foreign investment, repress unions, and loyally support U.S. foreign policy (a set of virtues that are frequently closely linked). Media that chose to feature Turkish violence against their own citizenry would have had to go to extra expense to find and check out information sources; they would elicit flak from government, business, and organized right-wing flak machines, and they might be looked upon with disfavor by the corporate community (including advertisers) for indulging in such a quixotic interest and crusade. They would tend to stand alone in focusing on victims that from the standpoint of dominant American interests were unworthy.

In marked contrast, protest over political prisoners and the violation of the rights of trade unions in Poland was seen by the Reagan administration and business elites in 1981 as a noble cause, and, not coincidentally, as an opportunity to score political points. Many media leaders and syndicated columnists felt the same way. Thus information and strong opinions on human-rights violations in Poland could be obtained from official sources in Washington, and reliance on Polish dissidents would not elicit flak from the U.S. government or the flak machines. These victims would be generally acknowledged by the managers of the filters to be worthy. The mass media never explain why Andrei Sakharov is worthy and Jose Luis Massera, in Uruguay, is unworthy—the attention and general dichotomization occur "naturally" as a result of the working of the filters, but the result is the same as if a commissar had instructed the media: "Concentrate on the victims of enemy powers and forget about the victims of friends."[2]

Based on the Propaganda Model, today one would still expect that dissidents in Russia would receive more attention than dissidents in either friendly or at least non-enemy countries. We have an opportunity to test out this hypothesis by comparing coverage of Russian dissidents—namely Alexei Navalny and the musical group Pussy Riot—to coverage given to Catalan independence politicians, such as those arrested after Catalonia's 2017 independence referendum, and Catalan independence activists, such as the rapper Pablo Hasél. Specifically dissidents in Spain, being largely an ally of the United States according to the Propaganda Model, would be expected to receive less coverage even if the oppression of the dissidents was equal to or even greater than that in Russia.

Background: Alexei Navalny and Catalan Independence

Alexei Navalny

Alexei Navalny has been an activist and dissident in Russia for over 20 years. His criticism has focused on the government of Vladmir Putin, its apparent corruption, and accusations of electoral fraud in the country. He has been the founder and leader of an opposition party in Russia, which has faced obstacles in registration and been prevented from fielding candidates in presidential elections.

Navalny has also faced legal trouble, allegedly due to his political activities. In 2013 he was convicted of embezzlement and sentenced to five years in prison. This sentence was suspended. Eventually the Supreme Court of Russia overturned the sentence, returning it to a lower court, who later confirmed it. Navalny was found guilty of other embezzlement charges in 2014 and given a three and a half year suspended sentence, a large fine, and requirements to pay renumeration for the victims of the alleged fraud. The European Court of Human Rights labelled the criminal proceedings in this case to be "arbitrary and unfair."[3]

While Navalny has frequently received coverage in the Western media for his dissident activities, the amount of this attention increased substantially in 2020 when Navalny became violently ill during a flight from the Siberian city of Tomsk to Moscow. Following the flight, Navalny was hospitalized and went in to a coma. It was suspected that tea which Navalny had drunk at the airport before his flight had been poisoned. Navalny was allowed to be flown to Germany to receive treatment where it was announced that Navalny was poisoned with a cholinesterase inhibitor. In early September, Navalny exited his coma and announced that he would return to Russia.

The poisoning resulted in sanctions against the Russian government from Western countries, who accused the government of being responsible. In mid-January Navalny returned to Russia. It is the three month period immediately preceding and coinciding with this return, and the events that followed, which I cover in this chapter.

Catalonia Independence

The position of the Spanish region of Catalonia within the Kingdom of Spain has been a controversial topic in Spanish politics for over a century. In the region, the most common language spoken is Catalan not Spanish, and many residents see themselves as having a culture distinct from the rest of Spain. Additionally, Catalonia is one of the most economically productive regions of Spain. Before the Spanish Civil War, Catalonia had a degree of autonomy which ended with the victory of the Fascists and the dictatorship of Francisco Franco. Some Catalan politicians opposed the new constitution that followed the end of Franco's reign because it declared indivisibility of Spain, while acknowledging rights to autonomy within the kingdom.

Since the early 2000s, parties which support Catalan independence have progressively gained more votes in regional, national, and European elections. In response to this increasing support for these independence-oriented parties, there have been two unsanctioned referendums held in Catalonia regarding independence. During the first referendum, in 2014, two questions were asked: "Do you want Catalonia to become a state?" and, to those who answered yes to the first question, "Do you want this state to become independent?"; with a turnout of about 40%, 80% of voters answered yes to both questions.

In the second referendum in 2019, with a turnout of over 40% despite some polling stations being closed by police because the referendum was declared unconstitutional, over 90% of voters supported independence. The election was boycotted by many in Catalonia who did not support independence for the region. Protests and a general strike in support of independence followed the referendum, which led to a police crackdown resulting in hundreds of injuries. The regional government of Catalonia led by Catalan President Carles Puigdemont signed a document declaring Catalan independence. However, immediately after the declaration of independence, Puigdemont suspended it with the goal of engaging in dialogue with the central Spanish government. The Spanish government reacted by dismissing Puigdemont's regional government.

This declaration of independence led to the events discussed in this chapter. Following the referendum and declaration of independence, Catalan independence politicians were arrested. Several politicians including Puigdemont entered exile to avoid arrest, but they still had charges filed against them. This chapter considers coverage of Catalan independence through 2019, which includes the trial of the Catalan independence politicians, their sentencing, the protests that followed and two Spanish general elections during which the situation in Catalonia was an important issue.

The Numbers

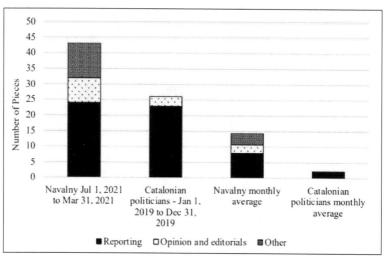

Figure 8. Coverage of 2021 Alexei Navalny Arrest, Trial and Protests and 2019 Catalan Independence Politicians Arrest, Trial, and Protests and Catalonia issues in general by time period and type of coverage

As shown in figure 8, during a three month period Navalny's arrest, trial, and the protests that followed received more coverage than the trial of the Catalan independence politicians and associated events over an entire year. There were 17 more pieces dealing with Navalny (43 total pieces) compared to the Catalan independence politicians (26 total pieces). On average, during the three month period considered, there were over 14 pieces published per month about Navalny compared to less than three per month for the Catalan independence politicians. The average coverage for Navalny was double the month that Catalonia received the most coverage (February) when there were seven pieces published. Navalny had more diversity in publications with eight opinion pieces (compared to three about Catalonia) and several videos showing his arrest and the protests that followed.

The Coverage

Alexei Navalny, January to March 2021

On January 13th, the *Times* reported that Navalny had announced that he would be returning to Russia. The possibility that he might be arrested upon his return was discussed:

> "The Kremlin has gone so far in its game of raising the stakes, sharply increasing expectations that Navalny will be arrested, that not arresting him will be seen by conservatives and security officials as a show of weakness," Tatiana Stanovaya, a nonresident scholar at the Carnegie Moscow Center, said in a post on *Telegram*. "They expected that he would not return."[4]

Navalny was indeed arrested three days later when he landed at the airport in Moscow.[5] The *Times* published videos of Navalny arriving at the airport and his arrest.[6,7] That same day, the *Times* Editorial Board published an article in support of Navalny.[8] Navalny was then ordered to be held until he could face charges for supposedly violating his parole for an earlier conviction while recovering in Germany.[9]

Shortly after his arrest, associates of Navalny published a video which claimed that an opulent palace being built on the Black Sea was being constructed for Putin. The video also called for protesters to come out in support of Navalny.[10] The protests were planned to happen the following Saturday. The *Times* reported that the Russian government was encouraging schools to create "counter programming" to keep young people away from the protests.[11]

During the day of the actual protests, the *Times* published live updates throughout the day with reports of over 3000 people arrested.[12] The *Times* also published videos of the protests featuring clashes between protesters and police.[13] The reporting about the protests acknowledged that it was not as large as some had hoped:

> Some protesters acknowledged that, despite the significance of Saturday's protests, it would take far greater numbers to change the course of the nation's politics. In neighboring Belarus, many more people protested for weeks last year against the authoritarian president, Aleksandr G. Lukashenko—a close ally of Mr. Putin's—without unseating him. "I'm a bit disappointed, honestly," said Nikita Melekhin, a 21-year-old nurse in Moscow. "I was expecting more."[14]

In a similar way, an opinion article in support of the protests was realistic regarding the prospects for their success:

> It would be foolish, however, to think they are going to lead to significant political changes or concessions from the state. If anything, as with the mass protests nearly a decade ago, they will probably just lead to more criminal cases and more repressive laws.[15]

Despite this sentiment that the protests were unlikely to have much of an impact, another opinion piece by columnist Bret Stephens advocated that supporting dissent and protest should be a primary focus of the then recently inaugurated Biden administration:

Dissidents matter to the U.S. strategically. The dictatorships that most threaten the free world are too powerful to be brought down militarily. Nor are they likely to moderate their behavior thanks to economic prosperity or reformers working within the system. Anyone in doubt on this score need only look at China's recent trajectory as an ever richer and ever more repressive regime.[16]

Following the protest, the *Times* covered the Kremlin taking a different tact with respect to Navalny and directly responding to his accusations including denial of the Black Sea palace.[17] At the same time, Russian authorities were reported to have begun raiding offices of organizations associated with Navalny.[18] The *Times* reported about how the protests were uniting opponents of Putin, including individuals with marginal opinions, such as monarchism. However, in this article, one democratic socialist critic of the Putin government indicated that support for Navalny was not a unifying aspect of the protests.

He says he finds Mr. Navalny just about as distasteful as he finds Mr. Putin, seeing both as beholden to the capitalist West. But he sees the current protests as the best chance to try to bring change, offering an opening for movements such as his own. And he called for solidarity with Mr. Navalny over his persecution by the state, cautioning that "what happened to him could happen to any of us." "People understand that this is Russia's Politician Number One," he said of Mr. Navalny. "If he calls for going into the streets, we all understand that people will come out, and other forces must make use of this."[19]

The *Times* reported that Russian police found it difficult to contain the protests, along with photos and videos of the police response,[20,21,22] and also information about the penalties that would be faced by those arrested during the protests.[23]

In early February, Navalny was sentenced to two years in prison for his alleged parole violation. When he was sentenced Navalny said:

> Hundreds of thousands cannot be locked up ... More and more people will recognize this. And when they recognize this—and that moment will come—all of this will fall apart, because you cannot lock up the whole country.[24]

In a typically bizarrely titled opinion piece Thomas Friedman argued that "Vladimir Putin Has Become America's Ex-Boyfriend From Hell."[25] The same day the Editorial Board gave their endorsement to Navalny and the protests in the country:

> But in this David v. Goliath saga, the 44-year-old Mr. Navalny has succeeded through raw courage and perseverance in putting Mr. Putin on the defensive. The imprisonment was Mr. Navalny's move. Mr. Putin had tried for years to give him only brief sentences to avoid making him a martyr. But by voluntarily returning from convalescence in Germany, and then releasing a devastating YouTube video showing the obscenely opulent palace Mr. Putin was building himself on the Black Sea, Mr. Navalny left the president little choice but to dispatch him to a labor camp, and thus transform him into a powerful symbol of resistance.[26]

Around the same time, the *Times* published excerpts from a speech Navalny gave at his trial.[27] The next day, an article discussed the possibility of Navalny's wife Yulia Navalnaya taking a more prominent role in opposition following Navalny's imprisonment.[28] Several European diplomats who were accused of participating in the protests were expelled from Russia.[29]

As Navalny began to serve his sentence, one article discussed how Navalny sympathizers had begun wearing red to show their solidary with him.[30] Another article provided a detailed description of the hierarchy in Russian penal colonies to which Navalny would soon be sent:[31]

A privileged group are leaders of criminal gangs, known as "thieves in law" or "authorities." A second elevated class are inmates known as "activists," who cooperate with corrections officers. Men who fall from favor or are sentenced for rape risk falling into the lowest class, known as the "degraded." They perform menial chores and many are sexually abused. The rest fall into a broad category called simply the "men," acquiescing to the gang leaders, refraining from cooperating with the guards and avoiding the abuse suffered by those at the bottom of the pecking order. A system of rituals keeps the hierarchy intact. Men, for example, never share silverware with the degraded.[32]

When Navalny was sent to Penal Colony No. 2, the *Times* provided a description of the conditions and procedures in the colony, primarily informed by information published by Navalny's organization.[33] Later, an article reported on Navalny's experience in prison. Quoting from an Instagram post from his account, Navalny compared the prison to *1984*.[34] Later in the month, the *Times* described Navalny's worsening health based on reports from his lawyer.[35] In response to complaints about the medical care that he was receiving, Navalny announced a hunger strike.[36]

A detailed profile of Navalny, which briefly described his participation in Russian nationalist movements a decade ago and condemned his past racist statements about people from Russia's predominantly Muslim Caucasus region, was also published.[37] Shortly after, the United Nations called for an investigation into Navalny's poisoning.[38] The US also announced sanctions against Russia in response to the poisoning. The sanctions were the first that Biden had introduced as president.[39,40]

Near the end of March, an interview with the *Times*'s Moscow Bureau Chief about Navalny was published. The Bureau Chief described how "Navalny's team has promised to organize another nationwide protest once 500,000 people sign up for it."[41] When these protests did occur on April 21 (outside of the months considered here), many fewer people showed up with Russian officials estimating 6000 supporters in Moscow and 4500 in St. Petersburg, while Navalny's office estimated between 13,000 to 14,000 participants in Yekaterinburg.[42]

Conclusion

Navalny's arrest, trial, and the protests that followed received substantial coverage through the three months considered, particularly in January and February. This coverage was generally sympathetic to Navalny and critical of the Russian government. During this period, multiple videos and photos were published that provided direct images of Navalny's arrest and the protests that followed. Opinion pieces were universally critical of the Russian government and portrayed Navalny as a leading opponent of Putin.

Catalonia, 2019

The first article dealing with the situation in Catalonia in 2019 discussed how the gains of the far-right Vox party in an election in the Spanish province of Andalusia were primarily driven by the hardline that they took against Catalan separatism.[43] In February there was a large protest in Madrid against talks between the Spanish government led by Prime Minister Pedro Sánchez and separatists in Catalonia with a goal of reducing conflict in the region. This article mentioned how the trial of Catalan separatists leaders would begin in two days.[44] On the day that the trial began, the *Times* published a primer about them with information about the lead-up to the trial, a listing of the defendants including the possible sentences facing each of them (such as the potential for 25 years faced by Oriol Junqueras), the denial of bail for the leaders, and how the trial would proceed.[45]

When the trial began, the *Times* noted the extensive coverage that it was receiving in Spain:

> The eagerly anticipated trial before the Spanish Supreme Court in Madrid has drawn enormous attention and is being broadcast live on national television.[46]

In addition to receiving attention because it dealt with a hot button issue in the country, it was also putting the government of Pedro Sánchez in a vulnerable situation, potentially threatening its viability.[47] This possibility was enhanced when Catalan parties refused to back Sánchez's budget plan,[48] which ultimately led to the fall of the Sánchez government.[49]

The first opinion piece about the situation in the country asked in its title: "Will Spain Become a Victim of the Catalan Separatists?" with a subtitle that claimed that separatists had "brought down a government. Now they could bring down the entire country." The author claimed that one of the goals of the separatists' party may be to provoke a violent response to their activities from right-wing parties in order to increase sympathy for their side:

> Why would the separatists possibly want this outcome? For the simple reason that a viable path to securing

Catalan independence remains elusive. Since 2011, both conservative and social democratic governments in Madrid have rejected a state sanctioned independence referendum for Catalonia. So Catalan separatists are now banking on political victimhood as the best strategy for rebooting the independence project. To do this, they need to depict Catalonia as the victim of Madrid's brutal oppression in the hopes that this would earn their cause international support.

Carles Puigdemont, the president of Catalonia until he fled to Belgium, where he remains today, to escape prosecution from Spanish authorities for having declared Catalonia an independent republic, has been exploiting the violence around the 2017 referendum to demonstrate the lengths that Madrid will go to deny Catalans the right to self-determination. On a recent trip to the United States, Quim Torra, Mr. Puigdemont's successor, accused the Spanish government of violating civil and political rights in Catalonia and of holding "political prisoners." At home, Catalan separatists have framed the trial that began this month of the 12 organizers of the illegal referendum on charges of rebellion and sedition as a persecution of Catalan nationalism.[50]

It is hard to imagine the *Times* running an opinion piece that accused Navalny or other opposition figures in official US state enemies of provoking state violence in order to generate sympathy for their cause. Such a claim would likely be framed as apologia or even defense of those state enemies. During the Hong Kong protests in 2019, the *Times* did publish an opinion piece that *advocated* for these methods (see Chapter 2).[51]

The first piece of reporting to deal directly with the trials I identified did not appear until two weeks after they began. The piece covered testimony from former Spanish Prime Minister Mariano Rajoy against the Catalan politicians. In his testimony echoing the earlier opinion piece, Rajoy put the blame for police violence following the referendum at the feet of the separatist politicians and not the central government, which he controlled at the time:

> In an attempt to turn the tables on Spain's central government, a defense lawyer for the separatists showed Mr. Rajoy television footage of the chaotic and unconstitutional referendum in October 2017, in which Spanish police officers were filmed hitting voters with their truncheons. "I have sadly seen many images of this kind during my life," Mr. Rajoy told the court. "What I would like to say is that the responsibility of political leaders is to avoid events like those that we have seen. If they acted by respecting the law, we would not have seen these images, nor other similar ones." "I greatly regret these images," he added. "If people had not been convened to an illegal referendum, nobody would have seen the injuries that some people suffered and members of the security forces," Mr. Rajoy said.[52]

A later article discussed historical aspects of the protests tracing the challenges in the region to the writing of the Spanish constitution in the post-Franco period, especially around the debate about its lack of recognition for "nations" within Spain.[53] I did not identify further coverage of the trials throughout the month of March or for most of April, even as the trial in March included testimony from other former members of the Spanish government and prominent Catalan politicians.

In an article about the snap general election that followed the collapse of the Sánchez government in April, the trials were presented as one heavily debated issue:

But the election also took place amid a continuing territorial conflict in the northeastern region of Catalonia and a landmark trial of separatist politicians from the region who were charged with rebellion and other crimes during a botched attempt to secede unilaterally in 2017. On Sunday, Esquerra Republicana, a pro-independence party, became the biggest representative of Catalonia in the Spanish Parliament, rising to 15 seats, from nine in the last election in 2016. Esquerra's leader, Oriol Junqueras, is among the jailed politicians who are on trial before the Spanish Supreme Court.[54]

In an opinion piece about the election, which contrasted the election of a left-wing government in Spain against the general rightward shift in European politics, the trial again was only briefly mentioned.[55] This pattern continued into May when the trial was briefly mentioned in one paragraph each in articles about local elections in Barcelona in which separatism was an important issue,[56] and socialist gains in local elections throughout the country.[57]

I did not identify another article focusing on the trials until mid-June when the trial closed (a verdict would not be reached until the fall). The article discussed the international component of the trials:

The case has also spilled over Spain's borders because the defendants have sought the backing of international institutions. Last month, the European Court of Human Rights, which is based in Strasbourg, unanimously rejected a case brought by Catalan separatist politicians who argued that Spain had violated their fundamental rights of freedom of expression and assembly.

Separately, however, a working group of the United Nations Human Rights Council issued a nonbinding report that demanded the release of Catalan politicians who it found had been jailed arbitrarily ahead of their trial. The Spanish government immediately denounced "mistakes and distortions" in the report, and also questioned its authors' impartiality.[58]

Two days later, the *Times* reported about how the Spanish Supreme Court banned Oriol Junqueras—a Catalan separatist politician who was jailed awaiting verdict in the trial—from joining the European Parliament to which he was elected.[59] Another gap in coverage followed with the next article identified appearing in September, when there were protests estimated to include 600,000 people in support of Catalonia independence. Despite the size of the protests, in the first paragraph of the article, the *Times* noted that they were "smaller than in previous years, underlining deep divisions within the independence movement."[60] I also did not identify any further coverage of these large protests. A week later, in reporting about the second general election in Spain that year which was called after the previous Spanish government coalition collapsed, the effect of the crisis in Catalonia and the upcoming verdict in the politicians' trial was discussed.[61]

In mid-October, the verdict in the cases of the twelve Catalan leaders was returned from the Spanish Supreme Court. As the *Times* reported

The court sentenced nine of the former leaders to prison for sedition, as well as for misusing public funds. The remaining three were sentenced for the lesser crime of disobedience during the events two years ago, which culminated in an unconstitutional referendum followed by a declaration of independence in October 2017.

Oriol Junqueras, the former Deputy Leader, received the longest sentence of 13 years and a new arrest warrant was issued for Puigdemont.[62] The verdict led to massive protests with hundreds of thousands of protesters and calls for a general strike. These protests were covered in about half of an article that provided an update to the situation in the region, with the other half focusing on the sentences themselves, the effect of the ruling on Spanish politics, and the impact on Puigdemont. Despite state violence occurring at the protests, the *Times* described the police response in this way:

> Mr. Sánchez's government has praised the national police force and the autonomous police force of Catalonia for cooperation in their approach to the demonstrations. The collaboration stands in stark contrast to 2017, when a rift between Spanish and Catalan police officers complicated an already tumultuous situation. The former police chief of Catalonia is still awaiting trial for failing to follow Madrid's orders at the time.[63]

In contrast, the next article about the protests focused on their "radicalized" nature:

> The violence on the streets of Barcelona and other Catalan cities since the Spanish Supreme Court ruling on Monday has raised fears that Catalonia's separatist politicians are now losing control over their supporters, some of them growing increasingly radicalized.

The effect of the protests on Barcelona were also discussed:

On Friday, protesters disrupted the region's transportation network, adding to the impact of a strike that had already forced the cancellation of many commuter trains and buses. They also erected barricades along major roads, including the main highway to France. The general strike, however, was a mitigated success for the independence movement, with the authorities reporting that less than half of government employees had heeded the call to stay away from work.[64]

The next article to deal with Catalonia appeared weeks later and discussed the situation in the region in the context of the general election where support from Catalan parties was seen as necessary for forming a coalition government.[65,66] One article presented the success of the right-wing Vox party in the election as at least partially a reaction to Catalan separatism.[67]

In December, the *Times* published an opinion piece from Puigdemont in which he argued for Catalan separatism and for democratic decisions about the nation's borders more broadly.[68] Finally, later in the month the *Times* reported about Quim Torra, a Catalan politician who a Spanish court determined could not hold office because he refused to stop wearing ribbons in support of Catalan independence.[69]

Conclusion

Coverage of the situations in Catalonia in 2019 was limited. Although some events did receive multiple stories, especially Spanish general elections, many other events were covered in less detail. Much of the discussion of the situation in Catalonia was framed around these elections. Coverage focusing specifically on the trial of the Catalan politicians and the associated protests was more limited. Fewer than ten articles during the year dealt with the trial and sentencing directly. Coverage, although not hostile, tended to be less sympathetic than coverage of other protests and featured frequent discussions of the violence of protesters. Opinion pieces were scant, with one asking whether Spain would be a *victim* of Catalan independence. However, the *Times* did publish a piece supportive of Catalan independence from Puigdemont.

Are the Situations Comparable?

An objection could be given that the alleged crimes committed by Navalny and the Catalan independence politicians are not the same and therefore comparing coverage of events related to those alleged crimes is not fair. The first part of this objection is true. Navalny was arrested and sentenced for a parole violation due to parole that he was on following an earlier conviction of fraud. Criticism has been offered in the case of both the fraud conviction and the parole violation. Indeed, the parole violation only occurred because Navalny was in Germany receiving treatment for a poisoning that agents of the Russian government have been accused of committing. In contrast, the Catalan politicians were charged with rebellion and other political crimes for supporting a referendum that allegedly violated Spanish law and for declaring independence from the Kingdom of Spain.

In the case of Navalny, his crimes were not explicitly political in nature. Many have convincingly argued that he was only being prosecuted because of his opposition to the Russian government. The alleged crimes of the Catalan independence leaders, however, were explicitly political in nature. The treatment of both Navalny and the Catalan leaders received criticism and condemnation from various international organizations.[70,71,72,73,74] One notable difference was that while the European Court of Human Rights did reject the trial and sentencing of Navalny and called for his immediate release,[75] in contrast the court rejected appeals from the Catalan leaders.[76] It is worth noting that when the European Court of Human Rights issued its opinion about the Navalny case, Russia was no longer a member because Russia was stripped of its voting rights in the Council of Europe (the body to which the court is a part) following its annexation of Crimea in 2014. In contrast, Spain is a full member of the Council of Europe and the European Council of Human Rights.

While the crimes in both cases are certainly different, it is hard to see how the accused crimes of Navalny are actually more worthy of attention than those of the Catalan leaders. While it is very possible to make an argument that the accused crimes of Navalny were political in nature, it is clear that those of the Catalan leaders were political in nature. Furthermore, in the case of the Catalan leaders, it could be argued that their accused crimes were committed with the backing of a large proportion of the people of Catalonia.

It may also be argued that the way the Russian and Spanish governments conducted the arrest and trials in the relevant cases may have meant that the case of Navalny deserved more attention. This poisoning angle to the Navalny story adds a dramatic element that would likely be attractive to reporters and indicate a more nefarious government in Russia. The poisoning could also be suspected to create a sympathetic perspective further encouraging coverage. However, especially in the United States, for which the right of declaring political independence is supposedly fundamental to the foundation of the country, one might expect a similar level of sympathy for the Catalan politicians. The trial of the Catalan politicians was also much longer than Navalny's trial, which should have theoretically given more time for coverage.

Additionally, many of the sentencings in the case of the Catalan politicians were longer than that received by Navalny. Following his 2021 arrest, Navalny was sentenced to two and half years in a penal colony. There were a total of 18 Catalan independence politicians tried. Fifteen of them received prison sentences much longer than Navalny, many over ten years with the longest being 13 years. So both in terms of the number of people sentenced and the length of sentencing (both cumulative and at the individual level), the sentencing in the case of the Catalan independence politicians was much harsher than in the case of Navalny. Navalny's sentencing would later be increased to nine years,[77] one year after his initial sentencing, but even this increase meant that his sentencing was still much shorter than many of the Catalan politicians. The imprisoned Catalan leaders would eventually be pardoned in 2021, outside of the period considered here.[78]

Another difference between the two situations that could have resulted in differentiations in coverage could be the protests associated with the trials and arrests. However, based on this criteria, it is more reasonable to expect that the Catalan trials would have received more coverage. While there were protests throughout 2019 in Catalonia, likely the largest were sparked in October when the verdict was returned in the case. In addition to the *Times* reporting 600,000 participants, the *Guardian* estimated that more than 500,000 people participated in these protests.[79] These protests involved over 600 hundred injuries[80] and hundreds of arrests.[81] While there were protests against the arrest of Navalny spread across much of Russia, the size of most of these protests was estimated to be in the thousands.[82] The largest size I found reported was an estimated 40,000 protesters in Moscow as reported by *Reuters*.[83] There may have been more arrests in the case of the Navalny protests, with the highest estimate I found being 5100 arrests.[84]

Conclusion

Navalny's arrest may have been more dramatic, because of the earlier poisoning, but the Catalan cases involved more individuals being arrested and a politically charged issue—a declaration of independence. Many of the sentencings in the Catalan trials were greater than in the Navalny case and the trial lasted longer. Additionally, the protests against the Catalan arrests were much larger with possibly more injuries although there may have been more arrests in the Navalny protests. With this in mind, the situations are comparable. If anything, the Catalan protests may have warranted more coverage because of the larger number of people involved. Additionally, the popularly elected leaders in Catalonia held more prominent positions in Catalan society, while a poll about Navalny in 2019 showed only 9% of Russians having a positive view of him, indicating that he is a relatively marginal figure within Russia.[85]

Reasons for Differences

This chapter has shown that the coverage given to Navalny's arrest, trial and the protests that followed over a three month period was greater than that given to the arrests of the Catalan politicians and the protests that followed over the period of one year. I argue that the coverage for Navalny was more sympathetic. I have also argued that the two situations are similar enough to each other that you would expect similar levels of coverage on the merits of the story. So now the question turns to why Navalny's situation may have received more coverage.

One hypothesis could be Navalny's circumstances. As noted above, Navalny had been poisoned and this poisoning has been blamed on the Russian government. Because of this alleged assassination attempt, Navalny had begun to receive more attention in the Western media in the months preceding his arrest. This higher baseline level of coverage may have resulted in more coverage for Navalny. While this explanation is reasonable, I do not think it can explain much of the increased levels of coverage. Catalonia had been in political turmoil before 2019—the year covered in this chapter, with an independence referendum, protests, and a harsh government crackdown occurring in the previous year. Also, while perhaps not as exciting as an alleged assassination attempt, the story of the Catalan politicians did involve politicians fleeing into exile to avoid arrest and efforts by the Spanish government to have them extradited.

Although it is not a very tenable argument, some may argue that the Catalan politicians' situation did not receive substantial attention because Spain is a non-English speaking country which is usually not seen as being politically relevant to the United States. This first premise of Spain being a non-English speaking country may explain part of the fact that the Catalan politicians' situation did not receive as much attention. I suspect that if something similar had been repeated with Scottish independence politicians, it would receive more attention. Indeed, it was sometimes difficult to find detailed reporting about the situation in Catalonia, especially the protests, in the English-language press. However, this hypothesis does not explain why Navalny received more attention, given that Navalny is from a Russian-speaking country, Russian being a language that many fewer people from the United States speak than Spanish.

The second part of this argument that political developments in Russia are more relevant to the United States than those in Spain is more tenable. I began this chapter with a discussion of how Russia has reemerged as a geopolitical rival of the United States over the past decade. Because this rivalry exists, which is not the case for Spain, which is a member of NATO and has been aligned, along with much of Western Europe, with the foreign policy goals of the United States, coverage of dissidents may be more expected. I agree that this argument is likely true, but I do not see it as being wholly distinguishable from the Worthy/Unworthy paradigm defined by Herman and Chomsky.

In reporting from the US media, Russia will be framed as a geopolitical foe of the United States, but that does not mean that internal dissidents in Russia are inherently tied to this geopolitical rivalry. Navalny may be a dissident in Russia, but his primary forms of dissent up to the period of his arrest were not directed against Russian foreign policy, but rather corruption of the Putin government. In some cases, Navalny has been supportive of the geopolitical actions of the Russian government, such as supporting Crimea remaining under Russian control.[86] So while the apparent relevance of Russia to the United States may compel more coverage, the reasons why Navalny may be more relevant than the Catalan politicians is because of the Worthy/Unworthy hypothesis. The utility of Navalny to the elements of US foreign policy opposed to Russia were clear in the coverage. Navalny was not just a sympathetic figure opposed to a tyrannical government, but was also someone who, despite being relatively marginal in Russian politics, was a threat to the Russian government and evidence of its weakness. For these reasons, I believe that the best explanation for much of the greater coverage of Navalny compared to the Catalan politicians is the fact that Navalny unlike the Catalan politicians is a dissident in an enemy state. A worthy dissident.

Background: Pussy Riot and Pablo Hasél

Pussy Riot

Pussy Riot is a Russian band (sometimes referred to as a "performance artist collective") that formed in 2011. The band's performance art focused on protesting different aspects of Russian politics and culture. In late February 2012 the band entered a Russian Orthodox cathedral in Moscow and filmed themselves on the altar jumping around and punching the air.

They were on the altar for only a short time before they were led away by security guards. This performance was filmed and then later combined with a song: "Mother of God Drive Putin Away." Following these events, three members of Pussy Riot were arrested and charged with hooliganism. They were held without bail. This chapter deals with a two month long period between June and August 2012, which coincides with the trial and sentencing of the band members.

Pablo Hasél

Pablo Hasél is a rapper from Catalonia. He has attracted legal attention for a variety of reasons throughout his adult life. In 2011 he was arrested for a song that praised an accused left-wing militant. In 2014, he was sentenced to two years in prison for lyrics in another song that dealt with militant organizations. In addition to being arrested for lyrics, he has also been arrested for attacking a stall of a right-wing political party and for pushing a journalist.

In 2018, he was again arrested and sentenced to two years in prison for Tweets and song lyrics that attacked the former King of Spain, Juan Carlos. This sentence was lowered to nine months. He refused to surrender himself to authorities and was only arrested after he barricaded himself with supporters inside of the University of Lleida. This arrest sparked protests in both Catalonia and other parts of Spain. In this chapter, any coverage of Hasél at any point in time is considered.

The Numbers

In a two month period between July 2012 (the first piece did not appear until over halfway through the month) and August 2012, Pussy Riot's trial and the protests associated with it received ten times as much coverage as any coverage related to Pablo Hasél at any time period. In total, during the two month period considered (which does not cover the period of their arrest), there were 24 pieces of reporting, five opinion pieces, and a series of photos about the trial and protests. With respect to coverage of Hasél at any point in time, there were two pieces of reporting and one video showing the protests against his arrest.

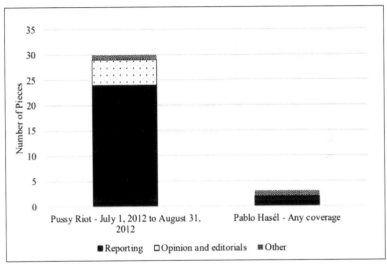

Figure 9. Coverage of two months of 2012 Pussy Riot trial and protests and any discussion of 2021 Pablo Hasél Arrest, Trial, by type of coverage

The Coverage

Pussy Riot

In the lead-up to the trial of the members of Pussy Riot, the *Times* published an article about the band's continued detention since their arrest in February. The article provided detail about the band's trial, including information about witnesses who testified against them during preliminary hearings and the potentially severe jail sentences they faced.[87] An opinion blog post argued that the prosecution against Pussy Riot was evidence for an increase in political prosecutions and show trials in Russia.[88]

When the trial itself began, the *Times* provided a detailed overview of the proceedings including direct quotes from the judge.[89] The *Times* covered musicians and bands who announced their support for Pussy Riot, including Sting and the Red Hot Chili Peppers.[90]

In an article about Russian views on the trial, the *Times* interviewed the reverend of the church where the band had protested, who said that he felt the time that they had already spent in jail was an adequate punishment and they should be given a suspended two year sentence. In the same article, Putin was quoted as saying, "I do not think that they should be judged severely for this."[91] Despite this seeming relatively noncommittal stance, a later opinion piece would declare:

> A case that should pivot on a specific legal question ("Does a violation of church protocol rise to the level of religious hatred?") instead hangs entirely on emotions, including those of Patriarch Kirill I and President Vladimir V. Putin, that the judge and the prosecution appear to be trying to divine.[92]

In early August the *Times* published an update about court proceedings, which were described as unruly with protesters outside and a barking rottweiler inside. Navalny was not allowed to testify after being called as a witness by the defense.[93] At a concert in Moscow, Madonna voiced her support for Pussy Riot.[94] Madonna's support for the band would receive coverage again a few weeks later.[95] A blog post discussed the details of the band's fashion, where Russian journalist Sergey Chernov was quoted as saying, "This case reminds us of both the 1930s

Stalinist show trials and medieval witch trials."[96] In a similar way, another blog post compared the trial of Pussy Riot to the "The Night of the Murdered Poets" when Soviet Jewish intellectuals were executed under Stalin.[97]

Later reporting discussed the reaction of the Russian Orthodox Church to the trial.[98] On the eve of the band's sentencing, the *Times* reported about a solidarity event held in Moscow where protesters read the band's "Punk Prayer."[99] Ultimately, the members of the band were sentenced to two years in prison, one year less than the three year sentence requested by prosecutors.[100] A slide show presented images from the trial.[101]

Following the verdict, a blog post declared, "To borrow the slogan of the world's most famous women's punk band, it seems we're all Pussy Riot now."[102] Russian authorities announced that they were still trying to find some members of the band,[103] who it was later reported fled the country.[104] During the sentencing, there were protests outside the courtroom,[105] and the band, who had never previously formally released a song, released a single called "Putin Stokes the Fires of Revolution."[106] Later reporting titled "Pussy Riot Was Carefully Calibrated for Protest" described the single:

> Titled, in translation, "Putin Lights Up the Fires," it's defiance set to bracing guitars and drum kicks. You can't seal us in a box, the women shout in a singsong as they demand more jail time. The chorus announces that the country is taking to the streets, bidding farewell to the regime, driven by a "feminist wedge." A few acolytes, complete with balaclavas, performed it in the courtroom during the sentencing. It's pure agitprop, and it's incredibly catchy.[107]

An insightful opinion piece did criticize some of the motivations for support for the band:

Yet there is something about the West's embrace of the young women's cause that should make us deeply uneasy, as Pussy Riot's philosophy, activism and even music quickly took second place to its usefulness in discrediting one of America's geopolitical foes. Twenty years after the end of the Cold War, are dissident intellectuals once again in danger of becoming pawns in the West's anti-Russian narrative?[108]

In contrast, a later opinion piece seemed to argue the exact perspective:

Pussy Riot struck at the sorest spot in modern Russia — which is why the group deserves praise, and not condemnation. The blow fell on the active merger of church and state into a single ideology, on the attempts to create a model of "Orthodox civilization" in Russia. The merger is intended to destroy the protest movement that has become a significant social phenomenon since December 2011 by depicting it as anti-Russian, as something alien to Russia's special way.[109]

A letter also acknowledged and defended the outsized attention that the trial received:

The women of Pussy Riot are a cause célèbre and so, by definition, they have received disproportionate media attention. Yet this outsized attention has served an important purpose. The outcry regarding their treatment has brought the world's attention to bear on the Kremlin's heavy-handed suppression not only of "radical" dissent, but of all opposition to Russia's current leadership.[110]

After the sentencing international shows of solidarity for the band continued with a *Times* blog post reporting about an

art exhibit about the band in New York.[111] Violent attacks by
culturally conservative activists on a Russian sex museum
were tied to a cultural backlash against Pussy Riot.[112] In late
August, at the scene of a double murder in Russia, someone left
the message "Free Pussy Riot" written on the wall in blood.[113]
Later reporting indicated that this was done to distract from the
actual motives of the crime.[114]

Conclusion

There was extensive coverage of the trial, the sentencing of Pussy
Riot and the protests that followed. This coverage portrayed the
band as a representative of opposition to the Putin government
and compared their trial and sentencing to past political trials in
Russia. Celebrity support for the band was frequently covered.

Pablo Hasél

I was only able to identify a total of three pieces—two articles
and one video associated with the second article—discussing
the case of Pablo Hasél anywhere in the *Times*'s archives. There
were no articles identified about his initial arrest or trial. The
first article described the protests following his 2021 arrest and
how Hasél "had barricaded himself inside a university to avoid
a prison sentence on charges that he had glorified terrorism
and denigrated the monarchy in Tweets and lyrics." The article
discussed violence at the protests and activists who declared
the arrest of Hasél as an assault on free speech.[115] Further
coverage of the protests focused on the young people who were
protesting, framing these protests around their dissatisfaction,
especially dissatisfaction associated with the pandemic:

Social isolation is as endemic as the contagion itself. Anxiety
and depression have reached alarming rates among young
people nearly everywhere, mental health experts and studies

have found. The police and mostly young protesters have also clashed in other parts of Europe, including last month in Amsterdam.

"It's not the same now for a person who is 60—or a 50-year-old with life experience and everything completely organized—as it is for a person who is 18 now and has the feeling that every hour they lose to this pandemic, it's like losing their entire life," said Enric Juliana, an opinion columnist with *La Vanguardia*, Barcelona's leading newspaper.[116]

A one and a half minute video accompanied this article showing protests in Barcelona against Hasél's arrest.[117]

Conclusion
Most of Hasél's arrests and sentencing were not covered by the *Times*. The 2021 arrest, which was notable because of the scale of protests that it sparked, received scant attention.

Are the Situations Comparable?
We now turn to whether the arrest and trial of Pussy Riot is really comparable to the arrests and trials of Pablo Hasél. In the case of Pussy Riot, their charges were only related to a single event, their performance in the Russian Orthodox Church in Moscow. For this performance, they were charged with "hooliganism" which is defined as "any deliberate behavior that violates public order and expresses explicit disrespect toward society."[118] Hasél had been charged and imprisoned on a variety of accused crimes including crimes involving assault. However, the first crime he was convicted of and the crimes that sparked the protests in 2021 were related to lyrics in his songs.

I believe a strong case can be made that the situations are comparable. While Pussy Riot was not convicted on an explicitly political crime, a standard interpretation of the events is that Pussy Riot was convicted for political reasons. This interpretation was reflected in the *Times*. In Hasél's case, while some of the charges he faced were not explicitly political, those related to lyrics in his songs were explicitly political. To the extent that there are differences between the two cases, it is that Hasél's charges were more explicitly political than those faced by Pussy Riot. International human rights organizations including Amnesty International and Human Rights Watch criticized both cases.[119,120,121,122]

Following the arrest of Hasél there were fairly large protests that lasted for multiple days throughout Spain, especially in Barcelona and Madrid. According to the BBC, the biggest protest was in Girona with over 5000 participants. The BBC also reported two other cities with 2000 protesters.[123] There were frequent clashes with police at these protests with multiple injuries and arrests.[124,125,126] In one notable incident, a woman was reported to have lost her eye after being hit with a projectile fired by police.[127]

With respect to the size of the protests in support of Pussy Riot, it is difficult to find clear estimates. One article from *Mother Jones* estimated about 1500 participants in what they characterized as an "anti-Putin/pro-Pussy Riot rally" in Moscow.[128] The small size of these protests within Russia is consistent with the fairly low levels of support that Pussy Riot had in the country. According to the *Moscow Times*, which is often seen as anti-Putin,[129] a poll of 1601 Russians found not one person reporting that they respect the band. Six percent of respondents sympathized with the band with 27% declaring some degrees of hostility.[130] A later poll by the Russian Public Opinion Study Center, a state-owned polling firm, found that 41% of respondents thought that there was an outside organization backing Pussy Riot.[131] There was also an international element to the Pussy Riot protests with small protests taking place across the United States[132,133] and the United Kingdom,[134] among other countries.[135] Celebrities also joined the calls for protests. Amnesty International thought Sting's protest of the trial was big enough news to release a press release about it.[136]

The situations of the trial and imprisonment of Pussy Riot and Hasél are comparable. The only factor that could have justified more attention for Pussy Riot just based on the facts of the case is that Pussy Riot's sentencing ended up being longer than Hasél following his appeal and the fact that the band had more members that were sentenced. The factors that one would expect to result in more coverage for Hasél are the explicitly political nature of the charges against him, the longer time that the case went through trials—with the case going all the way up to the supreme court—and the large protests following his imprisonment in 2021.

With respect to the trial and the sentencing, Pussy Riot's case was tried in a district court over the course of a few weeks. The three defendants faced a maximum sentence of seven years in prison and they were ultimately sentenced to two years. Although this occurred past the period reviewed in this chapter, one of the defendants had her conviction converted to two years of probation on appeal. As mentioned, Hasél had much more extensive interactions with the Spanish legal system, most of which were not covered at all by the *Times*. For the accusation that sparked the protests covered in this chapter, Hasél was initially sentenced to two years in prison, which was then reduced to nine months by the Spanish Supreme Court.[137] Hasél's initial sentence was comparable to those of the members of Pussy Riot.

Worthy and Unworthy Dissidents

Reasons for Differences

If Pussy Riot had been a successful and popular band in Russia or globally before their arrest that may have also justified the increased media attention that they received. In fact, Pussy Riot had only been founded in late 2011, a few months before their arrest.[138] While the band had done some public performances, they had not released any songs until during their trial. In contrast, Hasél had released dozens of albums and even books of poetry before his 2021 imprisonment.

With these factors in mind, the Worthy/Unworthy hypothesis for similar reasons to those made for why Navalny received more attention than the Catalan independence politicians discussed above remains a valid explanation for the increased attention received by Pussy Riot in comparison to Hasél.

Conclusion

The arrest and trial of Pussy Riot members received much more attention than the arrest and trial Pablo Hasél. Coverage of the Pussy Riots cases was very sympathetic with opinion pieces in support of the band. The coverage of Hasél was too scant to characterize in a meaningful way. The two cases are reasonably comparable. The Worthy/Unworthy paradigm is a viable hypothesis for explaining the differences in coverage.

171

Chapter 5

Worthy and Unworthy Interventions: Russia in Syria and Saudi Arabia in Yemen

The conflicts in the Middle East that followed the Arab Spring protests have resulted in a complex series of overlapping alliances pitting regional and global powers against each other. For the United States, regional enemies include countries like Iran and Syria and organizations like Hezbollah. Among the United States' allies are most of the Gulf Monarchies, especially Saudi Arabia, and Israel.

The conflicts in the region present an opportunity to examine the Worthy and Unworthy paradigm, especially as they relate to foreign interventions in these conflicts. In particular, this chapter will explore how coverage differs between Russia's intervention in Syria and Saudi Arabia's intervention in Yemen. As a geopolitical foe, according to the Worthy and Unworthy hypothesis one would expect more coverage to be given to Russia's intervention and less to be given to Saudi Arabia's, and for the coverage of Russia's intervention to be more negative than coverage of Saudi Arabia's.

Background

Russian Intervention in Syria
The conflict in Syria stretches back to the early days of the Arab Spring when protests against the government of President Bashar al-Assad began. Assad had ruled the country since 2000 after taking over from his father Hafez al-Assad whose reign began in 1971. These protests called for political reforms in the country and, in some cases, the end of Assad's control

of Syria. While many segments of society were involved, they were especially concentrated among Sunnis (Assad being from the Shia Alawite sect) and Kurds. There were counterprotests among Assad supporters and eventually a government crackdown on protests began. The conflict progressively escalated into an armed Civil War between many parties, but especially between the Assad government and their opponents, which eventually became loosely organized into the "Free Syria Army."

The United States and many other Western countries supported opponents of Assad. In August 2011, President Obama called on Assad to "step aside." The United States became more involved in the conflict with covert arming of rebels by the CIA. Foreign involvement in the country would grow to include countries like Saudi Arabia, Qatar, and Turkey. Other Western countries began also supporting opponents of Assad. Turkey used the opportunity to strike at Kurdish groups in Syria. Iran and Lebanon's Hezbollah were Assad's most prominent supporters.

The conflict became more complicated with the rapid rise of the militant Islamic State of Iraq and Syria (ISIS). While also seeking to overthrow Assad, the organization had conflicts with other rebel groups and Kurdish fighters. The United States had avoided direct military intervention in Syria preferring instead to support rebels; eventually as the threat of ISIS grew along with their self-proclaimed caliphate in Syria and Iraq and they then inspired other Islamic State groups around the world, the United States started intervening against ISIS militarily. Despite this intervention, ISIS continued to gain territory. It is important to note that while ISIS was the most prominent Islamist group operating in Syria during the Syrian Civil War, there were many other organizations with similar ideologies that were not necessarily allied with ISIS, most notably the Al-Nusra Front, an offshoot of Al-Qaeda. In some cases arms supplied by the United States to other rebels were reported to have fallen into the hands of Al-Nusra.[1]

Because the United States intervention was primarily motivated by ISIS's threat to other rebel organizations, the Assad government was still threatened as ISIS moved closer to the capital of Damascus in 2015. Such a threat eventually led to Russia, an ally (although often a distant ally) of Syria, to begin bombing campaigns against Islamist rebels in Syria in late September 2015.

Saudi Arabian Intervention in Yemen, April and May 2015

Yemen has been in political turmoil since the Arab spring when a protest was launched that overthrew the then President Ali Abdullah Saleh. In the subsequent presidential election, a Saudi-backed candidate Abdrabbuh Mansur Hadi ran unopposed and won. Houthis, a Shia political group in the north of Yemen, boycotted the election. Protests against the election led to armed resistance and the eventual overthrow of the Hadi government in early 2014. After a peace deal between the Houthis and the government of Hadi expired, the Hadi government fled to a city in the south of Yemen, Aden, which was declared Yemen's new capital with Hadi claiming to still run the government. The Houthis began to close in on Aden in late March, and Hadi called for an international intervention to stop them from overthrowing his government. In response Saudi Arabia led an intervention of other Gulf and Arab countries to counter the Houthi rebels. Saudi Arabia's intervention against the Houthis is often viewed as a method to prevent Iran from spreading its influence on the Arabian Peninsula, because Iran has supported the Houthis.

The Numbers

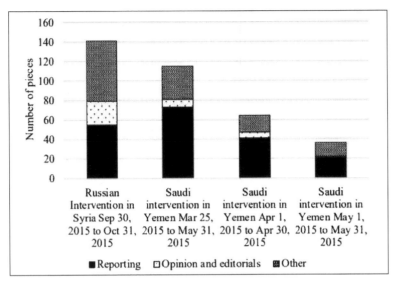

Figure 10. Coverage of 2015 Russian intervention in Syria and Saudi Arabian intervention in Yemen by type of coverage

As shown in figure 10, one month of coverage of Russia's intervention in Syria received more attention than two months of coverage of Saudi Arabia's intervention in Yemen. In the case of Russia's intervention, one day in September was included, and in the case of Saudi Arabia's intervention several days at the end of March were included. In both cases, these extra days were included because the interventions started at the end of the month. There were 141 pieces dealing with Russia's intervention and 115 dealing with Saudi Arabia's. With respect to Saudi Arabia's intervention, in April there were 64 pieces and in May there were 36 pieces.

A substantial share of Russia's coverage fell into the "other" category due to the large number of videos about the intervention that were published. However, even when only considering reporting articles, Russia's intervention had more articles published about it (73) than either month of Saudi Arabia's intervention (41 in April and 21 in May) or both months combined. There were also many more opinion pieces (opinion articles, editorials, and letters) dealing with Russia's intervention (24 total), compared to Saudi Arabia's intervention (8 total).

The Coverage

Russian Intervention in Syria

On just the first day of airstrikes (September 30, 2015), I identified 16 pieces dealing with Russia's intervention in Syria. One of these early articles titled "Russians Strike Targets in Syria, But Not ISIS Areas." This claim that Russia was not targeting ISIS, but rather other organizations like "one and possibly more Syrian opposition groups that have been secretly armed and trained by the C.I.A.," was coming from "American officials" and not directly from reporting about the targets of the strikes. The title of the article does not clarify this source and treats it as objective that Russia was not targeting ISIS.[2] However, that same day a spokesman from the White House said that they were reviewing the targets and that "it is too early to be sure what targets Russia is hitting inside Syria"[3] while the Secretary of Defense Ash Carter said that "it does appear" that the strikes were in areas where there were not ISIS fighters.[4] Other spokespeople doubted that Russia was attacking ISIS.[5] Assad opponents in Syria supported the United States' claims about who Russia was targeting.[6] Russian officials countered that they were indeed targeting ISIS. When the *Times* reported Russia's claims about their targets, it was attributed directly to officials from the country.[7] Russian Foreign Minister Sergey Lavrov further disputed US claims about Russia not targeting ISIS telling the media "don't listen to Pentagon about the Russian strikes."[8]

A video showed then Secretary of State John Kerry at the United Nations saying that the United States was willing to work with Russia in targeting ISIS and other terrorist groups, but not other opponents of the Assad government.[9] The *Times* reported about investigations studying Russian footage of airstrikes in order to determine whether they were targeting ISIS. One of the investigators that the *Times* discussed was posting on the website LiveJournal.[10]

On the second day of strikes the possibility was that if all of Russia's strikes were not targeting ISIS, they may have been targeting another Islamicist group namely the Al-Nusra Front:

> The Russian state news agency RIA reported on Thursday that airstrikes by the Syrian military, which is working with the Russian Air Force, had killed 107 militants, including three commanders of the Nusra Front, Al Qaeda's branch in Syria, near Homs.[11]

Later reporting would further discuss the identity of other groups that Russia was targeting:

> Russia has focused its earliest operations on the insurgent coalition known as the Army of Conquest, or Jaish al-Fatah, rather than on the Islamic State, according to the official from the pro-government alliance, because it is the Army of Conquest's positions that most urgently threaten the crucial government-held coastal province of Latakia, while Islamic State forces are farther to the east and can later be isolated and hit.[12]

As earlier reported by the paper, the Army of Conquest "consists of a number of mostly Islamist factions, including the Nusra Front, Al Qaeda's Syrian affiliate; Ahrar al-Sham, another large group; and more moderate rebel factions that have received covert arms support from the intelligence services of the United States and its allies."[13] Later reporting would also indicate that Russia's intervention led to increased funding to "help certain C.I.A.-vetted insurgent groups battle the Syrian government." This support was contrasted with less successful support from the Pentagon:

> The C.I.A. program that delivered the TOWs (an acronym for tube-launched, optically tracked, wire-guided missiles) is separate from—and significantly larger than—the failed $500 million Pentagon program that was canceled last week after it trained only a handful of fighters. That was unsuccessful largely because few recruits would agree to its goal of fighting only the militant Islamic State and not Mr. Assad.[14]

We are left wondering whether recipients of CIA support—in contrast to Pentagon support—did not need to agree to only fight Islamic State militants.

Lavrov said that Russia would only target terrorist groups and said that it did not consider the Western-backed Assad opponents Free Syrian Army to be a terrorist group, adding that the Free Syrian Army should be involved in the political solution in the country.[15] Despite this statement, in a later video, President Obama seemingly ignored this position saying that "we reject Russia's theory that everybody opposed to Assad is a terrorist."[16] Later Lavrov said that Russia was ready to support the Free Syrian Army[17] while calling for elections in the country.[18] Turkey, which had been accused of supporting Islamist groups in Syria, also accused Russia of not targeting ISIS[19] and expressed concerns that Russia was supporting Kurdish militias in Syria.[20] The European Union later joined with the criticism of Russia's intervention.[21] Additionally a Free Syrian Army commander was quoted as saying (Daesh is an Arabic acronym for ISIS):

Daesh has exploited the Russian airstrikes and the preoccupation of the Free Syrian Army in its battles in Hama, and advanced in Aleppo.[22]

Despite the claims that Russia was not primarily targeting ISIS, representatives from the terror organization threatened to attack Russia.[23] Later in the month, an alleged terrorist cell operating in Russia was reported to have been detained by Russia's Federal Security Services. A mortar shell also landed near Russia's embassy in Syria. Later in the month, security services in the country reported that they had foiled an ISIS plot to bomb a train in Russia. Putin declared that Russia was ready to defend against terrorist threats.

While a video was published showing Syrian opposition groups' claims that Russian strikes were harming civilians,[24] Putin claimed that no civilians had been hurt during Russia's airstrikes.[25]

The *Times* even provided a detailed overview of Putin's activities on his birthday:

It would be hard to imagine a more perfect birthday for Vladimir V. Putin, the president of Russia, who turned 63 on Wednesday.

After receiving a report from his defense minister that Russia had launched a major cruise missile strike on Syria—a move further confounding American policy in the Middle East—Mr. Putin celebrated his birthday by playing a game of hockey with N.H.L. veterans, and winning.[26]

Much of this coverage of the debate around who Russia was targeting appeared on the first days of the intervention. Initial coverage during this period also included an explainer article which discussed the complex relationship of the different countries intervening in Syria,[27] a video of the Russian

Duma approving the airstrikes, and videos of the airstrikes themselves.[28,29,30]

Russian Intervention and US Domestic Politics

The intervention became a topic for domestic politics in the United States. In the early stages of the 2016 Republican Presidential Primary, then candidate Donald Trump who was earlier reported as saying with respect to Syria, "I would go in and take the oil, and I'd put troops to protect the oil … I would absolutely go, and I'd take the money source away. And believe me, they would start to wither and they would collapse," voiced support for the Russian strikes saying, "Let Russia take care of ISIS."[31]

Chris Christie labelled President Obama a "weakling" for not instituting a no-fly zone.[32] The call for a "no-fly zone" was used by many of the candidates to try to prove their toughness even as it would risk direct conflict between Russia and the United States. Candidates were quoted as saying:

Senator Lindsey Graham: "Anybody who rides around on a horse without their shirt, I can handle that guy."

Former Governor Jeb Bush: "The argument is, 'Well, we'll get into conflict with Russia' … Well, maybe Russia shouldn't want to be in conflict with us. I mean, this is a place where American leadership is desperately needed."

Governor Chris Christie: "My first phone call would be to Vladimir, and I'd say to him, 'Listen, we're enforcing this no-fly zone … And I mean we're enforcing it against anyone, including you. So don't try me. Don't try me. 'Cause I'll do it.'"[33]

An infographic showed the position of Republican and Democratic candidates with respect to a "no-fly zone" with all the Republic candidates who had taken a position (Trump did not) except for Rand Paul supporting a "no-fly zone," while Clinton was the only Democrat in support. In addition to Paul, Bernie Sanders and Martin O'Malley also opposed a "no-fly zone."[34] In a video, Hillary Clinton was shown advocating for more confrontation with Russia in Syria during a Democratic debate.[35]

In contrast to the position of many presidential candidates, Putin pushed for coordination between Russia and the United States:[36]

"Syria, despite the dramatic situation there now, might become a model for partnership for the sake of our joint interests, for the resolution of our problems, which concern everyone, for working out an effective system of risk management," Mr. Putin said, seemingly laying out a broader plan for global cooperation with the United States and the West in general.

"We had this chance once after the end of the Cold War; unfortunately, we didn't use it," Mr. Putin told the annual gathering of academics and other Russia experts known as the Valdai Discussion Club. Another chance was missed during the terrorist upsurge in the early 2000s, he said.[37]

Reporting indicated that the Obama administration was taking a cautious approach with respect to Russia's intervention, but was comforted by the fact that they could not solve the decades long deadly civil war in the country:

Frustrated by their own inability to resolve the crisis over more than four years, the president and his team express a quiet confidence that Moscow almost certainly will be no more successful.[38]

Russian and US Motivations

The *Times* Editorial Board cast doubt on Russia's claims that their goal in intervening in Syria was to defeat ISIS:

> Mr. Putin's claim that the primary motivation for the bombing is to fight and destroy terrorists, including the Islamic State, is dubious. It is more likely that the Russian leader's main objective is to rescue President Bashar al-Assad of Syria, whose hold on power has weakened as the Syrian Army has lost ground not only to the Islamic State, which is trying to establish a caliphate in Syria and Iraq, but also to a coalition of insurgent groups that is opposed to the Islamic State.[39]

In a similar way, President Obama criticized Russian operations in the country as a way to support both Iran and Assad:

> An attempt by Russia and Iran to prop up Assad and try to pacify the population is just going to get them stuck in a quagmire and it won't work.[40]

In another interesting comparison with United States officials' claims that Russia's interventions were not about stopping ISIS, but rather propping up Assad, Obama further stated that:

> "The problem here is Assad and the brutality he's inflicted on the Syrian people," Mr. Obama said. While the United States will work with "all parties" to broker a transition, he said, "we are not going to cooperate with a Russian campaign to simply try to destroy anybody who is disgusted and fed up with Mr. Assad's behavior."[41]

The United States had also been intervening in Syria with the alleged goal of stopping ISIS and not overthrowing Assad.

This seeming hypocrisy was not pointed out in the article.[42] The UK Foreign Minister Philip Hammond joined in with the criticism of Russia, suggesting that Russia's bombing would drive members of the opposition to the arms of ISIS.[43] Later Secretary of State John Kerry would welcome the potential for Russia to help in the fight against ISIS, while still criticizing the country for allegedly targeting "moderate" opposition.[44,45] Throughout the conflict, videos showing Russian strikes were published.[46,47,48,49,50,51,52,53,54] The *Times* also published a detailed overview of the weapons that Russia was using in Syria.[55] In an article and an accompanying video, the Russian intervention was put into the context of Putin's political career and his theories about maintaining order and preventing chaos.[56,57]

US Response

Shortly after Russia's intervention began, the Obama administration announced plans to increase support for opposition groups in the country with the goal of defeating ISIS.[58] When discussing these plans, Foreign Minister Lavrov criticized US efforts against ISIS and their efforts to support rebels against Assad:

> The administration's position was ridiculed Monday by Sergey V. Lavrov, Russia's foreign minister, who said the American airstrikes, which began more than a year ago, had done little militarily. In comments carried by Russia's official Tass news agency, Mr. Lavrov said that even the Americans had acknowledged their faltering efforts to create a force of so-called moderate insurgents in Syria.
>
> "Nobody knows about these people," he said. "Nobody's really heard about the moderate opposition."[59]

Almost confirming Lavrov's claims, later in the month, a *Times* editorial described how the United States had begun performing less vetting on the opposition groups that it was supporting:

> The Pentagon will stop putting rebel fighters through training in neighboring countries, a program that was designed to ensure that fighters were properly vetted before they could get their hands on American weapons and ammunition. The new plan will simply funnel weapons through rebel leaders who are already in the fight and appear to be making some headway.[60]

When Russia announced that volunteer ground forces would be entering Syria, the *Times* framed the issue around the perspective of the United States and Saudi Arabia, who also opposed Russia's intervention:

> The Americans see the Islamic State as the most dangerous immediate threat. They view Russia's moves as prolonging and possibly widening the war, even if Russian forces also are hitting Islamic State targets as the Russians assert.
>
> Russia's intervention already appears to have subverted diplomatic efforts to halt the war, led by a special United Nations envoy, Staffan de Mistura. Forty-one rebel factions that oppose Mr. Assad said in a statement on Monday that Russia's "brutal occupation has cut the road to any political solution."
>
> Criticism of Russia also flowed from Saudi Arabia, which strongly opposes Mr. Assad and his Alawite sect, a Shiite Muslim offshoot. Reuters reported that 53 Saudi clerics issued a statement on Monday calling Russia's immersion in the conflict a Christian crusade against Sunni Muslims, the majority sect in Syria.[61]

The *Times* Editorial Board joined with this criticism, in particular questioning whether the volunteer ground forces that Russia was sending to the country were truly voluntary: "What is clear is that these 'volunteers' are there about as voluntarily as were the Russian soldiers ordered into Crimea or eastern Ukraine. Russians might want to ask why young Russians are being sent to face mortal danger in the Middle East in service of Mr. Putin's very dangerous gamble."[62]

While the board declared that it was "clear" that the forces were not voluntary, no evidence was offered for this assertion.

Russia and Other Countries

Russia's interactions with other countries in Syria was a frequent topic of coverage in the *Times*. Initially, the United States only agreed to coordinate with Russia in efforts to ensure safety in the air.[63] However, despite this air coordination, US plans were reported to have needed to change course because there were "Russian aircraft operating nearby."[64] Putin criticized the United States for not coordinating more in Syria.[65] Later in the month, a formal memorandum of understanding was issued seeking to avoid safety incidents.[66,67]

In a meeting with his Defense Minister, a video showed Putin suggesting that non-Islamist members of the Free Syrian Army might unite with the government forces to defeat ISIS and Al-Nusra.[68]

The Russian intervention seemed to have an impact as the Syrian Military began to take control of territory that they had previously lost.[69] However, at the same time groups opposing Assad began to feel more confident as increased US arms came into the country. One fighter said:

We can get as much as we need and whenever we need them … Just fill in the numbers.[70]

Around this same time, a Russian fighter jet briefly entered Turkish airspace, which sparked a response from NATO of which Turkey is a member[71,72,73] and strained Turkish-Russian relations.[74] A few days later NATO made its position with respect to Russia's operation in Syria clear:

> "We are implementing the biggest reinforcement of our collective defense since the end of the Cold War," NATO's secretary general, Jens Stoltenberg, said before a meeting of defense ministers here on Thursday. After the meeting, he said, "All of this sends a message to NATO citizens: NATO will defend you, NATO is on the ground, NATO is ready."[75]

Later in the conflict, Turkey shot down a drone near its border, which anonymous United States officials claimed was Russian.[76]

White House Press Secretary Josh Earnest claimed that Russia's intervention was turning itself into a "target of Sunni Muslims."[77] Such criticism was supported by Sunni religious leaders:

> The Saudi clerics, denigrating their longtime adversaries, including Shiite Muslims and Alawites, who practice an offshoot of Shiite Islam, also took aim at the "Orthodox crusader Russia," which they said was picking up where the Soviet force driven from Afghanistan by Muslims more than a generation ago had left off.
>
> In an online statement signed by 55 clerics, they warned that if the "holy warriors" were defeated in Syria, Sunni nations would also fall "one after the other."[78]

Coverage from the *Times* often tried to make sense of the complicated alliances in the conflict. Many Shia in Iraq expressed support for Russia's intervention,[79] while the Sunni Saudi

Arabian government and an archnemesis of Syrian ally Iran continued to express concerns about Russia's intervention.[80] In an odd series of infographics, the *Times* depicted the overlapping conflicts occurring in Syria. According to the graphic, rebels in general were the Assad government's main adversary, while ISIS, which also sought to take down the regime and was the most successful at capturing territory, was only a secondary enemy. While the infographic did acknowledge US support for rebels who targeted Assad, it did not list Assad, who President Obama had said must transition from power as an adversary. Most strangely, Kurds in Syria who the *Times* acknowledged had been bombed by Turkey were only listed as a "concern" for the Turkish government.[81]

Despite the claims that ISIS was not a primary target for Russia as frequently stated by US government officials, the *Times* reported that Russia was helping the Syrian government to retake an airport held by ISIS.[82] At this same time, Assad visited Putin.[83,84,85,86] This meeting may have contributed to the two countries moving towards a data sharing agreement.[87]

International Reactions and Calls for a Ceasefire

Following the United Nations Deputy Secretary-General's call for a ceasefire,[88] the *Times* discussed the failure of the United Nations Security Council to stop the conflict in Syria and in other parts of the world.[89]

Russia was blamed for increases in civilians fleeing Syria, especially the city of Homs. The piece describing the increase in civilian departures acknowledged how Russian strikes were welcomed by those in areas threatened by rebels:

For many Syrians in government-held areas, Russia's intervention, on Sept. 30, came just in time, shoring up the flagging Syrian Army and staving off the threat from the rebels. But in parts of central and northern Syria, where the violence has recently spiked, residents said Russia had exacerbated the suffering.[90]

Following advocacy by Russia, Iran was eventually invited to peace talks being held in Vienna.[91] An editorial considered this to be a positive development.[92] At the end of the month, discussion of Russia's intervention in Syria was overshadowed by the crash of a Russian plane over the Sinai desert.

Opinion Pieces

Several opinion pieces and letters[93,94] appeared on the first days of the intervention including one where Thomas Friedman wrote:

> Putin stupidly went into Syria looking for a cheap sugar high to show his people that Russia is still a world power. Well, now he's up a tree. Obama and John Kerry should just leave him up there for a month—him and Assad, fighting ISIS alone—and watch him become public enemy No. 1 in the Sunni Muslim world. "Yo, Vladimir, how's that working for you?"[95]

Some opinion pieces did offer perspectives outside of the seeming foreign policy consensus. In one, the authors advocated for engagement between the United States and Russia:

> Washington and Moscow could take advantage of their respective ties with the regional powers that actually have the manpower and operating space to act: Turkey, Saudi Arabia, Iran, Iraq, the Gulf states and the Kurds. While any coalition would have internal tensions—most notably between Turkey and the Kurds—combined Russian and American pressure

could help convince all parties to focus on the Islamic State today and leave other concerns for later.[96]

The authors of this piece also argued that the United States should be open to other ways of ending the conflict:

The United States should have two goals in Syria. First, bring order to those parts of the country that the Islamic State does not control. Second, strive to build a coalition of forces that can contain the Islamic State and eventually replace it. Russia's "intrusion" could offer a chance to achieve both.[97]

Another interpreted Putin's actions in Syria in a more nuanced light than the majority of the coverage:

It's more accurate to say that the Kremlin is in Syria for pedagogical reasons: It wants to teach Americans a lesson, and a valuable one. It wants to show that America should either be prepared to intervene in any civil war that follows a troubled revolution inspired by its lofty rhetoric, or it should quit goading people to revolt. "Do you realize, what you have done?" was the most memorable line of President Vladimir Putin's speech at the United Nations General Assembly.[98]

A later letter to the editor criticized this article.[99] Another opinion piece, however, framed Russia's intervention in cultural and religious terms:

Today, President Vladimir V. Putin has many motives in Syria, but we should keep in mind Russia's vision of its traditional mission in the Middle East, and how it informs the Kremlin's thinking. And not just the Kremlin: Russia's Orthodox Church spokesman said that Mr. Putin's intervention was part of "the special role our country has always played in the Middle East."[100]

Still another claimed that Russia's ultimate goal was the partition of Syria:

Russia's unspoken but unmistakable message is that Moscow is trying one—and perhaps the only—way of ending the conflict by means of a Lebanese-style segregation of Syria into zones controlled by rival militias. To Washington's perennial concern in any Middle Eastern imbroglio, "Tell me how this ends," Moscow responds: The Syrian conflict will be "resolved" on Russia's terms, even if Mr. Assad proves dispensable to the Kremlin in the long run.[101]

A later opinion piece lamented the seeming lack of concern for what was happening in Syria among many Russians.[102]

One opinion piece from former Ambassador to Russia Michael McFaul characterized Putin's intervention as a strategic mistake:

In the short term, Russia's Syrian bombing campaign has energized the Syrian Army and its allies to launch a counteroffensive against opposition rebels—that is, against everyone except the Islamic State. But in the long run, Russian airstrikes alone cannot restore Mr. Assad's authority over the whole country.[103]

A reasonable opinion piece by former President Jimmy Carter proposed a plan for achieving peace in Syria:

Iran outlined a general four-point sequence several months ago, consisting of a cease fire, formation of a unity government, constitutional reforms and elections. Working through the United Nations Security Council and utilizing a five-nation proposal, some mechanism could be found to implement these goals.

The involvement of Russia and Iran is essential. Mr. Assad's only concession in four years of war was giving up chemical weapons, and he did so only under pressure from Russia and Iran. Similarly, he will not end the war by accepting concessions imposed by the West, but is likely to do so if urged by his allies.[104]

An opinion piece summarized the author's feelings about the ultimate effect of Russia's intervention:

Overall, the Russian efforts will worsen the violence, inflame terrorism and risk dragging the Russians into a quagmire. The consequences are likely to be bad for Russia, for the United States and, worst of all, for Syria and its neighbors.[105]

Conclusion

Russia's intervention in Syria received extensive and detailed coverage throughout the month of October. Most days multiple pieces, including many videos, were published. Coverage of the intervention was generally very negative. Notably, coverage was very skeptical of claims that the intervention would target ISIS, and instead focused on suggesting that the primary goal of the intervention was to weaken other rebel groups opposed to Assad. The fact that many of these rebel groups were also Islamist in nature was rarely discussed in the *Times* coverage.

Saudi Intervention in Yemen

The first reports of Saudi Arabia's intervention appeared on March 25 and described how "Saudi Arabia announced on Wednesday night that it had begun military operations in

Yemen, launching airstrikes in coordination with a coalition of 10 nations." This initial article mostly focused on Houthi rebels' territorial gains in Yemen and less on the nature of the new Saudi intervention.[106] That same day, the *Times* published a Twitter post from people in Sanaa, the capital of Yemen, commenting about the bombing with little additional context,[107] something that they would do at other points during the intervention.[108,109] In one of these series, none of the Tweets mentioned Saudi Arabia.[110]

A video showed the effects of the beginning of the airstrikes, including burning vehicles. The video emphasized how the conflict was becoming a regional proxy war with Iran.[111] An analysis described the complicated situation in the Middle East following the bombing:

In Yemen, the Obama administration is supporting a Saudi-led military campaign to dislodge Iranian-backed Houthi rebels despite the risks of an escalating regional fight with Iran. But in Iraq and Syria, the United States is on the same side as Iran in the fight against the Islamic State, contributing airstrikes to an Iranian-supported offensive on Tikrit on Thursday even while jostling with Iran for position in leading the operation.[112]

As Houthi rebels gained territory in Yemen, the Saudi-allied Egyptian government said that it was willing to send troops to the country[113] with a meeting in Cairo ultimately leading to many Arab nations creating a joint military force, which they claimed sought to counter Iranian influence in the region.[114] The regional component of the conflict was further emphasized in an article that framed the conflict around Saudi Arabia's opposition to Iran as talks about Iran's nuclear program continued.[115] To try to make sense of the conflict, the *Times* published three maps showing countries aligned with Iran and Saudi Arabia.[116]

The former leader of Yemen, Ali Abdullah Saleh, who was seen as being allied with the Houthis, called for dialogue to end the airstrikes.[117] In contrast, while speaking on *Face the Nation* the Saudi Ambassador to the United States announced that Saudi Arabia had not ruled out sending ground forces into Yemen.[118]

Despite the intervention, the Houthis continued to make progress, taking the port city of Aden.[119] At the same time, the Saudi bombing campaign was reported to be used in Saudi Arabia to hype the image of Crown Prince Mohammed bin Salman:

> The Saudi news media has played up Prince Mohammed's role as the architect and overseer of the Yemen campaign, turning it into a pivotal test. "There is a huge public relations campaign about how wonderful and brilliant the son is, and if the war were to stop now, he would come out looking great, but not if they start taking casualties," Mr. Haykel said.[120]

A piece about the problems faced by Yemenis did not mention Saudi Arabia's intervention until the seventh paragraph.[121] Despite this seeming lack of focus on the role of Saudi Arabia in the conflict, a video characterized the airstrikes as creating a "ghost town" in parts of Yemen.[122] Further videos showing the effects of the bombing were released during the conflict.[123] Another video showed Yemenis protesting Saudi airstrikes.[124]

Efforts to end the conflict continued. Although the Iraqi Prime Minister offered criticism of the Saudi intervention,[125] a day later he would soften his stance.[126] The challenges of finding a resolution to the conflict led a UN mediator to resign.[127]

While a Security Council resolution banned the sales of weapons to the Houthi rebels,[128] US arms sales to Saudi Arabia were described as fueling the conflict.[129] The US sent an aircraft carrier off the Yemen coast to deter Iran from providing arms to the Houthis.[130] This naval convoy was credited with causing an Iranian ship, allegedly carrying aid to the Houthis, to turn back.[131] However, Houthi leader Abdul-Malik al-Houthi remained defiant during the conflict[132] and the intervention continued. In late April, a Saudi bombing was reported to have killed 25[133] as airstrikes continued to hit the capital of Sanaa.[134]

Brief Bombing Halt and Resumption

After nearly a month of bombing, Saudi Arabia announced a halt to the bombing campaign claiming that the operation "had achieved its objectives."[135,136] The *Times* published Tweets of Yemeni reacting to this news.[137] However, only a few days after this announcement bombing was resumed,[138,139] which again led to the *Times* publishing more Tweets of locals' reactions. The renewed campaign was renamed from Decisive Storm to Renewal of Hope.[140] A video showed the intensifying fighting.[141] The fighting continued to prompt Yemenis to flee the country, including some using wooden boats to sail across the Red Sea to Djibouti.[142] The fighting was suspected to be weighing on attempts for the United States to establish a nuclear deal with Iran.[143]

It was not just the military activity that was reported to be impacting aid reaching the country, but also the inspection standards implemented by Saudi Arabia.[144] Around the same time, another airstrike was estimated to have killed 20 civilians.[145] Some reporting provided details about the Saudi-led operation. The coalition had used cluster bombs, "which are banned by much of the world, though not by the United States, Saudi Arabia or Yemen," as part of their offensive.[146] While

Saudi Arabia sought to avoid sending ground troops to Yemen, it was reported that Yemen soldiers trained in Saudi Arabia had been sent to fight in Yemen.[147] Soon after Yemeni rebels would strike a Saudi border town.[148]

During a visit from representatives of the Saudi monarchy including Mohammed bin Salman, President Obama praised the role the country played in conflicts in the region.[149] Around this same time, Saudi airstrikes continued to kill civilians including five Ethiopian migrants.[150] The *Times* published a video showing women and children protesting in opposition to Saudi bombing and in support of the Houthi rebels.[151] A few days later there would be another large protest march.[152]

A brief article described a report from Amnesty International describing how munitions fire by Houthi rebels had killed civilians.[153] The *Times* published two videos showing further airstrikes close to the end of the month,[154,155] including the destruction of a sports complex.[156] It was reported that several civilians from the US were being detained by Houthi rebels.[157]

Humanitarian Catastrophe

The years long conflict in Yemen has been one of the world's worst humanitarian catastrophes. The *Times* described some aspects of this emerging crisis. Saudi airstrikes killed dozens of civilians at a displaced persons camp.[158,159] A later video of the aftermath of another airstrike showed a dairy factory in flames.[160]

The humanitarian situation continued to worsen in Yemen throughout early April. As many as eleven civilians may have been killed in one airstrike.[161] A video from a Houthi channel was published showing Saudi bombings.[162] A Chinese effort to evacuate foreign nations from the chaos in Yemen was reported to have assisted the country in improving its image.[163]

Despite the worsening humanitarian situation in the country, there was little action from the international community. In a one paragraph report, the *Times* described the Russian ambassador at the UN Security Council criticizing the United States for not supporting a call for a humanitarian pause to the bombing.[164] Despite still supporting the Saudi-led intervention, Kerry did eventually call for a humanitarian pause to the fighting. Human rights organizations reported that, "The harsh restrictions on importations imposed by the coalition for the past six weeks, added to the extreme fuel shortages, have made the daily lives of Yemenis unbearable."[165] As a *Times* article acknowledged the Saudi government was largely dependent on US support,[166] which may have contributed to them proposing a five day truce for aid to enter the Yemen,[167] which Kerry welcomed.[168] The Houthis agreed to the ceasefire.[169] Despite this cease-fire, fighting in the country continued.[170] When the truce expired aid groups called for it to expanded due to concerns that aid was not reaching vulnerable Yemenis.[171] However, strikes soon resumed. During this time, the leader of the Houthis announced that he was open to talks with Saudi Arabia.[172]

Through the end of May, the humanitarian situation in the country continued to deteriorate with another airstrike estimated to have killed at least 80. The World Health Organization warned that "roughly one-third of the country's population was in urgent need of medical care."[173]

Role of Iran

The role of the war in Yemen as a proxy conflict between Saudi Arabia and Iran was frequently discussed. In an editorial that was critical of the Saudi intervention in Yemen, the Editorial Board discussed the role of Iran in the conflict:

Saudi Arabia and other Sunni Arab states have reason to worry about Iran's disruptive, sometimes brutal, policies, including its help in keeping President Bashar al-Assad in power in Syria despite a civil war that has killed more than 200,000 people, most of them Sunnis. Even so, the Arab states have their own checkered history in fueling extremists and regional unrest. The Saudis appear to be overreacting to Iran's role in Yemen, which involves financing the Houthis but little else, according to American officials.[174]

An opinion piece challenged the Saudi narrative, often echoed by US politicians, that the Houthis were primarily succeeding because of Iranian support:

While the Houthis are Shiites, their Zaydi faith is theologically distinct from the Shiite practices of most Iranians. Historically, this has limited ties between them and Tehran. And although Iran has given the Houthis some financial support, it has not been directly involved in the conflict. In fact, many of the Houthis' recent gains are a result of their alliance with Sunni supporters of Mr. Hadi's predecessor, Ali Abdullah Saleh, who was removed from power in 2012, during the Arab Spring.[175]

The *Times* reported about Secretary of State Kerry declaring that Washington was not "not going to stand by while the region is destabilized" in response to Iran's support for the Houthis,[176] while his country continued to provide military aid to Saudi Arabia. Iran labelled Saudi airstrikes as being genocide amid strong criticism of Saudi Arabia's intervention.[177,178] Later Saudi Arabia would reject Iran's calls to end the intervention in Yemen.[179] Iran continued to criticize Saudi Arabia, particularly its alleged targeting of civilian infrastructure. The Iranian Foreign Minister said that while Saudi Arabia and Iran needed to talk, the conflict should be decided through "intra-Yemeni" dialogue. He also advocated for a ceasefire.[180,181] In contrast the

Saudi Ambassador to the United States said that the Houthis "will fail."[182] Following complaints from Iranians that "the Saudi Embassy stopped issuing visas, and at least two flights transporting pilgrims from Iran to Jeddah, Saudi Arabia, were denied permission to land," the Iranian government halted Iranians going to Mecca for minor pilgrimages.[183] A Saudi airstrike on an airport in Yemen during the second half of the conflict[184,185,186] was justified as being a way to prevent the landing of an Iranian plane.[187]

Foreign Support for Saudi Arabia and Al-Qaeda Operations

The conflict was not only between Saudi Arabia and the Houthi rebels. Different governments and terrorist organizations like Al-Qaeda were also involved in the conflict. In early April, Saudi Arabia requested the help of Pakistan amid the fighting.[188] The Pakistani parliament would later reject providing this support.[189] In contrast, the US continued to provide to support to Saudi Arabia by expediting the shipment of weapons to the country. Future Secretary of State Anthony Blinken, who was then a deputy Secretary of State: "praised the Saudis for 'sending a strong message to the Houthis and their allies that they cannot overrun Yemen by force.'"[190]

Amidst the chaos in Yemen, Al-Qaeda forces were able to capture the city of Al Mukalla.[191] Later the US Defense Secretary admitted that the turmoil caused by Saudi airstrikes had created a situation that Al-Qaeda was able to exploit.[192] Another article had the same message:

> the Saudi assaults on the Houthis have indirectly helped empower Al Qaeda in ways the group had not enjoyed before. Its fighters are now developing relations with Yemeni tribal leaders who share antipathy for the Houthis and their allies, said Jamal Benomar, the United Nations diplomat who had unsuccessfully sought to achieve a political reconciliation in Yemen.[193]

A US drone strike in Yemen was reported to have killed a Saudi citizen who was a member of Al-Qaeda.[194] Another Al-Qaeda leader would be killed by a US strike later in the conflict.[195] Despite these operations, concerns about Al-Qaeda grew as they got close to capturing oil fields.[196]

Opinion Pieces

An opinion piece, that drew comparison between former Egyptian President Gamal Abdel Nasser's intervention in Yemen in the 60s and Iran's support for the Houthi rebels, argued that it was in the interests of the United States to support Saudi Arabia in the conflict:

> Ultimately, the Obama administration will have to choose whether to accommodate Iran's leaders at the expense of America's traditional allies or align with the Saudis and Egyptians against them. In the context of a coherent regional strategy, the crisis in Yemen could supply a useful pressure point on Iran that might enhance the chances of success in the ongoing nuclear negotiations.
>
> An American red line in Yemen, backed by Saudi and Egyptian air power, would signal to the Iranians that relief from sanctions is contingent on ending their support for violent proxies from Yemen to Iraq and beyond. That was true of Egypt in the 1960s. It is true of Iran today.[197]

In an opinion piece written from Riyadh, Saudi Arabia, the President of Yemen Abdrabbuh Mansur Hadi supported the Saudi intervention and characterized the country as being:

> under siege by radical Houthi militia forces whose campaign of horror and destruction is fueled by the political and military support of an Iranian regime obsessed with regional domination. There is no question that the chaos in Yemen has

been driven by Iran's hunger for power and its ambition to control the entire region...

Operation Decisive Storm, the campaign by a coalition of nations led by Saudi Arabia, is coming to the aid of Yemen at the request of my government. If the Houthis do not withdraw and disarm their militia and rejoin the political dialogue, we will continue to urge the coalition to continue its military campaign against them.[198]

Another opinion piece rejected both the Houthi rebels and the foreign intervention in Yemen:

Like other democratic activists, I am in a third group—one that has been rendered nearly invisible. We reject external military intervention absolutely. We also reject the Houthis' coup and their vengeful campaign against Yemenis in the north and the south. Our brief hope for a peaceful democratic transition, after Mr. Saleh officially ceded power more than three years ago, has given way to despair.[199]

An editorial that lamented the devastating toll of the Saudi campaign ("more than 1,000 civilians killed, more than 4,000 wounded, and 150,000 displaced. Meanwhile, the fighting and a Saudi-led blockade have deprived Yemenis of food, fuel, water and medicines, causing what a Red Cross official called a humanitarian catastrophe") primarily focused on the perceived strategic failure of the bombing.[200] One letter to the editor by a high school student argued that the *Times* had a double standard in their reporting about Yemen compared to the Israel-Palestine conflict.[201]

Conclusion

The conflict in Yemen was covered throughout the first two months of Saudi Arabia's operations. Much of this reporting did not center around the intervention itself, but rather focused on the larger conflict in the country. Coverage reported on the humanitarian consequences of the Saudi intervention and strikes from Houthi rebels. The perspective that Saudi intervention was meant to counter Iranian influence in the country was often presented.

Are the Situations Comparable?

The lower amount of coverage given to Saudi Arabia's intervention in Yemen compared to Russia's intervention in Syria could be justified based on Russia's intervention being more deserving of coverage. However, based on my review of the conflicts, it is very difficult to make such an argument. While the Civil War in Syria had been going on since 2011 compared to 2014 for the Yemen Civil War, Yemen has suffered from political instability, including acts of political violence, since 2011. Both of the conflicts involved military support being given to different sides in the conflict from both regional and global powers. Additionally, both conflicts were taking place in the politically unstable Middle East. Geopolitically speaking, it could even be argued that the Yemen Civil War had greater implications because Yemen is adjacent to the Gulf of Aden waterway, an important shipping lane for the thousands of ships that pass through the Suez Canal and Red Sea every year.

More attention to the Russian intervention may also be justified *if* the Russian strikes were on a larger scale. Quantifying the scale of a military intervention is not easy to do. In the case of Russia and Saudi Arabia's intervention, because they were both focused around the use of airstrikes, one method can be to assess the average number of airstrikes. According to data published by the *Syrian Archive*, which receives support from Western organizations, there were a total of 173 airstrikes against civilian targets between the beginning of the Russian intervention and the end of October (the period covered in this chapter). Although I was not able to gain access to the whole database and therefore assess the number of civilians killed through the end of October, I could access the number estimated to have been killed until September 9, 2018. To that date, nearly three years after the intervention began, there were reportedly 704 civilian casualties caused by Russian airstrikes. During the whole period, the website lists a total of 1418 airstrikes.[202]

According to data published by the Yemen Data Project, there were a total of 6095 Coalition airstrikes in Yemen between the beginning of the intervention and the end of April. Over 600 occurred in just a few days in March, over 2500 in April and nearly 3000 in May. To make these numbers comparable to the Syria numbers, I restricted the database to only attacks against nonmilitary targets, because the Russian database described strikes on civilian targets. This resulted in a total of 454 airstrikes from the beginning of the conflict to the end of May. These airstrikes resulted in 3515 civilian casualties and 1319 civilian fatalities of which 87 were reported to be among women and 148 among children.[203] Both in terms of the number of airstrikes and casualties, the Saudi intervention would seem to warrant more coverage.

It may also be argued that the Russian airstrikes were of a different nature than the Saudi airstrikes. This position is not tenable. In both cases, the countries claimed that they were targeting rebel groups operating in the target countries and both countries faced accusations of also striking civilians.

Some may also argue that the Russian intervention was more worthy of attention because Russia was intervening on behalf of a dictator while Saudi Arabia was not. This position is also not tenable. The President of Yemen that the Houthi rebels overthrew—Abdrabbuh Mansur Hadi—ended up in office following an election in which he was the only candidate. The Houthis had called for boycotting this election. Even in the 2014 Syrian Presidential election, there was at least a token opposition candidate.

Conclusion

The Saudi Arabian intervention was much larger than that of Russia with many more airstrikes and more civilian casualties caused by Saudi Arabia in the two month window considered compared to the entirety of Russia's intervention through 2018. Both sides faced claims of attacking civilian infrastructure and supported leaders who could be described as obtaining power through undemocratic means. Based on this assessment, the situations are comparable, and if anything, based on the nature of the intervention, Saudi Arabia's intervention may be considered worthy of receiving more attention.

Reasons for Differences

It could be argued that Russia's intervention received more attention because Russia is not a Middle Eastern country, therefore their intervention in a conflict in the Middle East is more worthy than Saudi Arabia's intervention in a conflict in its neighbor. There may be some merit to this argument, but I do not think it can really be expected to explain the magnitude in the difference in coverage. Russia was not the first non-Middle Eastern country to intervene in Syria, with the US and other Western countries intervening against ISIS.

Geopolitical factors can be reasonably argued to account for much of the differences in coverage. The victims of Russia's intervention would in this case be considered worthy victims of an increasing geopolitical foe of the United States. In the case of victims of Saudi's intervention, they would be unworthy or, at least, less worthy victims. There are two reasons why this would be the case. First Saudi Arabia is one of the United States' main geopolitical allies in the Middle East. Much of the arms used by Saudi Arabia in the intervention were supplied by the United States. This military support has continued for years, even as the humanitarian toll of the invasion increased. Second, the Houthi movement received some support from the United States' main geopolitical rival in the Middle East—Iran. The United States is incentivized to aid Saudi Arabia in the conflict because that can help to weaken a geopolitical foe. Much of the coverage of Russia's intervention focused on whether they were actually targeting ISIS and framing the intervention around its effort to maintain the Assad government. While the *Times* did not fully adopt the notion of the Houthis being simply an Iranian proxy, there was not as much questioning of the motives behind the intervention.

Conclusion

The coverage given to Russia's intervention in Syria was much higher in quantitative terms than that given to Saudi Arabia's intervention in Yemen. This greater coverage occurred despite the fact that Saudi Arabia's intervention in terms of civilian infrastructure targeted and civilian deaths were greater than Russia's intervention. In general, the *Times* coverage was critical of both interventions. However, in the case of Russia's intervention this criticism was basically universal, whereas there were some supporting opinions offered for Saudi Arabia's intervention. In the case of Russia's intervention there were more frequent charges that the claims made by Russia about the intervention were false. In this way, the two interventions fit into the Worthy and Unworthy hypothesis. The impact of Russia's intervention was a "worthy" story, receiving attention, at least partially as I argue, due to the geopolitical position of Russia as a state enemy, whereas Saudi Arabia's received less attention because of its position as an ally of the United States.

Chapter 6

Worthy and Unworthy Disputes: the Chagos Islands, the South China Sea, and the East China Sea

Territorial disputes are a perennial issue in international relations. Many countries have disputes with their neighbors. Even the United States has some unsettled border disputes with Canada. However, unlike the relative benign border disputes between these two neighbors, the forces of history and politics can sometimes turn these disputes into conflicts. The seas around Asia have been hotspots for such conflicts in the post-World War II period. Due to the complexities of establishing borders at the end of the Second World War and during the period of decolonization, many countries in the region have disputed claims to different areas in the region both on land and sea.

In this chapter, I will compare coverage of different conflicts in this region with a focus on understanding how the *Times* reported about the position and actions of a US geopolitical foe (China) compared to other regional powers. In particular, I will compare how the *Times* covered one international court's ruling with respect to China's claims in the South China Sea to coverage of three separate court cases and two rulings about the United Kingdom's claimed control of the Chagos Islands and surrounding ocean territory in the Indian Ocean. I will also compare coverage of island building in the South China Sea and conflicts over islands in the seas east of Asia.

Background: Philippines South China Sea Court Case and Chagos Islands

Philippines South China Sea Court Case

Sovereignty disputes in the South China Sea have existed through much of the 20th century. These disputes have become more intense in the past few decades due to increased military operations, island construction, and the discovery of resources, including oil, in the sea. Many of the disputes are related to overlapping claims of sovereignty in the region. These overlapping claims are especially related to sea territory that the countries in the region claim as part of their Exclusive Economic Zones (EEZs) where they have exclusive rights to engage in economic activities, such as fishing and resource exploration. EEZs are supposed to extend 200 miles from a country's coast, including coasts of islands. In the South China Sea, these claims are complicated due to both naturally occurring islands in the region (in particularly the Spratly Islands in the southern part of the sea and Paracel Islands in the northern part of the sea), and the construction of artificial islands around reefs and atolls. In general an island must be always above water and be capable of supporting life to permit the establishment of an EEZ. Many of these reefs and atolls, before construction began on them, did not meet the requirement.

The most well-known claim in the South China Sea is the so-called nine-dash line, which describes the mapped line delineating territorial claims in the South China Sea by both the government of the People's Republic of China and the Republic of China (Taiwan). This claim encompasses much of the South China Sea and is based on the Chinese governments' claims of traditionally controlling islands and fishing in the area throughout Chinese history. However, other countries have overlapping claims in the region including Vietnam (which has an EEZ like that claimed by the Chinese governments which extends far beyond its mainland borders), Malaysia, Brunei, and the Philippines. Indonesia, while not having overlapping claims in the region, has been a part of the conflict due to cases of fishing vessels from the claimant countries entering their territory.

While the diplomatic conflict over the territory in the seas has remained persistent, there have been efforts to establish accords to allow for safe conduct in the South China Sea. The most significant such accord is the Declaration on the Conduct of Parties in the South China Sea, which was agreed to by the claimant countries in 2011. In this declaration, the parties agreed "to resolve their territorial and jurisdictional disputes by peaceful means, without resorting to the threat or use of force, through friendly consultations and negotiations by sovereign states directly concerned, in accordance with universally recognized principles of international law, including the 1982 UN Convention on the Law of the Sea."[1]

In 2015, the Philippines challenged some of China's claims in the region that overlapped with their own in the Permanent Court of Arbitration based on alleged violations of the United Nations Convention on the Law of the Sea. The cases focused on the area around land controlled by China in the Spratly Islands. The court considered maritime claims and not land claims in the region. In 2016, the court issued its ruling in favor of the Philippines. The most significant aspects of the court's ruling was that some of the territories controlled by China in the South China Sea did not meet the requirements for establishing an EEZ around them. In this chapter, I will consider *Times* coverage of the court's decision in July and August 2016.

Chagos Islands

The Chagos Islands are an archipelago in the Indian Ocean. The islands have a long history of being used by countries in the regions including the Maldives and European explorers. Visits from Europeans have led to different claims to the islands. The French claimed the islands in the 1600s as they began to expand their control in the Indian Ocean. Later in the 1700s, the British made claim to the islands. The islands were officially ceded to the British Empire by France after the defeat of Napoleon in 1814. Beginning in 1903, the islands were ruled from the British colony of Mauritius.

In the late 1700s, the British began enslaving people from Africa to work on coconut plantations on the islands. When Mauritius gained independence in 1965, the Chagos Islands were officially separated from the territory. Shortly after, the United States and the United Kingdom began negotiations to create a naval base on Diego Garcia—one of the Chagos Islands. In order to avoid challenges that the islands must be decolonized, without consulting the roughly 1000 people who lived on these islands, the British forcibly depopulated the islands after they determined that only military personnel were allowed to occupy the area. In a particularly ugly statement about the population of the island, Denis Greenhill, a British Undersecretary of Foreign Affairs, wrote of the depopulation: "Unfortunately along with the birds go some few Tarzans or Men Fridays whose origins are obscure and who are being hopefully whisked on to Mauritius etc. When this has been done I agree we must be very tough."[2] The islanders were eventually moved to the United Kingdom, where some would receive compensation for their forced removal from the Chagos Islands.

These islands have continued to be militarily important for projecting United States and United Kingdom military power in the region. During the War on Terror, the military base on Diego Garcia was used for extraordinary rendition of prisoners and likely torture.[3] In 2010, the British established the "Chagos Marine Protected Area" around the islands, which limited human activity and banned fishing. A cable from the US State

Department published by Wikileaks revealed that the purpose of the establishment of this marine reserve was seen by the United States as the "most effective long-term way to prevent any of the Chagos Islands' former inhabitants or their descendants from resettling."[4] Despite the existence of the marine protected area, it still allowed for environmental damage caused by military activities on the islands.

The Chagos Islanders have filed a number of legal claims about their forced removal from the islands in courts in the United States and in the United Kingdom. Additionally, three separate cases have been tried in international courts related to various aspects of the United Kingdom's control of the islands. The first case was brought to the Permanent Court of Arbitration (the same court that ruled in the Philippines versus China case regarding claims in the South China Sea) in 2010 by Mauritius. This case challenged the declaration of the Marine Protected Area based on the 1982 United Nations Convention on the Law of the Sea. In 2015, the court ruled unanimously in favor of Mauritius that the declaration of the Marine Protected Area did not follow the Law of the Sea. In 2017, a case was brought to the International Court of Justice to decide on the legitimacy of the British claims for control of the Chagos Islands. In its decision in 2019, the court ruled that ending control of the Chagos Islands was a part of decolonization and that therefore the United Kingdom must end its control of the islands. In 2019 another case was brought to the International Tribunal for the Law of the Sea to determine the borders between Mauritius and the Maldives. At the time of this writing, the case is still ongoing. However, as part of initial judgments in the case the tribunal determined that the Chagos Islands belong to Mauritius.[5] In this chapter, I consider any coverage of the Chagos Islands from 2010 to 2021 when all of these court cases were tried and two were decided.

The Numbers

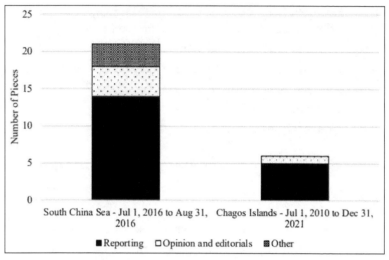

Figure 11. Coverage of 2016 Permanent Court of Arbitration ruling regarding the South China Sea and any coverage of Chagos Islands between 2010 and 2021 by type of coverage

In the two month period around the Permanent Court of Arbitration ruling about China's claims in the South China Sea there were a total of 21 articles dealing with the South China Sea, including 14 reporting pieces, 4 opinion pieces, and 3 cases of other types of coverage. In an over decade long period that included three separate international court cases and two rulings about the Chagos Islands, there were a total of six articles published about the Chagos Islands, including five pieces of reporting and one opinion piece.

Clearly more attention was given to the South China Sea dispute during a relatively short time period compared to over a decade of coverage regarding the Chagos Islands. Looking at the period from January 2010 to December 2021, there were a total of 1802 mentions of the "South China Sea" in the *Times*, compared to only 15 mentions of "Chagos." I did a separate search of the term

"Diego Garcia" to see if there were any articles that discussed this important island, without mentioning the Chagos Islands overall, and did not identify additional pieces to include.

The Coverage

South China Sea Court Decision

In early July, before the court ruling in the China versus Philippines case was issued, the *Times* printed several pieces in anticipation of the ruling. The first article described China's refusal to participate in the hearing, and naval exercises China held on and around the Paracel Islands in the South China Sea, which the *Times* presented as being in response to the looming verdict. The Paracel Islands are in the South China Sea, but are far north of the Filipino claim. They are disputed between China and Vietnam. The article also discussed the United States' role in the dispute:

> Sensing an opportunity, the Obama administration has begun a diplomatic push of its own, backing the tribunal and persuading allies to speak out for a "rules-based order at sea" and the use of international law to settle territorial disputes.[6]

The United States is not a party to the Convention on the Law of the Sea, which the case was tried under.

In a Q and A about the tribunal the *Times* characterized China's eventual response to the ruling as being: "a test of what kind of country it is becoming—a global leader committed to international law and institutions, or a superpower willing to take unilateral action against its neighbors."

The Q and A also described how the United States might respond to the ruling: "But the United States, the region's dominant military power, could use the decision to justify more naval patrols in the area, to recruit new allies and give more support to old ones, and to rally world opinion against Beijing's behavior."[7]

A *Times* reporter travelled with a Filipino boat into the South China Sea in order to observe interactions between the Filipino ship and Chinese naval vessels patrolling the waters. The reporter had to ask multiple sailors before a crew was found willing to go into the disputed waters. This reported included a sort of video essay with clips of sailing in the sea along with narration.[8]

Eventually the tribunal issued its finding in support of the Philippines' claim, which the *Times* characterized as "a sweeping rebuke ... of China's behavior in the South China Sea, including its construction of artificial islands, and found that its expansive claim to sovereignty over the waters had no legal basis." The Chinese government, as stated before the ruling was issued, did not accept the tribunal's authority.[9] The Philippines' Minister of Foreign Affairs welcomed the ruling.[10] The *Times* published the full decision from the tribunal.[11]

In an editorial in support of the decision, the Editorial Board echoed earlier reporting: "How China reacts to the sweeping legal defeat over its claims to the South China Sea will tell the world a lot about its approach to international law," and provided unsolicited advice to nations in the region arguing that they "need to join the Philippines in endorsing the tribunal decision and then proceed, if necessary, with their own arbitration cases."[12]

The Republic of China/Taiwan government, which shares the People's Republic of China's claims in South China Sea, reacted negatively to the ruling. Before the launch of a ship into the South China Sea President Tsai Ing-wen said, "The mission of this voyage is to display Taiwan people's resolve in defending the national interest."[13] The PRC did not send ships to the South China Sea, but did land two civilian aircrafts on artificial islands in the sea.[14]

A letter to the editor pointed out the hypocrisy of the United States supporting the tribunal's ruling, while not being a party to the United Nations Convention on the Law of the Sea, which the tribunal's existence is predicated on.[15] The *Times* published an "explainer" about the South China Sea dispute. The piece characterized the conflict as such: "At its most basic level, this is a contest between China and several Southeast Asian nations over territorial control in the South China Sea." This claim is not inaccurate, but misses the fact that these governments also have disputed and overlapping claims with each other, and that the ROC government has the same claims as the PRC. This piece did offer some effort to understand the Chinese position:

Something Americans often miss is that for China, this is in part defensive. The history of Western imperialism looms large. Chinese leaders often distrust the United States' intentions, and consider their country to be the far weaker party. Extending Chinese control is a way to stave off perceived threats.[16]

An article reported how the reaction of many Filipinos to the ruling was muted by the fact that the government did not show any major plans to act on it.[17] A cartoon about the ruling represented China in the South China Sea as a giant dragon.[18] There were some protests in China against the ruling.[19]

The *Times* published a detailed profile of one of the lawyers who had represented the Philippines in the case—Paul S. Reichler. Reichler had previously represented the Sandinista government of Nicaragua against the United States, but saw the United States' failing in this case as an anomaly:

The Nicaragua case is an exception, a big exception and a terrible exception ... I consider the Reagan administration to be an anomaly in terms of respect for international law. The United States does have a history of complying with the judgments of the International Court of Justice.

Reichler also represented Mauritius in a case against the UK involving the Chagos Islands (see the next section).[20]

In an article discussing how China had instituted miliary air patrols in the South China Sea, the *Times* published maps of the overlapping claims in the South China Sea. While it showed most of the countries in the disputes' claims, it did not show Vietnam's, which extends from the country's mainland and overlaps with other countries to a similar extent to China's.[21]

China announced plans for joint military exercises with Russia in the South China Sea.[22] Former Filipino president Fidel Ramos went to China with the goal of rekindling relations between the two countries.[23] Photos were published showing claimed military infrastructure on the Spratly Islands.[24]

In mid-August, another editorial criticized China's role in the South China Sea conflict. While acknowledging the role of other countries in the conflict, it placed China as the main instigator:

China is not alone in engaging in risky maneuvers. On Wednesday Reuters reported that Vietnam had recently stationed new mobile rocket launchers on five bases in the Spratly Islands. Fortunately, none of the claimants, which also include the Philippines, Indonesia, Brunei and Malaysia, have tried to take the sort of action that could cause a full-blown crisis, such as China's threat to declare an air defense zone over the sea and to insist that all planes obtain permission before crossing through it.[25]

Chagos Islands

In 2010, the *Times* published a one paragraph report about Mauritius's lawsuit against the UK where Mauritius argued that UK's declaration of the Chagos Islands as a marine reserve was in violation of the United Nations Convention of the Law of the Sea.[26] Although this case was adjudicated and decided in favor of Mauritius in the succeeding years, I could not find any further reports about it.

The next coverage of the Chagos Islands came seven years later in 2017 when the United Nations General Assembly voted 94 to 15 to ask the International Court of Justice to determine whether the United Kingdom or Mauritius had sovereignty over the Chagos Islands. The United Kingdom's opposition to the vote was supported by the United States.[27] This case was decided in 2019, when the next report about the islands was published. The International Court of Justice ruled 13 to 1 that the United Kingdom must "as rapidly as possible" cease to control the Chagos Islands. Only Judge Joan E. Donoghue from the United States offered a dissenting vote.[28] Following this decision, the United Nations General Assembly voted to demand that the United Kingdom give up its control of the Chagos Islands. This vote was even more lopsided than the vote referring the case to the International Court of Justice, with 116 countries supporting the resolution and 6 (the United Kingdom joined by US, Hungary, Israel, Australia and the Maldives[29]) opposing it.[30]

Later in 2019, an article dealing with Pope Francis had one paragraph that described his stance that the United Kingdom should leave the Chagos Islands.[31] An opinion piece appeared in 2019 entitled "Britain Holds On to a Colony in Africa, With America's Help"; the piece contrasted the United States' stance on the South China Sea with that of the Chagos Islands:

Yet anyone who wants to weaponize the rule of law first needs to have their own house in order, and that includes being sure their closest allies do, too. Britain's current approach to international law — especially the law of the sea — poses a serious problem for America. The British government recently published a foreign policy review on "Global Britain." The 100-plus-page document signals a shift away from Europe and toward the Indo Pacific region, premised on a military alliance with the United States: No relationship is "more valuable," it says. In particular, the paper asserts Britain's "absolute commitment to upholding the U.N. Convention on the Law of the Sea in all its dimensions."[32]

Are the Situations Comparable?

The cases of China's dispute with the Philippines in the South China Sea and disputes around sovereignty of the Chagos Islands are clearly different from each other. In the case of the China-Philippines dispute, the question before the tribunal was only about control of water in the South China Sea and not China's or any other country's control of islands. In the three cases tried for the UK and Chagos Islands dispute, there were questions about both control of water around the island and the sovereignty of the islands themselves. Additionally, in the case of the Chagos Islands there were individuals who had been forcibly removed from the territory, while in the case of the South China Sea, while there certainly have been issues with the treatment of fishermen in the region (see next section), there was nobody removed from the territory in the region. Additionally, with respect to the China-Philippines dispute there was only one international court case, whereas with respect to the Chagos Islands there were three court cases. Finally, the case of the Chagos Islands involved two votes from the United Nations General Assembly, first referring the case to the international criminal court and then voting for the decolonization of the Chagos Islands to proceed following the decision. So while there are certainly differences in the two cases, all of the differences enumerated here would be expected to contribute to *more* attention being given to the Chagos Islands not less attention, especially when considering an over decade long period when the Chagos Island court cases were tried, compared to a review of only two months of the South China Sea dispute.

One could make an argument that the South China Sea dispute is also distinct from the Chagos Islands, because it involves more countries, a larger territory, and a more important geopolitical location. On the first point about the dispute involving more countries, it is true that the disputes in the South China Sea do not just involve China and the Philippines, but also several other countries with claims in the region. However, it is also true that the Chagos Islands disputes do not just involve the United Kingdom and the people of the Chagos Islands, but also Mauritius (a country that claims sovereignty over the islands), the Maldives (whose border dispute with Mauritius is a topic of the International Tribunal for the Law of the Sea case), and the United States (who jointly run the military base on Diego Garcia with the United Kingdom). The direct involvement of the United States in the case would seem to warrant more coverage from a US newspaper. Additionally, while disputes in the South China Sea do involve other countries, the court case decided in the summer of 2016 only involved China and the Philippines. While the United States has involvement in the South China Sea dispute through "freedom of navigation" navy operations in the sea and has called on China to respect the ruling of the Permanent Court of Arbitration (despite not being a signatory to the United Nations Convention on the Law of the Sea), the United States does not occupy any territory in the South China Sea.

With respect to the size of the area in question, the South China Sea as a whole is certainly larger than the area in dispute with respect to the Chagos Islands dispute. The South China Sea is about 1.4 million square miles (the nine-dash line encompasses about 90% of this area), while the Chagos Marine Protected Area is about 250,000 square miles. However, the area in dispute in the China-Philippines case is much smaller, encompassing the overlapping claims between the Philippines and China, which is a smaller proportion of the overall South China Sea. The findings of the case may also set a precedent for the other territorial claims based on China's control of certain Spratly Islands, which would expand the relevant area, but it would still be smaller than the overall territory.

Additionally, the South China Sea certainly has major importance as a shipping lane, with estimates of one-third of global shipping going through the sea, accounting for trillions of dollars in value.[33] However, the Indian Ocean where the Chagos Islands and the claimed Maritime Protection Area are located also has enormous geopolitical importance as well. It has been reported that the Indian Ocean accounts "for around half of the world's container traffic, a third of its cargo bulk and 80% of maritime oil shipments."[34] The geopolitical importance of the islands is also clear based on the efforts of the United States and United Kingdom to maintain their base on the islands and their use during military invasions and engagements in the Middle East.

Reasons for Differences

From my perspective, the only viable reason other than the Worthy/Unworthy explanation for the increased coverage of the South China Sea compared to the Chagos Islands is the fact that there is just more going on in the South China Sea. This increased activity may mean that there is an inclination to report on this region more. The South China Sea being in a busy area means that more attention will be given to the region. This attention will increase interest and reporters on the South China Sea "beat" and then contribute to more coverage. These factors may explain some of the increased coverage and result in a higher amount of coverage overall, but it is hard to understand how these factors explain the fact that the South China Sea received so much more attention in a short two month time period compared to the Chagos Islands over more than a decade during which many important developments occurred. The court cases received minimal coverage, while some developments, such as the establishment of the Marine Protected Area and the use of the Diego Garcia military base, received basically no attention.

I believe the geopolitical explanation remains the most viable reason for the differences in coverage. Because China is often and increasingly perceived as a geopolitical foe of the United States and the South China Sea is of geopolitical interest to the United States, conflicts in that area attracted more attention. In contrast, the United Kingdom is a geopolitical ally of the United States. The United States also has strong geopolitical interests in the Chagos Islands because of the presence of a US military base on them.

Conclusion

The increased attention given to one international court ruling regarding the South China Sea over a two month period compared to any coverage given to the Chagos Islands over more than a decade long period suggests that these two cases fit well within the Worthy/Unworthy hypothesis. In particular, the South China Sea dispute is an example of a worthy dispute that warranted fairly extensive and detailed coverage from the *Times*. In contrast, the Chagos Islands are an example of an unworthy dispute and the Chagossians most impacted by are it are unworthy victims, who therefore received minimal coverage from the *Times*.

South China Sea Disputes

The disputes in the South China Sea do not just involve China and the Philippines, but also several other countries in the region that lay claim to islands, reefs, and atolls scattered throughout the South China Sea and EEZs surrounding them. This activity in the South China Sea has created controversy due to countries engaging in island building activities, such as adding sand and building up reefs so that they are always above water, and construction activity on these islands, including the adding of military equipment to them. At the same time, the number of ships in the South China Sea, both military and civilian, has created the risk for conflicts between ships from different nations. These conflicts can be seen particularly when the coast guard or navy from one country try to prevent fishing in their claimed waters by another country.

Such conflicts involve interactions between many of the countries in the region, not just China. China, for example, was not the first country to begin island construction in the region, with most construction prior to the mid-2010s being done by the Philippines and Vietnam.[35] As Kishore Mahbubani writes in *Has China Won? The Chinese Challenge to American Primacy* while discussing conflict in the South China Sea:

The problem occurs over less than 0.01 percent of the world's ocean surfaces. Even in the South China Sea, there is no disagreement as most of the sea lanes are open international waters through which many naval vessels cross without problem or hindrance. And of the disputed rocks and reefs in the South China Sea, China controls only a minority. Vietnam occupies between forty-nine and fifty-one outposts across twenty-seven features; by contrast, China only has twenty outposts in the Paracel Islands. Similarly, in the Spratlys, China controls eight maritime features, such as islands, reefs, and low-tide elevations, while the Philippines occupies nine and Malaysia occupies five. Taiwan controls only one outpost in the Spratlys, Itu Aba Island. When Malaysia, the Philippines, and Vietnam began reclaiming land around their features, China decided to follow suit. However, while Malaysia, the Philippines, and Vietnam could only reclaim a few acres around their features, China could reclaim up to two thousand acres with its massive resources.[36]

The United States itself, although often focused on China's claims in the South China Sea, has at times challenged other countries' claims, for example when the US Navy conducted naval operations to challenge what it deemed Vietnam's "excessive maritime claims" in the South China Sea.[37]

However, according to the Worthy/Unworthy hypothesis we would expect China's activities in the region to receive more attention. In this section, we review coverage of both artificial island building and construction in the South China Sea, and also conflicts between different countries in the region to see whether the hypothesis holds true and China's activities receive more attention than other countries.

The Numbers

As shown in figure 12, between 2015 and 2021 there was more coverage of island building and construction activities involving China compared to coverage of such activities involving any other countries. In particular, during this period there were 20 articles that dealt primarily with China's island building activities. Among these 20 articles, I identified three that briefly

The clusters of Chinese vessels busily dredge white sand and pump it onto partly submerged coral, aptly named Mischief Reef, transforming it into an island. Over a matter of weeks, satellite photographs show the island growing bigger, its few shacks on stilts replaced by buildings. What appears to be an amphibious warship, capable of holding 500 to 800 troops, patrols the reef's southern opening.[38]

Along with this report were satellite images of the building operations. The article did briefly acknowledge other countries' activities in the South China Sea:

While other countries in Southeast Asia, like Malaysia and Vietnam, have used similar techniques to extend or enlarge territory, none have China's dredging and construction power.[39]

A Chinese government spokesperson defended these island building activities:

Hua Chunying said at a regularly scheduled news conference in Beijing that the construction work was being used for maritime purposes and not aimed at making claims at the expense of other nations. China says large sections of the South China Sea are its territory, including the waters containing the Spratly and Paracel Islands, despite competing claims from Malaysia, the Philippines, Vietnam and other nations.[40]

The *Times* published the spokesperson's full response where she discussed the hypocrisy of the seeming lack of interest in other countries' building operations in the area:

we note that some countries have kept silent while other countries have illegally occupied China's Nansha islands and reefs and even constructed major structures on the islands, but then made irresponsible remarks as China conducted normal activities in its own territory. This behavior reflects a total double standard, is unfair and not constructive. I hope the relevant parties will earnestly abide by their own promise not to take sides on the South China Sea issue and commit themselves to promote regional peace and stability.[41]

A spokesperson from the Philippines criticized China's building activities:

China has pursued these activities unilaterally, disregarding people in the surrounding states who have depended on the sea for their livelihood for generations.[42]

Other satellite images would show the apparent construction of a runway on Fiery Cross Reef. Interestingly, the size of the runway was contrasted with that on Diego Garcia, part of the Chagos Islands, with no mention of the sovereignty dispute regarding those islands.[43] A video showed satellite images of the construction of the runway and protests in the Philippines in response to it.[44] Two months later the Chinese government would announce that they would halt island building activities in the South China Sea.[45] In September, satellite images showed the construction of new airstrips.[46]

An article in July 2015 provided detailed satellite images of China's construction activities in the South China Sea. The article also briefly acknowledged some other countries' building activities in the region.[47] China's military buildup in the South China Sea was described as potentially resulting in China gaining complete control of the region.[48] Later in 2016 satellite images were also published that were claimed to show Chinese military installations on one of the Spratly Islands.[49]

In 2016, the Pentagon reported the deployment of missiles on Chinese controlled islands in the South China Sea.[50,51] A video showed leaders from different countries responding to China's deployment.[52] An editorial labelled the deployment as a "provocation."[53] China was also reported to be installing a radar station on an artificial island in the Spratly Islands.[54] Extensive discussion of construction in the South China Sea did not appear again until 2018 when anonymously obtained photos showed construction on islands in the sea, which were not independently verified.[55]

During the time period considered here, I only identified three articles that primarily focused on other governments' building activities in the South China Sea. Two from 2017 described the Philippines construction in the region. The first of which described President Rodrigo Duterte walking back an earlier comment where he suggested that the Philippines military should "occupy uninhabited islands" in the South China Sea.[56] Later in the year, Duterte ordered construction in the South China Sea to halt, which was framed as an effort to appease China.[57]

Another article described Taiwan's work in the region, which the article contrasted with the mainland Chinese government's activities:

China has built artificial islands out of the reefs and shoals it controls and, according to analysts poring over satellite photographs, armed them with radars and missiles. Taiwan, by contrast, is soliciting competitive bids from companies to rebuild its small hospital here, bolstering sorely needed search and rescue facilities in the event of maritime disaster in the heavily trafficked sea.

The article also seemed to challenge some of the determinations of the International Court of Arbitration's ruling regarding the Chinese claims in the South China Sea:

The panel, adjudicating a claim brought by the Philippines against China's claims, declared it a "rock" instead, meaning it cannot sustain human habitation or economic activity. The demotion from being an "island" means that Taiwan can no longer claim exclusive economic control over a wide swath of waters around Itu Aba. It is, to be sure, a nice "rock."

On either side of the runway, which was built in 2007 and expanded in 2012, dense growths include banana and coconut trees. Signs along the pathways warn of falling coconuts. The place is teeming with sea birds, and is a nesting ground for green sea turtles.[58]

Conflicts in the South China Sea

In 2016, several articles were published that dealt with conflicts between China and Indonesia in the South China Sea. The first such article described an incident when a Chinese Coast Guard vessel rammed a Chinese fishing boat that had been seized by Indonesian ships for illegally fishing in Indonesia's exclusive economic zone in order to free it.[59] A few weeks later, the *Times* published a more detailed description of the events including quotes from the captain of the ship that was detained by Indonesia authorities.[60] In June, another Chinese fishing vessel was seized, resulting in diplomatic protests from China who accused Indonesia of violating international law.[61,62]

An article a year later described Indonesia's increasingly more assertive position in the conflict. While focusing on the relationship between China and Indonesia, this article briefly acknowledged that Indonesia had conflicts with fishing vessels from other nations:

The administration of the Indonesian president, Joko Widodo, whose top administrative priorities since taking office in October 2014 include transforming his country into a maritime power, has ordered the authorities to blow up

227

hundreds of foreign fishing vessels seized while illegally fishing in Indonesian waters.[63]

In 2019, coverage shifted to conflicts between China and the Philippines in the region. That year the Filipino defense secretary accused China of ramming and sinking a Filipino fishing vessel whose crew were later rescued by a fishing vessel from Vietnam.[64] In later reporting about the incident, the Chinese government did not commit to whether a Chinese vessel caused the sinking, but stated that the escape of the Chinese vessel following the sinking "should be condemned."[65] A week later, President Duterte indicated that an investigation revelated the sinking was "an ordinary maritime mishap." Antonio Carpio, a Filipino Supreme Court Justice, disagreed with this assessment.[66]

In 2020, further conflicts between China and Indonesia were described when a report detailed Chinese fishing vessels with the support of the Chinese Coast Guard driving off Indonesia fishing vessels and the evolution of the China-Indonesian conflict in the South China Sea.[67] A year later, another similar detailed account would describe China and the Philippines conflict in the South China Sea.[68]

During the period considered, I only identified one article that described a conflict in the South China Sea that did not involve China. The article described a case where two Vietnamese fishermen were shot and killed after being pursued by a Filipino naval vessel. The government of the Philippines promised a full investigation into the killings.[69]

Because there was so little attention given to conflicts not involving China in the South China Sea, I also searched for articles dealing with a notable incident that occurred in the period before 2015—the shooting of two fishermen from Taiwan by the Philippine Navy. The first article about this incident described a demand from the government in Taiwan to apologize for the killing. The mainland China government joined with these calls for an apology. A Filipino military official was quoted as saying: "If somebody died, they deserve our sympathy but not an apology ... This is part of Philippine waters."[70]

Although the Philippines did later offer an "informal apology" this gesture was considered inadequate, and the representative from the government in Taiwan was withdrawn in protest.[71] An analysis of the situation focused less on the actual shooting, but instead on the response of the government in Taiwan which was described as potentially being evidence of "Han Chauvinism."[72] Eventually prosecutors in the Philippines would recommend that charges be brought against the crew responsible for the shooting.[73] The last piece of reporting about the incidence in 2013 described the government in Taiwan ending sanctions against the Philippines which had followed the incident. The Filipino government agreed to pay compensation to the family of the man who was killed.[74] In 2019, eight of the crewmen responsible for the incident were sentenced to between eight and 15 years in prison and ordered to pay a fine.[75] I did not identify coverage of this event in the *Times*.

Are the Situations Comparable?

It could be argued that it is reasonable that the *Times* reported more on Chinese island building and construction activities in the South China Sea and interstate conflicts between China and other countries in the South China Sea because China is more involved in these activities. With respect to island building, the scale of China's activities in the region may be larger than other individual countries, but the activities of other countries have still been extensive. The Asia Maritime Transparency Initiative, which is part of the Center for Strategic and International Studies, an organization which receives funding from multiple governments including the United States, Japan and Taiwan, as well as defense contractors like Northrop Grumman, Lockheed Martin Corporation, and Raytheon,[76] tracks island building activity in the region. While much of their attention is given to China's activities, they also describe activities of other countries.

Throughout the period discussed here, other countries including Vietnam and Malaysia engaged in oil operations in disputed territory.[77,78] According to the institute, China has reclaimed more acres of territory than Vietnam[79] and China's largest runway is larger than those of other countries in the region.[80] Countries in the region also engaged in construction activities on the islands including the Philippines.[81,82,83] Most of the claimant nations also have military stationed on at least some of their islands.[84] The case can be made that China's activities in the South China Sea are more extensive than other nations, but not to the extent that justifies the disproportionate attention given to these activities. Additionally, it is important to keep in mind that as already mentioned, China controls only a minority of the disputed territory in the South China Sea with Vietnam having control of more rocks and reefs in the Paracel Islands and the Philippines controlling more in the Spratly Islands. China was also not the first country to begin reclamation activities. (See page 221, note 36.)

Turning to conflicts between states in the South China Sea, I believe an even stronger case can be made that during the period considered (2015 to 2021) there were more incidents and more severe incidents involving other countries, many of which were not covered or only covered minimally by the *Times*. For example, during the time period considered, conflicts between Indonesia and Chinese fishing boats and the Chinese navy received extensive attention. However, an Indonesian newspaper *Kompas* reported that between late 2015 and 2019 Indonesian authorities sank a total of 556 ships of which only three were Chinese. More sunken ships were from Vietnam

(312), the Philippines (91), and Malaysia (87).[85] These sinkings, although extensive, did not receive attention from the *Times* that I could identify. Even in a notable case when two Vietnamese fishermen were killed by the Philippine Navy, the incident only was covered in one article. While other incidents that did not result in death involving China received more attention.

Reasons for Differences

The Worthy/Unworthy explanation seems to be the best explanation for the differences in coverage between China and other activities in the South China Sea. While it could be argued that Chinese construction may be worthy of more coverage for being more extensive, the almost complete lack of coverage of other construction activities suggests that it is not just that China gets more coverage, but also other countries in the region are not extensively covered. Part of the explanation could be "momentum" meaning that the *Times* perceives that its readers are more familiar with China's activities in the region and therefore feels compelled to cover those actions more. This may be an explanation, but it is not a justification. Furthermore, this familiarity may be caused by geopolitical reasons: the United States government focuses on criticizing China's activities in the South China Sea much more than other countries, and so this may create a feedback loop compelling more coverage from the *Times* and other media sources.

Conclusion

China's activities in the South China Sea, whether island building, construction on islands, or conflicts with other countries, received substantially more coverage than other countries involved in disputes in the region. While China's claims in the region are extensive, Vietnam and the government in Taiwan's claims in the region also stretch far beyond their mainland borders. Other countries have engaged in extensive building activities and there have been numerous cases of conflict between countries, most notably the sinking of hundreds of Vietnamese ships by Indonesia. Also, conflicts involving countries other than China have frequently been more violent than those involving China, with at least two incidents where the Philippine Navy has been found responsible for killing fishermen in the sea. The lopsided coverage may contribute to false impressions about the region which suggest that China is the only country with disputes with other countries. Such coverage may serve to justify the United States' focus on China in the region and as rationalization for naval operations in the South China Sea.

East China Sea/Philippine Sea

North of the South China Sea and east of the Asian mainland is the East China Sea. Much like its southern neighbor, the East China Sea has also been a site of territorial disputes between countries in the region—especially China (including both the People's Republic of China and the Republic of China government in Taiwan), Japan, and South Korea. North Korea is a party to the conflicts, but has not been as active in them. The origins of many of these conflicts stretch back to the end of World War II when the sovereignty over territories that Japan had taken over during its colonial expansion in the decades before the war were decided. In many cases, the ownerships of these territories came into dispute.

In this section, I will focus on two of these disputes. The first is between China and Japan over sovereignty of the Diaoyu/Senkaku Islands. These islands lie northeast of Taiwan and southwest of the Ryukyu Islands controlled by Japan. The Chinese side's claim to the islands is related to them having allegedly been a part of China going back to the 16th century, with Japan only taking control of them during the First Sino-Japanese War at the end of the 19th century. The Chinese argument asserts that because these islands were not those enumerated as not being required to be decolonized following the Potsdam Declaration, which defined Japan's terms of surrender, the islands should have been returned to China at the end of the Second World War. Japan, on the other hand, rejects that China controlled the islands before the First Sino-Japanese War and asserts that people from Okinawa have been visiting and working on the islands since the late 19th century. Following a 1971 agreement with the United States, Japan has exercised sovereignty over the islands. I will review coverage of the dispute in one particularly active year—2012—in this section.

The second dispute is over the Liancourt Rocks also known as the Dokdo or Takeshima islands, which are claimed by both Japan and South Korea. South Korea bases its claims to the two rocky islands based on ancient documents and maps that appear to refer to the islands and show them as being part of territory controlled by Korea. Japan disputes these historical accounts. The islands became part of Japan following the country's colonization of Korea in the early 20th century. Japan disputes whether the islands were included when it renounced its control of occupied territories after World War II. South Korea has maintained sovereignty over the islands since 1952. In this section, I will review any coverage of this dispute between 2010 and 2021.

I also review coverage of Okinotorishima/Parece Vela. Although this territory is not in the East China Sea (laying to the east in the Philippine Sea) and is not involved in sovereignty disputes, Japan has used its control of the reef to claim an EEZ in the area around it. This claim that the reef (which Japan has built up over time) meets the requirements for the establishment of an EEZ has been challenged by regional governments including China and South Korea, similar to how China's claims in the

South China Sea were challenged by the Philippines. I will review any coverage of the Parece Vela dispute at any point in time.

Based on the Worthy/Unworthy hypothesis, we would expect that coverage of the Diaoyu/Senkaku dispute involving China and Japan will receive more attention than the Liancourt Rocks/Dokdo/Takeshima dispute involving Japan and South Korea, and also questions about Japan's claimed EEZ around Okinotorishima/Parece Vela.

The Numbers

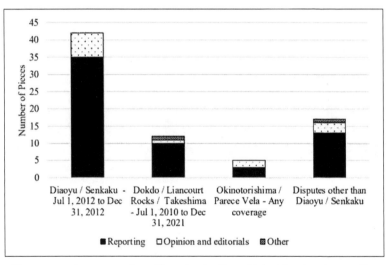

Figure 14. Coverage of conflicts in the East China Sea by the conflict

As shown in figure 14, in 2013 there were a total of 42 pieces dealing with the Diaoyu/Senkaku dispute. Most of these pieces were reporting articles. In comparison, from 2010 to 2021, there were only 12 pieces dealing with the Dokdo/Liancourt Rock/ Takeshima dispute. At any point in time, there were only five pieces that dealt with Japan's claims around Okinotorishima/ Parece Vela. In one year, there was more than twice as much coverage of the Diaoyu/Senkaku dispute than over ten years of reporting about Dokdo/Liancourt Rocks/Takeshima and any reporting of Okinotorishima/Parece Vela combined.

The Coverage

Diaoyu/Senkaku Islands Dispute

In 2012, the first article focusing on the Diaoyu/Senkaku dispute was a short piece that described Japan's detention of 14 Chinese citizens who had landed on one of the islands on a vessel that launched from Hong Kong. Those arrested included journalists covering the landing.[86] Following this incident, the *Times* described the origins of the disputes in the East China Sea and the reaction in China to the detention of the protesters.[87] The Chinese government urged the Japanese government to release the protesters,[88] which they did shortly after.[89] In response to this arrest, protests launched in several cities in China. The piece discussed the Chinese government's efforts to rein in nationalistic protests in the past:

> The demonstrations appeared to be sanctioned and chaperoned by the police, who generally prohibit public protests unless they suit the needs of the Communist Party. In the past, Beijing has allowed nationalist sentiment to bubble up into street demonstrations, but the authorities usually keep them contained out of concern they might spiral out of control or turn into popular antigovernment sentiment.[90]

Another piece provided details about the response to the arrests in the Chinese media:

> An editorial in *People's Daily* called for people to "remain calm and unflustered," although it noted that the island

issue would remain "very possibly a grindstone for stored-up feelings in Chinese hearts."

Other *People's Daily* commentaries referenced "the anguish of millions of Chinese" over the islands, which "have belonged to China since ancient times, but were stolen by Japan."

"Japan has never sincerely admitted its past sins of aggression and still clings to the notion of one day retracing its past error of militarism," the paper wrote. "It's wrong and risky to continue playing with the Diaoyu Islands by naively relying on strengthening its military alliance with the United States."[91]

In the midst of one of these protests, a man had his skull smashed and ended up temporarily paralyzed, because he was driving a Japanese manufactured Toyota car.[92]

The Hong Kong based group that led the visit to the disputed island announced plans to continue the protests in September during the anniversary of the Manchurian Incident, which launched the Second Sino-Japanese War.[93] In response to the Chinese protesters, ten Japanese protesters landed on the island and planted the Japanese flag. The protest was described as part of Japan's fears of a rising China:

> But the activists are also tapping into a widespread anxiety over China, which intensified two years ago during the last major flare-up over the Senkakus. China retaliated then for Japan's arrest of a fishing captain by starving Japan of the rare earths needed for its already struggling electronics industry.[94]

An opinion piece argued that some of the anger at the protests in China was also directed at the United States:

And although Chinese nationalist rage is primarily aimed at Japan, it is also directed toward the United States. As Chinese nationalists see it, America is the cause of China's continuing problems with both Taiwan and Japan. If it were not for the "American imperialists" inserting the United States Seventh Fleet in the Taiwan Strait during the Korean War, they say, Taiwan would long ago have been reunified with mainland China, erasing that "national humiliation." And Japan's continuing impertinence is also America's fault: the United States' alliance with Japan gives Japanese nationalists the gumption to defy a rising China.[95]

A letter to the editor argued that the Permanent Court of Arbitration would be an effective mechanism to solve the conflict over the Diaoyu/Senkaku Islands' other disputes in the East China Sea.[96]

Then Secretary of State Hillary Clinton's plan to visit China and other countries in the region was framed around the dispute.[97] The US's position on the island was ambiguous: "In a public display of displeasure with Washington over the East China Sea disputes, China reacted quickly to a comment last week by the State Department's spokeswoman, Victoria Nuland, that the United States refers to the islands as the Senkakus, as the Japanese do. She said the islands were under the administrative control of the government of Japan since they were 'part of the reversion of Okinawa' in 1972, and thus fell under the United States-Japan defense treaty.

Pressed by a Chinese reporter on whether Washington regarded the islands as part of Japanese territory, Ms. Nuland confusingly said, 'We don't take a position on the islands, but we do assert that they are covered under the treaty'."[98]

The conflict around the islands continued to be fueled when the Japanese government announced plans for buying the islands from their current private owners,[99] which the government later did, amid accusations of theft from the Chinese government.[100]

The *Times* speculated that the Chinese government would begin arming fishermen in response to the crisis, based on a single comment from the owner of a Chinese fishing company.[101] In a seeming effort to diffuse the situation, the Hong Kong government stopped another vessel from travelling to the islands.[102] However, shortly after Chinese maritime patrol vessels entered the waters around the islands, to the protest of Japan.[103] Further reporting described the reactions of Chinese people to the developments.[104,105] The Chinese government was reported to be sympathetic to the protests, while arguing that they should be "rational" and "peaceful."[106] An opinion piece argued that these protests were representative of rising nationalism in China.[107] The conflict was reported to interfere with "panda diplomacy," where China loans pandas to zoos in foreign countries, between the Japan and China.[108] Protests also led to declining Japanese car sales in China[109] and Chinese officials deciding not to attend a financial meeting in Tokyo.[110]

The *Times* invited a scholar to make the case for the islands properly being Chinese territory, arguing that the Japanese took the islands as "booty of war" following the First Sino-Japanese War.[111] The *Times* later invited a Japanese scholar to respond to this argument. The second scholar argued that because China had previously supported self-determination for the Ryukyu Islands, it was inconsistent for them to later argue that the islands were part of China.[112]

Another opinion piece argued that the conflict could be resolved by all parties renouncing their claims to the islands:

It would require a bold new kind of diplomacy, but the Senkaku/Diaoyu rocks could be established as a kind of "international zone" surrounded, say, by a 12-mile cordon sanitaire. The islets would belong to no specific nation, much like the legal status of the Moon. No fishing or tourist boats would be allowed to encroach. No military drilling, no oil drilling. And in the spirit of a negotiated settlement, the currently unmanned lighthouse on Uotsuri, the principal islet, could be occupied by a trilateral rotation of keepers.[113]

An article reported that many in Japan were concerned that the rising tensions between the two countries could harm their mutually beneficial economic ties.[114] Another article described the tensions from the perspective of Japan including how Japanese officials tried to prevent protesters from landing on the island.[115] The conflict continued as fishing boats from Taiwan entered the waters around the island. These boats and the Japanese navy both fired water cannons at each other.[116,117]

Eventually protests morphed into negotiations between both sides.[118,119] A group of former "national security officials" from the United States took a trip to Japan and China to try to defuse the situation.[120] Despite these diplomatic overtures, then leader of the opposition and future Prime Minister Shinzo Abe visited the Yasukuni Shrine where Japanese war criminals from the Second World War who committed atrocities against Chinese people and others in Asia are honored.[121] Later in the year, when Abe was to be sworn in as Prime Minister, his nationalistic policies were viewed as risking further escalation of the conflict.[122] A former Chinese diplomat also suggested that the United States should do more to restrain Japan in the conflict.[123]

Throughout the conflict, Chinese ships continued to patrol the areas around the island, while being warned by Japanese Coast Guard ships.[124] In another incident, Japan scrambled jets after Chinese planes entered airspace considered to be part of Japanese held territory around the islands.[125,126] While this chapter only considered coverage of the Diaoyu/Senkaku dispute in 2012, similar incidents would continue in to 2013.

Liancourt Rocks

The Liancourt Rocks controversy was discussed in 2011 when a diplomatic dispute erupted between Japan and South Korea after the South Korean government denied three Japanese politicians entry to the country, because they planned to travel close to the Liancourt Rocks. Outside the airport, South Koreans protested the politicians:

> … members of South Korean civic groups opposed to Japan's claims shouted for the Japanese politicians to come out. They displayed three wooden coffins they said they would use to "arrest" them.
>
> A shoving match erupted with the riot police when the activists tried to barge into the customs zone. One activist dumped a large pot of curry sauce in protest.[127]

The most extensive coverage of the dispute began in 2012. Conflict began that year began when South Korean President Lee Myung-bak visited the disputed islands, which led to Japan recalling its ambassador to South Korea. During the visit President Lee declared: "Dokdo is truly our territory, and it's worth defending with our lives."[128] Around the same time as the President's visit to the island, a South Korean soccer player was denied a bronze medal at the 2012 Olympics in London following his team's defeat of the Japanese team, because after the match he held up a sign declaring: "Dokdo is our territory" in reference to the conflict.[129]

A detailed report about the island including the history dispute made it clear how important it was to many. One of the few residents on the island said: "If the Japanese come to take this place by force ... I say, 'Give me a rifle.'" One of the military personnel tasked with protecting the island while discussing frequent trips by Japanese Coast Guard ships to the vicinity of the islands said: "It's not supposed to come within 12 miles of Dokdo ... If it does, we will warn it and then ram it, or worse. But so far nothing like that has happened."[130]

The South Korean government later tried to return a letter sent to their President from the Prime Minister of Japan protesting President Lee's visit to the islands. While trying to return the letter in Japan, the diplomat was met with protests:

> as the diplomat tried to deliver the letter, a group of Japanese nationalists with a loudspeaker made comments characterizing as "prostitutes" the South Korean women who were forced into sexual servitude by the Japanese military during World War II. That subject, like the disputed islets, remains for South Koreans a highly emotional issue from the years of Japanese rule.[131]

The conflict continued to escalate as the Japanese Prime Minister went on TV to promise to bring the issue to the international community to get a decision about sovereignty.[132] An opinion piece discussed the importance of maintaining cordial relations between Japan and South Korea for the geopolitical interests of the United States.[133]

In 2014, a video was published showing "Day of Dokdo" protests against Japan.[134] The next discussion of the islands came in 2019 when Russian and Chinese planes during a joint military drill allegedly entered airspace around the islands. In response, a South Korean jet fired warning shots and Japan was reported to have scrambled jets.[135] Later that year, South Korea held its biannual military drills on the islands, to the protests of the Japanese government.[136] A week later South Korean lawmakers visited the islands.[137]

Parece Vela

Two articles about Parece Vela were published in 1988. The first article written in a somewhat tongue-in-cheek tone ("to call Okinotorishima an island is somewhat akin to describing a rowboat as a vessel—true but grandiose") described Japanese efforts to build up Parece Vela. The article acknowledged that the purpose of Japan's efforts were to enlarge the country's exclusive economic zone, but did not acknowledge questions about whether the territory met the requirements necessary to maintain an exclusive economic zone around it.[138] A few weeks later, the *Times* published a letter to the editor that made the point that the islet did not meet the requirements for establishing an exclusive economic zone:

> Article 121(3) of the 1982 Law of the Sea Convention, which Japan has signed, states that "Rocks which cannot sustain human habitation or economic life of their own shall have no exclusive economic zone or continental shelf." Okinotorishima—which consists of two eroding protrusions no larger than king-size beds—certainly meets the description of an uninhabitable rock that cannot sustain economic life of its own. It is not, therefore, entitled to generate a 200-mile exclusive economic zone.[139]

The next story about the islet appeared in 2005 when the nationalist Governor of Tokyo Shintaro Ishihara visited it. During his visit, the governor was described as "referring to China as 'Shina'—the derogatory term used during Japan's occupation of the country in the 1930s and 40s." In the article, disputes around the islet were framed as being due to China's economic interests in the areas around it.[140]

In 2007, further efforts to bolster Japan's exclusive economic zone around the island occurred when officials arrived at the island to plant coral.[141] The last discussion of the islet I found in the *Times* used it as an example of an ephemeral island and further described Japan's efforts to protect the territory from the ocean eroding it.[142]

Are the Situations Comparable?

In the case of the Diaoyu/Senkaku Islands and Liancourt comparison, the disputes are fairly comparable involving East Asian countries in disagreement about sovereignty of islands in areas close to them with historic debates about the legitimacy of each of the countries' claims. In both cases, throughout the period considered, there were multiple instances of these issues flaring up due to a variety of precipitating events. In the case of the Diaoyu/Senkaku Islands, only one year of coverage was considered and still that controversy received more attention.

Justification for more coverage given to the Diaoyu/Senkaku dispute could be based on the larger size of those disputed islands. However, the larger size does not necessarily make them more important. It is worth noting that, presently, no one lives on the Diaoyu/Senkaku Islands, while the Liancourt Rocks have people living on them and include military installations. It could also be argued that the Diaoyu/Senkaku dispute in 2013 received more coverage due to large-scale protests in China, which frequently turned violent, that year. With that said, there are frequent and ongoing protests in South Korea against Japan's stance on the islands, including the annually held Dokdo Day protests,[143] which does not seem to be the case in China.

There were many notable events that occurred in the time period considered involving the Liancourt Rocks of which I did not identify coverage from the *Times* including further visits to the islands by lawmakers and other officials to the islands,[144,145,146] military drills around the islands,[147,148] controversy about

Japanese textbooks which some in South Korea accused of distorting the conflict,[149] and protests from Japan about "Dokdo Shrimp" being served when Donald Trump visited South Korea.[150]

The Parece Vela controversy is distinct, because it is not a sovereignty dispute, but rather a dispute about Japan's rights to claim an EEZ around the territory, analogous to similar concerns about EEZs and land reclamation in the South China Sea. It was included here, because China and South Korea[151] have complained about Japan's claims and because it is located in an approximately similar geographical area. At least one notable incident involving the islands was not covered by the *Times* when protesters from Taiwan were detained while sailing to the territory to protest Japan's claims. Those on the fishing boat were only released after paying a $54,440 security deposit to the Japanese government.[152]

Reasons for Differences

The case can be made that the dispute which involves China directly receives more attention for geopolitical reasons. Japan has been the United States' strongest geopolitical ally in Asia since the end of World War II and China has taken on an increasing role as the United States' primary foe. While the disputes involve both sides, China often (although not always) was portrayed in a negative light. In much of the coverage, the dispute was presented as a way to distract from other problems in China. China was often portrayed in more militaristic terms, such as the suggestion that China may start arming fishermen.

Conclusion

The *Times* coverage of the disputes in the seas around East Asia fit well within the "Worthy/Unworthy" hypothesis. Consistently China gets more attention, even when smaller time periods are considered, and the coverage tends to portray China in a more negative light. As with the other disputes discussed in this chapter, these differences can serve to increase support as the United States takes a harder line against China, which is often portrayed as a unique threat. The understanding that there are other countries in the region with similar conflicts can serve as a counter to this narrative.

Chapter 7

Worthy and Unworthy Around the World

Introduction

In the preceding chapters, I have tried to select cases of suspected worthy and unworthy events that are designed to be as closely paralleled to one another as possible. I have done this because by comparing the coverage of two comparable events, it is possible to test the Worthy and Unworthy hypothesis in a somewhat systematic way. However, most historical and newsworthy events will not provide such comparisons. Even the ones discussed in the preceding chapters, as I review, are not perfectly comparable. Still, the Worthy and Unworthy hypothesis would be expected to be seen in coverage of events without fitting comparisons as well. In this chapter, I discuss other events that I believe fit with this Worthy/Unworthy paradigm in how they were covered, but that do not perfectly parallel each other. In the previous chapters, I focused on both the quantitative (how much coverage was received) and the qualitative (the nature of that coverage) of the coverage. In this chapter I focus on the qualitative side of the coverage.

Worthy

Ukraine, 2013–2014

Ukraine's Euromaidan protests and the subsequent fleeing and ousting of President Viktor Yanukovych has had impacts on Ukraine and the world that have been felt for a decade. The protests followed a decision by Yanukovych to slow down negotiations for a trade deal with the European Union and move towards a trade deal with Russia. Because of the fact that the protests were viewed as being both Pro-Europe and Anti-Russia, they would be expected to fall into the category of worthy protests. In this section, I review some of the *Times* coverage of the protests with a focus on how they reported about the European and Russian deals and the reasoning behind Yanukovych favoring the Russian offer, violence during the protests, Yanukovych's ousting, and a fire during intra-Ukrainian clashes that killed over 40 protesters who favored closer ties with Russia.

Euromaidan Protest

In November of 2013, protests were launched as the Ukrainian government rejected the European Union trade deal. As the *Times* reported:

> Prime Minister Mykola Azarov of Ukraine told enraged opposition lawmakers on Friday that his government's decision to walk away from far-reaching political and trade agreements with the European Union was based on fiscal imperatives, and ultimately prompted by the International Monetary Fund's overly harsh terms for an aid package.[1]

This interpretation of the government's decision was rejected by a later piece, which characterized the decision to move away from the trade deal as the Ukrainian government "buckling under pressure from Moscow."[2] As the article elaborates:

> For the second time in a decade, Ukraine is in turmoil, with tens of thousands of protesters in recent days loudly demanding that the country shake off its post-Soviet identity and move once and for all into the orbit of a more prosperous Europe. They exploded in anger last week when their leaders,

buckling under pressure from Moscow, said they would walk away from a deal that many here, especially the young, see as a vital step in escaping the clutches of the Kremlin and joining fellow ex-satellite countries of Eastern Europe on a path to modernization and greater wealth.[3]

An opinion piece made the same argument even more bluntly:

Ukraine faces a stark choice. It can embrace modernity by signing an association agreement with the European Union. It can, instead, drift into obsolescence by signing on to Russia's customs union.[4]

An editorial offered similar criticism of the decision to slow down the European Union Deal.[5] In even more forceful terms, one piece accused Russia's pressure during the negotiations of trying "to drag Ukraine back into the Middle Ages with it" in contrast to Europe, which "promises a future of openness and progress."[6]

Despite this reframing of the issue, the actual situation was more nuanced and aligned more closely with the earlier coverage. Far from being simply a Russian stooge, President Yanukovych had spent much of his term working on negotiating the trade deal with the European Union[7] including pardoning members of the past administrations who the European Union held were imprisoned for political reasons and set their release as a precondition for negotiating a deal.[8] However, as the initial reporting suggested, the Yanukovych administration felt that the requirements of EU were too stringent. At least one opinion piece did criticize the action of the EU in the trade deal negotiations:

Instead of adopting a strategy that would have allowed Ukraine to capitalize on its close cultural, religious and economic ties with Russia, and which could have also served to build deeper ties between Western Europe and Russia, from the outset European negotiators went out of their way to turn Union association into a loyalty test.

First, they rejected Ukraine's suggestion—to which Russia initially had no objection—that accession to the European Union could be compatible with membership in the Customs Union, the precursor to a Eurasian Union linking former Soviet states. Now they have apparently also rejected President Viktor Yanukovich's proposal to resolve the remaining issues (the main one being the very real possibility of European goods being dumped into Russia through Ukraine) through a three-way format that would include efforts to curb cross-border smuggling—something one would think would also concern Brussels.[9]

Pro-European trade deal protests launched in response to Yanukovich government's decision regarding the deal. As the *Times* reported: "In a sign of solidarity with the protesters, one of the country's main news sites, Ukrainska Pravda—Ukrainian Truth—changed the name at the top of its home page to Evropeiska Pravda: European Truth."[10]

An article described a scene where Angela Merkel, the German Chancellor who was often seen as a representative of the Europe projected, seemed to criticize Yanukovich to his face:

Ms. Merkel, holding a glass of white wine, stood in front of Mr. Yanukovich, a beefy man who is at least a head taller. "We see you here," said Ms. Merkel, nodding her head and giving a disapproving shrug. "But we expected more." Next to her, Ms. Grybauskaite nodded in assent. Mr. Yanukovich had nowhere to turn.[11]

In the early days before the protests expanded, there was often some acknowledgement of Yanukovich's tough position. For example, the same article that discussed the Merkel-Yanukovich scene also described the often harsh terms of trade deals with Europe: "it was not clear that the I.M.F. would be willing to ease its requirements, which include a number of painful austerity steps, such as increasing public utility rates."[12]

Articles in the *Times* often gave the impression that there was wide support for further integration with Europe. For example, in one opinion piece the author wrote: "Polls showed that a strong majority of Ukrainians supported integration with Europe, even in the East, the region most oriented toward Russia."[13] The article did not link to any of the polls as a reference. In my own research, polling on the question of the trade deal at the time tended to show a very divided nation. While some polls had shown wider support, one poll from the Kyiv International Institute of Sociology published just a few days before the opinion piece, which compared the support for the European trade deal and the Russian Customs Union, found that "Ukraine is split practically 50/50 over the accession to the European Union or the Customs Union. Europe is favored by 39 percent of Ukrainians, and 37 percent prefer the Customs Union."[14] Far from showing support for the deal in the east, this poll found that "the Customs Union is more popular in the southern and eastern regions."[15] Even when considering the country overall, while some polls did show majority support for European integration, the country was still fairly divided. One poll in October of 2013 showed 53% supported European Integration,[16] while a November poll showed 58% support for integration.[17]

Despite this division, a *Times* editorial stated that "The West's duty, meanwhile, is to give full support to the Ukrainians who are fighting for everything that an association with Europe represents to them: the commitment to democracy, the rule of law, honest government, human rights and a better future."[18]

As the protests continued, the *Times* described in detail the often violent methods used to disperse protesters in Kyiv along with the United States embassy's response to this violence: "The United States condemns the violence against protesters on Independence Square early this morning ... We urge the government of Ukraine to respect the rights of civil society and the principles of freedom of speech and freedom of assembly."[19] Videos showed the violent scenes at the protest.[20] One piece meticulously reviewed different footage of violence at the protests to document police violence.[21]

In an interview, President Yanukovich suggested that the issues could be decided democratically: "If we want European standards, we must do everything within the framework of the law — this is the principle of democracy ... Elections are coming," he said. "People will determine. Whoever is elected, so be it."[22] An article described support from the Kyiv Patriarch of the Ukrainian Orthodox Church for the protests, which presaged later controversies that would ultimately result in the church being granted autocephaly, essentially independence, from the Moscow Patriarch.[23]

While counter protests were covered, this coverage often focused on their perceived opposition to European values:

Marchers said they favored allegiance to Russia rather than Europe because Russia more closely matches the cultural and religious heritage of Ukraine, once part of the Soviet Union. They intend to draw attention to what they characterize as overly liberal European social values, they said.[24]

The *Times* reported about Ukrainian oligarchs' internal battle with respect to the protests, including future president Petro Poroshenko's support:

Mr. Poroshenko has been joined by Victor Pinchuk, the billionaire son-in-law of a former president, Leonid Kuchma, who on Wednesday joined several former

Ukrainian presidents in signing a letter of support for the demonstrations. Ukraine's wealthiest man, Rinat Akhmetov, is usually seen as a staunch backer of Mr. Yanukovich. But Mr. Akhmetov's company, System Capital Management, issued a largely neutral statement saying Ukraine should seek integration with both Russia and Europe.

The trade deal with Europe, Mr. Poroshenko said, "is a way to modernize the country, to fight corruption, the way to have a fair court, freedom of press, democracy." "Modernization of the country is possible," he said. "And unfortunately, by not signing, somebody is stealing the hope of the people," the wealthy included.

In December, the initial stages of the protest died down, but did not end, after another government crackdown.[25]

Yanukovych Overthrown

In early 2014, the protests were rekindled. In mid-February, these events escalated into what has been referred to both as the Revolution of Dignity and the Euromaidan Revolution. The *Times* published videos and satellite images of these escalating protests[26,27,28,29,30] which included attacks on the presidential headquarters.[31] In notable incidents, at least 25 people were reported to have been killed during the clashes.[32,33] Russia blamed the Ukrainian opposition for the violence,[34] while the White House urged President Yanukovych to deescalate the situation.[35]

There was a brief truce in the conflict,[36] which was soon broken with more clashes between protesters and police.[37] The government labelled the protests as a coup attempt. The European Union reacted by freezing bank activities in Ukraine.[38] A graphic video showed a woman who was shot in western Ukraine outside of a building of the National Security Service.[39] President Obama said that the US held the Ukrainian government primarily responsible for the violence, while calling for protests to remain peaceful.[40] Clashes between police and protesters continued.[41,42] There were efforts to find a peaceful resolution to the conflict, while the opposition met with Western leaders.[43]

An explainer video discussed the east-west division in the Ukraine, with more Uranian speakers in the west and Russian speakers in the east, and briefly showed protesters attacking security personnel.[44] Many protesters reacted negatively to another truce, which among other initiatives involved an agreement to an early election, while "a militant leader threatening armed attacks if President Viktor F. Yanukovych did not step down by morning."[45,46]

Unexpectedly after this deal, Yanukovych left Kyiv.[47] Although Yanukovych reported that he was not resigning or leaving the country[48] and called on international mediators to ensure his security,[49] the Ukrainian parliament voted to remove him from office.[50,51] The *Times* published a video showing celebrations following the vote.[52] This coverage did not report about controversy regarding the constitutionality of Yanukovych's removal, which according to the Ukraine constitution was meant to follow an investigation and obtain 75% support from the Verkhovna Rada, the Ukraine parliament. The actual vote was just short at 73% of deputies. The parliament, rather than following the normal impeachment process, instead said that by leaving Kyiv, Yanukovych had removed himself from power and called early elections.

The Odessa Fire

The Maidan Protests and the removal of Yanukovych from power would have far reaching consequences throughout Ukraine. Soon after a rebellion would break out in the eastern Donbass region of the country and Russia would invade and annex Crimea. The city of Odessa in Ukraine's south became a focus of conflict between Pro and Anti-Maidan activists. In one particularly ugly incident during these clashes, Anti-Maidan activists were forced out of an encampment and took refuge in a trade union hall. During this clash between the two sides a fire started in the hall, which ultimately killed 48 people.

The initial *Times* report of the incident was one paragraph in a larger piece dealing with the clashes in Odessa:

> Violence also erupted Friday in the previously calmer port city of Odessa, on the Black Sea, where dozens of people died in a fire related to clashes that broke out between protesters holding a march for Ukrainian unity and pro-Russian activists. The fighting itself left four dead and 12 wounded, Ukraine's Interior Ministry said. Ukrainian and Russian news media showed images of buildings and debris burning, fire bombs being assembled, and men armed with pistols.[53]

In a video report about Ukraine, the fire was briefly mentioned, with no description of the fact that most of those killed were Anti-Maidan activists.[54] In a more detailed video report about the incident, again the position of those killed in the blaze was not mentioned. At the same time, the report indicated that the violence started when Anti-Maidan activists attacked a "pro-Kyiv" march.[55]

A later article describing the clashes in the south did finally give some indication of the political position of those killed:

> An official in the city said 46 people had died as a result of street battles between pro-Russia and pro-Ukraine groups; many of the dead were pro-Russia militants who had retreated into a trade union building that was then set on

fire. If confirmed, the death toll would be the highest since the struggles in February between pro-Europe demonstrators and the pro-Russia Ukrainian government of the ousted President Viktor F. Yanukovych.

Until Friday, Odessa, a Black Sea port in southern Ukraine, had been mostly calm. Amid the chaos, which included the lobbing of firebombs, it was not immediately clear who had started the blaze, though a report from a pro-Ukraine national newspaper, Ukrainska Pravda, suggested that Ukrainian activists had done nothing to help those inside. "As the building burned, the Ukrainian activists continued to scream mottos about Putin and sing the Ukrainian national anthem," the article said, referring to President Vladimir V. Putin of Russia.

The same article quoted Ukrainian officials blaming Russia for the violence:

Ukraine's Foreign Ministry blamed the day of violence on provocateurs "paid by the Russian special services," while Russia's Foreign Ministry blamed a Ukrainian nationalist group, Right Sector.[56]

Another report described the incident in these terms:

Many in the pro-Russian group carried bowie knives, photographs show. Four people died on and around Deribasovskaya Street. The pro-Russians, outnumbered by the Ukrainians, fell back, abandoning their tent camp on Kulikovo Square, which was burned by their opponents. Many then sought refuge in the trade union building.

Yanus Milteynus, a 42-year-old construction worker and pro-Russian activist, said he watched from the roof as the pro-Ukrainian crowd threw firebombs into the building's lower windows, while those inside feared being beaten to death by the crowd if they tried to flee.[57]

Despite people in the "pro-Russian" camp also being Ukrainians, the article described their opponents as the "Ukrainians." Additionally, despite the Anti-Maidan activists being the main victims of the violence in the city, the description of the incident starts with a discussion of the weapons that the Anti-Maidan side had.

A video showed pro-Kyiv groups burning a Russian flag outside of the hall.[58] A long article describing pro-Kyiv militants fighting Anti-Maidan militants and separatists described them in these terms:

> With popular support but little police backup, pro-Ukrainian civilian groups confronted the pro-Russian activists storming government buildings and protesting on Kulikovo Square in central Odessa.

The UN called for a deeper investigation into what happened during the Odessa fire.[59]

Belarus Election Protest, 2020

In August 2020, Alexander Lukashenko, Belarus's only President who had been in power since 1994, faced off against Sviatlana Tsikhanouskaya. Tsikhanouskaya rose to prominence after the jailing of her husband, dissident Sergei Tsikhanouski. Lukashenko has faced criticism throughout his presidency for accruing dictator-like powers. In the official election results Lukashenko won 81% of the vote compared to 10% for Tsikhanouskaya. Tsikhanouskaya declared that she was the actual winner and called for negotiations between her and Lukashenko. Protests occurred in Belarus, especially in the capital of Minsk, against the election results. Shortly after Tsikhanouskaya was forced into exile.

There was extensive coverage of the election protests in *The New York Times*. On the night that the election results were announced, the *Times* published videos of protesters clashing with police and other security personnel.[60,61,62] Early in the protests, one protester was killed.[63] The *Times* reported that Tsikhanouskaya was under duress after she went on TV reading a statement calling on supporters not to protest.[64] After reaching exile in Lithuania, Tsikhanouskaya explained that she had made the statement amid threats from the government.[65] Later the *Times* published a detailed profile of Tsikhanouskaya that discussed different aspects of her life including time spent in Ireland as a child where she developed her English skills.[66]

The *Times* indicated that as many as 200,000 may have participated in these initial protests.[67] Journalists covering the protests were arrested with reports of beatings from the police.[68] Workers at state-run facilities joined in with the protests, which were covered by an in-depth report.[69,70,71]

The *Times* published several opinion pieces in support of the protests[72] including one from a leader in a Belarusian Trade Union who joined the protests.[73] In an editorial, the *Times* Editorial Board gave Western governments advice on how to handle the election:

The West's sympathies and unquestionable support must be with people of Belarus who have had enough of Mr. Lukashenko's willful, cruel and illegitimate rule. The European Union and the United States have made a good start by painting the Belarus election as neither free nor fair and condemning the crackdown on demonstrators. They can do more: They can warn Mr. Lukashenko that they do not accept the official results and will not recognize him as the winner unless he calls off his thugs and there is a new and credible election. To underscore the point, Washington should hold off sending a new ambassador to Minsk.[74]

The European Union did eventually formally reject the election results, and indicated plans to introduce sanctions. Several European countries also called for new elections.[75]

Although before the election there were reports about an increasingly strained relationship between Belarus and Russia, including Belarus not strongly supporting Russia's actions in Ukraine over the past six years and at one point Belarus expelling the Russian ambassador, the *Times* coverage described a shift in this relationship with Putin congratulating Lukashenko shortly after the election results and reports that Putin promised support amid the protests.[76] In late August, Putin indicated a willingness to intervene if the situation in Belarus continued to deteriorate.[77]

A detailed video analysis from the *Times* documented cases of police violence including beatings inflicted on protesters who had been taken into custody.[78] Lukashenko continued to reject negotiating with the protesters.[79] A video showed Lukashenko exiting a plane holding an assault rifle and receiving applause from security forces.[80]

The brief success of a protest in a town near the Polish border was covered.[81] By the end of August, coverage indicated that the prospects of Lukashenko being overthrown anytime soon were dim:

But a path to unseating Mr. Lukashenko, who insists the West is fomenting the demonstrations, remains far from clear. He faced a backlash after mass beatings and the detention of thousands of protesters in the days after the election and is now avoiding scenes of violent repression that could discredit him further.[82]

Belarus Plane Grounding

Months after the 2020 Belarussian election and the protests that followed another notable incident occurred when a Ryanair flight from Athens, Greece to Vilnius, Lithuania was forced to land in Belarus after an alleged bomb threat on the plane. The plane was carrying Roman Protasevich, a Belarussian activist. Many believe that the government of Belarus fabricated the bomb threat in order to force the plane to land and then arrest Protasevich.

The *Times* covered this incident extensively. Coverage included the reports of the initial grounding of the plane[83] and a profile of Protasevich with a listing of the charges that he faced.[84] The grounding led the European Union to consider instituting new sanctions against Belarus[85] and airlines began avoiding Belarussian airspace.[86] Russia responded by rejecting some flight plans that avoided Belarussian airspace.[87] The US later added more sanctions against Belarus.[88] The *Times* reported that Lukashenko reacted to the efforts to isolate Belarus by instituting more efforts to curb dissidence in the country.[89] A description of the plane before landing included a quote from Protasevich where he said: "I know that death penalty awaits me in Belarus."[90]

Ursula von der Leyen, the European Commission President, referred to the grounding as a "State Hijacking."[91] In similar way the *Times* Editorial Board characterized the grounding as a "skyjacking." In that same editorial, the board discussed comparisons to the Morales grounding (see the Unworthy section below):

Mr. Lukashenko was unfazed and on Monday went on with business as usual—signing laws further cracking down on dissent. Russia promptly came to Mr. Lukashenko's defense, with a Foreign Ministry spokeswoman recalling that several years ago the United States pressured a plane carrying Bolivia's president, Evo Morales, to make an unscheduled stop in Vienna after European countries refused it permission to fly over. That's whataboutism, of course, but it is worth revisiting the facts. In 2013, Mr. Snowden had made his way to Moscow, where Mr. Morales went to attend an international conference. On the suspicion that Mr. Morales would grant Mr. Snowden asylum and had taken him aboard his flight home, the president's plane was barred from flying over some European countries and forced to land in Austria. When officials determined that Mr. Snowden was not on board, Mr. Morales was allowed to continue. The outcry, especially from Latin America, was fierce. Much of the criticism leveled at the Obama administration at the time was warranted. But there is a difference between denying overflight to a plane and forcing a commercial jetliner to land over a false alarm, accompanied by a warplane.[92]

The *Times* published a detailed profile of Protasevich, which included information about a short video in which "Mr. Protasevich confessed—under duress, his friends say—to taking part in the organization of 'mass unrest' last year in Minsk, the Belarus capital."[93] The grounding was discussed in light of Lukashenko drawing closer to Putin's Russia. While Western politicians framed Lukashenko as essentially always serving Putin's interests, activists in Belarus saw the situation differently:

Some Western politicians, such as Senator Ben Sasse, Republican of Nebraska, have called for sanctions on Russia over the Ryanair incident. Mr. Lukashenko, the senator said on Monday, "doesn't use the bathroom without asking for

Moscow's permission." But the reality is more complicated, Mr. Lukashenko's Belarusian opponents and critics say. In a flurry of diplomacy this week, Belarus's opposition has been urging Western governments to stay focused on Minsk—not Moscow—in their response, insisting that Mr. Lukashenko should not be seen as Mr. Putin's puppet.

"Lukashenko doesn't listen to anyone," Mr. Viacorka said, rejecting the idea that the ruler must have sought the Kremlin's permission before forcing down the Ryanair plane. "He's an absolutely unpredictable, rather impulsive person."

There seemed to be some evidence to this claim, with Putin reportedly saying that Russia should remain neutral in the situation.[94] Later attention turned to Protasevich's girlfriend, Russian Sofia Sapega, who was also detained following the grounding.[95] In June, a video was published of Protasevich which the *Times* characterized in this way: "He appeared nonchalant or tried his best to show no outward sign of duress. He wore civilian clothes and sat calmly beside the generals as cameras rolled. The news conference had not been announced beforehand."[96]

Cuba Protest, 2021
In July 2021, protests broke out in Cuba. The protesters were against chronic economic problems on the island and issues with the government's handling of the resurgent COVID-19 pandemic. Reporting indicated that these protests may have been the largest since the 1990s Maleconazo protests which occurred at a time of particular economic hardship for the island following the collapse of the Soviet Union.

Throughout the month of July, the *Times* published several reports about the protests. The earliest reports described scenes from the protests that were shown streaming online.[97] Videos from the protests presented protesters walking down streets in the city and security forces taking protesters in to custody.[98] Shortly after they began, President Biden indicated his support for the protests.[99] While some claimed that the longstanding US embargo of Cuba was responsible for the protest, the *Times* quoted the leader of a Cuban organization in Miami to counter this claim:

> "The truth is that if one wanted to help Cuba, the first thing that should be done is to suspend the blockade of Cuba," Mexico's president, Andrés Manuel López Obrador, told reporters on Monday. "That would be a truly humanitarian gesture."
>
> But some Cuban activists in the United States, including those who oppose the embargo, were quick to challenge that narrative.
>
> "There's no food, there's no medicine, there's nothing, and this isn't a product of the American embargo, which I do not support," said Ramón Saúl Sánchez, president of the Movimiento Democracia advocacy group in Miami. He noted that the embargo does allow Cuba to buy food from the United States, though restrictions on financing present significant barriers to the amount.[100]

The *Times* described a rap song "Patria y Vida" which became an anthem of the protests.[101] Another article described continued protests despite a government crackdown.[102] A podcast episode of the *Times* podcast "The Daily" was devoted to the protests.[103] Two opinion pieces were published about the protests; one did not discuss the embargo as contributing to the protests,[104] while the other briefly acknowledged it while arguing that other factors were more important contributors:

For more than six decades, the Cuban regime has denied its people the basic building blocks of the human spirit and body. Of course, the U.S. embargo that's been in place nearly as long doesn't help. Government restrictions on the tiny private sector hurt Cubans even more. Businesses, including grocery stores and restaurants, are barred from taking out bank loans or importing products. Food has always been rationed, and now with the pandemic, restrictions are even stricter.[105]

Protests in sympathy with the Cuban protests occurred in Florida, where many Cuban exiles live as protests within Cuba began to die down.[106] In response to the protests, the US government introduced further sanctions against Cuban officials and security forces.[107] While announcing the sanctions, Ned Price, the State Department Spokesman, announced that the United States would stand with the protesters.[108] Activists reported that Cuban security officials continued to take many into custody.[109] Protests were mostly over by July 17th, about a week after they started.

Unworthy

Assam Detention Centers
The National Register of Citizens (NRC) is an Indian registration system that is meant to contain the names of all citizens of the country. The NRC has been controversial in recent years because of efforts to validate the citizenship of Indian residents based on the list. In 2019 and 2020 this became particularly controversial when an amendment was passed that made it more difficult for Muslim refugees to get on the role. This amendment sparked protests throughout India during which dozens of citizens were killed.

The NRC of the Indian state of Assam has been particularly controversial. Assam borders Bangladesh and has therefore had refugees and immigrants, mostly Muslims, coming across the border from Bangladesh into Assam, especially in the post-Partition period and during the 1971 war between Indian and Pakistan, which coincided with Bangladesh's independence from Pakistan. In 1983, there was a massacre of immigrants in the state, known as the Nellie Massacre, when at least 2000 people were killed with estimates of the numbers dead going in to the tens of thousands. Assam's process of updating its NRC has attracted particular attention.

When Assam finalized its NRC in 2019 nearly 1.9 million residents of the state were not included potentially turning them into stateless people.[110] Many of those left off the roles were longtime residents of Assam with families who had lived in the state for generations.[111]

In 2008, Assam began building detention centers to house those whose citizenship was challenged. The use of these detention centers increased in 2019 with the changes to the NRC in the state. In some cases, people are held in detention for multiple years if they cannot prove their citizenship. It is difficult to determine the number held in detention, but at least one report indicated that the numbers reached a high of over 3000 in 2020. It was also reported that millions of Muslims in Assam feared their citizenship being challenged and being held in the camps.[112] At least 31 detainees died while in custody between 2016 and 2021.[113] Through 2022 residents of Assam continue to be declared foreign and therefore face deportation.[114]

While articles in the *Times* did report about the Citizenship Amendment and the violent protests that followed, over the course of the existence of the Assam detention centers, there were not many articles published in the *Times* dealing directly with the centers. Although the detention centers pre-dated the changes to the citizenship register by about a decade, the first two articles I found discussing the detention centers appeared in 2018 amid discussions of the changes to the citizenship registry.[115] An opinion piece compared India's citizenship registry to Myanmar's prosecution of Rohingya Muslims in the country, who also faced accusations of not actually being citizens of Myanmar.[116]

Coverage did increase in 2019, the year of the Citizenship Amendment Protests, with mentions of the detention centers amid discussions of the larger citizenship protests in several articles.[117,118,119,120,121] Plans for building more detention camps in Assam were also described.[122] An article detailed the process of trying to register as a citizen and the complexities involved.[123] An opinion piece very critical of the Indian government described the detention centers as one planned way to deal with those who could not prove their citizenship.[124] Another opinion piece used the camps as evidence of Prime Minister's Modi's alleged bigotry.[125] Later reporting would describe Modi defending his policies and denying the existence of detention camps.

> He beseeched the crowd to resist their "evil game." He accused protesters of attacking school buses, targeting the police (whom he called "martyrs") and spreading rumors about the fate of Indian Muslims. He made no mention of protesters who had been killed or injured. He denied that detention centers existed.
>
> The law "has nothing to do with Muslims who are made out of the soil of India, whose ancestors are the sons of Mother India," he said, adding: "No Indian Muslims are being sent to detention camps."[126]

In 2020, the *Times* described plans to build further detention centers.[127] Finally, in 2021, *The New York Times Magazine* published a detailed report about the camps and the citizenship situation in Assam more broadly.[128]

Indian Farmers' Protest, 2020–2021

Throughout much of 2020 and almost all of 2021, India was hit by protests in response to bills passed by the Indian Parliament that would potentially end price floors for the sale of food. Farmers feared that the removal of these price floors would have a detrimental impact on their finances. Protests by farmers against the proposal started regionally, but soon went nationwide when farmers began marching towards India's capital, New Delhi. In November 2020, a general strike was called in solidarity with the farmers. Talks between the government and farmers did not result in an agreement. The protests continued throughout 2021 with the government finally repealing the law in 2021, over a year after they began.

While the *Times* did cover the protests, the coverage was relatively scant throughout the over yearlong protest period. In September 2020, the *Times* reported on farmer suicides in India, which was seen as a consequence of the economic difficulties facing farmers in the country.[129] A video showed the early protests as well as Prime Minister Narendra Modi's response.[130] In December, the *Times* reported about farmers from across India converging on New Delhi.[131] In response to the protests, it was reported that opposition leaders were being detained.[132] One article described the system the protesters put in place to ensure that their numbers did not diminish:

> The protesters, which one leader estimated at about 50,000, have organized a rotation to ensure their numbers don't shrink. When protesters tire, or fall sick, they often arrange for replacements from their village before they leave the site.[133]

After the Indian Supreme Court temporarily suspended the implementation of the law in early January, it was announced that the protests would continue.[134] Shortly after, the *Times* published an opinion piece that was sympathetic to the protests.[135]

Although there was substantial violence during the protests, this was not a frequent topic in *Times* coverage of them. One article reported on clashes between police and farmers that resulted in at least one death.[136] In October, another article reported on an incident when at least eight protesters were killed. The incident was described in this way:

> Mr. Mishra, who represents the district in Parliament, warned the protesters to "behave, or we will teach you how to behave. It will take just two minutes," according to local newspaper reports.
>
> In an apparent response to the statement, protesters tried on Sunday to block a visit by Mr. Mishra and a state minister from Mr. Modi's party.
>
> As Mr. Mishra's convoy was traveling past the site, a vehicle occupied by his son and others deliberately plowed into the farmers, according to farmers' union leaders.[137]

Modi's efforts to control dissent including police crackdowns and Internet controls, such as blocking Twitter,[138,139] was briefly covered.[140] In May 2021, representatives of India's antiterrorism office visited the offices of Twitter in the country to accuse the company of allowing fake news.[141] Arrests of journalists continued throughout 2021.[142] The *Times* covered the eventual success of the protests, some of which was attributed to foreign support.[143]

Morales Plane Grounding

In 2013, after his release of secret information about the National Security Agency's mass surveillance of people in the US and other surveillance activities including surveillance directed at foreign governments, Edward Snowden fled the country. Eventually after being stuck in transit while in Russia, Snowden would be granted asylum by the Russian government. Before he was granted Russian asylum, four Latin American countries had offered him asylum: Ecuador, Nicaragua, Bolivia, and Venezuela. The US put pressure on countries along routes between Russia and any of the potential asylum countries to detain Snowden, making it difficult for him to take asylum in those countries.

During the period in the summer of 2013 when Snowden was still trying to seek asylum, President of Bolivia Evo Morales attended a conference in Russia. While seeking to fly back to Bolivia, Morales's plane was forced to land in Austria after France, Spain, and Italy denied the flight access to their airspace. Although officially the plane landed for "technical reasons," the landing occurred because the US had put pressure on these countries to deny the flight access to their airspace, believing that Edward Snowden may be onboard the plane. Following the forced landing, the plane was searched by authorities in Austria. Snowden was not on the plane. The flight was then allowed to proceed to Bolivia. The French and Spanish governments later apologized for the incident.

Given the fact that the incident involved a head of state, a fugitive sought by the US justice system, and several foreign countries, the incident received relatively little coverage in the *Times* even compared to the similar incident involving Belarus (see above). One article described the initial incident, including the Bolivian Foreign Minister's statement's about it.[144] Heads of State throughout Latin America were reported to have reacted negatively to the grounding of Morales's plane.[145] The incident was briefly mentioned in two articles about Venezuela's offer of asylum to Snowden,[146,147] the US's effort to pressure Latin American countries not to offer Snowden asylum,[148] and the impact of Snowden on Russia-US relations.[149] In September

2013, the US denied a flight from Venezuela to China rights to fly over Puerto Rico, which received comparisons to the Morales incident from earlier in the year.[150]

Conclusion

While this chapter does not take the systematic comparison approach of the preceding chapters, in the brief case studies discussed here, it does appear that the predictions of the Worthy/Unworthy paradigm hold true. In particular, protests and government actions in countries with friendlier relations to the United States tend to receive less coverage and less critical coverage than protests and government actions in countries with less friendly relations with the United States.

Conclusion

This book has presented case studies comparing the coverage of political events in countries around the world in *The New York Times* in order to test Worthy/Unworthy hypothesis articulated by Herman and Chomsky in *Manufacturing Consent*. Based on a qualitative and quantitative assessment of this coverage, I argue that this paradigm holds true. This assessment showed that stories involving geopolitical enemies of the United States (Worthy stories) tended to get more coverage than similar stories from geopolitical allies or at least states who are not enemies (Unworthy stories). I also argue that the coverage of geopolitical enemies tended to be more negative. I make the case that the comparisons were fair, meaning that simply based on the merits of the case you would not expect the Worthy stories to be more deserving of significantly more coverage. In fact, in several cases, the merit of the stories seemed to warrant more attention being given to the Unworthy stories. These case studies came from different corners of the world, occurred in different time periods, and involved different types of political events. While I only engage in a systematic comparison for the *Times*, as shown in the appendix, at least in quantitative terms, the *Times* is not alone.

In this conclusion, I ask four questions about this book. First, "How?" meaning what is the mechanism that results in the "worthy" stories receiving more coverage than the "unworthy" stories. In response to this question, I can only speculate and offer hypotheses. Similarly and based on my argument that the geopolitical explanation is an important driver of the increased attention to the "Worthy" stories, I try to answer "Why" by discussing what purpose these differences in coverage might serve. Third, I try to answer, "So what?" meaning what are the implications of the argument presented in the book. Finally, I ask, "What to do?" meaning what can be done to change the lopsided coverage and how an understanding of this lopsided attention to "Worthy" stories can help us as we try consume and understand media coverage.

How?

The goal of this book is to document the persistence of the Worthy/Unworthy paradigm of media coverage rather than to focus on why these differences in coverage occur. As mentioned in the introduction, Herman and Chomsky laid out the five filters that help to explain the Propaganda Model. To briefly review, these are:

Ownership: Media companies are mostly large corporations with the fundamental imperative to make a profit. These companies are disincentivized from covering topics that may threaten their profit.

Advertising: In a similar way, almost all media companies are dependent on advertising for their revenue. Therefore, media companies are also disincentivized from covering topics that may lose them advertisers.

Sourcing: Media outlets frequently use official, government sources for their information. These sources will tend to reflect the biases of the government.

Flak: Individuals who provide dissenting viewpoints will often face concerted campaigns to discredit them. These campaigns will make journalists less likely to decide to cover stories that may result in such flak, including those that may portray allies of the United States in a negative light.

Anti-Communism/Fear: Reporting will often play into the fears of official enemies (Communists during the Cold War, Islamic Terrorism during the War on Terror, etc.). Playing into these fears will often mean that official state enemies will receive more coverage.

I believe that these filters remain an important explanation for explaining the observations about media coverage in this book with three through five, in my opinion, likely being the most important. For example, with respect to sourcing, much of the coverage in the "worthy" category was complemented by statements from US officials, while there were often no such statements, or far fewer, in the "unworthy" stories. This sourcing may indicate that because government officials are sources that can be consulted relatively easily then the perspective offered by US government officials will more often be reflected in media coverage. Additionally, journalists may be incentivized to challenge US government perspectives less because it may make it more difficult to use these officials as sources in the future.

Flak may also explain a lot of these differences in coverage as well. Some journalists may fear being labelled a stooge of foreign nations if they critique coverage of that country in the United States. To give just one example, the journalist Aaron Maté has been accused (without evidence) of conducting journalism supported by foreign governments, because his reporting frequently counters the US government's official position, especially with respect to Russia and Syria.

Ideology plays an important role as well. While it may not be as intellectual as commitment to capitalism (although that still matters), there is still certainly ideological understanding that some countries fall in the "Bad" category and they will be covered one way, and other countries, although they may not necessarily be in a "Good" category, by virtue of not being in the "Bad" category will be covered less negatively.

Still, these filters leave questions that deserve to be answered. How are these filters enacted? Is it a question of the stories that journalists choose to cover? Meaning that at the baseline, fewer reporters are doing reporting that falls into the "unworthy" category. Are editors making decisions about what to cover? Are there many reporters who want to cover the "unworthy" stories, but are being led away from them by editors? Or are these stories being written, but not published either due to editorial decisions or due to pressure from ownership? These are important questions that should be answered if the tendencies described in this book are to change.

Why?

The question of why these differences in coverage occur is intrinsically connected to the question of how. To answer the why questions requires a deeper understanding of the relationship of media with the state and corporations that may benefit financially from foreign conflicts. I do not presume to answer that central question here, but a few hypotheses are worth considering.

First, one could just consider following the Worthy/Unworthy paradigm as the path of least resistance. It requires challenging fewer narratives to present state enemies in a negative light and to portray other states in a better (although not always good) light. Reporting will not need to challenge preconceived notions of readers or editors. State officials will be likely to give you background information about the position. There are also a rich array of think-tanks (often funded by the state or defense contractors) willing to provide support. Presenting stories that challenge the dominant narrative may be perceived as antagonistic and make it less likely to have access to these sources in the future.

Second, it may be that the media actually sees its purpose as reflecting dominant narratives. The leadership of *The New York Times* and other media outlets, although private, may believe through notions of patriotism or other ideology that their primary job is to reflect the perspective of the United States government.

Finally (and related to second filter of advertising), media sponsors' interests may be aided by stories that conform to the Worthy/Unworthy paradigm. For example, defense contractors benefit when enemies are perceived negatively, making the seeming need for having a strong military more likely.

Again, the "why" is an open question, but these hypotheses may help future work seeking to find an answer.

So What?

You could follow along with the analysis and arguments in this book and agree with all my conclusions and still ask a central question: So what? Why does this matter? We live in an age where we are almost gagging on information, why should we care that the media tends to cover negative stories about state enemies more often, compared to negative stories about other countries? Is it not possible to find out the information that is not being reported as much?

While it is true that information has become more diffuse in the digital age, most stories that are shared on social media are still stories that originate with major news companies. There are many people on YouTube doing commentary and this commentary is often a very effective method for revealing media bias, but this commentary is still based around reporting that is often conducted by major news companies. For better or worse, the spread of social media has not resulted in an increase in reporters, but rather just more people offering their opinion about stories generated by reporters that work for the major media producers. This situation means that biases in coverage that are reflected in those media sources will still filter through.

So why care about these biases? As I argued in the introduction, I believe that these biases contribute to creating an environment where people are prepared to support antagonistic policies directed towards state enemies. While it has persuasively been argued that democratic control of government has substantially been reduced in recent years and that foreign policy is one of the areas most insulated from popular control (see Aaron Good's brilliant book *American Exception: Empire and the Deep State* for a discussion of this issue), the opinion of the populace still matters to a limited extent. In the lead-up to the Iraq War, for example, the Bush administration still needed to engage in propaganda exercises directed at popular opinion which involved media outlets like the *Times*, even if the decision to invade the country had already been made. A press that often reflects the dominant views of government will make it that much easier to bring the people along on endeavors like that, as it did in the lead-up to the Iraq War.

How much do negative stories about Iran and Venezuela make it easier for the government to institute sanctions on these countries? How much does reporting about South China Sea make it easier to expand military budgets? How much do negative reports about Russian involvement in Syria encourage further US military engagement in the Middle East? How does not hearing as many negative stories about countries like Saudi Arabia, Colombia, and India further promote the interests of their governments? These are questions that further research should consider.

What to Do?

Most of us are consumers of media and not creators of it, so our first task is to consider the issue of differences in portrayal of "worthy and unworthy" stories when reading, watching, or listening to media. Having a healthy skepticism of all stories is helpful, but is even more so when those stories are about state enemies. Additionally, when one does consume or hear about potentially "unworthy" stories learning as much about them by seeking reporting from different media sources, especially those in the country where the stories originate, can be helpful.

The more daunting task is actually how the media's conformity to the "Worthy and Unworthy" paradigm can be altered. Even large media outlets have been shrinking making first-person reporting scarce. This contraction can mean that any coverage of unworthy stories that might have existed might be reduced. Alternative media with limited resources can only have so much power to do such reporting. Supporting alternative media in the countries where unworthy sources might originate can be a way to fight against this tendency.

Conclusion

I began this book with the story of Jeju Island and the massacre there that was barely reported by *The New York Times* in the late 1940s. Such silence about the massacre was not unique. For years the Jeju Uprising was a taboo topic in South Korea. In a similar way, the memories of Jeju (like many of the memories discussed in this book's first chapter) have barely registered in *The New York Times*.

In the late 2000s, Jeju Island itself became a geopolitically important issue as the South Korean government began contemplating building a naval base on the island. From the initial proposal to build the base in 2007 through its completion in the mid-2010s and the time since when it has been in use, the base has received very little coverage from the *Times*. This lack of coverage existed despite the fact that the base was very controversial among Jeju islanders with active protests against its construction. Much of this controversy surrounds fears that the base may be used to house US missiles.

In 2011, several opinion pieces were published about the base; some of which opposed it.[1,2,3] The *Times* published a South

Korean government-authored letter in response to these opinion pieces.[4] A further response to this letter contradicted many of the claims made in it.[5] Another article described the controversy on the island. This article referenced the tens of thousands killed on Jeju Island.[6] In September 2011, after South Korean police crackdown on protests against the base,[7] coverage of the base in the *Times* basically ended, even as controversy and construction continued.

After 2011, articles were published describing the island including concerns about there being too many Chinese tourists on the island, which briefly referenced the base[8] and refugees from Yemen on the island.[9,10] In one of the articles about Yemen refugees there was a one sentence description of the uprising. During this period, the only other time the uprising was discussed was in an article describing increased tourism to Jeju studying the history of the uprising.[11]

The base eventually opened in 2016. I did not identify coverage from the *Times* about its opening. Telling, in any of the mentions of the Jeju Uprising I also did not identify any references to the involvement of the United States military in permitting the massacres to proceed as a South Korean government report concluded. Even after the base's completion, protests against it have continued.[12]

In contrast to the relatively little attention given to the memory of the Jeju Uprising even in light of present controversies on the island, the memory of the Berlin airlift, which I used as an example of a Worthy Story in the introduction, was frequently mentioned by the *Times*. The memory would appear in articles discussing the Berlin airport.[13,14,15,16,17,18,19,20,21] In one these articles it was labelled a "symbol of freedom to West Berliners."[22] In another article, then senator John McCain was quoted bringing up the Berlin airlift in defense of there being a greater "military dimension" to the United States involvement in the Russia-

Ukraine conflict.[23] During the coronavirus pandemic, the Berlin airlift was used as a model for a plan to move patients from places with surging cases to parts of the countries with resources to treat them[24] and referenced in an article about evacuating Afghanis during the fall of Kabul.[25] The *Times* even developed a history module about it.[26]

Worthy stories, like the Berlin airlift, are indeed worthy. The media attention given to them can make it possible to develop new historical understandings and, hopefully, for us to learn from the past. Unfortunately, such an examination will not occur for unworthy stories. Even in 2022, survivors of the Jeju Uprising were still seeking an apology from the United States for its role in the massacre.[27] It is not surprising that many on the island would be skeptical of promises that the US military would not have a permanent presence on the Jeju naval base or that the base would not host US missiles.

Unworthy events are experienced by unworthy victims. Whether those victims are Jeju islanders or any of the other victims of the US military or US allied regimes, their stories should be heard. Otherwise the silence about them might reverberate into the future.

Appendix

In this appendix, I present the amount of coverage given to stories covered in this book by select major media outlets other than *The New York Times*. These media outlets are the *Washington Post*, *The Wall Street Journal*, *CNN*, *Fox News*, and *NPR*. The amount of coverage was determined by measuring how many "hits" certain key phrases related to these stories received on the website of the selected media organizations during time periods when the stories were occurring, which was determined using Google searches of their websites. All of these "hits" do not refer to the stories themselves, and some articles, videos, opinion pieces, etc. about these stories may not have shown up in these searches. Because of the dynamic nature of the Internet, the exact number of hits may change from day-to-day. The numbers are presented to give a rough estimate of the extent of the coverage.

As shown in figure 1a, with respect the coverage of the 30th anniversary of the historical events discussed in Chapter 1 (20th in the case of the Gujarat riots, because the 30th anniversary has not yet occurred), the anniversary of the Tiananmen Square Protests and crackdown received far more coverage than any of the other events both when all the five news sources are aggregated together and across the five media sources considered. *CNN*, *The Wall Street Journal*, and the *Washington Post* all had over 20 "hits" for the Tiananmen anniversary, while *Fox News* and *NPR* each had several. During the anniversaries of Caracazo and Gwangju there was at most one hit with some news sources having none. Gujarat had more related "hits" than the two other non-Tiananmen events with a total of nine across the media sources.

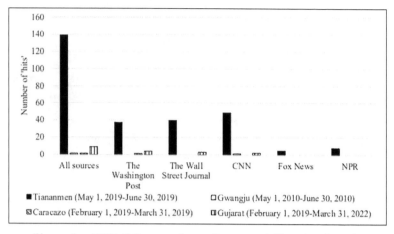

Figure 1a. "Hits" for search results potentially related to the anniversaries of the selected historical events discussed in Chapter 1 by media source

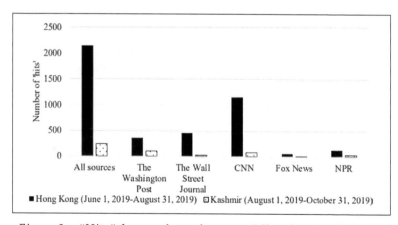

Figure 2a. "Hits" for search results potentially related to the Hong Kong and Kashmir protests discussed in Chapter 2 by media source

As shown in figure 2a, there was a much higher volume of coverage potentially related to the Hong Kong protests in 2019 compared to potential coverage of the Kashmir protests in 2019. Across all media outlets, there were over 2000 hits for a search of "Hong Kong"; in comparison there were fewer than 300 "hits" for a search of "Kashmir." This same pattern existed for all of the media sources considered with the greatest disparity in potential coverage existing for *CNN*, which had over 1000 more hits for Hong Kong compared to Kashmir.

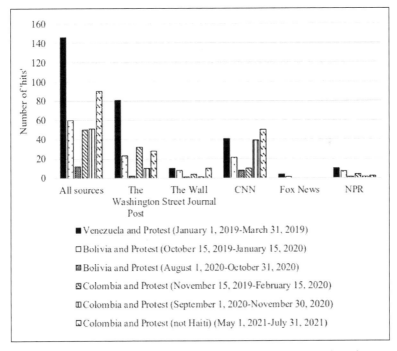

Figure 3a. "Hits" for search results potentially related to the Venezuelan, Bolivian, and Colombian protests discussed in Chapter 3 by media source

As shown in figure 3a, the 2019 Venezuelan protests covered in Chapter 3 had more potentially related "hits" than the two protests in Bolivia and the three protests covered in Colombia. There were a few exceptions to this pattern. In *The Wall Street Journal* there were an equal number of hits potentially related to the Venezuelan protests and the third round of Colombian protests. *CNN* also had more hits for the third round of Colombian protests compared to the Venezuelan protests, and there were only two fewer hits for second round of Colombian protests compared to the Venezuelan protests. For my search of the third round of Colombian protests, I excluded hits that mentioned Haiti, because during the same period as those protests, the former president of Haiti—Jovenel Moïse—was assassinated allegedly by a team of mercenaries that included Colombians.

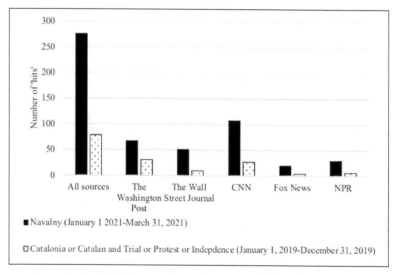

Figure 4a. "Hits" for search results potentially related to Alexei Navalny and the Catalan trial and protests discussed in Chapter 4 by media source

As shown in figure 4a, during a three month period corresponding to his arrest, trial, and the beginning of his imprisonment, there were over three times as many hits for coverage potentially related to Alexei Navalny—the Russian dissident discussed in Chapter 4—than hits for more than one year of coverage potentially related to the trial of Catalan independence leaders and the related protests. This general same pattern was seen across the media outlets considered with the biggest discrepancy for *The Wall Street Journal*, which had five times more hits potentially related to Navalny than the Catalan story.

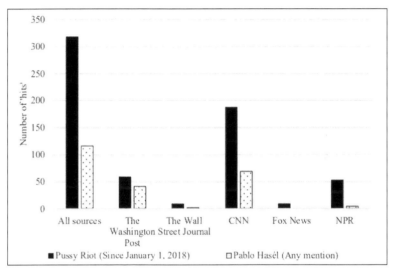

Figure 5a. "Hits" for search results potentially related to Pussy Riot and Pablo Hasél discussed in Chapter 4 by media source

As shown in figure 5a, the Russian protest band Pussy Riot since 2018 received more potential coverage than any mention of the Catalan protest rapper Pablo Hasél. It should be noted that post-2018 was used for Pussy Riot because this was the period when some coverage of Hasél began. Although this period was not the most active one for Pussy Riot, the arrest, trial, and imprisonment of their members having happened years earlier, they still received more coverage than any mention of Hasél across the media sources. The greatest discrepancy was seen for *NPR*, which had more than 13 times as many hits potentially related to Pussy Riot as compared to Hasél.

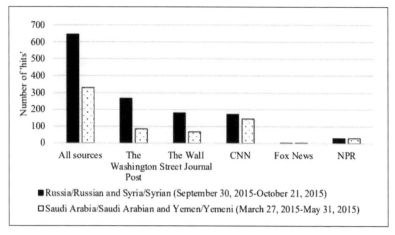

Figure 6a. "Hits" for search results potentially related to the Russian intervention in Syria and the Saudi Arabian intervention in Yemen discussed in Chapter 5 by media source

As shown in figure 6a, the first month of Russia's intervention in Syria had nearly twice as many potentially related hits as the first two months of Saudi Arabia's intervention in Yemen. The pattern of increased coverage for the Saudi intervention was seen across the different media sources except for *NPR*, which had one more "hit" potentially related to the Saudi intervention and *Fox News*, which had an equal number of potentially related "hits," although *Fox News* had a low number in general with three "hits" for each story. Keep in mind that more time was included for potential hits for Saudi Arabia, meaning the monthly average coverage for the Russian intervention was higher across the media sources.

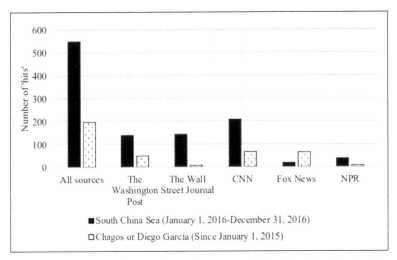

Figure 7a. "Hits" for search results potentially related to the South China Sea and Chagos Islands disputes discussed in Chapter 6 by media source

As shown in figure 7a, one year of coverage potentially related to the South China Sea (the year that included the court decision discussed in Chapter 6) received nearly three times as many hits as hits potentially related to the Chagos Islands disputes since 2015, a period which includes three court cases and two court decisions about the Chagos Islands. The biggest discrepancy was for the *Washington Post* which had over 17 times as many hits potentially related to the South China Sea as the Chagos Islands. Interestingly, the only exception to this pattern was *Fox News*, which had more "hits" potentially related to Chagos. Briefly reviewing this coverage, much of it was related to the military on Diego Garcia and not the territorial dispute. Because of the longer time period considered for the Chagos Islands, the average monthly coverage from *Fox News* was still greater for the South China Sea.

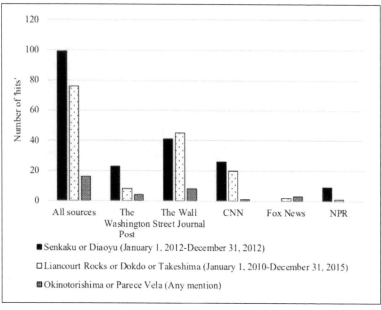

Figure 8a. "Hits" for search results potentially related to the island disputes involving China, South Korea, and Japan discussed in Chapter 6 by media source

As shown in figure 8a, one year of coverage of the dispute between China and Japan over Senkaku/Diaoyu (January 1, 2012–December 31, 2012) received more potentially related hits than six years of the dispute between South Korea and Japan over the Liancourt Rocks/Dokdo/Takeshima or any "hits" potentially related to questions about Japan's claimed Exclusive Economic Zone around Okinotorishima/Parece Vela. The only exception to this pattern was *The Wall Street Journal*, which had more hits potentially related to the South Korea-Japan dispute than the China-Japan dispute. Keep in mind that there were many more years considered for the South Korea-Japan dispute, meaning that the average annual coverage would still be lower compared to the China-Japan dispute. Additionally for *Fox News*, I did not identify hits potentially related to the China-Japan dispute.

References

Introduction

1. Jeju Peace Foundation. (2018). *The Jeju 4.3 Mass Killing: Atrocity, Justice, and Reconciliation*. Yonsei University Press.
2. National Committee for the Investigation of the Truth about the Jeju April 3 Incident. (2003). *The Jeju 4.3 Incident Investigation Report*.
3. Herman, E.S., & Chomsky, N. (2010). *Manufacturing Consent: The Political Economy of the Mass Media*. Random House.
4. Herman, E.S., & Chomsky, N. (2010). *Manufacturing Consent: The Political Economy of the Mass Media*. Random House.
5. Democratic Party. (2016). *2016 Democratic Party Platform—Democratic National Committee*. Retrieved April 15, 2023, from https://democrats.org/wp-content/uploads/2018/10/2016_DNC_Platform.pdf
6. Republican Party. (2016, July 18). *2016 Republican Party Platform*. 2016 Republican Party Platform | The American Presidency Project. Retrieved April 15, 2023, from https://www.presidency.ucsb.edu/documents/2016-republican-party-platform
7. Majid, A. (2023, April 13). "Top 50 News Sites in the US in March: Substack Traffic Up by a Third While *New York Times* Suffers Continued Drop." *Press Gazette*. Retrieved April 15, 2023, from https://pressgazette.co.uk/media-audience-and-business-data/media_metrics/most-popular-websites-news-us-monthly-3/
8. NewsWhip. (2021, February 24). "The 25 Most Engaged Sites on Facebook in February 2018." *NewsWhip*. Retrieved

April 15, 2023, from https://www.newswhip.com/2018/03/facebook-publishers-febraury-2018/

9. Gallup. (2023, April 5). "Country Ratings." *Gallup.com*. Retrieved April 15, 2023, from https://news.gallup.com/poll/1624/perceptions-foreign-countries.aspx

Chapter 1. Worthy and Unworthy Memories

1. Hilberg, R. (1996). *The Politics of Memory: The Journey of a Holocaust Historian*.

2. Burkhalter, H. (1990, May 3). "A Way to Pressure Beijing." *The New York Times*. Retrieved April 17, 2023, from https://www.nytimes.com/1990/05/03/opinion/a-way-to-pressure-beijing.html

3. Binyan, L. (1990, June 3). "China's Long Wall of Silence." *The New York Times*. Retrieved April 17, 2023, from https://www.nytimes.com/1990/06/03/opinion/chinas-long-wall-of-silence.html

4. Kristof, N. (1990, June 3). "China's Untold Story: Who Died in the Crackdown?" *The New York Times*. Retrieved April 17, 2023, from https://www.nytimes.com/1990/06/03/world/china-s-untold-story-who-died-in-the-crackdown.html

5. Basler, B. (1990, June 4). "Hong Kong Honors Beijing's Victims." *The New York Times*. Retrieved April 17, 2023, from https://www.nytimes.com/1990/06/04/world/hong-kong-honors-beijing-s-victims.html

6. Kristof, N. (1990, June 4). "Hundreds March in a Protest at Beijing University." *The New York Times*. Retrieved April 17, 2023, from https://www.nytimes.com/1990/06/04/world/hundreds-march-in-a-protest-at-beijing-university.html

7. Rasky, S.F. (1990, June 5). "Bush Nudges China on Anniversary of Crackdown." *The New York Times*. Retrieved April 17, 2023, from https://www.nytimes.com/1990/06/05/world/bush-nudges-china-on-anniversary-of-crackdown.html

8. Kristof, N. (1991, May 5). "Escape from Tiananmen Square: A Chinese Odyssey." *The New York Times*. Retrieved April 17, 2023, from https://www.nytimes.com/1991/05/05/magazine/escape-from-tiananmen-square-a-chinese-odyssey.html

9. Wudunn, S. (1991, May 30). "Beijing Students Issue Leaflets on Democracy." *The New York Times*. Retrieved April 17, 2023, from https://www.nytimes.com/1991/05/30/world/beijing-students-issue-leaflets-on-democracy

10. Wudunn, S. (1991, June 4). "Beijing University Students Mark the 1989 Crackdown." *The New York Times*. Retrieved April 17, 2023, from https://www.nytimes.com/1991/06/04/world/beijing-university-students-mark-the-1989-crackdown.html

11. Woodman, W.F. (1991, June 16). "Remember Those Who Almost Changed China." *The New York Times*. Retrieved April 17, 2023, from https://www.nytimes.com/1991/06/16/opinion/l-remember-those-who-almost-changed-china-406491.html

12. The New York Times. (1994, May 14). "Tiananmen Leader is Set Free by China." *The New York Times*. Retrieved April 17, 2023, from https://www.nytimes.com/1994/05/14/world/tiananmen-leader-is-set-free-by-china.html

13. Tyler, P.E. (1994, May 14). "In a Surprise Gesture, China Releases a Major Dissident." *The New York Times*. Retrieved April 17, 2023, from https://www.nytimes.com/1994/05/14/world/in-a-surprise-gesture-china-releases-a-major-dissident.html

14. The New York Times. (1994, May 15). "Wife Makes Plea for Jailed Chinese Official." *The New York Times*. Retrieved April 17, 2023, from https://www.nytimes.com/1994/05/15/world/wife-makes-plea-for-jailed-chinese-official.html

15. Tyler, P.E. (1994, May 27). "Ex-Leaders of '89 Uprising Send a Petition to Beijing." *The New York Times*. Retrieved

April 17, 2023, from https://www.nytimes.com/1994/05/27/world/ex-leaders-of-89-uprising-send-a-petition-to-beijing.html

16. Hayes, P. (1994, May 26). "China: Will Clinton Yield?" *The New York Times*. Retrieved April 17, 2023, from https://www.nytimes.com/1994/05/26/opinion/IHT-chinawill-clinton-yield-letters-to-the-editor.html

17. The New York Times. (1994, June 5). "Symbol of Tiananmen Square is Resurrected." *The New York Times*. Retrieved April 17, 2023, from https://www.nytimes.com/1994/06/05/us/symbol-of-tiananmen-square-is-resurrected.html

18. Tyler, P.E. (1994, June 5). "China Tries to Blot Out Memories of 1989." *The New York Times*. Retrieved April 17, 2023, from https://www.nytimes.com/1994/06/05/world/china-tries-to-blot-out-memories-of-1989.html

19. Eckholm, E., & Chen, D. (1999, June 1). "Kin of the Dead Seeking Inquiry on Tiananmen." *The New York Times*. Retrieved April 17, 2023, from https://www.nytimes.com/1999/06/01/world/kin-of-the-dead-seeking-inquiry-on-tiananmen.html

20. Mirsky, J., International Herald Tribune. (1999, June 3). "We are Many Who Know the Truth about June 1989 at Tiananmen." *The New York Times*. Retrieved April 17, 2023, from https://www.nytimes.com/1999/06/03/opinion/IHT-we-are-many-who-know-the-truth-about-june-1989-at-tiananmen.html

21. Eckholm, E. (1999, June 3). "Party Paper in China Makes Rare Mention of '89 Protests." *The New York Times*. Retrieved April 17, 2023, from https://www.nytimes.com/1999/06/03/world/party-paper-in-china-makes-rare-mention-of-89-protests.html

22. Zimbalist, A. (1999, June 2). "Riot, Revolution and Reform." *The New York Times*. Retrieved April 17, 2023, from

https://web.archive.org/web/20110416223652/https://
learning.blogs.nytimes.com/1999/06/02/riot-revolution-
and-reform/

23. Eckholm, E. (1999, June 4). "In Beijing, Reminders of '89 Protest are Few." *The New York Times*. Retrieved April 17, 2023, from https://www.nytimes.com/1999/06/04/world/in-beijing-reminders-of-89-protest-are-few.html

24. Rosenthal, E. (1999, June 4). "Memories of June 4 Fade, Stunted by Public Silence." *The New York Times*. Retrieved April 17, 2023, from https://www.nytimes.com/1999/06/04/world/memories-of-june-4-fade-stunted-by-public-silence.html

25. Yi, T. (1999, June 5). "Still No Room for Dissent." *The New York Times*. Retrieved April 17, 2023, from https://www.nytimes.com/1999/06/05/opinion/still-no-room-for-dissent.html

26. Rosenthal, E. (1999, June 6). "Former Insider Still Hopes Leaders Will Rethink the 1989 Tiananmen Crackdown." *The New York Times*. Retrieved April 17, 2023, from https://www.nytimes.com/1999/06/06/world/former-insider-still-hopes-leaders-will-rethink-the-1989-tiananmen-crackdown.html

27. Faison, S. (1999, June 4). "The Persistent Mystery: How Many Died in 1989?" *The New York Times*. Retrieved April 17, 2023, from https://www.nytimes.com/1999/06/04/world/the-persistent-mystery-how-many-died-in-1989.html

28. Landler, M. (1999, June 5). "A Quiet Tiananmen Anniversary in China." *The New York Times*. Retrieved April 17, 2023, from https://www.nytimes.com/1999/06/05/world/a-quiet-tiananmen-anniversary-in-china.html

29. Rosenthal, E. (1999, June 4). "Memories of June 4 Fade, Stunted by Public Silence." *The New York Times*. Retrieved

April 17, 2023, from https://www.nytimes.com/1999/06/04/world/memories-of-june-4-fade-stunted-by-public-silence.html

30. The New York Times. (1999, June 6). "May 30-June 5; on Anniversary of Massacre, Silence and Introspection." *The New York Times*. Retrieved April 17, 2023, from https://www.nytimes.com/1999/06/06/weekinreview/may-30-june-5-on-anniversary-of-massacre-silence-and-introspection.html

31. Rosenthal, A.M. (1999, June 4). "On My Mind; Meeting at Tiananmen." *The New York Times*. Retrieved April 17, 2023, from https://www.nytimes.com/1999/06/04/opinion/on-my-mind-meeting-at-tiananmen.html

32. Wines, M. (2009, May 13). "China Holds an Ex-Leader of '89 Rallies, Family Says." *The New York Times*. Retrieved April 17, 2023, from https://www.nytimes.com/2009/05/14/world/asia/14china.html

33. Ziyang, Z. (2009, May 13). "Excerpts from Zhao Ziyang's 'Prisoner of the State.'" *The New York Times*. Retrieved April 17, 2023, from https://www.nytimes.com/2009/05/15/world/asia/15zhao-transcript.html

34. Eckholm, E. (2009, May 14). "Secret Memoir Offers Look Inside China's Politics." *The New York Times*. Retrieved April 17, 2023, from https://www.nytimes.com/2009/05/15/world/asia/15zhao.html

35. Ansfield, J. (2009, May 23). "Openness in China About Memoir Proves Short-Lived." *The New York Times*. Retrieved April 17, 2023, from https://www.nytimes.com/2009/05/23/world/asia/23beijing.html

36. Wines, M. (2009, May 13). "China Holds an Ex-Leader of '89 Rallies, Family Says." *The New York Times*. Retrieved April 18, 2023, from https://www.nytimes.com/2009/05/14/world/asia/14china.html

37. LaFraniere, S. (2009, May 21). "Tiananmen Now Seems Distant to China's Students." *The New York Times*. Retrieved April 18, 2023, from https://www.nytimes.com/2009/05/22/world/asia/22tiananmen.html

38. Hua, Y. (2009, May 30). "China's Forgotten Revolution." *The New York Times*. Retrieved April 18, 2023, from https://www.nytimes.com/2009/05/31/opinion/31yuhua.html

39. Li, Y. (2009, May 30). "Dance with Democracy." *The New York Times*. Retrieved April 18, 2023, from https://www.nytimes.com/2009/05/31/opinion/31yiyun.html

40. Zhang, L. (2009, May 30). "Here Come the Workers!" *The New York Times*. Retrieved April 18, 2023, from https://www.nytimes.com/2009/05/31/opinion/31lijia.html

41. Jin, H. (2009, May 30). "Exiled to English." *The New York Times*. Retrieved April 18, 2023, from https://www.nytimes.com/2009/05/31/opinion/31hajin.html

42. Witty, P. (2009, June 3). "Behind the Scenes: Tank Man of Tiananmen." *The New York Times*. Retrieved April 18, 2023, from https://lens.blogs.nytimes.com/2009/06/03/behind-the-scenes-tank-man-of-tiananmen/

43. Ansfield, J. (2009, June 5). "English-Language Chinese Newspaper Breaks Silence on Tiananmen Crackdown." *The New York Times*. Retrieved April 18, 2023, from https://www.nytimes.com/2009/06/05/world/asia/05globaltimes.html

44. LaFraniere, S., & Bradsher, K. (2009, June 4). "Hong Kong Pays Tribute to Tiananmen Protesters While Beijing Stays Silent." *The New York Times*. Retrieved April 18, 2023, from https://www.nytimes.com/2009/06/05/world/asia/05beijing.html

45. Bradsher, K. (2009, June 4). "Thousands Gather in Hong Kong for Tiananmen Vigil." *The New York Times*. Retrieved

April 18, 2023, from https://www.nytimes.com/2009/06/05/world/asia/05hong.html

46. Wong, E. (2009, June 2). "India: Tibetans Plan Tiananmen Vigil." *The New York Times*. Retrieved April 18, 2023, from https://www.nytimes.com/2009/06/02/world/asia/02briefs-brfIndia.html

47. Wines, M., & Jacobs, A. (2009, June 2). "To Shut Off Tiananmen Talk, China Disrupts Sites." *The New York Times*. Retrieved April 18, 2023, from https://www.nytimes.com/2009/06/03/world/asia/03china.html

48. Mackey, R. (2009, June 2). "China's Great Firewall Blocks Twitter." *The New York Times*. Retrieved April 18, 2023, from https://thelede.blogs.nytimes.com/2009/06/02/chinas-great-firewall-blocks-twitter/

49. The New York Times. (2009, June 3). "Tight Security for Tiananmen Anniversary." *The New York Times*. Retrieved April 18, 2023, from https://www.nytimes.com/video/multimedia/1194840673965/tight-security-for-tiananmen-anniversary.html

50. Jacobs, A. (2009, June 4). "Tiananmen Square Scars Soldier Turned Artist." *The New York Times*. Retrieved April 18, 2023, from https://www.nytimes.com/2009/06/04/world/asia/04soldier.html

51. Wines, M. (2009, June 4). "After Tiananmen and Prison, a Comfortable but Uneasy Life in the New China." *The New York Times*. Retrieved April 18, 2023, from https://www.nytimes.com/2009/06/04/world/asia/04protester.html

52. Tung, T. (2009, June 3). "June 4: A Chinese Expatriate Remembers Tiananmen." *The New York Times*. Retrieved April 18, 2023, from https://www.nytimes.com/2009/06/04/opinion/l04china.html

53. The Editors. (2009, June 3). "China's New Rebels." *The New York Times*. Retrieved April 18, 2023, from https://

roomfordebate.blogs.nytimes.com/2009/06/02/chinas-new-rebels/

54. Morrison, D. (2009, June 3). "Who Really Won Tiananmen?" *The New York Times*. Retrieved April 18, 2023, from https://www.nytimes.com/2009/06/04/opinion/04iht-edmorrison.html

55. LaFraniere, S. (2009, June 3). "Chinese Activist Tries to Surrender." *The New York Times*. Retrieved April 18, 2023, from https://www.nytimes.com/2009/06/04/world/asia/04china.html

56. Kristof, N. (2009, June 3). "Bullets Over Beijing." *The New York Times*. Retrieved April 18, 2023, from https://www.nytimes.com/2009/06/04/opinion/04kristof.html

57. Buckley, C. (2019, May 28). "30 Years After Tiananmen, a Chinese Military Insider Warns: Never Forget." *The New York Times*. Retrieved April 18, 2023, from https://www.nytimes.com/2019/05/28/world/asia/china-tiananmen-square-massacre.html

58. Theroux, P. (2019, June 7). "Paul Theroux: Truth and Tiananmen." *The New York Times*. Retrieved April 18, 2023, from https://www.nytimes.com/2019/06/07/opinion/letters/tiananmen-china-paul-theroux.html

59. May, T. (2019, May 30). "Photos of the Tiananmen Square Protests Through the Lens of a Student Witness." *The New York Times*. Retrieved April 18, 2023, from https://www.nytimes.com/2019/05/30/world/asia/tiananmen-square-protest-photos.html

60. Buckley, C. (2019, June 3). "He Stayed at Tiananmen to the End. Now He Wonders What It Meant." *The New York Times*. Retrieved April 18, 2023, from https://www.nytimes.com/2019/06/03/world/asia/tiananmen-zhou-duo.html

61. The New York Times. (2019, June 3). "Witnessing China's 1989 Protests, 1,000 Miles from Tiananmen Square." *The*

New York Times. Retrieved April 18, 2023, from https://www.nytimes.com/2019/06/02/world/asia/china-1989-protests-chengdu-andy-levin.html

62. Kristof, N. (2019, June 1). "When China Massacred Its Own People." *The New York Times*. Retrieved April 18, 2023, from https://www.nytimes.com/2019/06/01/opinion/sunday/tiananmen-square-protest.html

63. Dan, W. (2019, June 1). "What I Learned Leading the Tiananmen Protests." *The New York Times*. Retrieved April 18, 2023, from https://www.nytimes.com/2019/06/01/opinion/sunday/tiananmen-protests-china-wang-dan.html

64. Buckley, C. (2019, May 31). "New Documents Show Power Games Behind China's Tiananmen Crackdown." *The New York Times*. Retrieved April 18, 2023, from https://www.nytimes.com/2019/05/30/world/asia/china-tiananmen-crackdown.html

65. Ramzy, A. (2019, June 4). "In Hong Kong, a Publisher Struggles to Document Tiananmen's Carnage." *The New York Times*. Retrieved April 18, 2023, from https://www.nytimes.com/2019/06/04/books/hong-kong-publishing-tiananmen.html

66. The New York Times. (2019, June 4). "The Tiananmen Square Anniversary: A Guide to Our Coverage." *The New York Times*. Retrieved April 18, 2023, from https://www.nytimes.com/2019/06/03/world/asia/the-tiananmen-square-anniversary-a-guide-to-our-coverage.html

67. UPI. (1981, May 22). "Around the World; 30 Priests in South Korea End 3-Day Hunger Strike." *The New York Times*. Retrieved April 19, 2023, from https://www.nytimes.com/1981/05/22/world/around-the-world-30-priests-in-south-korea-end-3-day-hunger-strike.html

68. UPI. (1981, May 21). "Around the World; Police in South Korea Battle Students in 2D Day of Protest." *The New York*

Times. Retrieved April 19, 2023, from https://www.nytimes. com/1981/05/21/world/around-the-world-police-in-south-korea-battle-students-in-2d-day-of-protest.html

69. Tharp, M. (1981, May 27). "A Year After Korean Uprising, Chun's Grip is Firm." *The New York Times*. Retrieved April 19, 2023, from https://www.nytimes.com/1981/05/27/ world/a-year-after-korean-uprising-chun-s-grip-is-firm. html

70. Stokes, H.S. (1982, May 30). "Dissident Predicts Ouster of Korean." *The New York Times*. Retrieved April 19, 2023, from https://www.nytimes.com/1982/05/30/world/dissident-predicts-ouster-of-korean.html

71. Stokes, H.S. (1982, June 16). "Political Trial Under Way in Korea." *The New York Times*. Retrieved April 19, 2023, from https://www.nytimes.com/1982/06/16/world/political-trial-under-way-in-korea.html

72. Choi, S.-I. (1985, May 11). "In Korea, Democracy is Still an Illusion." *The New York Times*. Retrieved April 19, 2023, from https://www.nytimes.com/1985/05/11/opinion/l-in-korea-democracy-is-still-an-illusion-233754.html

73. Henderson, G. (1985, May 11). "Our Military Role." *The New York Times*. Retrieved April 19, 2023, from https://www. nytimes.com/1985/05/11/opinion/l-in-korea-democracy-is-still-an-illusion-our-military-role-231206.html

74. AP. (1985, May 18). "South Korean Students Mark '80 Kwangju Riots." *The New York Times*. Retrieved April 19, 2023, from https://www.nytimes.com/1985/05/18/world/ around-the-world-south-korean-students-mark-80-kwangju-riots.html

75. Reuters. (1985, May 21). "Seoul Students Burn a Car." *The New York Times*. Retrieved April 19, 2023, from https:// www.nytimes.com/1985/05/21/world/seoul-students-burn-a-car.html

76. Chira, S. (1985, May 24). "60 Students in Seoul Occupy U.S. Office." *The New York Times*. Retrieved April 19, 2023, from https://www.nytimes.com/1985/05/24/world/60-students-in-seoul-occupy-us-office.html

77. Chira, S. (1985, May 25). "Korean Students Continue U.S. Office Sit-In." *The New York Times*. Retrieved April 19, 2023, from https://www.nytimes.com/1985/05/25/world/korean-students-continue-us-office-sit-in.html

78. Chira, S. (1985, May 26). "Seoul Protesters Leave U.S. Office." *The New York Times*. Retrieved April 19, 2023, from https://www.nytimes.com/1985/05/26/world/seoul-protesters-leave-us-office.html

79. Chira, S. (1985, May 27). "Students in Seoul Arrested After Leaving U.S. Office." *The New York Times*. Retrieved April 19, 2023, from https://www.nytimes.com/1985/05/27/world/students-in-seoul-arrested-after-leaving-us-office.html

80. UPI. (1985, May 29). "25 Students Arrested in Seoul." *The New York Times*. Retrieved April 19, 2023, from https://www.nytimes.com/1985/05/29/world/25-students-arrested-in-seoul.html

81. The Associated Press. (1985, May 31). "More Than 60 Detained in South Korean Protest." *The New York Times*. Retrieved April 19, 2023, from https://www.nytimes.com/1985/05/31/world/around-the-world-more-than-60-detained-in-south-korean-protest.html

82. The New York Times. (1990, May 19). "Protesters Hail 1980 Uprising in Korea." *The New York Times*. Retrieved April 19, 2023, from https://www.nytimes.com/1990/05/19/world/protesters-hail-1980-uprising-in-korea.html

83. The Associated Press. (1990, May 21). "Korean Protesters and Police Clash for 3D Day." *The New York Times*. Retrieved April 19, 2023, from https://www.nytimes.

com/1990/05/21/world/korean-protesters-and-police-clash-for-3d-day.html

84. Sterngold, J. (1990, May 27). "The Tear Gas Clears, the Tensions Remain." *The New York Times*. Retrieved April 19, 2023, from https://www.nytimes.com/1990/05/27/weekinreview/the-world-the-tear-gas-clears-the-tensions-remain.html

85. The New York Times. (1990, June 13). "Korean Students Attack a U.S. Site." *The New York Times*. Retrieved April 19, 2023, from https://www.nytimes.com/1990/06/13/world/korean-students-attack-a-us-site.html

86. Myers, B.R. (2010, May 28). "South Korea's Collective Shrug." *The New York Times*. Retrieved April 19, 2023, from https://www.nytimes.com/2010/05/28/opinion/28myers.html

87. The New York Times. (1990, February 11). "How Latin America's Economies Look After a Decade's Decline." *The New York Times*. Retrieved April 19, 2023, from https://www.nytimes.com/1990/02/11/weekinreview/the-world-how-latin-america-s-economies-look-after-a-decade-s-decline.html

88. Fuerbringer, J. (1990, March 21). "Venezuela Agrees to Debt Proposal." *The New York Times*. Retrieved April 19, 2023, from https://www.nytimes.com/1990/03/21/business/venezuela-agrees-to-debt-proposal.html

89. Brooke, J. (1990, August 24). "Venezuela to Increase Oil Production by 25%." *The New York Times*. Retrieved April 19, 2023, from https://www.nytimes.com/1990/08/24/business/venezuela-to-increase-oil-production-by-25.html

90. Fuerbringer, J. (1990, December 29). "Big Swings of Fortune from Rise in Oil Price." *The New York Times*. Retrieved April 19, 2023, from https://www.nytimes.com/1990/12/29/business/big-swings-of-fortune-from-rise-in-oil-price.html

91. Brooke, J. (1991, September 16). "Venezuela is Surging Again After a Period of Difficulties." *The New York Times.* Retrieved April 19, 2023, from https://www.nytimes.com/1991/09/16/business/venezuela-is-surging-again-after-a-period-of-difficulties.html

92. Krauss, C. (1999, February 3). "New Chief to Battle Venezuela's 'Cancer.'" *The New York Times.* Retrieved April 19, 2023, from https://www.nytimes.com/1999/02/03/world/new-chief-to-battle-venezuela-s-cancer.html

93. Rohter, L. (2002, April 20). "Venezuela's 2 Fateful Days: Leader Is Out, and In Again." *The New York Times.* Retrieved April 19, 2023, from https://www.nytimes.com/2002/04/20/world/venezuela-s-2-fateful-days-leader-is-out-and-in-again.html

94. Kurmanaev, A. (2020, May 15). "From Nearly Free to Out-of-Reach: Gasoline's Crazy Price Swing in Venezuela." *The New York Times.* Retrieved April 19, 2023, from https://www.nytimes.com/2020/05/15/world/americas/venezuela-gasoline-shortage.html

95. Mishra, P. (2003, February 2). "The Other Face of Fanaticism." *The New York Times.* Retrieved April 19, 2023, from https://www.nytimes.com/2003/02/02/magazine/the-other-face-of-fanaticism.html

96. Weiss, S.A., & International Herald Tribune. (2003, March 25). "Meanwhile: Secularism Must Unite India's Religious Public." *The New York Times.* Retrieved April 19, 2023, from https://www.nytimes.com/2003/03/25/opinion/IHT-meanwhile-secularism-must-unite-indias-religious-public.html

97. Kumar, H. (2003, February 7). "Asia: India: Arrest in Burning of Hindus on Train." *The New York Times.* Retrieved April 19, 2023, from https://www.nytimes.com/2003/02/07/world/world-briefing-asia-india-arrest-in-burning-of-hindus-on-train.html

98. Rai, S. (2003, March 6). "Court in India Orders Archaeological Study of Disputed Holy Site." *The New York Times*. Retrieved April 19, 2023, from https://www.nytimes.com/2003/03/06/world/court-in-india-orders-archaeological-study-of-disputed-holy-site.html

99. Waldman, A. (2003, March 26). "Ex-Minister in Indian Province is Shot and Killed." *The New York Times*. Retrieved April 19, 2023, from https://www.nytimes.com/2003/03/26/international/asia/exminister-in-indian-province-is-shot-and-killed.html

100. Waldman, A. (2003, March 26). "Former Minister Assassinated in India." *The New York Times*. Retrieved April 19, 2023, from https://www.nytimes.com/2003/03/26/international/former-minister-assassinated-in-india.html

101. The New York Times. (2003, March 27). "Former State Minister Assassinated in India." *The New York Times*. Retrieved April 19, 2023, from https://www.nytimes.com/2003/03/27/world/former-state-minister-assassinated-in-india.html

102. Outlook India. (2022, February 5). "A Midnight Meeting on Feb 27 and a Murdered Minister." *Outlook India*. Retrieved April 19, 2023, from https://www.outlookindia.com/magazine/story/a-midnight-meeting-on-feb-27-and-a-murdered-minister/235982

103. Sengupta, S. (2007, February 21). "Response to the Film 'Parzania' Raises the Question: Can Gujarat Confront Its Brutal Past?" *The New York Times*. Retrieved April 19, 2023, from https://www.nytimes.com/2007/02/21/arts/21iht-indfilm.html

104. Macintyre, B. (2007, February 4). "Midnight's Grandchildren." *The New York Times*. Retrieved April 19, 2023, from https://www.nytimes.com/2007/02/04/books/review/Macintyre.t.html

105. Sengupta, S. (2007, February 19). "India and Pakistan Condemn Train Blasts - Asia - Pacific - International Herald Tribune." *The New York Times*. Retrieved April 19, 2023, from https://www.nytimes.com/2007/02/19/world/asia/19iht-india.4649061.html

106. Sengupta, S. (2007, February 19). "Old Foes Join in Anger Over India Train Bombing." *The New York Times*. Retrieved April 19, 2023, from https://www.nytimes.com/2007/02/19/world/asia/19cnd-india.html

107. Sengupta, S. (2007, February 20). "Old Foes Join in Anger as Train Bombing's Toll Rises to 66." *The New York Times*. Retrieved April 19, 2023, from https://www.nytimes.com/2007/02/20/world/asia/20india.html

108. Joseph, M. (2012, February 15). "Shaking Off the Horror of the Past in India." *The New York Times*. Retrieved April 19, 2023, from https://www.nytimes.com/2012/02/16/world/asia/16iht-letter16.html

109. The New York Times. (2012, February 27). "From the Archives: Godhra, February 2002." *The New York Times*. Retrieved April 19, 2023, from https://archive.nytimes.com/india.blogs.nytimes.com/2012/02/27/from-the-archives-godhra-february-2002/

110. Gottipati, S. (2012, March 4). "Newswallah: Long Reads Edition." *The New York Times*. Retrieved April 19, 2023, from https://archive.nytimes.com/india.blogs.nytimes.com/2012/03/04/newswallah-long-reads-edition-23/

111. Schmall, E. (2022, March 5). "Build a New City or New Humans? A Utopia in India Fights Over Future." *The New York Times*. Retrieved April 19, 2023, from https://www.nytimes.com/2022/03/05/world/asia/auroville-india.html

112. Mashal, M., Raj, S., & Kumar, H. (2022, February 8). "As Officials Look Away, Hate Speech in India Nears Dangerous Levels." *The New York Times*. Retrieved April 19, 2023, from

https://www.nytimes.com/2022/02/08/world/asia/india-hate-speech-muslims.html

113. Anand, G. (2017, March 11). "Narendra Modi's B.J.P. Party Wins Big in Uttar Pradesh, India's Largest State." *The New York Times*. Retrieved April 19, 2023, from https://www.nytimes.com/2017/03/11/world/asia/narendra-modis-party-wins-big-in-uttar-pradesh-indias-largest-state.html

114. Hazarika, S. (1990, January 6). "11 Kashmir Cities Get Curfew to Counter Militants." *The New York Times*. Retrieved April 19, 2023, from https://www.nytimes.com/1990/01/06/world/11-kashmir-cities-get-curfew-to-counter-militants.html

115. Reuters. (1990, January 9). "Police Kill 12 in Kashmir Riots." *The New York Times*. Retrieved April 19, 2023, from https://www.nytimes.com/1990/01/09/world/police-kill-12-in-kashmir-riots.html

116. Crossette, B. (1990, January 22). "35 Reported Dead as Indian Army Opens Fire on Kashmir Protesters." *The New York Times*. Retrieved April 19, 2023, from https://www.nytimes.com/1990/01/22/world/35-reported-dead-as-indian-army-opens-fire-on-kashmir-protesters.html

117. Gargan, E.A. (1992, November 22). "Where Violence Has Silenced Verse." *The New York Times*. Retrieved April 19, 2023, from https://www.nytimes.com/1992/11/22/magazine/where-violence-has-silenced-verse.html

118. Gargan, E.A. (1993, January 7). "Indian Troops Reportedly Kill 40 in Kashmir Raid." *The New York Times*. Retrieved April 19, 2023, from https://www.nytimes.com/1993/01/07/world/indian-troops-reportedly-kill-40-in-kashmir-raid.html

119. Gargan, E.A. (1993, May 19). "Srinagar Journal; From the Editor's Chair, a Bleak View of Kashmir." *The New York Times*. Retrieved April 19, 2023, from https://www.nytimes.

com/1993/05/19/world/srinagar-journal-from-the-editor-s-chair-a-bleak-view-of-kashmir.html

120. Zhao, D. (2001). *The Power of Tiananmen: State-Society Relations and the 1989 Beijing Student Movement.* University of Chicago Press.

121. MacroTrends. (ND). "Beijing, China Metro Area Population 1950–2023." *MacroTrends.* Retrieved April 19, 2023, from https://www.macrotrends.net/cities/20464/beijing/population

122. Katsiaficas, G. (2006, September 19). "The Gwangju Uprising, 1980." *libcom.org.* Retrieved April 19, 2023, from https://libcom.org/article/gwangju-uprising-1980

123. MacroTrends. (ND). "Gwangju, South Korea Metro Area population 1950–2023." *MacroTrends.* Retrieved April 19, 2023, from https://www.macrotrends.net/cities/21750/gwangju/population

124. May 18 Democratic Archive. (2021). "Spring of Democratization on 1980." *May 18 Democratic Archive.* Retrieved April 19, 2023, from https://www.518archives.go.kr/eng/?PID=008

125. Szczepanski, K. (2019, January 23). "The History of the Gwangju Massacre in South Korea." *ThoughtCo.* Retrieved April 19, 2023, from https://www.thoughtco.com/the-gwangju-massacre-1980-195726

126. Koerner, L. (2019, July 27). "Venezuelans Commemorate 26th Anniversary of the Caracazo." *Venezuelanalysis.com.* Retrieved April 19, 2023, from https://venezuelanalysis.com/news/11240

127. Maya, M.L. (2003). "The Venezuelan Caracazo of 1989: Popular Protest and Institutional Weakness." *Journal of Latin American Studies, 35*(1), 117–137.

128. Chenoy, K.M., Nagar, V., Bose, P., & Krishnan, V. (2002, March). "Ethnic Cleaning in Ahmedabad: A Preliminary Report." Retrieved April 19, 2023, from https://web.

archive.org/web/20030210234712/http://www.mnet.fr/
aiindex/sahmatreport032002.html

129. Brass, P.R. (2011). *The Production of Hindu-Muslim Violence
in Contemporary India*. University of Washington Press.

130. Weber, I.M. (2021). *How China Escaped Shock Therapy: The
Market Reform Debate*. Routledge.

131. Ahn, J.-C., Byun, J., & Baker, D. (2003). *Contentious Kwangju:
The May 18 Uprising in Korea's Past and Present*. Rowman &
Littlefield.

132. Oh, S.-min. (2020, December 22). "Soldiers Killed During
Gwangju Uprising Recognized as Dead on Duty, Not War
Dead." *Yonhap News Agency*. Retrieved April 19, 2023, from
https://en.yna.co.kr/view/AEN20201222005500325

133. Zhao, D. (2001). *The Power of Tiananmen: State-Society
Relations and the 1989 Beijing Student Movement*. University
of Chicago Press.

134. Zhao, D. (2001). *The Power of Tiananmen: State-Society
Relations and the 1989 Beijing Student Movement*. University
of Chicago Press.

135. Zhao, D. (2001). *The Power of Tiananmen: State-Society
Relations and the 1989 Beijing Student Movement*. University
of Chicago Press.

136. Zhao, D. (2001). *The Power of Tiananmen: State-Society
Relations and the 1989 Beijing Student Movement*. University
of Chicago Press.

137. Zhao, D. (2001). *The Power of Tiananmen: State-Society
Relations and the 1989 Beijing Student Movement*. University
of Chicago Press.

138. Pandey, S. (2002, March 17). "Riots Hit All Classes,
People of All Faith." *Times of India*. Retrieved April 20,
2023, from https://timesofindia.indiatimes.com/city/
ahmedabad/Riots-hit-all-classes-people-of-all-faith/
articleshow/4007683.cms

139. BBC. (2005, May 11). "South Asia | Gujarat Riot Death Toll Revealed." *BBC News*. Retrieved April 20, 2023, from http://news.bbc.co.uk/2/hi/south_asia/4536199.stm

140. Kristof, N. (1989, June 21). "A Reassessment of How Many Died in the Military Crackdown in Beijing." *The New York Times*. Retrieved April 20, 2023, from https://www.nytimes.com/1989/06/21/world/a-reassessment-of-how-many-died-in-the-military-crackdown-in-beijing.html

141. Fisher, M. (2014, June 3). "25 Years after Tiananmen, Most Chinese University Students Have Never Heard of It." *Vox*. Retrieved April 20, 2023, from https://www.vox.com/2014/6/3/5775918/25-years-after-tiananmen-most-chinese-univeristy-students-have-never

142. Kristof, N.D. (1990, June 3). "China's Untold Story: Who Died in the Crackdown?" *The New York Times*. Retrieved April 20, 2023, from https://www.nytimes.com/1990/06/03/world/china-s-untold-story-who-died-in-the-crackdown.html

143. Richelson, J.T., & Evans, M.L. (eds.). (1999, June 1). "Tiananmen Square, 1989: The Declassified History." *National Security Archive*. Retrieved April 20, 2023, from https://nsarchive2.gwu.edu/NSAEBB/NSAEBB16/

144. Time Inc. (1990, June 4). "How Many Really Died? Tiananmen Square Fatalities." *Time*. Retrieved April 20, 2023, from https://content.time.com/time/subscriber/article/0,33009,970278,00.html

145. Sik, C.K., Chun Nam University. (1999). "The Kwangju Popular Uprising and the May Movement." Retrieved April 20, 2023, from https://web.archive.org/web/20090207032303/http://www.kimsoft.com/1997/43kwang.htm

146. Tennant, R. (1996). *A History of Korea*. Routledge.

147. Maya, M.L. (2003). "The Venezuelan Caracazo of 1989: Popular Protest and Institutional Weakness." *Journal of Latin American Studies*, 35(1), 117–137.

148. Vidal, L. (2017, February 28). "'El Caracazo' Riots are Still at the Center of Venezuelan Debate 28 Years Later." *Global Voices*. Retrieved April 20, 2023, from https://globalvoices.org/2017/02/28/el-caracazo-riots-are-still-at-the-center-of-venezuelan-debate-28-years-later/

149. BBC. (2005, May 11). "South Asia | Gujarat Riot Death Toll Revealed." *BBC News*. Retrieved April 20, 2023, from http://news.bbc.co.uk/2/hi/south_asia/4536199.stm

150. Jaffrelot, C. (2003). "Communal Riots in Gujarat: The State at Risk?"

151. Gilinskiy, Y. et al. (2009). *The Ethics of Terrorism: Innovative Approaches from an International Perspective (17 Lectures)*. Charles C. Thomas Publisher.

152. Kuhn, R.L. (2004). *The Man Who Changed China: The Life and Legacy of Jiang Zemin*. Crown Publishers.

153. Times of India. (2005, March 18). "No Entry for Modi into US: Visa Denied." *Times of India*. Retrieved April 20, 2023, from https://web.archive.org/web/20110713025332/http://articles.timesofindia.indiatimes.com/2005-03-18/india/27866126_1_business-visa-gujarat-riots-immigration-and-nationality-act

154. Jacobs, A., & Buckley, C. (2013, June 4). "Elite in China Molded in Part by Tiananmen." *The New York Times*. Retrieved April 20, 2023, from https://www.nytimes.com/2013/06/04/world/asia/chinas-new-leadership-has-ties-to-tiananmen-era.html

155. Watts, J. (2011, May 31). "China Tried to Pay Off Tiananmen Square Family, Activists Claim." *Guardian*. Retrieved April 20, 2023, from https://www.theguardian.com/world/2011/may/31/tiananmen-square-china-pay-off

156. Anderlini, J. (2012, March 20). "Wen Lays Ground for Tiananmen Healing." *Financial Times*. Retrieved April 20, 2023, from https://www.ft.com/content/13c6fcb2-7285-11e1-9be9-00144feab49a

157. Newzfirst. (2013, April 16). "Gujarat Riots Not Sudden and Spontaneous, SIT Probe Biased." *Newzfirst*. Retrieved April 20, 2023, from https://web.archive. org/web/20160905065319/http://www.newzfirst.com/ web/guest/full-story/-/asset_publisher/Qd8l/content/ gujarat-riots-not-sudden-and-spontaneous-sit-probe-biased?redirect=%2Fweb%2Fguest%2Ffull%20story

158. Lee, W. (2018, July 6). "South Korean Military Planned Crackdown on Protesters of Ex-President." *UPI*. Retrieved April 20, 2023, from https://www.upi.com/Top_News/ World-News/2018/07/06/South-Korean-military-planned-crackdown-on-Park-protesters/6941530861760/?ur3=1

159. EFE. (2018, July 20). "Plan to Activate Martial Law in South Korea Included Arrests of Lawmakers." *www.efe.com*. Retrieved April 20, 2023, from https://web.archive.org/ web/20210308042539/https://www.efe.com/efe/english/ world/plan-to-activate-martial-law-in-south-korea-included-arrests-of-lawmakers/50000262-3696788

Chapter 2. Worthy and Unworthy Protests in Asia: Hong Kong and Kashmir, 2019

1. Chomsky, N., & Herman, E.S. (2009, November). "The Propaganda Model after 20 Years: Interview with Edward S. Herman and Noam Chomsky." *Chomsky Info*. Retrieved April 20, 2023, from https://chomsky.info/200911__/

2. For a nuanced understanding of the 2019 Hong Kong Protests, I recommend Vittachi, N. (2020). *The Other Side of the Story: A Secret War in Hong Kong*. YLF Hong Kong; Vukovich, D. (2020). "A Sound and Fury Signifying Mediatisation: On the Hong Kong Protests, 2019." *Javnost– The Public*, 27(2), 200–209; Vukovich, D. (2020). "A City and a SAR on Fire: As if Everything and Nothing Changes." *Critical Asian Studies*, 52(1), 1–17.

3. Ramzy, A. (2019, March 4). "Murder Case Poses Dilemma for Hong Kong on Sending Suspects to China." *The New York Times*. Retrieved April 20, 2023, from https://www.nytimes.com/2019/03/04/world/asia/hong-kong-china-extradition.html

4. Lague, D., Torode, G., & Pomfret, J. (2019, December 20). "How Murder, Kidnappings and Miscalculation Set Off Hong Kong Revolt." *Reuters*. Retrieved April 20, 2023, from https://www.reuters.com/investigates/special-report/hongkong-protests-extradition-narrative/

5. Government of the Hong Kong Special Administrative Region. (2019). "Fugitive Offenders and Mutual Legal Assistance in Criminal Matters Legislation (Amendment) Bill 2019 to be Submitted to LegCo." Retrieved April 20, 2023, from https://www.info.gov.hk/gia/general/201903/26/P2019032600708.htm

6. Government of the Hong Kong Special Administrative Region. (2019). "Fugitive Offenders and Mutual Legal Assistance in Criminal Matters Legislation (Amendment) Bill 2019 to be Submitted to LegCo." Retrieved April 20, 2023, from https://www.info.gov.hk/gia/general/201903/26/P2019032600708.htm

7. Citizen News. (2019, April 2). "Observations of the Hong Kong Bar Association on the Fugitive Offenders and Mutual Legal Assistance in Criminal Matters Legislation (Amendment) Bill 2019: CitizenNews op-ed." *Citizen News*. Retrieved April 20, 2023, from https://web.archive.org/web/20220903055717/https://www.hkcnews.com/article/19529/bar_association-fugitives_bill-19529/observations-of-the-hong-kong-bar-association-on-the-fugitive-offenders-and-mutual-legal-assistance-in-criminal-matters-legislation-amendment-bill-2019

8. ANI. (2021, May 20). "Activists in Exile Urge EU States to Suspend Extradition Treaties with China." *ANI News*. Retrieved April 20, 2023, from https://www.aninews.in/news/world/europe/activists-in-exile-urge-eu-states-to-suspend-extradition-treaties-with-china20210521011633/

9. Population U. (2023). "Ladakh population." *World Population*. Retrieved April 20, 2023, from https://www.populationu.com/in/ladakh-population

10. Lin, G. (2020, March 31). "CUHK Survey Finds Nearly 40% of Young Hongkongers Want Independence after 2047." *Hong Kong Free Press HKFP*. Retrieved April 20, 2023, from https://hongkongfp.com/2016/07/25/17-hongkongers-support-independence-2047-especially-youth-cuhk-survery/

11. Ramzy, A. (2019, June 9). "Hong Kong March: Vast Protest of Extradition Bill Shows Fear of Eroding Freedoms." *The New York Times*. Retrieved April 20, 2023, from https://www.nytimes.com/2019/06/09/world/asia/hong-kong-extradition-protest.html

12. Marcolini, B. (2019, June 9). "Scenes From the Protest in Hong Kong." *The New York Times*. Retrieved April 20, 2023, from https://www.nytimes.com/video/world/asia/100000006548975/hong-kong-extradition-protest-video.html

13. Stephens, B. (2019, June 13). "Hong Kong and the Future of Freedom." *The New York Times*. Retrieved April 20, 2023, from https://www.nytimes.com/2019/06/13/opinion/hong-kong-protests-trump.html

14. The Editorial Board. (2019, June 10). "The Hong Kong Protests Are About More Than an Extradition Law." *The New York Times*. Retrieved April 20, 2023, from https://www.nytimes.com/2019/06/10/opinion/hong-kong-protests.html

15. The New York Times. (2019, June 12). "Bricks, Bottles and Tear Gas: Protesters and Police Battle in Hong Kong." *The New York Times*. Retrieved April 20, 2023, from https://www.nytimes.com/2019/06/12/world/asia/hong-kong-protest-extradition.html

16. The New York Times. (2019, June 13). "Police Violence Puts Hong Kong Government on Defensive." *The New York Times*. Retrieved April 20, 2023, from https://www.nytimes.com/2019/06/12/world/asia/hong-kong-protests.html

17. Ives, M., & Stevenson, A. (2019, June 13). "Hong Kong Police Face Criticism Over Force Used at Protests." *The New York Times*. Retrieved April 20, 2023, from https://www.nytimes.com/2019/06/13/world/asia/hong-kong-extradition.html

18. The New York Times. (2019, June 13). "Police Violence Puts Hong Kong Government on Defensive." *The New York Times*. Retrieved April 20, 2023, from https://www.nytimes.com/2019/06/12/world/asia/hong-kong-protests.html

19. Ramzy, A. (2019, June 9). "Hong Kong March: Vast Protest of Extradition Bill Shows Fear of Eroding Freedoms." *The New York Times*. Retrieved April 20, 2023, from https://www.nytimes.com/2019/06/09/world/asia/hong-kong-extradition-protest.html

20. Ives, M., & May, T. (2019, June 11). "Hong Kong Residents Block Roads to Protest Extradition Bill." *The New York Times*. Retrieved April 20, 2023, from https://www.nytimes.com/2019/06/11/world/asia/hong-kong-protest.html

21. Ives, M. (2019, June 12). "Extradition Protesters in Hong Kong Face Tear Gas and Rubber Bullets." *The New York Times*. Retrieved April 20, 2023, from https://www.nytimes.com/2019/06/12/world/asia/hong-kong-extradition-protest.html

22. Bradsher, K. (2019, June 12). "In Battle for Hong Kong, the Field Has Tilted Toward Beijing." *The New York Times*.

Retrieved April 20, 2023, from https://www.nytimes. com/2019/06/12/world/asia/hong-kong-china.html

23. The New York Times. (2019, June 13). "Police Violence Puts Hong Kong Government on Defensive." *The New York Times*. Retrieved April 20, 2023, from https://www.nytimes. com/2019/06/12/world/asia/hong-kong-protests.html

24. Ives, M., & Stevenson, A. (2019, June 13). "Hong Kong Police Face Criticism Over Force Used at Protests." *The New York Times*. Retrieved April 20, 2023, from https:// www.nytimes.com/2019/06/13/world/asia/hong-kong-extradition.html

25. Bradsher, K. (2019, June 14). "Carrie Lam: A 'Good Fighter' in the Crisis Over the Hong Kong Extradition Bill." *The New York Times*. Retrieved April 20, 2023, from https:// www.nytimes.com/2019/06/14/world/asia/carrie-lam-hong-kong.html

26. Hong Kong Public Opinion Research Institute Project Citizens Foundation. (2019, December 13). "Anti-Extradition Bill Movement People's Public Sentiment Report." Retrieved April 20, 2023, from https://web.archive. org/web/20210629105737/https://static1.squarespace.com/ static/5cfd1ba6a7117c000170d7aa/t/5df3158f04b7db043c7d a1bd/1576211867361/PCF_Anti_Extradition_Bill_Stage+3_ rpt_2019dec13_first+edition.pdf

27. Scarr, S., Sharma, M., & Hernandez, M. (2019, July 4). "Hong Kong Protests: How Many Protesters Took to the Streets on July 1?" *Reuters*. Retrieved April 20, 2023, from https:// graphics.reuters.com/HONGKONG-EXTRADITION-CROWDSIZE/0100B05W0BE/index.html

28. Ives, M., & May, T. (2019, June 11). "Hong Kong Residents Block Roads to Protest Extradition Bill." *The New York Times*. Retrieved April 20, 2023, from https://www.nytimes. com/2019/06/11/world/asia/hong-kong-protest.html

29. Ives, M. (2019, June 12). "Extradition Protesters in Hong Kong Face Tear Gas and Rubber Bullets." *The New York Times*. Retrieved April 20, 2023, from https://www.nytimes.com/2019/06/12/world/asia/hong-kong-extradition-protest.html?searchResultPosition=59

30. Bradsher, K. (2019, June 12). "In Battle for Hong Kong, the Field Has Tilted Toward Beijing." *The New York Times*. Retrieved April 20, 2023, from https://www.nytimes.com/2019/06/12/world/asia/hong-kong-china.html

31. Ives, M., & Stevenson, A. (2019, June 13). "Hong Kong Police Face Criticism Over Force Used at Protests." *The New York Times*. Retrieved April 20, 2023, from https://www.nytimes.com/2019/06/13/world/asia/hong-kong-extradition.html

32. Bradsher, K., & Stevenson, A. (2019, June 15). "Hong Kong's Leader, Yielding to Protests, Suspends Extradition Bill." *The New York Times*. Retrieved April 20, 2023, from https://www.nytimes.com/2019/06/15/world/asia/hong-kong-protests-extradition-law.html

33. Chan, Y.Y. (2019, June 15). "Why Hong Kong Is Still Marching." *The New York Times*. Retrieved April 20, 2023, from https://www.nytimes.com/2019/06/15/opinion/hong-kong-extradition-protests.html

34. Ives, M., & Li, K. (2019, June 17). "For Hong Kong's Youth, Protests are 'A Matter of Life and Death.'" *The New York Times*. Retrieved April 20, 2023, from https://www.nytimes.com/2019/06/17/world/asia/hong-kong-protests-youth.html

35. Hernández, J.C. (2019, July 1). "Hong Kong Protesters Storm Legislature, Dividing the Movement." *The New York Times*. Retrieved April 20, 2023, from https://www.nytimes.com/2019/07/01/world/asia/china-hong-kong-protest.html

36. Stevenson, A., & Hernández, J.C. (2019, July 2). "China Calls Hong Kong Protesters Who Stormed Legislature 'Extreme

Radicals.'" *The New York Times*. Retrieved April 20, 2023, from https://www.nytimes.com/2019/07/02/world/asia/hong-kong-protestors.html

37. Ho-fai, F.C. (2019, June 30). "Opinion: A Hong Kong Protester's Tactic: Get the Police to Hit You." *The New York Times*. Retrieved April 20, 2023, from https://web.archive.org/web/20190701001955/https://www.nytimes.com/2019/06/30/opinion/hong-kong-protests-police-violence.html

38. Stevenson, A., & Hernández, J.C. (2019, July 2). "China Calls Hong Kong Protesters Who Stormed Legislature 'Extreme Radicals.'" *The New York Times*. Retrieved April 20, 2023, from https://www.nytimes.com/2019/07/02/world/asia/hong-kong-protestors.html

39. Lim, L. (2019, July 2). "Hong Kong Has Nothing Left to Lose." *The New York Times*. Retrieved April 20, 2023, from https://www.nytimes.com/2019/07/02/opinion/hong-kong-protest.html

40. Sautman, B., & Yan, H. (2015). "Localists and 'Locusts' in Hong Kong: Creating a Yellow-Red Peril Discourse." *Maryland Series in Contemporary Asian Studies*, *2015*(2), 1.

41. CNN. (2019, November 11). "Hong Kong Protests Leave Flights Canceled, Roads Blocked." *CNN*. Retrieved April 20, 2023, from https://www.cnn.com/asia/live-news/hong-kong-strike-protest-intl-hnk/index.html

42. Lee, D., Ting, V., & Leung, K. (2019, August 15). "How a Terrifying Night Unfolded at Hong Kong Airport." *South China Morning Post*. Retrieved April 20, 2023, from https://www.scmp.com/news/hong-kong/politics/article/3022838/how-terrifying-night-hong-kong-international-airport

43. South China Morning Post. (2019, October 5). "Attack on JPMorgan Banker in Hong Kong Sparks Outrage in Mainland China." *South China Morning Post*. Retrieved

April 20, 2023, from https://www.scmp.com/news/china/
society/article/3031708/attack-jpmorgan-banker-hong-
kong-sparks-outrage-mainland-china

44. Zhu, J. (2019, October 30). "Mainlanders in Hong
     Kong Worry as Anti-China Sentiment Swells." *Reuters*.
     Retrieved April 20, 2023, from https://www.reuters.com/
     article/us-hongkong-protests-mainlanders/mainlanders-
     in-hong-kong-worry-as-anti-china-sentiment-swells-
     idUSKBN1X90Q8

45. BBC. (2019, August 12). "Hong Kong Protests: How Badly Has
     Tourism Been Affected?" *BBC News*. Retrieved April 20, 2023,
     from https://www.bbc.com/news/world-asia-china-49276259

46. "Chapter II - Relationship between the Central Authorities
     and the Hong Kong Special Administrative Region." (1997).
     Basic Law, Chapter II (EN). Retrieved April 20, 2023, from
     https://www.basiclaw.gov.hk/en/basiclaw/chapter2.html

47. Myers, S.L., & Hernández, J.C. (2019, August 19). "With
     Troop Buildup, China Sends a Stark Warning to Hong
     Kong." *The New York Times*. Retrieved April 20, 2023, from
     https://www.nytimes.com/2019/08/19/world/asia/hong-
     kong-china-troops.html

48. Pickrell, R. (2019, August 16). "Chinese Armed Police
     are Drilling at a Stadium Outside Hong Kong in a 'Clear
     Warning' to Protesters." *Business Insider*. Retrieved
     April 20, 2023, from https://www.businessinsider.com/
     china-paramilitary-force-drills-a-clear-warning-to-hong-
     kong-2019-8

49. McGregor, R. (2019, August 14). "Is a Crackdown Coming
     in Hong Kong?" *The New York Times*. Retrieved April 20,
     2023, from https://www.nytimes.com/2019/08/14/opinion/
     hong-kong-protest.html

50. South China Morning Post. (2019, November 16). "PLA
     Soldiers Sent onto Hong Kong Streets to Help Clear

Roadblocks." *South China Morning Post*. Retrieved April 20, 2023, from https://www.scmp.com/news/hong-kong/politics/article/3038049/pla-soldiers-sent-streets-hong-kong-first-time-protests

51. Prasad, E.S. (2019, July 3). "Why China No Longer Needs Hong Kong." *The New York Times*. Retrieved April 20, 2023, from https://www.nytimes.com/2019/07/03/opinion/hong-kong-protest.html

52. Ip, R. (2019, July 5). "Hong Kong is a Work in Progress." *The New York Times*. Retrieved April 20, 2023, from https://www.nytimes.com/2019/07/05/opinion/hong-kong-protests-china-one-country-two-systems.html

53. Lian, Y.-Zheng. (2019, August 21). "The People's War Is Coming in Hong Kong." *The New York Times*. Retrieved April 20, 2023, from https://www.nytimes.com/2019/08/21/opinion/hong-kong-protest.html

54. Gettleman, J., Raj, S., Schultz, K., & Kumar, H. (2019, August 5). "India Revokes Kashmir's Special Status, Raising Fears of Unrest." *The New York Times*. Retrieved April 21, 2023, from https://www.nytimes.com/2019/08/05/world/asia/india-pakistan-kashmir-jammu.html

55. The Editorial Board. (2019, August 6). "India Tempts Fate in Kashmir, 'the Most Dangerous Place in the World.'" *The New York Times*. Retrieved April 21, 2023, from https://www.nytimes.com/2019/08/05/opinion/kashmir-article-370.html

56. Gettleman, J., Schultz, K., Kumar, H., & Raj, S. (2019, August 6). "In Kashmir Move, Critics Say, Modi is Trying to Make India a Hindu Nation." *The New York Times*. Retrieved April 21, 2023, from https://www.nytimes.com/2019/08/06/world/asia/jammu-kashmir-india.html

57. Schultz, K., Raj, S., & Masood, S. (2019, August 7). "Pakistan Hits Back at India Over Kashmir Move, Targeting Bilateral Trade." *The New York Times*. Retrieved April 21, 2023,

from https://www.nytimes.com/2019/08/07/world/asia/
pakistan-kashmir-india.html

58. Yasir, S., Raj, S., & Gettleman, J. (2019, August 10). "Inside Kashmir, Cut Off from the World: 'A Living Hell' of Anger and Fear." *The New York Times*. Retrieved April 21, 2023, from https://www.nytimes.com/2019/08/10/world/asia/kashmir-india-pakistan.html

59. Yasir, S., & Gettleman, J. (2019, August 12). "With Pens, Paper and Motorcycles, Journalists Chronicle Kashmir Crackdown." *The New York Times*. Retrieved April 21, 2023, from https://www.nytimes.com/2019/08/12/world/asia/kashmir-crackdown-newspapers.html

60. Yasir, S., Raj, S., & Gettleman, J. (2019, August 10). "Inside Kashmir, Cut Off from the World: 'A Living Hell' of Anger and Fear." *The New York Times*. Retrieved April 21, 2023, from https://www.nytimes.com/2019/08/10/world/asia/kashmir-india-pakistan.html

61. Yasir, S., & Gettleman, J. (2019, August 12). "With Pens, Paper and Motorcycles, Journalists Chronicle Kashmir Crackdown." *The New York Times*. Retrieved April 21, 2023, from https://www.nytimes.com/2019/08/12/world/asia/kashmir-crackdown-newspapers.html

62. Schultz, K., & Raj, S. (2019, August 16). "India Says It Will Ease Restrictions in Kashmir." *The New York Times*. Retrieved April 21, 2023, from https://www.nytimes.com/2019/08/16/world/asia/kashmir-india.html

63. Special Correspondent. (2020, June 8). "2G Mobile Internet Services Restored in J&K." *Hindu*. Retrieved April 21, 2023, from https://www.thehindu.com/news/national/2g-mobile-internet-restored-in-kashmir-from-midnight/article30650005.ece

64. Singh, K.D., Khan, A., Collier, N., & Laffin, B. (2019, August 23). "What's Happening in Kashmir? Our Cameras

Contradict India's Official Story." *The New York Times.* Retrieved April 21, 2023, from https://www.nytimes. com/video/world/asia/100000006676350/kashmir-india-article370.html

65. Gettleman, J., Schultz, K., Yasir, S., & Raj, S. (2019, August 23). "India's Move in Kashmir: More Than 2,000 Rounded Up With No Recourse." *The New York Times.* Retrieved April 21, 2023, from https://www.nytimes.com/2019/08/23/ world/asia/kashmir-arrests-india.html

66. Schultz, K., Raj, S., & Masood, S. (2019, August 7). "Pakistan Hits Back at India Over Kashmir Move, Targeting Bilateral Trade." *The New York Times.* Retrieved April 21, 2023, from https://www.nytimes.com/2019/08/07/world/asia/ pakistan-kashmir-india.html

67. Gladstone, R. (2019, August 12). "Pakistan's Envoy Suggests Kashmir Crisis Could Affect Afghan Peace Talks." *The New York Times.* Retrieved April 21, 2023, from https://www. nytimes.com/2019/08/12/world/asia/pakistan-afghanistan-taliban-kashmir.html

68. Gettleman, J., & Raj, S. (2019, September 4). "Teenager Dies in Kashmir Amid Protests After Autonomy Was Revoked." *The New York Times.* Retrieved April 21, 2023, from https:// www.nytimes.com/2019/09/04/world/asia/kashmir-protest-death.html

69. Raj, S., & Gettleman, J. (2019, September 15). "Abused by Soldiers and Militants, Kashmiris Face Dangers in Daily Life." *The New York Times.* Retrieved April 21, 2023, from https://www.nytimes.com/2019/09/15/world/asia/kashmir-india-militants.html

70. Abi-Habib, M., Mughal, J., & Masood, S. (2019, September 19). "In Pakistan-Held Kashmir, Growing Calls for Independence." *The New York Times.* Retrieved April 21, 2023, from https://www.nytimes.com/2019/09/19/world/ asia/pakistan-kashmir-independence.html

71. Loke, A., & Gettleman, J. (2019, September 30). "In Kashmir, Growing Anger and Misery." *The New York Times*. Retrieved April 21, 2023, from https://www.nytimes.com/2019/09/30/world/asia/Kashmir-lockdown-photos.html

72. Venkataraman, A., & Gettleman, J. (2019, September 20). "As Narendra Modi Heads to U.S., Controversy Follows Him." *The New York Times*. Retrieved April 21, 2023, from https://www.nytimes.com/2019/09/20/world/asia/narendra-modi-bill-gates-foundation.html

73. Gladstone, R., & Virella, K. (2019, September 27). "Imran Khan Warns of Kashmir 'Blood Bath' in Emotional U.N. Speech." *The New York Times*. Retrieved April 21, 2023, from https://www.nytimes.com/2019/09/27/world/asia/khan-modi-united-nations.html

74. Yasir, S., & Gettleman, J. (2019, October 7). "In Kashmir, a Race Against Death, with No Way to Call a Doctor." *The New York Times*. Retrieved April 21, 2023, from https://www.nytimes.com/2019/10/07/world/asia/kashmir-doctors-phone.html

75. Yasir, S. (2019, October 12). "India Vows to Restore Mobile Service in Kashmir." *The New York Times*. Retrieved April 21, 2023, from https://www.nytimes.com/2019/10/12/world/asia/india-kashmir-cellphones.html

76. Yasir, S. (2019, October 14). "Cell Service Returns to Kashmir, Allowing First Calls in Months." *The New York Times*. Retrieved April 21, 2023, from https://www.nytimes.com/2019/10/14/business/kashmir-cellphone-service-restored.html

77. Yasir, S., & Gettleman, J. (2019, October 15). "As Militants Kill in Kashmir, People Are Afraid to Go to Work." *The New York Times*. Retrieved April 21, 2023, from https://www.nytimes.com/2019/10/15/world/asia/kashmir-militants.html

78. Schultz, K., & Yasir, S. (2019, October 30). "Militants Kill 5 Laborers in Kashmir, Expanding Threat to Civilians." *The New York Times*. Retrieved April 21, 2023, from

https://www.nytimes.com/2019/10/30/world/asia/kashmir-militants-civilians.html

79. Abi-habib, M. (2019, October 29). "India Finally Lets Lawmakers into Kashmir: Far-Right Europeans." *The New York Times.* Retrieved April 21, 2023, from https://www.nytimes.com/2019/10/29/world/asia/india-kashmir-european.html

80. Yasir, S., & Gettleman, J. (2019, October 31). "Anxious and Cooped Up, 1.5 million Kashmiri Children Are Still Out of School." *The New York Times.* Retrieved April 21, 2023, from https://www.nytimes.com/2019/10/31/world/asia/kashmir-school-children.html

81. The Editorial Board. (2019, August 6). "India Tempts Fate in Kashmir, 'the Most Dangerous Place in the World.'" *The New York Times.* Retrieved April 21, 2023, from https://www.nytimes.com/2019/08/05/opinion/kashmir-article-370.html

82. The Editorial Board. (2019, October 2). "The U.N. Can't Ignore Kashmir Anymore." *The New York Times.* Retrieved April 21, 2023, from https://www.nytimes.com/2019/10/02/opinion/editorials/kashmir-india-pakistan-un.html

83. Mattoo, P. (2019, September 12). "We Never Moved Back to Kashmir, Because We Couldn't." *The New York Times.* Retrieved April 21, 2023, from https://www.nytimes.com/2019/09/12/opinion/we-never-moved-back-to-kashmir-because-we-couldnt.html

84. Shringla, H.V. (2019, September 19). "India Is Building a More Prosperous Kashmir." *The New York Times.* Retrieved April 21, 2023, from https://www.nytimes.com/2019/09/19/opinion/india-pakistan-kashmir-jammu.html

85. Kumar, R., & Lacy, A. (2020, March 16). "India Lobbies to Stifle Criticism, Control Messaging in U.S. Congress Amid Rising Anti-Muslim Violence." *Intercept.* Retrieved

April 21, 2023, from https://theintercept.com/2020/03/16/india-lobbying-us-congress/

86. Bradnock, R.W., & Schofield, R. (2010). *Kashmir: Paths to Peace*. London: Chatham House.

87. Chung, T.-Y., Pang, K.-L., Lee, W.-Y., & Tai, C.-F. (2019, December 27). "Survey on Hong Kong People's Views Regarding the Anti-Extradition Bill Movement (Round 1)." *Hong Kong Public Opinion Research Institute*. Retrieved April 21, 2023, from https://www.pori.hk/wp-content/uploads/2021/01/reuters_anti_elab_round1_ENG_v3_pori.pdf

88. Chung, T.-Y., Pang, K.-L., Lee, W.-Y., & Tai, C.-F. (2019, December 27). "Survey on Hong Kong People's Views Regarding the Anti-Extradition Bill Movement (Round 1)." *Hong Kong Public Opinion Research Institute*. Retrieved April 21, 2023, from https://www.pori.hk/wp-content/uploads/2021/01/reuters_anti_elab_round1_ENG_v3_pori.pdf

89. Masood, B. (2015, October 11). "Art 370 Permanent … Cannot Be Repealed or Amended: HC." *Indian Express*. Retrieved April 21, 2023, from https://indianexpress.com/article/india/india-news-india/j-k-high-court-says-article-370-is-permanent-cant-be-abrogated-repealed-or-amended/

90. BBC. (2019, June 17). "Hong Kong Protest: 'Nearly Two Million' Join Demonstration." *BBC News*. Retrieved April 21, 2023, from https://www.bbc.com/news/world-asia-china-48656471

91. Ghoshal, D., & Bukhari, F. (2019, August 9). "Thousands Protest in Indian Kashmir Over New Status Despite Clampdown." *Reuters*. Retrieved April 21, 2023, from https://www.reuters.com/article/india-kashmir-370-idINKCN1UZ0OO

92. Al Jazeera. (2019, August 28). "Kashmir Saw 500 Protests, Hundreds Injured in Three Weeks: Report." *Al Jazeera.* Retrieved April 21, 2023, from https://www.aljazeera.com/news/2019/8/28/kashmir-saw-500-protests-hundreds-injured-in-three-weeks-report

93. Gettleman, J., Raj, S., Schultz, K., & Kumar, H. (2019, August 5). "India Revokes Kashmir's Special Status, Raising Fears of Unrest." *The New York Times.* Retrieved April 21, 2023, from https://www.nytimes.com/2019/08/05/world/asia/india-pakistan-kashmir-jammu.html

94. Al Jazeera. (2019, August 28). "Kashmir Saw 500 Protests, Hundreds Injured in Three Weeks: Report." *Al Jazeera.* Retrieved April 21, 2023, from https://www.aljazeera.com/news/2019/8/28/kashmir-saw-500-protests-hundreds-injured-in-three-weeks-report

95. Marlow, I., Li, F., & Tan, S. (2019, July 25). "Hong Kong Police Deny Permit for Saturday Protest after Attacks." *Bloomberg.com.* Retrieved April 21, 2023, from https://www.bloomberg.com/news/articles/2019-07-25/hong-kong-police-deny-permit-for-saturday-protest-after-violence?leadSource=uverify+wall

96. Frayer, L. (2019, September 9). "With Kashmir Lockdown, India Violates Freedom of the Press, Advocates Say." *NPR.* Retrieved April 21, 2023, from https://www.npr.org/2019/09/09/759157602/kashmiri-journalists-find-creative-workarounds-to-media-blackout

97. Schultz, K., & Raj, S. (2019, August 16). "India Says It Will Ease Restrictions in Kashmir." *The New York Times.* Retrieved April 21, 2023, from https://www.nytimes.com/2019/08/16/world/asia/kashmir-india.html

98. Yasir, S. (2019, October 12). "India Vows to Restore Mobile Service in Kashmir." *The New York Times.* Retrieved April 21, 2023, from https://www.nytimes.com/2019/10/12/world/asia/india-kashmir-cellphones.html

99. Wong, B. (2021, January 9). "Hong Kong Protests: Open Verdict on Death of Student in Car Park Fall." *South China Morning Post.* Retrieved April 21, 2023, from https://web. archive.org/web/20210216105750/https://www.scmp.com/ news/hong-kong/law-and-crime/article/3117071/hong-kong-protests-open-verdict-recorded-death-student

100. Wang, J. (2020, April 22). "Hong Kong Charges Teens with Murder Tied to Protests." *The Wall Street Journal.* Retrieved April 21, 2023, from https://www.wsj.com/ articles/hong-kong-charges-teens-with-murder-tied-to-protests-11587562477

101. Wong, B. (2020, July 9). "Man Set on Fire in Hong Kong Protests Says He Was Standing Up for Justice." *South China Morning Post.* Retrieved April 21, 2023, from https://www.scmp.com/news/hong-kong/law-and-crime/ article/3092549/hong-kong-protests-man-set-fire-says-he-was-standing

102. Jammu Kashmir Coalition of Civil Society, & Association of Parents of Disappeared Persons. (2019, December 31). *Annual Human Rights Review 2019: A Review of Human Rights Situation in Jammu and Kashmir.* Jammu Kashmir Coalition of Civil Society. Retrieved April 21, 2023, from https:// kashmirscholars.files.wordpress.com/2019/12/jkccs-2019-human-rights-report.pdf

103. Sidiq, N. (2019, December 31). "69 Deaths in Kashmir Since Aug. 5, Rights Group Says." *Anadolu Ajansı.* Retrieved April 22, 2023, from https://www.aa.com.tr/en/asia-pacific/69-deaths-in-kashmir-since-aug-5-rights-group-says/1688788

104. Ramzy, A., & Mullany, G. (2019, August 12). "Over 150 Flights Canceled as Hong Kong Airport is Flooded by Protesters." *The New York Times.* Retrieved April 22, 2023, from https://www.nytimes.com/2019/08/12/world/asia/ hong-kong-airport-protest-cancellations.html

105. Myers, S.L., & Mozur, P. (2019, August 13). "China is Waging a Disinformation War Against Hong Kong Protesters." *The New York Times*. Retrieved April 22, 2023, from https://www.nytimes.com/2019/08/13/world/asia/hong-kong-protests-china.html

106. Ives, M., Cheung, E., & Chen, E. (2019, August 13). "Chaos Grips Hong Kong's Airport as Police Clash with Protesters." *The New York Times*. Retrieved April 22, 2023, from https://www.nytimes.com/2019/08/12/world/asia/hong-kong-airport-protest.html

107. Ramzy, A., & Zhong, R. (2019, August 18). "Hong Kong Protesters Defy Police Ban in Show of Strength After Tumult." *The New York Times*. Retrieved April 22, 2023, from https://www.nytimes.com/2019/08/18/world/asia/hong-kong-protest.html

108. Brooks, D. (2019, August 27). "The One United Struggle for Freedom." *The New York Times*. Retrieved April 22, 2023, from https://www.nytimes.com/2019/08/26/opinion/hong-kong-protest.html

109. Leung, K. (2021, June 4). "Hong Kong Protester at Centre of Eye-Injury Case Revealed to Have Left for Taiwan." *South China Morning Post*. Retrieved April 22, 2023, from https://www.scmp.com/news/hong-kong/politics/article/3134828/hong-kong-protests-controversial-woman-centre-eye-injury

110. Hernández, J.C. (2019, June 19). "With Hymns and Prayers, Christians Help Drive Hong Kong's Protests." *The New York Times*. Retrieved April 22, 2023, from https://www.nytimes.com/2019/06/19/world/asia/hong-kong-extradition-protests-christians.html

111. The New York Times. (2019, June 20). "A Protest Song in Hong Kong." *The New York Times*. Retrieved April 22, 2023, from https://www.nytimes.com/video/world/

asia/100000006569070/hong-kong-extradition-protests-christians-video.html

112. Bradsher, K., Victor, D., & Ives, M. (2019, June 26). "Why Hong Kong's Protesters Are Turning to G-20 Leaders for Help." *The New York Times*. Retrieved April 22, 2023, from https://www.nytimes.com/2019/06/26/world/asia/hong-kong-protests.html

113. Victor, D., Qin, A., & May, T. (2019, July 5). "What Denise Ho, Jackie Chan and Others Think About the Hong Kong Protests." *The New York Times*. Retrieved April 22, 2023, from https://www.nytimes.com/2019/07/05/world/asia/denise-ho-hong-kong-protests.html

114. Qin, A. (2019, July 7). "Hong Kong Protesters Take Their Message to Chinese Tourists." *The New York Times*. Retrieved April 22, 2023, from https://www.nytimes.com/2019/07/07/world/asia/hong-kong-protests-chinese-tourists.html

115. Ives, M., & Li, K. (2019, July 14). "Hong Kong Protesters' New Target: A News Station Seen as China's Friend." *The New York Times*. Retrieved April 22, 2023, from https://www.nytimes.com/2019/07/14/world/asia/hong-kong-protests-tvb.html

116. May, T. (2019, August 2). "Hong Kong's Civil Servants Protest Their Own Government." *The New York Times*. Retrieved April 22, 2023, from https://www.nytimes.com/2019/08/02/world/asia/hong-kong-civil-servants-protest.html

117. Li, K., & Ives, M. (2019, August 2). "Fueling the Hong Kong Protests: A World of Pop-Culture Memes." *The New York Times*. Retrieved April 22, 2023, from https://www.nytimes.com/2019/08/02/world/asia/hong-kong-protests-memes.html

118. Victor, D. (2019, August 19). "Hong Kong Protesters Love Pepe the Frog. No, They're Not Alt-Right." *The New York*

Times. Retrieved April 22, 2023, from https://www.nytimes.com/2019/08/19/world/asia/hong-kong-protest-pepe-frog.html

119. Wu, J., Singhvi, A., & Kao, J. (2019, June 21). "A Bird's-Eye View of How Protesters Have Flooded Hong Kong Streets." *The New York Times*. Retrieved April 22, 2023, from https://www.nytimes.com/interactive/2019/06/20/world/asia/hong-kong-protest-size.html

120. Rebecca, K.K. (2019, June 28). "Protesters in Hong Kong Have Changed Their Playbook. Here's How." *The New York Times*. Retrieved April 22, 2023, from https://www.nytimes.com/interactive/2019/06/28/world/asia/hong-kong-protests.html

121. Rebecca, K.K. (2019, July 3). "How A.I. Helped Improve Crowd Counting in Hong Kong Protests." *The New York Times*. Retrieved April 22, 2023, from https://www.nytimes.com/interactive/2019/07/03/world/asia/hong-kong-protest-crowd-ai.html

122. Marcolini, B., Willis, H., Hernández, J.C., May, T., Chen, E., Jordan, D., & O'Neill, S. (2019, July 14). "Did Hong Kong Police Use Violence Against Protesters? What the Videos Show." *The New York Times*. Retrieved April 22, 2023, from https://www.nytimes.com/video/world/asia/100000006602584/hong-kong-police-protest-video-investigation.html

123. Yasir, S., Raj, S., & Gettleman, J. (2019, August 10). "Inside Kashmir, Cut Off From the World: 'A Living Hell' of Anger and Fear." *The New York Times*. Retrieved April 22, 2023, from https://www.nytimes.com/2019/08/10/world/asia/kashmir-india-pakistan.html

124. Goel, V., Singh, K.D., & Yasir, S. (2019, August 14). "India Shut Down Kashmir's Internet Access. Now, 'We Cannot Do Anything.'" *The New York Times*. Retrieved April 22, 2023,

from https://www.nytimes.com/2019/08/14/technology/india-kashmir-internet.html

125. Gettleman, J., Schultz, K., Yasir, S., & Raj, S. (2019, August 23). "India's Move in Kashmir: More Than 2,000 Rounded Up With No Recourse." *The New York Times*. Retrieved April 22, 2023, from https://www.nytimes.com/2019/08/23/world/asia/kashmir-arrests-india.html

126. Raj, S., & Gettleman, J. (2019, September 15). "Abused by Soldiers and Militants, Kashmiris Face Dangers in Daily Life." *The New York Times*. Retrieved April 22, 2023, from https://www.nytimes.com/2019/09/15/world/asia/kashmir-india-militants.html

127. Loke, A., & Gettleman, J. (2019, September 30). "In Kashmir, Growing Anger and Misery." *The New York Times*. Retrieved April 22, 2023, from https://www.nytimes.com/2019/09/30/world/asia/Kashmir-lockdown-photos.html

128. The New York Times. (2019, June 13). "Police Violence Puts Hong Kong Government on Defensive." *The New York Times*. Retrieved April 22, 2023, from https://www.nytimes.com/2019/06/12/world/asia/hong-kong-protests.html

129. The New York Times. (2019, June 13). "Video of Police Response in Hong Kong Stirs Outrage." *The New York Times*. Retrieved April 22, 2023, from https://www.nytimes.com/video/world/asia/100000006556470/police-violence-hong-kong.html?searchResultPosition=72

130. Ives, M., & Stevenson, A. (2019, June 13). "Hong Kong Police Face Criticism Over Force Used at Protests." *The New York Times*. Retrieved April 22, 2023, from https://www.nytimes.com/2019/06/13/world/asia/hong-kong-extradition.html

131. Ives, M. (2019, June 24). "Hong Kong Police, Once Called 'Asia's Finest,' Are Now a Focus of Anger." *The New York Times*. Retrieved April 22, 2023, from https://www.nytimes.com/2019/06/24/world/asia/hong-kong-police-protest.html

132. Marcolini, B., Willis, H., Hernández, J.C., May, T., Chen, E., Jordan, D., & O'Neill, S. (2019, July 14). "Did Hong Kong Police Use Violence Against Protesters? What the Videos Show." *The New York Times*. Retrieved April 22, 2023, from https://www.nytimes.com/video/world/asia/100000006602584/hong-kong-police-protest-video-investigation.html

133. Leung, C. (2021, June 29). "Hong Kong Police Seize Explosive Substances and Weapons, Arrest Two." *South China Morning Post*. Retrieved April 22, 2023, from https://www.scmp.com/news/hong-kong/law-and-crime/article/3139218/explosive-substances-weapons-seized-hong-kong-police

134. Ghoshal, D., & Pal, A. (2019, September 12). "Thousands Detained in Indian Kashmir Crackdown, Official Data Reveals." *Reuters*. Retrieved April 22, 2023, from https://www.reuters.com/article/us-india-kashmir-detentions/thousands-detained-in-indian-kashmir-crackdown-official-data-reveals-idUSKCN1VX142

135. Mahtani, S., & Shih, G. (2019, August 30). "Hong Kong Intensifies Crackdowns with Arrests of Pro-Democracy Leaders." *Washington Post*. Retrieved April 22, 2023, from https://www.washingtonpost.com/world/student-leader-joshua-wong-arrested-in-hong-kong/2019/08/29/9d35e1fc-ca98-11e9-9615-8f1a32962e04_story.html

136. Deutsche Welle. (2019, August 30). "Hong Kong Release Activists on Bail." *DW.com*. Retrieved April 22, 2023, from https://www.dw.com/en/hong-kong-democracy-activist-joshua-wong-released-on-bail-after-arrest/a-50223068

137. Leung, C., & Lau, C. (2019, October 21). "Call for Special Hong Kong Court to Fast-Track Protesters' Cases." *South China Morning Post*. Retrieved April 22, 2023, from https://www.scmp.com/news/hong-kong/law-and-crime/

article/3033775/hong-kong-protests-growing-number-repeat-arrests

138. Ghoshal, D., & Pal, A. (2019, September 12). "Thousands Detained in Indian Kashmir Crackdown, Official Data Reveals." *Reuters*. Retrieved April 22, 2023, from https://www.reuters.com/article/us-india-kashmir-detentions/thousands-detained-in-indian-kashmir-crackdown-official-data-reveals-idUSKCN1VX142

139. The New York Times. (2019, June 13). "Police Violence Puts Hong Kong Government on Defensive." *The New York Times*. Retrieved April 22, 2023, from https://www.nytimes.com/2019/06/12/world/asia/hong-kong-protests.html

140. Ives, M., & Li, K. (2019, June 19). "Hong Kong Official Defends Police's Use of Force Against Protesters." *The New York Times*. Retrieved April 22, 2023, from https://www.nytimes.com/2019/06/19/world/asia/hong-kong-protests.html

141. Hernández, J.C., Marcolini, B., Willis, H., Jordan, D., Felling, M., May, T., & Chen, E. (2019, June 30). "Did Hong Kong Police Abuse Protesters? What Videos Show." *The New York Times*. Retrieved April 22, 2023, from https://www.nytimes.com/2019/06/30/world/asia/did-hong-kong-police-abuse-protesters-what-videos-show.html

142. Victor, D. (2019, August 15). "Trump Says 'Hong Kong Is Not Helping' in Trade War with China." *The New York Times*. Retrieved April 22, 2023, from https://www.nytimes.com/2019/08/15/world/asia/donald-trump-hong-kong.html

143. The New York Times. (2019, June 13). "Police Violence Puts Hong Kong Government on Defensive." *The New York Times*. Retrieved April 22, 2023, from https://www.nytimes.com/2019/06/12/world/asia/hong-kong-protests.html

144. Victor, D. (2019, August 15). "Trump Says 'Hong Kong Is Not Helping' in Trade War with China." *The New York*

Times. Retrieved April 22, 2023, from https://www.nytimes. com/2019/08/15/world/asia/donald-trump-hong-kong. html

145. Victor, D., & Li, K. (2019, August 20). "Hong Kong Police Officers Arrested Over Beating of Man in Hospital." *The New York Times.* Retrieved April 22, 2023, from https:// www.nytimes.com/2019/08/20/world/asia/hong-kong-police-arrested-beating.html

146. Victor, D. (2019, August 15). "Trump Says 'Hong Kong Is Not Helping' in Trade War with China." *The New York Times.* Retrieved April 22, 2023, from https://www.nytimes. com/2019/08/15/world/asia/donald-trump-hong-kong. html

147. Gettleman, J., Schultz, K., Venkataraman, A., & Yasir, S. (2019, May 23). "India Election Gives Modi a 2nd Term. Here Are 5 Takeaways." *The New York Times.* Retrieved April 22, 2023, from https://www.nytimes.com/2019/05/23/ world/asia/india-election-narendra-modi.html

148. Yasir, S. (2019, May 24). "Violent Protests Erupt in Kashmir After Indian Forces Kill Militant." *The New York Times.* Retrieved April 22, 2023, from https://www.nytimes. com/2019/05/24/world/asia/kashmir-militant-protests. html

149. Mattoo, P. (2019, September 12). "We Never Moved Back to Kashmir, Because We Couldn't." *The New York Times.* Retrieved April 22, 2023, from https://www.nytimes. com/2019/09/12/opinion/we-never-moved-back-to-kashmir-because-we-couldnt.html

150. National Endowment for Democracy. (ND). "Hong Kong (China) 2019." *National Endowment for Democracy.* Retrieved April 22, 2023, from https://web.archive.org/ web/20200608213548/https://www.ned.org/region/asia/ hong-kong-china-2019/

151. Lamb, K. (2019, August 27). "Why is the National Endowment for Democracy Fueling the Hong Kong protests?" *CGTN*. Retrieved April 22, 2023, from https://news.cgtn.com/news/2019-08-27/Why-is-the-NED-fueling-the-Hong-Kong-protests--JtMb2yKKWc/index.html

Chapter 3. Worthy and Unworthy Protests in South America: 2019 Venezuelan Protests, 2019–2020 Bolivian Protests, and 2019–2021 Colombian Protests

1. Biden, J. (2022, January 20). "Remarks by President Biden in Press Conference." *The White House*. Retrieved April 22, 2023, from https://www.whitehouse.gov/briefing-room/speeches-remarks/2022/01/19/remarks-by-president-biden-in-press-conference-6/

2. Forero, J. (2004, December 3). "Documents Show C.I.A. Knew of a Coup Plot in Venezuela." *The New York Times*. Retrieved April 22, 2023, from https://www.nytimes.com/2004/12/03/washington/world/documents-show-cia-knew-of-a-coup-plot-in-venezuela.html

3. Borger, J., & Bellos, A. (2002, April 17). "US 'Gave the Nod' To Venezuelan Coup." *Guardian*. Retrieved April 22, 2023, from https://www.theguardian.com/world/2002/apr/17/usa.venezuela

4. Campbell, D. (2002, April 29). "American Navy 'Helped Venezuelan Coup.'" *Guardian*. Retrieved April 22, 2023, from https://www.theguardian.com/world/2002/apr/29/venezuela.duncancampbell

5. Vulliamy, E. (2002, April 21). "Venezuela Coup Linked To Bush Team." *Guardian*. Retrieved April 22, 2023, from https://www.theguardian.com/world/2002/apr/21/usa.venezuela

6. WOLA. (ND). *15th Anniversary of Plan Colombia: Learning From Its Successes and Failures*. "U.S. Aid to Colombia."

WOLA. Retrieved April 22, 2023, from https://www.wola.org/files/1602_plancol/content.php?id=us_aid

7. Specia, M. (2019, January 4). "Envoys Denounce Venezuela's Maduro and Urge Him To Cede Power." *The New York Times*. Retrieved April 22, 2023, from https://www.nytimes.com/2019/01/04/world/americas/diplomats-venezuela-maduro.html

8. Herrero, A.V., & Specia, M. (2019, January 10). "Venezuela is in Crisis. So How Did Maduro Secure a Second Term?" *The New York Times*. Retrieved April 22, 2023, from https://www.nytimes.com/2019/01/10/world/americas/venezuela-maduro-inauguration.html

9. The New York Times. (2019, January 24). "The Crisis in Venezuela Was Years in the Making. Here's How It Happened." *The New York Times*. Retrieved April 22, 2023, from https://www.nytimes.com/2019/01/23/world/americas/venezuela-news-noticias.html

10. Pozzebon, S., & Hu, C. (2021, February 13). "US-Led Sanctions on Venezuela 'Devastating' to Human Rights, Says UN Report." *CNN*. Retrieved April 22, 2023, from https://edition.cnn.com/2021/02/12/world/us-venezuela-sanctions-alina-douhan-intl/index.html

11. Herrero, A.V. (2019, January 13). "Venezuela Opposition Leader is Arrested after Proposing to Take Power." *The New York Times*. Retrieved April 22, 2023, from https://www.nytimes.com/2019/01/13/world/americas/venezeula-juan-guaido-arrest.html

12. Herrero, A.V., & Londoño, E. (2019, January 15). "Venezuela Opposition Declares Maduro Illegitimate, and Urges Defections." *The New York Times*. Retrieved April 23, 2023, from https://www.nytimes.com/2019/01/15/world/americas/guaido-maduro-venezuela.html

13. Wong, E. (2019, January 22). "Pence Tells Venezuelans that U.S. Backs Efforts To Oust Maduro." *The New York Times*. Retrieved April 23, 2023, from https://www.nytimes.com/2019/01/22/world/americas/venezuela-usa-nicolas-maduro.html

14. Herrero, A.V. (2019, January 23). "After U.S. Backs Juan Guaidó as Venezuela's Leader, Maduro Cuts Ties." *The New York Times*. Retrieved April 23, 2023, from https://www.nytimes.com/2019/01/23/world/americas/venezuela-protests-guaido-maduro.html

15. The Associated Press. (2019, January 23). "Venezuela Opposition Leader Swears Himself in as Interim President." *The New York Times*. Retrieved April 23, 2023, from https://www.nytimes.com/video/world/americas/100000006322287/venezuela-opposition-leader-swears-himself-in-as-president.html

16. The Associated Press. (2019, January 24). "Pompeo to O.A.S. Members: Recognize Guaidó as Venezuela's New President." *The New York Times*. Retrieved April 23, 2023, from https://www.nytimes.com/video/world/americas/100000006324044/pompeo-venezuela-guaido.html

17. Semple, K. (2019, January 25). "Echoes of the Past in Venezuela Crisis, But Heard More Lightly." *The New York Times*. Retrieved April 23, 2023, from https://www.nytimes.com/2019/01/24/world/americas/venezuela-latin-america.html

18. Herrero, A.V., & Macfarquhar, N. (2019, January 24). "Russia Warns U.S. Not to Intervene in Venezuela as Military Backs Maduro." *The New York Times*. Retrieved April 23, 2023, from https://www.nytimes.com/2019/01/24/world/americas/venezuela-news-maduro-russia.html

19. Baker, P., & Wong, E. (2019, January 24). "Intervening Against Venezuela's Strongman, Trump Belies 'America first.'" *The New York Times*. Retrieved April 23, 2023, from https://www.nytimes.com/2019/01/24/world/americas/donald-trump-venezuela.html

20. Reuters. (2019, January 24). "Venezuela Defense Minister: 'A Coup is Taking Place.'" *The New York Times*. Retrieved April 23, 2023, from https://www.nytimes.com/video/world/americas/100000006324867/venezuela-defense-minister-coup.html

21. Herrero, A.V. (2019, January 21). "Venezuela Detains National Guard Members Accused of Turning on Maduro." *The New York Times*. Retrieved April 23, 2023, from https://www.nytimes.com/2019/01/21/world/americas/venezuela-maduro-national-guard.html

22. Fisher, M. (2019, January 24). "A Short, Simple Primer on What's Happening in Venezuela." *The New York Times*. Retrieved April 24, 2023, from https://www.nytimes.com/2019/01/24/world/americas/noticias-venezuela-protests-maduro-guaido.html

23. Tabrizy, N., & Tiefenthäler, A. (2019, January 25). "Two Leaders. Two Messages. Inside the Battle for Venezuela." *The New York Times*. Retrieved April 24, 2023, from https://www.nytimes.com/video/world/americas/100000006324144/two-leaders-two-messages-inside-the-battle-for-venezuela.html

24. Baker, P., & Wong, E. (2019, January 26). "On Venezuela, Rubio Assumes U.S. Role of Ouster in Chief." *The New York Times*. Retrieved April 24, 2023, from https://www.nytimes.com/2019/01/26/world/americas/marco-rubio-venezuela.html

25. Wong, E., & Casey, N. (2019, January 28). "U.S. Targets Venezuela with Tough Oil Sanctions During Crisis of Power." *The New York Times*. Retrieved April 24, 2023,

from https://www.nytimes.com/2019/01/28/us/politics/ venezuela-sanctions-trump-oil.html

26. The New York Times. (2019, January 29). "The U.S. Role in Venezuela's Turmoil." *The New York Times*. Retrieved April 24, 2023, from https://www.nytimes.com/2019/01/29/ opinion/letters/us-venezuela.html

27. Wong, E. (2019, January 29). "Venezuelan Opposition Leader Guaidó Controls U.S. Bank Accounts, State Dept. Says." *The New York Times*. Retrieved April 24, 2023, from https://www.nytimes.com/2019/01/29/us/politics/ venezuela-bank-accounts-guaido-pompeo.html

28. Herrero, A.V., & Krauss, C. (2019, January 30). "Opposition Leader, and Oil, Become Focus of Venezuela-U.S. Struggle." *The New York Times*. Retrieved April 24, 2023, from https:// www.nytimes.com/2019/01/29/world/americas/venezuela-juan-guaido-oil-assets.html

29. Casey, N. (2019, January 26). "Within Venezuelan Military Ranks, a Struggle Over What Leader to Back." *The New York Times*. Retrieved April 24, 2023, from https://www. nytimes.com/2019/01/25/world/americas/venezuela-military-maduro.html

30. Semple, K. (2019, January 26). "With Spies and Other Operatives, a Nation Looms Over Venezuela's Crisis: Cuba." *The New York Times*. Retrieved April 24, 2023, from https://www.nytimes.com/2019/01/26/world/americas/ venezuela-cuba-oil.html

31. The Associated Press. (2019, January 28). "'All Options Are on the Table' in Venezuela, Says Bolton." *The New York Times*. Retrieved April 24, 2023, from https://www. nytimes.com/video/world/americas/100000006330127/ bolton-trump-venezuela-sanctions.html

32. Herrero, A.V., & Ramzy, A. (2019, January 30). "Maduro Sounds Conciliatory But Warns: U.S. Intervention Would

Be Worse Than Vietnam." *The New York Times*. Retrieved April 26, 2023, from https://www.nytimes.com/2019/01/30/world/americas/maduro-venezuela-talks-opposition.html

33. The New York Times. (2019, February 1). "How is Venezuela's Political Crisis Affecting You?" *The New York Times*. Retrieved April 26, 2023, from https://www.nytimes.com/2019/02/01/reader-center/how-is-venezuelas-political-crisis-affecting-you.html

34. The New York Times. (2019, February 1). "How is Venezuela's Political Crisis Affecting You?" *The New York Times*. Retrieved April 26, 2023, from https://www.nytimes.com/2019/02/01/reader-center/how-is-venezuelas-political-crisis-affecting-you.html

35. Herrero, A.V., & Specia, M. (2019, February 1). "Venezuela Voices: 'We Are Starving Here.'" *The New York Times*. Retrieved April 26, 2023, from https://www.nytimes.com/2019/02/01/world/americas/venezuela-voices-protests.html

36. Oliveros, L. (2020, October). "The Impact of Financial and Oil Sanctions on the Venezuelan Economy." *WOLA*. Retrieved April 26, 2023, from https://www.wola.org/wp-content/uploads/2020/10/Oliveros-report-summary-ENG.pdf

37. Londoño, E. (2019, February 4). "Guaidó Steers Venezuela to a Perilous Crossroads." *The New York Times*. Retrieved April 26, 2023, from https://www.nytimes.com/2019/02/03/world/americas/guaido-venezuela-maduro.html

38. Kurmanaev, A., & Krauss, C. (2019, February 8). "U.S. Sanctions are Aimed at Venezuela's Oil. Its Citizens May Suffer First." *The New York Times*. Retrieved April 26, 2023, from https://www.nytimes.com/2019/02/08/world/americas/venezuela-sanctions-maduro.html

39. Herrero, A.V., & Casey, N. (2019, February 2). "Venezuelans Opposed to Maduro Pour into Streets for Day of Protests." *The New York Times*. Retrieved April 26, 2023, from https://

www.nytimes.com/2019/02/02/world/americas/venezuela-protests-opposition-maduro.html

40. Marcolini, B., Tabrizy, N., López, M.A., & Reneau, N. (2019, February 8). "Some Venezuelans Have Turned on Maduro, and Paid with Their Lives." *The New York Times*. Retrieved April 26, 2023, from https://www.nytimes.com/video/world/americas/100000006331824/maduro-venezuela-poor-protests.html

41. Wong, E., & Casey, N. (2019, February 1). "Venezuela's Dueling Diplomats Lobby Nations to Pick Sides in Conflict." *The New York Times*. Retrieved April 26, 2023, from https://www.nytimes.com/2019/02/01/world/americas/venezuela-maduro-guaido-diplomats.html

42. Herrero, A.V. (2019, February 4). "In Fight for Venezuela, Who Supports Maduro and Who Backs Guaidó?" *The New York Times*. Retrieved April 26, 2023, from https://www.nytimes.com/2019/02/04/world/americas/venezuela-support-maduro-guaido.html

43. Pérez-Peña, R. (2019, February 4). "European Countries Recognize Guaidó as Venezuela's Leader, Joining U.S." *The New York Times*. Retrieved April 26, 2023, from https://www.nytimes.com/2019/02/04/world/americas/venezuela-juan-guaido.html

44. Gladstone, R. (2019, February 15). "Venezuela's Top Diplomat Enlists Support from Dozens of Nations to Counter U.S." *The New York Times*. Retrieved April 26, 2023, from https://www.nytimes.com/2019/02/14/world/americas/venezuela-united-nations-support.html

45. Fisher, M. (2019, February 5). "Who is Venezuela's Legitimate President? A Messy Dispute, Explained." *The New York Times*. Retrieved April 26, 2023, from https://www.nytimes.com/2019/02/04/world/americas/venezuela-maduro-guaido-legitimate.html

46. Horowitz, J. (2019, February 5). "Pope Francis Says He's Willing to Mediate in Venezuela if Both Sides Want." *The New York Times*. Retrieved April 26, 2023, from https://www.nytimes.com/2019/02/05/world/europe/pope-francis-abu-dhabi-maduro.html

47. Kurmanaev, A., Herrero, A.V., & Londoño, E. (2019, February 5). "Venezuela's Opposition Plans to Deliver Aid, Undermining Maduro." *The New York Times*. Retrieved April 26, 2023, from https://www.nytimes.com/2019/02/05/world/americas/venezuela-humanitarian-aid.html

48. The Editorial Board. (2019, February 5). "Venezuela's Crisis Spreads Beyond Its Borders." *The New York Times*. Retrieved April 26, 2023, from https://www.nytimes.com/2019/02/05/opinion/venezuela-maduro-guaido-trump.html

49. The Editorial Board. (2019, February 20). "Venezuela's Border Standoff." *The New York Times*. Retrieved April 26, 2023, from https://www.nytimes.com/2019/02/19/opinion/venezuela-border-maduro-trump.html

50. Casey, N., & Kurmanaev, A. (2019, February 13). "Humanitarian Aid Stalls, Testing Venezuela's Opposition." *The New York Times*. Retrieved April 26, 2023, from https://www.nytimes.com/2019/02/13/world/americas/aid-to-venezuela.html

51. Casey, N. (2019, February 20). "Venezuela Closes Border to 3 Caribbean Islands Ahead of Aid Showdown." *The New York Times*. Retrieved April 26, 2023, from https://www.nytimes.com/2019/02/20/world/americas/venezuela-borders-aid.html

52. Casey, N. (2019, February 21). "Maduro Closes Venezuela's Border with Brazil to Block Aid." *The New York Times*. Retrieved April 26, 2023, from https://www.nytimes.com/2019/02/21/world/americas/venezuela-aid-block-brazil.html

53. Marcolini, B., Koettl, C., & Botti, D. (2019, February 22). "How a Border Bridge Became a Flashpoint in Venezuela's Crisis." *The New York Times*. Retrieved April 26, 2023, from https://www.nytimes.com/video/world/americas/100000006360134/venezuela-border-bridge-guaido-maduro.html

54. Londoño, E. (2019, February 16). "U.S. Military Starts Flying Aid for Venezuela to Colombia." *The New York Times*. Retrieved April 26, 2023, from https://www.nytimes.com/2019/02/16/world/americas/venezuela-aid-us-airforce.html

55. Karni, A., Casey, N., & Kurmanaev, A. (2019, February 18). "Trump Delivers Blunt Warning to Venezuela Military Over Aid Impasse." *The New York Times*. Retrieved April 26, 2023, from https://www.nytimes.com/2019/02/18/world/americas/venezuela-guaido-maduro-trump.html

56. McDonald, B., Rhyne, E., & De Guzman, O. (2019, February 20). "Maduro is Denying Venezuelans U.S. Aid. His Opposition Sees an Opportunity." *The New York Times*. Retrieved April 26, 2023, from https://www.nytimes.com/video/world/100000006353977/maduro-venezuela-us-aid-colombia.html

57. Casey, N., & McDonald, B. (2019, February 26). "Desertions Reflect Discontent with Maduro, But Not Enough to Topple Him." *The New York Times*. Retrieved April 26, 2023, from https://www.nytimes.com/2019/02/26/world/americas/venezuela-defectors.html

58. Casey, N., Kurmanaev, A., & Londoño, E. (2019, February 22). "At Venezuela's Border, a Strange and Deadly Showdown Over Aid." *The New York Times*. Retrieved April 26, 2023, from https://www.nytimes.com/2019/02/22/world/americas/brazil-venezuela-border-shooting.html

59. Casey, N., Linares, A., & Kurmanaev, A. (2019, February 23). "Some Aid from Brazil Pierces Venezuela's Blockade,

But Deadly Violence Erupts." *The New York Times*. Retrieved April 26, 2023, from https://www.nytimes.com/2019/02/23/world/americas/venezuela-aid-border-maduro.html

60. The New York Times. (2019, February 23). "As Venezuela Aid Standoff Turns Deadly, Maduro Severs Ties with Colombia." *The New York Times*. Retrieved April 26, 2023, from https://www.nytimes.com/2019/02/23/world/americas/venezuela-aid-live.html

61. Tiefenthäler, A. (2019, February 23). "Scenes from Venezuela: Violence Erupts at Border." *The New York Times*. Retrieved April 26, 2023, from https://www.nytimes.com/video/world/americas/100000006376314/venezuela-aid-news.html

62. Casey, N., & Linares, A. (2019, February 25). "With Aid Blocked at Border, What's Next Move for Venezuela's Opposition?" *The New York Times*. Retrieved April 26, 2023, from https://www.nytimes.com/2019/02/24/world/americas/venezuela-aid-maduro-guaido.html

63. Collier, N., De Guzman, O., & Laffin, B. (2019, February 25). "Venezuela Crisis: Hope and Aid Blocked at Border." *The New York Times*. Retrieved April 26, 2023, from https://www.nytimes.com/video/world/americas/100000006332149/hope-thwarted-along-with-aid-at-venezuelas-border.html

64. Casey, N. (2019, February 26). "The Venezuela Battle Border." *The New York Times*. Retrieved April 26, 2023, from https://www.nytimes.com/2019/02/25/world/americas/venezuela-border-photos.html

65. Casey, N., & González, J.C. (2019, February 20). "A Staggering Exodus: Millions of Venezuelans are Leaving the Country, on Foot." *The New York Times*. Retrieved April 26, 2023, from https://www.nytimes.com/2019/02/20/world/americas/venezuela-refugees-colombia.html

66. Kurmanaev, A., & Herrera, I. (2019, February 22). "As Venezuela's Politicians Fight Over Aid, Patients Die Without It." *The New York Times*. Retrieved April 26, 2023, from https://www.nytimes.com/2019/02/22/world/americas/venezuela-patients-hospital.html

67. Rogers, K. (2019, February 25). "Pence, in Colombia to Meet Guaidó, Announces New Venezuela Sanctions." *The New York Times*. Retrieved April 26, 2023, from https://www.nytimes.com/2019/02/25/world/americas/pence-guaido-venezuela-colombia.html

68. The Associated Press. (2019, February 25). "'We Are with You 100 Percent': Pence Shows Support for Guaidó." *The New York Times*. Retrieved April 26, 2023, from https://www.nytimes.com/video/world/americas/100000006379210/pence-guaido-venezuala.html

69. Gladstone, R. (2019, February 27). "Cold War-Style Accusations Fly as Security Council Meets on Venezuela." *The New York Times*. Retrieved April 26, 2023, from https://www.nytimes.com/2019/02/26/world/americas/venezuela-security-council-abrams.html

70. Gladstone, R. (2019, February 27). "U.S. Urges New Venezuela Elections. One Obstacle: Russia." *The New York Times*. Retrieved April 26, 2023, from https://www.nytimes.com/2019/02/27/world/americas/venezuela-russia-security-council.html

71. Schwirtz, M. (2019, March 1). "Russia Blocks Venezuela Measure at U.N., Calling It a U.S. Ploy for Regime Change." *The New York Times*. Retrieved April 26, 2023, from https://www.nytimes.com/2019/02/28/world/americas/russia-venezuela-veto-united-nations.html

72. Rogers, K. (2019, March 1). "U.S. Issues New Penalties Against Venezuelan Officials, Vowing 'Maduro Must Go.'" *The New York Times*. Retrieved April 26, 2023, from https://

www.nytimes.com/2019/03/01/world/americas/venezuela-
sanctions-white-house.html

73. Casey, N. (2019, February 26). "Jorge Ramos, Univision
Anchor, Said He was Detained by Venezuelan Government."
The New York Times. Retrieved April 26, 2023, from https://
www.nytimes.com/2019/02/25/world/americas/jorge-
ramos-venezuela-maduro.html

74. Ramos, J. (2019, February 27). "Jorge Ramos: The Dictator of
Venezuela Earns His Title." *The New York Times*. Retrieved
April 26, 2023, from https://www.nytimes.com/2019/02/27/
opinion/jorge-ramos-venezuela.html

75. The Editorial Board. (2019, March 4). "Venezuela's Hunger
Games." *The New York Times*. Retrieved April 26, 2023, from
https://www.nytimes.com/2019/03/03/opinion/venezuela-
maduro-guaido.html

76. Herrero, A.V., Casey, N., & Rogers, K. (2019, March 4).
"Juan Guaidó Returns to Venezuela, Facing Threat of
Arrest." *The New York Times*. Retrieved April 26, 2023, from
https://www.nytimes.com/2019/03/04/world/americas/
juan-guaido-venezuela.html

77. The Associated Press. (2019, March 4). "Guaidó Returns
to Venezuela." *The New York Times*. Retrieved April 26,
2023, from https://www.nytimes.com/video/world/
americas/100000006392885/guaido-venezuela.html

78. Corrales, J. (2019, March 4). "How to Tackle Venezuela's
Military Problem." *The New York Times*. Retrieved April 26,
2023, from https://www.nytimes.com/2019/03/04/opinion/
venezuela-military-maduro-guaido.html

79. Yuhas, A. (2019, March 8). "As Blackout Plunges Venezuela
in Darkness, Maduro Blames the U.S." *The New York Times*.
Retrieved April 26, 2023, from https://www.nytimes.
com/2019/03/07/world/americas/venezuela-power-outage-
blackout-apagon.html

80. Kurmanaev, A., Herrera, I., & Krauss, C. (2019, March 8). "Venezuela Blackout, in 2nd Day, Threatens Food Supplies and Patient Lives." *The New York Times*. Retrieved April 26, 2023, from https://www.nytimes.com/2019/03/08/world/americas/venezuela-blackout-power.html

81. Kurmanaev, A., & Herrera, I. (2019, March 9). "Power Still Flickering, Venezuelans Take to Streets to Protest." *The New York Times*. Retrieved April 27, 2023, from https://www.nytimes.com/2019/03/09/world/americas/venezuela-power-protests.html

82. Kurmanaev, A., & Herrera, I. (2019, March 11). "No End in Sight to Venezuela's Blackout, Experts Warn." *The New York Times*. Retrieved April 27, 2023, from https://www.nytimes.com/2019/03/11/world/americas/venzuela-blackout-maduro.html

83. Sanger, D.E., Kurmanaev, A., & Herrera, I. (2019, March 12). "Pompeo Accuses Cuba and Russia of Propping Up Venezuelan Ruler." *The New York Times*. Retrieved April 27, 2023, from https://www.nytimes.com/2019/03/11/us/politics/us-venezuela-pompeo.html

84. Casey, N. (2019, March 17). "'It is Unspeakable': How Maduro Used Cuban Doctors to Coerce Venezuela Voters." *The New York Times*. Retrieved April 27, 2023, from https://www.nytimes.com/2019/03/17/world/americas/venezuela-cuban-doctors.html

85. Jones, J., & Guy, J. (2019, March 12). "The Struggle to Live Through Venezuela's Blackouts." *CNN*. Retrieved April 27, 2023, from https://www.cnn.com/2019/03/12/americas/venezuela-struggle-power-intl/index.html

86. Rogers, K. (2019, March 14). "Trump Administration Warns Venezuela Not to Arrest Opposition Leader." *The New York Times*. Retrieved April 27, 2023, from

https://www.nytimes.com/2019/03/14/world/americas/
trump-venezuela-warning.html

87. Kurmanaev, A. (2019, March 21). "Venezuela Crisis Escalates as Guaidó's Chief of Staff is Arrested." *The New York Times*. Retrieved April 27, 2023, from https://www. nytimes.com/2019/03/21/world/americas/guaido-Roberto-Marrero.html

88. Casey, N. (2019, March 22). "Maduro Digs In. It's an Old Strategy, But It May Work." *The New York Times*. Retrieved May 1, 2023, from https://www.nytimes.com/2019/03/22/world/americas/maduro-guaido-venezuela.html

89. The New York Times. (2019, March 22). "How Maduro Keeps Power in Venezuela, Even with the Lights Out." *The New York Times*. Retrieved May 1, 2023, from https://www. nytimes.com/2019/03/22/video/the-dispatch-venezuela-blackout.html

90. Kurmanaev, A. (2019, March 25). "2 Russian Military Planes Land in Venezuela, Exacerbating Political Tension." *The New York Times*. Retrieved May 1, 2023, from https:// www.nytimes.com/2019/03/25/world/americas/russian-planes-caracas.html

91. Rogers, K. (2019, March 28). "Trump Warns Russia to 'Get Out' of Venezuela." *The New York Times*. Retrieved May 1, 2023, from https://www.nytimes.com/2019/03/27/us/politics/trump-russia-venezuela.html

92. C-SPAN. (2019, March 28). "Russia 'Has to Get Out' of Venezuela, Trump Says." *The New York Times*. Retrieved May 1, 2023, from https://www.nytimes.com/video/us/politics/100000006433602/trump-venezuela-russia.html

93. Schwirtz, M. (2019, March 27). "U.N. Appeals to Maduro and Guaidó to End Battle Over Humanitarian Aid." *The New York Times*. Retrieved May 1, 2023, from https:// www.nytimes.com/2019/03/27/world/americas/venezuela-united-nations.html

References

94. Kurmanaev, A., & Herrera, I. (2019, March 29). "Red Cross Granted Access to Deliver Aid in Venezuela." *The New York Times*. Retrieved May 1, 2023, from https://www.nytimes.com/2019/03/29/world/americas/red-cross-venezuela-aid.html

95. Kurmanaev, A., & Ramírez, M. (2019, March 30). "As Venezuelan Economy Unravels, Maduro Opponents Hope Downturn Will Topple Him." *The New York Times*. Retrieved May 1, 2023, from https://www.nytimes.com/2019/03/30/world/americas/venezuelan-economy-maduro.html

96. Rodríguez, F. (2019, July 10). "Trump Doesn't Have Time for Starving Venezuelans." *The New York Times*. Retrieved May 1, 2023, from https://www.nytimes.com/2019/07/10/opinion/venezuela-sanctions.html

97. Robles, F., & Jordan, M. (2019, January 25). "Venezuelans Living in America Watch Crisis Back Home with Hope and Caution." *The New York Times*. Retrieved May 1, 2023, from https://www.nytimes.com/2019/01/24/us/venezuelans-florida-noticias-news.html

98. Mazzei, P. (2019, February 10). "'Dangerous Territory' for Democrats as Republicans Seize Venezuela Moment in Miami." *The New York Times*. Retrieved May 1, 2023, from https://www.nytimes.com/2019/02/10/us/venezuelans-miami-republicans.html

99. Karni, A., & Mazzei, P. (2019, February 19). "Trump, in Miami, Attacks Maduro, and Some See Bid for Florida Votes." *The New York Times*. Retrieved May 1, 2023, from https://www.nytimes.com/2019/02/18/world/americas/trump-maduro-miami-speech.html

100. Stephens, B. (2019, January 26). "Yes, Venezuela is a Socialist Catastrophe." *The New York Times*. Retrieved May 1, 2023, from https://www.nytimes.com/2019/01/25/opinion/venezuela-maduro-socialism-government.html

101. The New York Times. (2019, February 4). "Is Venezuela Failing Because of Socialism?" *The New York Times*. Retrieved

May 1, 2023, from https://www.nytimes.com/2019/02/04/opinion/letters/venezuela-socialism.html

102. Krugman, P. (2019, January 29). "The Venezuela Calumny." *The New York Times*. Retrieved May 1, 2023, from https://www.nytimes.com/2019/01/29/opinion/the-venezuela-calumny.html

103. The New York Times. (2019, January 24). "'The Venezuelan People Are Feeling Hopeful.'" *The New York Times*. Retrieved May 1, 2023, from https://www.nytimes.com/2019/01/24/opinion/letters/venezuela-united-states-maduro-guaido.html

104. Shifter, M. (2019, January 24). "Can Venezuela Have a Peaceful Transition?" *The New York Times*. Retrieved May 1, 2023, from https://www.nytimes.com/2019/01/24/opinion/venezuela-guaido-maduro.html

105. The Editorial Board. (2019, January 25). "Venezuela: Between Maduro and a Hard Place." *The New York Times*. Retrieved May 1, 2023, from https://www.nytimes.com/2019/01/24/opinion/venezuela-maduro-trump.html

106. Iber, P. (2019, January 31). "The U.S. Needs to Stay Out of Venezuela." *The New York Times*. Retrieved May 1, 2023, from https://www.nytimes.com/2019/01/31/opinion/us-intervention-venezuela.html

107. Velasco, A. (2019, February 5). "A Geopolitical Showdown in Venezuela Will Only Make Things Worse." *The New York Times*. Retrieved May 1, 2023, from https://www.nytimes.com/2019/02/05/opinion/venezuela-guaido-trump-united-states.html

108. Castañeda, J.G. (2019, February 6). "The U.S. Can Help Solve the Venezuelan Crisis By Not Being a Bully." *The New York Times*. Retrieved May 1, 2023, from https://www.nytimes.com/2019/02/06/opinion/venezuelan-maduro-guaido.html

109. González, F. (2019, February 14). "Felipe González: We Must Not Fail the Venezuelan People." *The New York Times*. Retrieved May 1, 2023, from https://www.nytimes.com/2019/02/14/opinion/felipe-gonzalez-venezuelan.html

110. Duarte, E. (2019, February 2). "Venezuela's Very Normal Revolution." *The New York Times*. Retrieved May 1, 2023, from https://www.nytimes.com/2019/02/02/opinion/sunday/venezuela-guaido-protests.html

111. Albertus, M. (2019, January 30). "Venezuela's Best Path to Democracy? Pay Off the Military." *The New York Times*. Retrieved May 1, 2023, from https://www.nytimes.com/2019/01/30/opinion/venezuela-military-guaido-maduro.html

112. Specia, M., & Casey, N. (2019, January 31). "Juan Guaidó Says Venezuelan Opposition Had Secret Talks with Military." *The New York Times*. Retrieved May 1, 2023, from https://www.nytimes.com/2019/01/31/world/americas/venezuelan-juan-guaido-military.html

113. Guaidó, J. (2019, January 31). "Juan Guaidó: Venezuelans, Strength is in Unity." *The New York Times*. Retrieved May 1, 2023, from https://www.nytimes.com/2019/01/30/opinion/juan-guaido-venezuela.html

114. Kronick, D. (2019, February 28). "A Backup Plan is Needed to Prevent Venezuelan Famine." *The New York Times*. Retrieved May 1, 2023, from https://www.nytimes.com/2019/02/28/opinion/venezuela-maduro-famine.html

115. Koettl, C., Acosta, D., Jordan, D., & Singhvi, A. (2019, March 10). "The U.S. Blamed Maduro for Burning Aid to Venezuela. New Video Casts Doubt." *The New York Times*. Retrieved May 1, 2023, from https://www.nytimes.com/video/world/americas/100000006385986/the-us-blamed-maduro-for-burning-aid-to-venezuela-new-video-casts-doubt.html

116. Casey, N., Koettl, C., & Acosta, D. (2019, March 10). "Footage Contradicts U.S. Claim that Nicolás Maduro Burned Aid Convoy." *The New York Times*. Retrieved May 1, 2023, from https://www.nytimes.com/2019/03/10/world/americas/venezuela-aid-fire-video.html

117. Londoño, E. (2019, October 20). "Bolivia's Evo Morales Faces Runoff, Early Election Returns Show." *The New York Times*. https://www.nytimes.com/2019/10/20/world/americas/bolivia-election-evo-morales.html

118. Londoño, E. (2019, October 21). "President Accused of Fraud in Bolivia Election as He Opens Big Vote Lead." *The New York Times*. https://www.nytimes.com/2019/10/21/world/americas/Bolivia-election-vote-count.html

119. Londoño, E. (2019, October 23). "'There Could Be a War': Protests Over Elections Roil Bolivia." *The New York Times*. https://www.nytimes.com/2019/10/23/world/americas/boliva-election-protests.html

120. Londoño, E. (2019, October 25). "Morales Averts Runoff in Bolivia, Officials Say, But Anger and Doubt Remain." *The New York Times*. https://www.nytimes.com/2019/10/25/world/americas/bolivia-election-president-evo-morales.html

121. Machicao, M., & Londoño, E. (2019, October 31). "Bolivia's Democracy Faces Pivotal Test as Unrest Spreads." *The New York Times*. https://www.nytimes.com/2019/10/31/world/americas/bolivia-election-protests.html

122. Machicao, M., & Semple, K. (2019, November 8). "Bolivian Mayor Assaulted by Protesters in Postelection Mayhem." *The New York Times*. https://www.nytimes.com/2019/11/07/world/americas/bolivia-mayor-protest-paint.html

123. Kurmanaev, A., Londoño, E., & Machicao, M. (2019, November 9). "Bolivian Leader Clings to Power as Police Join Protesters." *The New York Times*. https://www.nytimes.com/2019/11/09/world/americas/bolivian-police-morales.html

124. Kurmanaev, A., Machicao, M., & Londoño, E. (2019, November 10). "Military Calls on President to Step Down After Election Dispute in Bolivia." *The New York Times*. https://www.nytimes.com/2019/11/10/world/americas/bolivia-election-evo-morales.html

125. Reuters. (2019, November 10). "Watch: President Evo Morales of Bolivia Resigns." *The New York Times*. https://www.nytimes.com/video/world/americas/100000006817420/watch-bolivian-president-evo-morales-resigns.html

126. Londoño, E. (2019, November 10). "Bolivian Leader Evo Morales Steps Down." *The New York Times*. https://www.nytimes.com/2019/11/10/world/americas/evo-morales-bolivia.html

127. Kurmanaev, A., Londoño, E., & Machicao, M. (2019, November 9). "Bolivian Leader Clings to Power as Police Join Protesters." *The New York Times*. https://www.nytimes.com/2019/11/09/world/americas/bolivian-police-morales.html

128. Krauss, C. (2019, November 11). "Evo Morales of Bolivia Accepts Asylum in Mexico." *The New York Times*. https://www.nytimes.com/2019/11/11/world/americas/bolivia-evo-morales.html

129. Castañeda, J.G. (2019, November 11). "Latin Americans are Clamoring for Equality—and Democracy." *The New York Times*. https://www.nytimes.com/2019/11/11/opinion/bolivia-evo-morales.html

130. The Editorial Board. (2019, November 12). "Evo Morales is Gone. Bolivia's Problems Aren't." *The New York Times*. https://www.nytimes.com/2019/11/11/opinion/evo-morales-bolivia.html

131. Krauss, C. (2019, November 12). "'I Assume the Presidency': Bolivia Lawmaker Declares Herself Leader." *The New York Times*. https://www.nytimes.com/2019/11/12/world/americas/evo-morales-mexico-bolivia.html

132. Fisher, M. (2019, November 12). "Bolivia Crisis Shows the Blurry Line Between Coup and Uprising." *The New York Times*. Retrieved May 4, 2023, from https://www.nytimes.com/2019/11/12/world/americas/bolivia-evo-morales-coup.html

133. Krauss, C. (2019, November 13). "Bolivia's Interim Leader Pledges to 'Reconstruct Democracy.'" *The New York Times*. Retrieved May 4, 2023, from https://www.nytimes.com/2019/11/13/world/americas/bolivia-morales-news.html

134. Corrales, J. (2019, November 15). "From Bolivia, Sad Lessons on How to Fix Semi-Democracies." *The New York Times*. Retrieved May 4, 2023, from https://www.nytimes.com/2019/11/15/opinion/bolivia-morales.html

135. Kurmanaev, A., & Krauss, C. (2019, November 15). "Ethnic Rifts in Bolivia Burst into View with Fall of Evo Morales." *The New York Times*. Retrieved May 4, 2023, from https://www.nytimes.com/2019/11/15/world/americas/morales-bolivia-Indigenous-racism.html

136. Kurmanaev, A., & Krauss, C. (2019, November 15). "Ethnic Rifts in Bolivia Burst into View with Fall of Evo Morales." *The New York Times*. Retrieved May 4, 2023, from https://www.nytimes.com/2019/11/15/world/americas/morales-bolivia-Indigenous-racism.html

137. Kurmanaev, A. (2019, November 16). "In Bolivia, Interim Leader Sets Conservative, Religious Tone." *The New York Times*. Retrieved May 4, 2023, from https://www.nytimes.com/2019/11/16/world/americas/bolivia-anez-morales.html

138. Kurmanaev, A., & Malkin, E. (2019, November 20). "As Violence Grips Bolivia, Congress Moves Toward New Elections." *The New York Times*. Retrieved May 4, 2023, from

https://www.nytimes.com/2019/11/20/world/americas/bolivia-deaths-sentaka.html

139. Malkin, E., & Cantú, E. (2019, November 23). "Evo Morales Raises a Fist, But Knows His Presidency is Over." *The New York Times.* Retrieved May 4, 2023, from https://www.nytimes.com/2019/11/23/world/americas/evo-morales-mexico.html

140. Kurmanaev, A., & Castillo, C.D. (2019, November 24). "How an Unknown Female Senator Came to Replace the Bolivian President Evo Morales." *The New York Times.* Retrieved May 4, 2023, from https://www.nytimes.com/2019/11/24/world/americas/how-an-unknown-female-senator-came-to-replace-the-bolivian-president-evo-morales.html

141. Kurmanaev, A., & Rios, F. (2019, November 27). "'Evo Morales is Like a Father to Us.'" *The New York Times.* Retrieved May 4, 2023, from https://www.nytimes.com/2019/11/27/world/americas/evo-morales-bolivia-coca.html

142. Kurmanaev, A. (2019, December 5). "Election Fraud Aided Evo Morales, International Panel Concludes." *The New York Times.* Retrieved May 4, 2023, from https://www.nytimes.com/2019/12/05/world/americas/evo-morales-election.html

143. Turkewitz, J. (2020, February 29). "M.I.T. Researchers Cast Doubt on Bolivian Election Fraud." *The New York Times.* Retrieved May 4, 2023, from https://www.nytimes.com/2020/02/28/world/americas/bolivia-election-fraud.html

144. The Editorial Board. (2019, December 10). "Restore Bolivian Democracy and Break Its History of Coups." *The New York Times.* Retrieved May 4, 2023, from https://www.nytimes.com/2019/12/09/opinion/evo-morales-bolivia.html

145. Kurmanaev, A., & Minder, R. (2019, December 30). "Bolivia Expels 3 Diplomats in Tiff with Mexico and Spain Over Morales Aides." *The New York Times*. Retrieved May 4, 2023, from https://www.nytimes.com/2019/12/30/world/americas/bolivia-mexico-spain-diplomats.html

146. Trigo, M.S., & Kurmanaev, A. (2020, August 7). "Bolivia Under Blockade as Protesters Choke Access to Cities." *The New York Times*. Retrieved May 4, 2023, from https://www.nytimes.com/2020/08/07/world/americas/bolivia-roadblock-blockade.html

147. Trigo, M.S., Kurmanaev, A., & McCann, A. (2020, August 22). "As Politicians Clashed, Bolivia's Pandemic Death Rate Soared." *The New York Times*. Retrieved May 4, 2023, from https://www.nytimes.com/2020/08/22/world/americas/virus-bolivia.html

148. von Vacano, D. (2020, September 9). "The Best Answer to Chaos in Bolivia is Socialism." *The New York Times*. Retrieved May 4, 2023, from https://www.nytimes.com/2020/09/09/opinion/contributors/bolivia-socialism-arce-elections-morales.html

149. Turkewitz, J. (2020, October 18). "In Election, Bolivia Confronts Legacy of Ousted Socialist Leader." *The New York Times*. Retrieved May 4, 2023, from https://www.nytimes.com/2020/10/18/world/americas/bolivia-election-evo-morales.html

150. Kurmanaev, A. (2020, September 18). "Bolivia's Interim President Pulls Out of Election." *The New York Times*. Retrieved May 4, 2023, from https://www.nytimes.com/2020/09/17/world/americas/bolivia-jeanine-anez.html

151. Turkewitz, J. (2020, October 19). "Evo Morales is Out. His Socialist Project Lives On." *The New York Times*. Retrieved May 4, 2023, from https://www.nytimes.com/2020/10/19/world/americas/morales-arce-bolivia-election.html

152. Turkewitz, J. (2020, October 23). "How Bolivia Overcame a Crisis and Held a Clean Election." *The New York Times*. Retrieved May 4, 2023, from https://www.nytimes.com/2020/10/23/world/americas/boliva-election-result.html

153. O'Boyle, B. (2020, October 27). "The Lesson from Bolivia for Latin American Politics." *The New York Times*. Retrieved May 4, 2023, from https://www.nytimes.com/2020/10/27/opinion/bolivia-election-arce-morales.html

154. Yuhas, A. (2019, November 27). "Death of Colombian Teenager Drives Protesters Back to Streets." *The New York Times*. Retrieved May 4, 2023, from https://www.nytimes.com/2019/11/26/world/americas/colombia-protests.html

155. Barbara, V. (2019, December 26). "Why Are Brazilian Streets So Calm?" *The New York Times*. Retrieved May 4, 2023, from https://www.nytimes.com/2019/12/26/opinion/latin-america-protests-brazil.html

156. Londoño, E., & Casado, L. (2019, December 28). "'The Pendulum Has Swung Back': Latin America's Corruption Fight Stalls." *The New York Times*. Retrieved May 4, 2023, from https://www.nytimes.com/2019/12/28/world/americas/latin-america-corruption.html

157. Turkewitz, J. (2020, September 10). "Violent Protests Erupt in Colombia After a Man Dies in Police Custody." *The New York Times*. Retrieved May 4, 2023, from https://www.nytimes.com/2020/09/10/world/americas/colombia-javier-ordonez-police.html

158. Turkewitz, J. (2020, September 10). "Violent Protests Erupt in Colombia After a Man Dies in Police Custody." *The New York Times*. Retrieved May 4, 2023, from https://www.nytimes.com/2020/09/10/world/americas/colombia-javier-ordonez-police.html

159. Turkewitz, J. (2020, September 13). "Colombia Sees Surge in Mass Killings Despite Historic Peace Deal." *The New York*

Times. Retrieved May 4, 2023, from https://www.nytimes.
com/2020/09/13/world/americas/colombia-massacres-
protests.html

160. Turkewitz, J., & Villamil, S. (2020, October 24). "Indigenous
Colombians, Facing New Wave of Brutality, Demand
Government Action." *The New York Times*. Retrieved
May 4, 2023, from https://www.nytimes.com/2020/10/24/
world/americas/colombia-violence-indigenous-protest.
html

161. Turkewitz, J. (2021, May 3). "Colombia Backs Off Pandemic
Tax Overhaul After Deadly Protests." *The New York Times*.
Retrieved May 4, 2023, from https://www.nytimes.
com/2021/05/03/world/colombia-backs-off-pandemic-tax-
overhaul-after-deadly-protests.html

162. The Associated Press. (2021, May 3). "Protests Prompt
Colombia to Abandon Tax Overhaul." *The New York Times*.
Retrieved May 4, 2023, from https://www.nytimes.com/
video/world/americas/100000007743240/colombia-tax-
protest.html

163. The Associated Press and Reuters. (2021, May 6). "Protests
Continue in Colombia." *The New York Times*. Retrieved
May 4, 2023, from https://www.nytimes.com/video/world/
americas/100000007748095/colombia-crisis-protest.html

164. Turkewitz, J., & Villamil, S. (2021, May 5). "Colombia Police
Respond to Protests with Bullets, and Death Toll Mounts."
The New York Times. Retrieved May 4, 2023, from https://
www.nytimes.com/2021/05/05/world/americas/colombia-
covid-protests-cali.html

165. Turkewitz, J., & Villamil, S. (2021, May 12). "Colombia's
Police Force, Built for War, Finds a New One." *The New York
Times*. Retrieved May 4, 2023, from https://www.nytimes.
com/2021/05/12/world/americas/colombia-protests-police-
brutality.html

166. Proulx, N. (2021, May 11). "Lesson of the Day: 'Colombia Police Respond to Protests with Bullets, and Death Toll Mounts.'" *The New York Times*. Retrieved May 4, 2023, from https://www.nytimes.com/2021/05/11/learning/lesson-of-the-day-colombia-police-respond-to-protests-with-bullets-and-death-toll-mounts.html

167. Isacson, A. (2021, May 12). "Colombia is in Turmoil. Biden Must Push It Toward Dialogue." *The New York Times*. Retrieved May 4, 2023, from https://www.nytimes.com/2021/05/12/opinion/international-world/colombia-protests-biden.html

168. Turkewitz, J. (2021, May 18). "Why are Colombians Protesting?" *The New York Times*. Retrieved May 4, 2023, from https://www.nytimes.com/2021/05/18/world/americas/colombia-protests-what-to-know.html

169. Cooper, S., Tabrizy, N., Triebert, C., McDonald, B., Laffin, B., Olmos, S., & Ismay, J. (2021, May 27). "Videos Show the Violent, and Deadly, Ways Colombian Police Quell Protests." *The New York Times*. Retrieved May 4, 2023, from https://www.nytimes.com/2021/05/27/video/colombia-protests-cali-police-video.html

170. Vigdor, N. (2021, June 22). "The Virus is Ravaging Colombia, Where the Death Toll Surpassed 100,000." *The New York Times*. Retrieved May 4, 2023, from https://www.nytimes.com/2021/06/21/world/colombia-covid-coronavirus-deaths-100000.html

171. Turkewitz, J. (2021, June 25). "Colombia's President is Shot at in Helicopter But Survives Attack." *The New York Times*. Retrieved May 4, 2023, from https://www.nytimes.com/2021/06/25/world/americas/colombia-ivan-duque-helicopter-attack.html

172. Jakes, L. (2021, July 12). "Latin America Unrest Forces Biden to Confront Challenges to Democracy Close to

Home." *The New York Times*. Retrieved May 4, 2023, from https://www.nytimes.com/2021/07/12/us/politics/biden-cuba-haiti-latin-america.html

173. United Nations Office of the Human Rights Commissioner. (2019, July 4). "UN Human Rights Report on Venezuela Urges Immediate Measures to Halt and Remedy Grave Rights Violations." *OHCHR*. Retrieved May 4, 2023, from https://www.ohchr.org/en/press-releases/2019/07/un-human-rights-report-venezuela-urges-immediate-measures-halt-and-remedy

174. Amnesty International. (2021, June 1). "Human Rights in the Americas. Review of 2019." *Amnesty International*. Retrieved May 4, 2023, from https://www.amnesty.org/en/documents/amr01/1353/2020/en/

175. Rampietti, A. (2020, September 12). "Colombia Police Brutality: Protests Rage for Third Day in Bogota." *Al Jazeera*. Retrieved May 4, 2023, from https://www.aljazeera.com/videos/2020/9/12/colombia-police-brutality-protests-rage-for-third-day-in-bogota

176. Toro, M. (2020, September 11). "13 Civiles Muertos y Más de 400 Heridos en dos Días de Protestas en Colombia por la Muerte de Javier Ordóñez." *CNN*. Retrieved May 4, 2023, from https://cnnespanol.cnn.com/2020/09/11/13-civiles-muertos-y-mas-de-400-heridos-en-dos-dias-de-protestas-en-colombia-por-la-muerte-de-javier-ordonez/

177. Human Rights Watch. (2022, January 13). "World Report 2022: Rights Trends in Colombia." *Human Rights Watch*. Retrieved May 4, 2023, from https://www.hrw.org/world-report/2022/country-chapters/colombia

178. La Silla Vacía. (2023, May 1). "Las Ong Son Más Transparentes que la Fiscalía con las Cifras de Muertos en el Paro." *www.lasillavacia.com*. Retrieved May 4, 2023, from https://www.lasillavacia.com/historias/silla-nacional/las-

ong-son-m%c3%a1s-transparentes-que-la-fiscal%c3%ada-con-las-cifras-de-muertos-en-el-paro

179. Internal Displacement Monitoring Centre. (2020, October 30). "The Last Refuge: Urban Displacement in Colombia." *Urban Displacement in Colombia.* Retrieved May 4, 2023, from https://story.internal-displacement.org/colombia-urban/index.html

180. Daniels, J.P. (2019, January 23). "Venezuela Protests: Thousands March as Military Faces Call to Abandon Maduro." *Guardian.* Retrieved May 4, 2023, from https://www.theguardian.com/world/2019/jan/23/venezuela-protests-thousands-march-against-maduro-as-opposition-sees-chance-for-change

181. The Economist Newspaper. (2019, February 2). "The Battle for Venezuela's Future." *Economist.* Retrieved May 4, 2023, from https://www.economist.com/leaders/2019/02/02/the-battle-for-venezuelas-future

182. Daniels, J.P. (2019, November 21). "Clashes in Colombia as Hundreds of Thousands Protest Against Government." *Guardian.* Retrieved May 4, 2023, from https://www.theguardian.com/world/2019/nov/21/colombia-protests-ivan-duque-government

183. Deutsche Welle. (2019, November 22). "Colombia: Clashes as Hundreds of Thousands Protest Govt." *DW.com.* Retrieved May 4, 2023, from https://www.dw.com/en/colombia-anti-government-protesters-clash-with-police/a-51360862

184. BBC News. (2020, September 10). "Colombia Protests: Death of Man Tasered by Police Sparks Deadly Clashes." *BBC News.* Retrieved May 4, 2023, from https://www.bbc.com/news/world-latin-america-54078852

185. Grattan, S. (2021, April 29). "Thousands March in Colombia over Tax Proposals, Rising Insecurity." *Al Jazeera.* Retrieved May 4, 2023, from https://www.aljazeera.com/

news/2021/4/29/thousands-march-in-colombia-over-tax-proposals-rising-insecurity

186. Kurmanaev, A., & Krauss, C. (2019, November 15). "Ethnic Rifts in Bolivia Burst into View with Fall of Evo Morales." *The New York Times*. Retrieved May 4, 2023, from https://www.nytimes.com/2019/11/15/world/americas/morales-bolivia-Indigenous-racism.html

187. CEIC. (2021). "Venezuela Crude Oil: Exports." Venezuela Crude Oil: Exports, 1980–2023. *CEIC*. Retrieved May 4, 2023, from https://www.ceicdata.com/en/indicator/venezuela/crude-oil-exports

188. CEIC. (2021). "Colombia Crude Oil: Exports." Colombia Crude Oil: Exports, 1980–2023. *CEIC*. Retrieved May 4, 2023, from https://www.ceicdata.com/en/indicator/colombia/crude-oil-exports

189. Ramos, D. (2019, February 6). "Bolivia Picks Chinese Partner for $2.3 Billion Lithium Projects." *Reuters*. Retrieved May 4, 2023, from https://www.reuters.com/article/us-bolivia-lithium-china/bolivia-picks-chinese-partner-for-2-3-billion-lithium-projects-idUSKCN1PV2F7

Chapter 4. Worthy and Unworthy Dissidents: Alexei Navalny, Catalan Independence Politicians, Pussy Riot, and Pablo Hasél

1. Gallup. (2023, March 29). "Russia." *Gallup.com*. Retrieved May 4, 2023, from https://news.gallup.com/poll/1642/russia.aspx

2. Herman, E., & Chomsky, N. (1988). "A Propaganda Model." A Propaganda Model, by Noam Chomsky (Excerpted from *Manufacturing Consent*). Retrieved May 4, 2023, from https://chomsky.info/consent01/

3. Saeed, S. (2017, October 17). "Human Rights Court: Kremlin Critic's Conviction 'Arbitrary and Unfair.'" *POLITICO*.

358

Retrieved May 4, 2023, from https://www.politico.eu/article/human-rights-court-kremlin-critics-conviction-arbitrary-and-unfair/

4. Troianovski, A. (2021, January 13). "Aleksei Navalny Says He'll Return to Russia on Sunday." *The New York Times*. Retrieved May 4, 2023, from https://www.nytimes.com/2021/01/13/world/europe/aleksei-navalny-russia-return.html

5. Troianovski, A., & Nechepurenko, I. (2021, January 17). "Navalny Arrested on Return to Moscow in Battle of Wills with Putin." *The New York Times*. Retrieved May 4, 2023, from https://www.nytimes.com/2021/01/17/world/europe/navalny-russia-return.html

6. The Associated Press. (2021, January 17). "Kremlin Critic Navalny Arrested on Arrival in Moscow." *The New York Times*. Retrieved May 4, 2023, from https://www.nytimes.com/video/world/europe/100000007556178/navalny-arrested-moscow.html

7. The Associated Press. (2021, January 19). "Navalny Arrested on Return to Moscow." *The New York Times*. Retrieved May 4, 2023, from https://www.nytimes.com/video/world/europe/100000007557797/aleksei-navalny-arrested-moscow-airport.html

8. The Editorial Board. (2021, January 18). "The Extraordinary Courage of Aleksei Navalny." *The New York Times*. Retrieved May 4, 2023, from https://www.nytimes.com/2021/01/17/opinion/aleksei-navalny-russia.html

9. Troianovski, A., & Nechepurenko, I. (2021, January 18). "Russian Court Orders Aleksei Navalny Held for 30 Days." *The New York Times*. Retrieved May 4, 2023, from https://www.nytimes.com/2021/01/18/world/europe/aleksei-navalny-russia.html

10. Troianovski, A. (2021, January 19). "Navalny, from Jail, Issues Report Describing an Opulent Putin 'Palace.'" *The*

New York Times. Retrieved May 4, 2023, from https://www. nytimes.com/2021/01/19/world/europe/navalny-putin.html

11. Troianovski, A., & Nechepurenko, I. (2021, January 22). "Russia Scrambles to Keep Young People Away from Navalny Protests." *The New York Times*. Retrieved May 4, 2023, from https://www.nytimes.com/2021/01/22/world/europe/russia-navalny-protests.html

12. Troianovski, A., Kramer, A.E., & Higgins, A. (2021, January 23). "In Aleksei Navalny Protests, Russia Faces Biggest Dissent in Years." *The New York Times*. Retrieved May 4, 2023, from https://www.nytimes.com/2021/01/23/world/europe/navalny-protests-russia.html

13. The Associated Press. (2021, January 23). "Tens of Thousands Protest Arrest of Russian Opposition Leader." *The New York Times*. Retrieved May 4, 2023, from https://www.nytimes.com/video/world/europe/100000007567216/russia-navalny-protests.html

14. Troianovski, A., & Higgins, A. (2021, January 23). "Pro-Navalny Protests Sweep Russia in Challenge to Putin." *The New York Times*. Retrieved May 4, 2023, from https://www.nytimes.com/2021/01/23/world/europe/russia-protests-navalny.html

15. Kovalev, A. (2021, January 25). "Something Special Just Happened in Russia." *The New York Times*. Retrieved May 4, 2023, from https://www.nytimes.com/2021/01/25/opinion/aleksei-navalny-russia-protests.html

16. Stephens, B. (2021, January 26). "Dissidents First: A Foreign Policy Doctrine for the Biden Administration." *The New York Times*. Retrieved May 4, 2023, from https://www.nytimes.com/2021/01/25/opinion/navalny-biden-russia.html

17. Troianovski, A. (2021, January 24). "As Protests Shake Russia, Kremlin Drops Its 'Navalny Who?' Tack." *The New*

York Times. Retrieved May 4, 2023, from https://www.nytimes.com/2021/01/24/world/europe/putin-navalny-russia-protests.html

18. Troianovski, A. (2021, January 27). "Navalny Allies and Offices Targeted in Raids as Kremlin Turns Up Pressure." *The New York Times*. https://www.nytimes.com/2021/01/27/world/europe/navalny-raids-russia.html

19. Troianovski, A. (2021, January 30). "As Protests Grip Russia, Putin Critics of Many Stripes Rally Around Navalny." *The New York Times*. https://www.nytimes.com/2021/01/30/world/europe/russia-protests-navalny-putin.html

20. Troianovski, A., Kramer, A.E., Nechepurenko, I., & Higgins, A. (2021, January 31). "Russia Protesters Defy Vast Police Operation as Signs of Kremlin Anxiety Mount." *The New York Times*. https://www.nytimes.com/2021/01/31/world/europe/russia-protests-navalny-live-updates.html

21. Ponomarev, S. (2021, January 31). "In Photos: Crowds of Police Couldn't Quell Russia's Pro-Navalny Protests." *The New York Times*. https://www.nytimes.com/2021/01/31/world/europe/russia-protest-photos.html

22. The Associated Press and Reuters. (2021, January 31). "Navalny Supporters are Met with Heavy Police Force Across Russia." *The New York Times*. https://www.nytimes.com/video/world/europe/100000007580025/navalny-protests-russia.html

23. Kramer, A.E. (2021, February 1). "Severe Punishment Awaits Protesters in Russia, Kremlin Says." *The New York Times*. https://www.nytimes.com/2021/02/01/world/europe/protesters-in-russia-punishment.html

24. Troianovski, A. (2021, February 2). "Russian Activist Navalny Sentenced to More Than 2 Years in Prison." *The New York Times*. https://www.nytimes.com/2021/02/02/world/europe/russia-navalny-putin.html

25. Friedman, T.L. (2021, February 3). "Vladimir Putin Has Become America's Ex-Boyfriend From Hell." *The New York Times*. https://www.nytimes.com/2021/02/02/opinion/vladimir-putin-russia-america.html

26. The Editorial Board. (2021, February 3). "Aleksei Navalny is Resisting Putin, and Winning." *The New York Times*. https://www.nytimes.com/2021/02/02/opinion/navalny-russia-prison-putin.html

27. Navalny, A. (2021, February 4). "Vladimir the Poisoner of Underpants." *The New York Times*. https://www.nytimes.com/2021/02/03/opinion/navalny-putin-speech.html

28. Kramer, A.E. (2021, February 4). "With Her Husband in Prison, Will Yulia Navalnaya Take the lead?" *The New York Times*. https://www.nytimes.com/2021/02/04/world/europe/yulia-navalnaya-navalny-wife.html

29. Troianovski, A. (2021, February 5). "Russia Expels European Diplomats Over Navalny Protests, Defying the West." *The New York Times*. https://www.nytimes.com/2021/02/05/world/europe/aleksei-navalny-russia-court.html

30. Friedman, V., & Safronova, V. (2021, February 9). "Wearing Red Takes on New Meaning in Russia." *The New York Times*. https://www.nytimes.com/2021/02/09/style/aleksei-navalny-red-supporters.html

31. Nechepurenko, I. (2021, February 20). "Russian Court Clears Way to Send Navalny to a Penal Colony." *The New York Times*. https://www.nytimes.com/2021/02/20/world/europe/russia-navalny-prison.html

32. Kramer, A.E. (2021, February 5). "What Awaits Navalny in Russia's Brutal Penal Colony System." *The New York Times*. https://www.nytimes.com/2021/02/05/world/europe/navalny-russia-penal-colony.html

33. Kramer, A.E., & Erlanger, S. (2021, March 1). "'Your Personality Deforms': Navalny Sent to Notoriously

Harsh Prison." *The New York Times*. https://www.nytimes.com/2021/03/01/world/europe/navalny-prison-russia.html

34. Troianovski, A. (2021, March 15). "Navalny Greets Supporters from Prison: 'Our Friendly Concentration Camp.'" *The New York Times*. https://www.nytimes.com/2021/03/15/world/europe/aleksei-navalny-prison-instagram.html

35. Kramer, A.E. (2021, March 25). "Navalny's Health is Deteriorating in Prison, His Lawyers Say." *The New York Times*. https://www.nytimes.com/2021/03/25/world/europe/navalny-health-prison.html

36. Nechepurenko, I. (2021, March 31). "Navalny Declares a Hunger Strike in Russian Prison Over Medical Care." *The New York Times*. https://www.nytimes.com/2021/03/31/world/europe/navalny-hunger-strike-prison.html

37. Troianovski, A. (2021, February 13). "A Life in Opposition: Navalny's Path from Gadfly to Heroic Symbol." *The New York Times*. https://www.nytimes.com/2021/02/13/world/europe/navalny-russia-putin.html

38. The Associated Press. (2021, March 1). "U.N. Calls for Investigation into Aleksei Navalny Poisoning." *The New York Times*. https://www.nytimes.com/video/world/europe/100000007630395/united-nations-navalny-poisoning-investigation.html

39. Sanger, D.E., & Erlanger, S. (2021, March 2). "Biden Administration Accuses Russian Intelligence of Poisoning Navalny, and Announces Its First Sanctions." *The New York Times*. https://www.nytimes.com/2021/03/02/us/politics/russia-navalny-biden.html

40. The Associated Press. (2021, March 2). "White House Imposes Sanctions on Russia Following Navalny Poisoning." *The New York Times*. https://www.nytimes.

com/video/us/politics/100000007632862/biden-russia-sanctions-aleksei-navalny.html

41. Moses, C. (2021, March 29). "Navalny vs. Putin." *The New York Times*. https://www.nytimes.com/2021/03/29/briefing/suez-canal-biden-covid-passport-mozambique.html

42. Romo, V. (2021, April 22). "At Least 1,700 Protesters in Russia Arrested after Nationwide Anti-Putin Rallies." *NPR*. https://www.npr.org/2021/04/22/989694331/at-least-1-700-protesters-in-russia-arrested-after-nationwide-anti-putin-rallies

43. Minder, R. (2019, January 8). "Far-Right, Anti-Immigrant Vox Party Gains a Toehold in Spain." *The New York Times*. https://www.nytimes.com/2019/01/08/world/europe/spain-vox-party.html

44. Minder, R. (2019, February 10). "Thousands Protest in Spain Against Catalonia Talks." *The New York Times*. https://www.nytimes.com/2019/02/10/world/europe/madrid-protest-spain-catalonia.html

45. Minder, R. (2019, February 11). "Catalan Separatists' Trial: How They Got Here, and What They Could Face." *The New York Times*. https://www.nytimes.com/2019/02/11/world/europe/catalonia-separatists-trial.html

46. Minder, R. (2019, February 12). "Catalan Leaders' Trial Starts, and Spain's Government Fights for Its Survival." *The New York Times*. https://www.nytimes.com/2019/02/12/world/europe/catalonia-trial.html

47. Minder, R. (2019, February 12). "Catalan Leaders' Trial Starts, and Spain's Government Fights for Its Survival." *The New York Times*. https://www.nytimes.com/2019/02/12/world/europe/catalonia-trial.html

48. Minder, R. (2019, February 13). "Elections in Spain Are Likely After Lawmakers Reject Budget." *The New York Times*. https://www.nytimes.com/2019/02/13/world/europe/spain-election-vote.html

49. Kingsley, P. (2019, February 15). "Yet Another Election for Spain Reveals Deeper Strains." *The New York Times*. https://www.nytimes.com/2019/02/15/world/europe/spain-snap-election.html

50. Encarnación, O.G. (2019, February 25). "Will Spain Become a Victim of the Catalan Separatists?" *The New York Times*. https://www.nytimes.com/2019/02/25/opinion/spain-catalonia-election.html

51. Ho-fai, F.C. (2019, June 30). "Opinion: A Hong Kong Protester's Tactic: Get the Police to Hit You." *The New York Times*. https://web.archive.org/web/20190701001955/https://www.nytimes.com/2019/06/30/opinion/hong-kong-protests-police-violence.html

52. Minder, R. (2019, February 27). "Spain's Former Premier Testifies Against Catalan Separatists." *The New York Times*. https://www.nytimes.com/2019/02/27/world/europe/spain-rajoy-testimony-catalan-separatists.html

53. Kingsley, P. (2019, March 2). "Roots of Spain's Crisis: One Word Fought Over at Birth of Constitution." *The New York Times*. https://www.nytimes.com/2019/03/02/world/europe/spain-constitution-election-catalonia.html

54. Minder, R. (2019, April 29). "Spain's Election Gives a Lift to the Left and a Warning to the Far Right." *The New York Times*. https://www.nytimes.com/2019/04/29/world/europe/spain-election-sanchez-vox.html

55. The Editorial Board. (2019, April 30). "As Europe Veers Right, Spain Stays the Socialist Course." *The New York Times*. https://www.nytimes.com/2019/04/29/opinion/spain-election.html

56. Minder, R. (2019, May 23). "Valls Puts 'Identity' at Center of Barcelona's Mayor Race." *The New York Times*. https://www.nytimes.com/2019/05/23/world/europe/barcelona-mayor-manuel-valls.html

57. Minder, R. (2019, May 27). "Spain's Socialists Make Gains in 3 Elections." *The New York Times.* https://www.nytimes.com/2019/05/26/world/europe/spain-elections-pedro-sanchez.html

58. Minder, R. (2019, June 12). "Trial of Catalan Independence Leaders Ends in Spain." *The New York Times.* https://www.nytimes.com/2019/06/12/world/europe/spain-catalan-leaders-trial.html

59. Minder, R. (2019, June 14). "Spain Blocks Jailed Catalan Leader from Joining European Parliament." *The New York Times.* https://www.nytimes.com/2019/06/14/world/europe/spain-oriol-junqueras-european-parliament.html

60. Minder, R. (2019, September 11). "600,000 Protesters in Barcelona Call for Independence from Spain." *The New York Times.* https://www.nytimes.com/2019/09/11/world/europe/spain-catalonia-independence.html

61. Minder, R. (2019, September 17). "Spain Heads to 4th Election in 4 Years After Failure to Form Government." *The New York Times.* https://www.nytimes.com/2019/09/17/world/europe/spain-election-government-collapse.html

62. Minder, R. (2019, October 14). "Catalan Separatist Leaders Get Lengthy Prison Terms for Sedition." *The New York Times.* https://www.nytimes.com/2019/10/14/world/europe/catalonia-separatists-verdict-spain.html

63. Minder, R. (2019, October 16). "With Catalan Fury Inflamed Anew, What Comes Next for Spain?" *The New York Times.* https://www.nytimes.com/2019/10/16/world/europe/catalonia-independence-spain.html

64. Minder, R. (2019, October 18). "Catalonia Protesters, Slipping the Reins of Jailed Leaders, Grow More Radicalized." *The New York Times.* https://www.nytimes.com/2019/10/18/world/europe/catalonia-separatist-belgium.html

65. Minder, R. (2019, November 9). "Another Election in Spain Threatens to Deepen the Political Deadlock." *The New York Times*. https://www.nytimes.com/2019/11/09/world/europe/spain-election.html

66. Minder, R. (2019, November 12). "Spain's Left Comes Up with Tentative Deal to Form a Government." *The New York Times*. https://www.nytimes.com/2019/11/12/world/europe/spain-government-sanchez-podemos.html

67. Minder, R. (2019, November 11). "Spain's Far Right Gains in Election." *The New York Times*. https://www.nytimes.com/2019/11/10/world/europe/spain-election.html

68. Puigdemont, C. (2019, December 3). "Outdated Borders are Strangling Liberal Democracy." *The New York Times*. https://www.nytimes.com/2019/12/03/opinion/border-vote-catalonia-brexit.html

69. Minder, R. (2019, December 19). "Spain Bars Catalan Leader from Public Office for 18 Months." *The New York Times*. https://www.nytimes.com/2019/12/19/world/europe/catalan-leader-immunity-eu.html

70. Amnesty International. (2021, January 17). "Russia: Aleksei Navalny Becomes Prisoner of Conscience After Arrest on Arrival in Moscow." *Amnesty International*. https://www.amnesty.org/en/latest/press-release/2021/01/russia-aleksei-navalny-becomes-prisoner-of-conscience-after-arrest-on-arrival-in-moscow/

71. Roth, K. (2021, April 20). "The Last Chance to Save Alexey Navalny." *Human Rights Watch*. https://www.hrw.org/news/2021/04/20/last-chance-save-alexey-navalny

72. Amnesty International. (2019, November 19). "Spain: Analysis of the Supreme Court's Ruling in the Case of Catalan Leaders." *Amnesty International*. https://www.amnesty.org/en/documents/eur41/1393/2019/en/

73. International Association of Democratic Lawyers. (2018, December 3). "IADL Calls for Release of Catalan Political Prisoners." *International Association of Democratic Lawyers.* https://iadllaw.org/2018/12/iadl-calls-for-release-of-catalan-political-prisoners/

74. Khattab, A. (2019, February 12). "Spain: Trial of Catalan Leaders Imperils Human Rights." *ICJ.* https://www.icj.org/spain-trial-of-catalonian-leaders-imperils-human-rights/

75. BBC. (2021, February 17). "Navalny Must be Freed, European Rights Court Tells Russia." *BBC News.* https://www.bbc.com/news/world-europe-56102257

76. Pérez, F.J., & Ayuso, S. (2019, May 29). "European Court Rejects Catalan Secession Leaders' Claims of Rights Violations." *EL PAÍS English.* https://english.elpais.com/elpais/2019/05/29/inenglish/1559114253_396007.html

77. BBC. (2022, March 22). "Russia Navalny: Putin Critic Given Nine-Year Jail Sentence in Trial Branded 'Sham.'" *BBC News.* https://www.bbc.com/news/world-europe-60832310

78. BBC. (2021, June 22). "Spain Pardons Catalan Leaders Over Independence Bid." *BBC News.* https://www.bbc.com/news/world-europe-57565764

79. Burgen, S., & Jones, S. (2019, October 18). "Violence Erupts After Pro-Catalan General Strike in Barcelona." *Guardian.* https://www.theguardian.com/world/2019/oct/18/catalonia-general-strike-protests-independence

80. France 24. (2019, October 27). "Catalan Separatists Stage Mass Rally in Barcelona." *France 24.* https://www.france24.com/en/20191026-catalan-separatists-stage-mass-rally-in-barcelona

81. Binnie, I. (2019, October 19). "Spanish Government Dismisses Call for Catalan Talks; Police Brace for More Unrest." *Reuters.* https://www.reuters.com/article/us-spain-politics-catalonia/spanish-government-dismisses-

call-for-catalan-talks-police-brace-for-more-unrest-idUSKBN1WY09Y

82. BBC. (2021, April 21). "Alexei Navalny: Thousands Across Russia Defy Ban on Protests." *BBC News.* https://www.bbc.com/news/world-europe-56834655

83. Zverev, A., & Osborn, A. (2021, January 22). "Police Crack Down on Russian Protests Against Jailing of Kremlin Foe Navalny." *Reuters.* https://www.reuters.com/article/idUSKBN29R10S

84. Heintz, J. (2021, January 31). "Over 5,100 Arrested at Pro-Navalny Protests Across Russia." *AP NEWS.* https://apnews.com/article/ap-top-news-moscow-coronavirus-pandemic-arrests-russia-085b16035e9c89ffb9919e4d94a2309c

85. Deutsche Welle. (2019, November 5). "Most Russians 'Don't Care' About Navalny's Work." *DW.com.* https://www.dw.com/en/alexei-navalny-most-russians-dont-care-about-his-work-poll-shows/a-51114579

86. Mackey, R. (2014, October 17). "Navalny's Comments on Crimea Ignite Russian Twittersphere." *The New York Times.* https://www.nytimes.com/2014/10/17/world/europe/navalnys-comments-on-crimea-ignite-russian-twittersphere.html

87. Barry, E., & Roth, A. (2012, July 20). "Punk Band Feels Wrath of a Sterner Kremlin." *The New York Times.* https://www.nytimes.com/2012/07/21/world/europe/russias-prosecution-of-punk-band-signals-a-shift.html

88. Gessen, M. (2012, July 23). "A New Age of Show Trials." *The New York Times.* https://archive.nytimes.com/latitude.blogs.nytimes.com/2012/07/23/russias-new-age-of-show-trials/

89. Herszenhorn, D.M., & Roth, A. (2012, July 30). "Musicians on Trial Over Crude Anti-Putin Song in Moscow Cathedral." *The New York Times.* https://www.nytimes.com/2012/07/31/

world/europe/musicians-on-trial-over-crude-anti-putin-song-in-moscow-cathedral.html

90. Schwirtz, M. (2012, July 31). "Musicians Voice Support for Jailed Russian Punk Group." *The New York Times.* https://archive.nytimes.com/thelede.blogs.nytimes.com/2012/07/31/musicians-voice-support-for-jailed-russian-punk-group

91. Herszenhorn, D.M. (2012, August 3). "Mixed Russian Feelings on Jailed Punk Rock Band." *The New York Times.* https://www.nytimes.com/2012/08/03/world/europe/putin-says-go-easy-on-punk-band-but-others-want-members-jailed.html

92. Idov, M. (2012, August 8). "Putin v. the Punk Rockers." *The New York Times.* https://www.nytimes.com/2012/08/07/opinion/on-trial-putin-v-pussy-riot.html

93. Roth, A. (2012, August 4). "Unruly Proceedings in Trial of Russian Punk Group." *The New York Times.* https://www.nytimes.com/2012/08/04/world/europe/russian-punk-bands-trial-inspires-protests.html

94. Herszenhorn, D.M. (2012, August 8). "In Russia, Madonna Defends a Band's Anti-Putin Stunt." *The New York Times.* https://www.nytimes.com/2012/08/08/world/europe/madonna-defends-pussy-riot-at-moscow-concert.html

95. Piepenburg, E. (2012, August 19). "Madonna Supports Russian Punk Band." *The New York Times.* https://www.nytimes.com/2012/08/20/arts/music/madonna-supports-russian-punk-band.html

96. Goldman, V. (2012, August 8). "The Riot Girls' Style." *The New York Times.* https://archive.nytimes.com/tmagazine.blogs.nytimes.com/2012/08/08/the-riot-girls-style/

97. Gessen, M. (2012, August 13). "The Stalin in Putin." *The New York Times.* https://archive.nytimes.com/latitude.blogs.nytimes.com/2012/08/13/the-stalin-in-putin/

98. Kishkovsky, S., & Herszenhorn, D.M. (2012, August 9). "Punk Band's Moscow Trial Offers Platform for Orthodox Protesters." *The New York Times*. https://www.nytimes. com/2012/08/09/world/europe/punk-bands-moscow-trial-offers-platform-for-orthodox-protesters.html

99. Ryzik, M. (2012, August 17). "On Eve of Sentencing, an Artistic Show of Solidarity for Russian Punk Band." *The New York Times*. https://www.nytimes.com/2012/08/18/ arts/music/in-new-york-a-show-of-solidarity-for-russian-punk-band.html

100. Herszenhorn, D.M. (2012, August 17). "Anti-Putin Stunt Earns Punk Band Two Years in Jail." *The New York Times*. https:// www.nytimes.com/2012/08/18/world/europe/suspense-ahead-of-verdict-for-jailed-russian-punk-band.html

101. The New York Times. (2012, August 18). "Russian Punk Band's Trial Spurs Protests." *The New York Times*. https:// www.nytimes.com/slideshow/2012/08/17/world/20120817-RIOT/s/20120817-RIOT-slide-OMUR.html?interstitial=true &prev=3&next=4&src=2

102. Morris, H. (2012, August 17). "We're All Pussy Riot Now." *The New York Times*. https://archive.nytimes.com/ rendezvous.blogs.nytimes.com/2012/08/17/were-all-pussy-riot-now/

103. Roth, A. (2012, August 20). "Russian Authorities Seek Others in Dissident Punk Band." *The New York Times*. https://www.nytimes.com/2012/08/21/world/europe/ russian-authorities-seek-others-in-pussy-riot-band.html

104. Kramer, A.E. (2012, August 26). "2 Band Members in Russia Said to Flee to Avoid Arrest." *The New York Times*. https:// www.nytimes.com/2012/08/27/world/europe/2-members-of-band-in-russia-may-have-fled-to-evade-arrest.html

105. Roth, A. (2012, August 18). "Protester Briefly Skitters Out of Russian Jurisdiction." *The New York Times*. https://www.

nytimes.com/2012/08/18/world/europe/russian-police-chase-pussy-riot-protester-into-turkish-space.html

106. Mackey, R. (2012, August 17). "With Defiance, Laughter and a New Single, Russian Riot Grrrls Go to Jail." *The New York Times*. https://archive.nytimes.com/thelede.blogs.nytimes.com/2012/08/17/with-defiance-laughter-and-a-new-single-russian-riot-grrrls-go-to-jail

107. Ryzik, M. (2012, August 22). "Pussy Riot Was Carefully Calibrated for Protest." *The New York Times*. https://www.nytimes.com/2012/08/26/arts/music/pussy-riot-was-carefully-calibrated-for-protest.html

108. Nikitin, V. (2012, August 20). "The Wrong Reasons to Back Pussy Riot." *The New York Times*. https://www.nytimes.com/2012/08/21/opinion/the-wrong-reasons-to-back-pussy-riot.html

109. Erofeyev, V. (2012, August 22). "A Verdict Against Russia." *The New York Times*. https://www.nytimes.com/2012/08/23/opinion/a-verdict-against-russia.html

110. Platt, K.M.F. (2012, August 23). "On Behalf of Stifled Russian Voices." *The New York Times*. https://www.nytimes.com/2012/08/24/opinion/on-behalf-of-stifled-russian-voices.html

111. Ryzik, M. (2012, August 28). "An Art Show for Pussy Riot." *The New York Times*. https://archive.nytimes.com/artsbeat.blogs.nytimes.com/2012/08/28/an-art-show-for-pussy-riot/

112. Mackey, R. (2012, August 30). "After Pussy Riot Verdict, Christian Culture Warriors Run Riot in Moscow." *The New York Times*. https://archive.nytimes.com/thelede.blogs.nytimes.com/2012/08/30/following-pussy-riot-verdict-christian-culture-warriors-run-riot-in-moscow/

113. Herszenhorn, D.M. (2012, August 31). "Russia: Crime-Scene Message About Convicted Band." *The New York Times*.

https://www.nytimes.com/2012/08/31/world/europe/russia-crime-scene-message-about-convicted-band.html

114. Kordunsky, A., & Herszenhorn, D.M. (2012, August 31). "Russians Call Pussy Riot Note at Murder Site a Diversion." *The New York Times*. https://www.nytimes.com/2012/09/01/world/europe/pussy-riot-murder-a-domestic-dispute.html

115. Minder, R., & Ives, M. (2021, February 18). "'You are Not Alone': Spanish Rapper's Arrest Sparks Free Speech Protests." *The New York Times*. https://www.nytimes.com/2021/02/18/world/europe/pablo-hasel-protest-spain.html

116. Casey, N. (2021, February 27). "Rapper's Arrest Awakens Rage in Spanish Youth Chafing in Pandemic." *The New York Times*. https://www.nytimes.com/2021/02/27/world/europe/barcelona-protests-pablo-hasel.html

117. The Associated Press and Reuters. (2021, February 27). "Protests in Barcelona Over Rapper's Arrest." *The New York Times*. https://www.nytimes.com/video/world/europe/100000007627935/spain-rapper-protests-pablo-hasel.html

118. O'Brien, J. (2012, August 17). "Pussy Riot's Hooliganism Explained." *The World* from PRX. https://theworld.org/stories/2012-08-17/pussy-riots-hooliganism-explained

119. Amnesty International. (2022, August 8). "Spain: Jailing of Rapper for Song Lyrics and Tweets 'Unjust and Disproportionate.'" *Amnesty International*. https://www.amnesty.org/en/latest/news/2021/02/spain-jailing-of-rapper-for-song-lyrics-and-tweets-unjust-and-disproportionate-2/

120. Human Rights Watch. (2021, January 13). "World Report 2021: Rights Trends in Spain." *Human Rights Watch*. https://www.hrw.org/world-report/2021/country-chapters/spain

121. Amnesty International. (2021, June 2). "Russian Federation: Open Letter of Support to Pussy Riot." *Amnesty International.* https://www.amnesty.org/en/documents/eur46/031/2013/en/

122. Denber, R. (2020, October 28). "Pussy Riot and Russia's Surreal 'Justice.'" *Human Rights Watch.* https://www.hrw.org/news/2012/08/17/pussy-riot-and-russias-surreal-justice

123. BBC. (2021, February 17). "Pablo Hasel Protests: Thousands Demand Rapper's Release in Spain." *BBC News.* https://www.bbc.com/news/world-europe-56082120

124. The Associated Press. (2021, February 18). "33 Injured, 14 Arrested in Violent Street Protests Over Spanish Rapper Pablo Hasel's Jailing." *Billboard.* https://www.billboard.com/music/music-news/street-protests-spanish-rapper-pablo-hasel-jailing-arrests-injuries-9526872/

125. Slotkin, J. (2021, February 21). "Violence Erupts in Barcelona on 5th Night of Protests Over Jailed Rapper." *NPR.* https://www.npr.org/2021/02/21/969958495/violence-erupts-in-barcelona-on-5th-night-of-protests-over-jailed-rapper

126. García, T. (2021, March 3). "Nearly 400 Arrested and Injured as Protesters Demand Spanish Rapper's Release from Prison." *Zenger News.* https://www.zenger.news/2021/03/02/nearly-400-arrested-and-injured-as-protesters-demand-spanish-rappers-release-from-prison/

127. Al Jazeera. (2021, February 18). "Spain Protests: Woman Hit by Police Rubber Bullet 'Loses Eye.'" *Al Jazeera.* https://www.aljazeera.com/news/2021/2/18/protester-loses-eye-as-police-crackdown-on-hasel-demos-report

128. Brownstone, S. (2012, August 1). "Pussy Riot Sentenced to 2 Years in Prison." *Mother Jones.* https://www.motherjones.com/politics/2012/07/what-is-pussy-riot-explained/

129. Luhn, A. (2015, February 5). "Hackers Target Russian Newspaper Site Accused of Being Anti-Putin." *Guardian.*

https://www.theguardian.com/world/2015/feb/05/russia-moscow-times-cyber-attack

130. The Moscow Times. (2023, May 16). "Russians Have No Respect for Pussy Riot, Poll Says." *Moscow Times.* https://www.themoscowtimes.com/2013/09/13/russians-have-no-respect-for-pussy-riot-poll-says-a27649

131. Russia Beyond. (2012, October 27). "Poll: Over 40% of Russians Suspect Mastermind Behind Pussy Riot Performance." *Russia Beyond.* https://web.archive.org/web/20210922213713/https://www.rbth.com/articles/2012/10/26/poll_over_40_of_russians_suspect_mastermind_behind_pussy_riot_perfor_19496.html

132. Velasco, S. (2012, August 17). "Pussy Riot Sentenced: Is Chorus of Support Helpful, or Just Fashionable?" *Christian Science Monitor.* https://www.csmonitor.com/USA/Society/2012/0817/Pussy-Riot-sentenced-Is-chorus-of-support-helpful-or-just-fashionable

133. Freed, B.R. (2023, May 16). "Pussy Riot and a Protest Legacy." *New Republic.* https://newrepublic.com/article/106288/benjamin-r-freed-pussy-riot-and-protest-legacy

134. Bauer, M. (2012, October 18). "Pussy Riot in Edinburgh." *HuffPost.* https://www.huffpost.com/entry/pussy-riot-in-edinburgh_b_1800461

135. CBC News. (2012, August 18). "Anti-Putin Pussy Riot Band Members Jailed for 2 Years." *CBC News.* https://www.cbc.ca/news/world/anti-putin-pussy-riot-band-members-jailed-for-2-years-1.1180933

136. Amnesty International. (2012, July 25). "Sting Condemns Russia's Treatment of Pussy Riot Musicians Ahead of Moscow Concert." *Amnesty International UK.* https://www.amnesty.org.uk/press-releases/sting-condemns-russias-treatment-pussy-riot-musicians-ahead-moscow-concert

137. López-Fonseca, Ó., & Cué, C.E. (2021, February 10). "After Rapper Pablo Hasél Gets Jail for Tweets, Spain Plans to End Prison Terms for Crimes Involving Freedom of Speech." *EL PAÍS English.* https://english.elpais.com/spanish_news/2021-02-10/after-rapper-pablo-hasel-gets-jail-for-tweets-spain-plans-to-end-prison-terms-for-crimes-involving-freedom-of-speech.html
138. Tochka, N. (2013). "Pussy Riot, Freedom of Expression, and Popular Music Studies After the Cold War." *Popular Music*, 32(2), 303–311.

Chapter 5. Worthy and Unworthy Interventions: Russia in Syria and Saudi Arabia in Yemen

1. Bacchi, U. (2014, November 4). "Syria: Al-Nusra Jihadists 'Capture US TOW Anti-Tank Missiles' from Moderate Rebels." *International Business Times UK.* https://www.ibtimes.co.uk/syria-al-nusra-jihadists-capture-us-weaponry-moderate-rebels-1472864
2. Cooper, H., Gordon, M.R., & Macfarquhar, N. (2015, September 30). "Russians Strike Targets in Syria, But Not ISIS Areas." *The New York Times.* https://www.nytimes.com/2015/10/01/world/europe/russia-airstrikes-syria.html
3. Reuters. (2015, September 30). "White House: Pentagon Reviewing Russia Strikes, Targets." *The New York Times.* https://www.nytimes.com/video/multimedia/100000003948135/white-house-pentagon-reviewing-russia-strikes-targets.html
4. Reuters. (2015, September 30). "Ash Carter: Russian Air Strikes in Syria Probably Not in Islamic State Areas." *The New York Times.* https://www.nytimes.com/video/multimedia/100000003948300/ash-carter-russian-air-strikes-in-syria-probably-not-in-islamic.html

5. Reuters. (2015, October 1). "U.S. Military Spokesman Casts Doubt on Russian Air Strike Claims." *The New York Times*. https://www.nytimes.com/video/multimedia/100000003950566/us-military-spokesman-casts-doubt-on-russian-air-strike-claims.html

6. Barnard, A. (2015, September 30). "Syrian Rebels Say Russia is Targeting Them Rather Than Isis." *The New York Times*. https://www.nytimes.com/2015/10/01/world/middleeast/syrian-rebels-say-russia-targets-them-rather-than-isis.html

7. Reuters. (2015, September 30). "Russian Airstrikes in Syria Underway: Moscow." *The New York Times*. https://www.nytimes.com/video/multimedia/100000003947579/russian-airstrikes-in-syria-underway-moscow.html

8. Reuters. (2015, September 30). "U.S. Questions Targets of Russian Air Strikes in Syria." *The New York Times*. https://www.nytimes.com/video/multimedia/100000003948402/us-questions-targets-of-russian-air-strikes-in-syria.html

9. Reuters. (2015, September 30). "U.S. Concerned About Russian Air Strikes in Syria: Kerry." *The New York Times*. https://www.nytimes.com/video/multimedia/100000003947976/us-concerned-about-russian-air-strikes-in-syria-kerry.html

10. Mackey, R. (2015, September 30). "Parsing YouTube Evidence of Russian Strikes in Syria." *The New York Times*. https://www.nytimes.com/2015/10/01/world/middleeast/parsing-youtube-evidence-of-russian-strikes-in-syria.html

11. Barnard, A., & Kramer, A.E. (2015, October 1). "Russia Carries Out Airstrikes in Syria for 2nd Day." *The New York Times*. https://www.nytimes.com/2015/10/02/world/middleeast/russia-syria-airstrikes-isis.html

12. Barnard, A., & Kramer, A.E. (2015, October 7). "Russian Cruise Missiles Help Syrians Go on the Offensive." *The New York Times*. https://www.nytimes.com/2015/10/08/world/middleeast/russia-syria-conflict.html

13. Hubbard, B. (2015, October 1). "A Look at the Army of Conquest, a Prominent Rebel Alliance in Syria." *The New York Times*. https://www.nytimes.com/2015/10/02/world/middleeast/syria-russia-airstrikes-rebels-army-conquest-jaish-al-fatah.html

14. Barnard, A., & Shoumali, K. (2015, October 12). "U.S. Weaponry is Turning Syria into Proxy War with Russia." *The New York Times*. https://www.nytimes.com/2015/10/13/world/middleeast/syria-russia-airstrikes.html

15. https://www.nytimes.com/video/us/100000008419463/san-antonio-migrant-deaths-tractor-trailer.html?playlistId=video/breaking-news

16. https://www.nytimes.com/video/multimedia/100000003954268/obama-says-russia-went-into-syria-out-of-weakness.html?searchResultPosition=58

17. Reuters. (2015, October 24). "Russia Wants Syrian Elections, Ready to Help Free Syrian Army: Lavrov." *The New York Times*. https://www.nytimes.com/video/multimedia/100000003997216/russia-wants-syrian-elections-ready-to-help-free-syrian-army-lav.html

18. Reuters. (2015, October 25). "Lavrov: Russia Wants Syria Elections." *The New York Times*. https://www.nytimes.com/video/multimedia/100000003997429/lavrov-russia-wants-syria-elections.html

19. Reuters. (2015, October 7). "Turkey: Russian Air Strikes Hitting Islamic State Opponents." *The New York Times*. https://www.nytimes.com/video/multimedia/100000003963154/turkey-russian-air-strikes-hitting-islamic-state-opponents.html

20. Arango, T., & Barnard, A. (2015, October 15). "Turkey Expresses Concern to U.S. and Russia Over Help for Syrian Kurds." *The New York Times*. https://www.nytimes.com/2015/10/15/world/middleeast/turkey-expresses-concern-to-us-and-russia-over-help-for-syrian-kurds.html

21. Reuters. (2015, October 12). "EU Condemns Russian Strikes on Syria, Demands They Stop." *The New York Times*. https://www.nytimes.com/video/multimedia/100000003973195/eu-condemns-russian-strikes-on-syria-demands-they-stop.html

22. Barnard, A., & Erdbrink, T. (2015, October 9). "Isis Makes Gains in Syria Territory Bombed by Russia." *The New York Times*. https://www.nytimes.com/2015/10/10/world/middleeast/hussein-hamedani-iran-general-killed-in-syria.html

23. Reuters. (2015, October 14). "Islamic State Urges Jihad Against Russians." *The New York Times*. https://www.nytimes.com/video/multimedia/100000003976771/islamic-state-urges-jihad-against-russians.html

24. Reuters. (2015, October 2). "Confusion Over Russia Air Strikes on Syria." *The New York Times*. https://www.nytimes.com/video/multimedia/100000003952356/confusion-over-russia-air-strikes-on-syria.html

25. Reuters. (2015, October 1). "Putin: No Syrian Civilians Hurt as Result of Russian Air Strikes." *The New York Times*. https://www.nytimes.com/video/multimedia/100000003951253/putin-no-syrian-civilians-hurt-as-result-of-russian-air-strikes.html

26. Kramer, A.E. (2015, October 8). "For Vladimir Putin's Birthday, Ice Hockey and a Missile Strike." *The New York Times*. https://www.nytimes.com/2015/10/08/world/europe/putins-birthday-gift-nhl-opponents-and-a-victory.html

27. The New York Times. (2015, September 30). "Who is Fighting Whom in Syria." *The New York Times*. https://www.nytimes.com/2015/10/01/world/middleeast/the-syria-conflicts-overlapping-agendas-and-competing-visions.html

28. Reuters. (2015, September 30). "Russian Parliament Approves Syrian Air Strikes." *The New York Times*. https://www.nytimes.com/video/multimedia/100000003947290/russian-parliament-approves-syrian-air-strikes.html

29. Reuters. (2015, September 30). "Russia Releases Video of Airstrikes in Syria." *The New York Times*. https://www.nytimes.com/video/multimedia/100000003948190/russia-releases-video-of-airstrikes-in-syria.html

30. Barnard, A., & Kramer, A.E. (2015, October 1). "Russia Carries Out Airstrikes in Syria for 2nd Day." *The New York Times*. https://www.nytimes.com/2015/10/02/world/middleeast/russia-syria-airstrikes-isis.html

31. Rappeport, A. (2015, October 1). "Shifting on Islamic State, Donald Trump Welcomes Russia's Moves in Syria." *The New York Times*. https://archive.nytimes.com/www.nytimes.com/politics/first-draft/2015/10/01/shifting-on-islamic-state-donald-trump-welcomes-russias-moves-in-syria/

32. Rappeport, A. (2015, October 12). "Calling Obama a 'Weakling,' Chris Christie Says He Would Shoot Down Russian Planes Over Syria." *The New York Times*. https://archive.nytimes.com/www.nytimes.com/politics/first-draft/2015/10/12/calling-obama-a-weakling-chris-christie-says-he-would-shoot-down-russian-planes-over-syria/

33. Kaplan, T. (2015, October 19). "G.O.P. Candidates Leading Charge in Call for Syrian No-Fly Zone." *The New York Times*. https://www.nytimes.com/2015/10/20/us/politics/gop-candidates-leading-charge-in-call-for-syrian-no-fly-zone.html

34. Kaplan, T., & Andrews, W. (2015, October 20). "Presidential Candidates on Syrian No-Fly Zone." *The New York Times*. https://www.nytimes.com/interactive/2015/10/19/us/

elections/presidential-candidates-on-syria-no-fly-zone.
html

35. Reuters. (2015, October 14). "Clinton: U.S. Must Make
Clear Putin's Actions in Syria 'Not Acceptable.'" *The
New York Times.* https://www.nytimes.com/video/
multimedia/100000003976148/clinton-us-must-make-clear-
putins-actions-in-syria-not-acceptabl.html

36. Reuters. (2015, October 23). "Putin on U.S. Cooperation
in Syria." *The New York Times.* https://www.nytimes.com/
video/world/100000003994247/putin-on-us-cooperation-
in-syria.html

37. Macfarquhar, N. (2015, October 23). "Putin, Citing
Key Moment, Prods West to Cooperate on Syria." *The
New York Times.* https://www.nytimes.com/2015/10/23/
world/europe/putin-citing-key-moment-prods-west-to-
cooperate-on-syria.html

38. Baker, P. (2015, October 9). "Wary of Escalation in Syria,
U.S. is Waiting Out Putin's Moves." *The New York Times.*
https://www.nytimes.com/2015/10/09/world/wary-of-
escalation-the-us-is-waiting-out-putins-moves.html

39. Editorial Board. (2015, October 2). "Russia's Dangerous
Escalation in Syria." *The New York Times.* https://www.
nytimes.com/2015/10/02/opinion/russias-dangerous-
escalation-in-syria.html

40. Baker, P., & Macfarquhar, N. (2015, October 2). "Obama
Sees Russia Failing in Syria Effort." *The New York Times.*
https://www.nytimes.com/2015/10/03/world/middleeast/
syria-russia-airstrikes.html

41. Baker, P., & Macfarquhar, N. (2015, October 2). "Obama
Sees Russia Failing in Syria Effort." *The New York Times.*
https://www.nytimes.com/2015/10/03/world/middleeast/
syria-russia-airstrikes.html

42. Baker, P., & Macfarquhar, N. (2015, October 2). "Obama Sees Russia Failing in Syria Effort." *The New York Times.* https://www.nytimes.com/2015/10/03/world/middleeast/syria-russia-airstrikes.html

43. Reuters. (2015, October 4). "Russia Cannot Fight IS and Also Support Assad in Syria: Britain." *The New York Times.* https://www.nytimes.com/video/multimedia/100000003956840/russia-cannot-fight-is-and-also-support-assad-in-syria-britain.html

44. Reuters. (2015, October 23). "Kerry Welcomes 'Constructive Role' by Russia." *The New York Times.* https://www.nytimes.com/video/multimedia/100000003995533/kerry-welcomes-constructive-role-by-russia.html

45. Rosenberg, M., & Macfarquhar, N. (2015, October 23). "U.S. and Russia Find Common Goals on Syria, If Not on Assad." *The New York Times.* https://www.nytimes.com/2015/10/24/world/middleeast/us-and-russia-find-common-goals-on-syria-if-not-on-assad.html

46. Reuters. (2015, October 2). "Strikes on Syria Could Last Months: Russian Parliament." *The New York Times.* https://www.nytimes.com/video/multimedia/100000003953744/strikes-on-syria-could-last-months-russian-parliament.html

47. Reuters. (2015, October 3). "Russian Jets in Third Day of Bombing in Syria." *The New York Times.* https://www.nytimes.com/video/multimedia/100000003955344/russian-jets-in-third-day-of-bombing-in-syria.html

48. Reuters. (2015, October 5). "Russian Airstrikes Hit Syria Targets." *The New York Times.* https://www.nytimes.com/video/multimedia/100000003957782/russian-airstrikes-hit-syria-targets.html

49. Reuters. (2015, October 7). "Russian Warships Launch Rockets on Islamic State in Syria." *The New York Times.* https://

www.nytimes.com/video/multimedia/100000003963703/
russian-warships-launch-rockets-on-islamic-state-in-syria.
html

50. Reuters. (2015, October 12). "Dramatic Videos Reveal Intensified Fighting in Syria." *The New York Times*. https://www.nytimes.com/video/multimedia/100000003972785/dramatic-videos-reveal-intensified-fighting-in-syria.html

51. Reuters. (2015, October 9). "Syrians, Russians Marching Forward in Offensive." *The New York Times*. https://www.nytimes.com/video/multimedia/100000003969285/syrians-russians-marching-forward-in-offensive.html

52. Reuters. (2015, October 17). "Russia Continues Airstrikes in Homs and Damascus After Period of Ease." *The New York Times*. https://www.nytimes.com/video/multimedia/100000003983768/russia-continues-airstrikes-in-homs-and-damascus-after-period-of.html

53. Reuters. (2015, October 19). "Damascus Bombed, Russian Jets Fly Over Aleppo - Activists." *The New York Times*. https://www.nytimes.com/video/multimedia/100000003986496/damascus-bombed-russian-jets-fly-over-aleppo-activists.html

54. Reuters. (2015, October 23). "Misery and Mayhem in Syria." *The New York Times*. https://www.nytimes.com/video/multimedia/100000003995513/misery-and-mayhem-in-syria.html

55. Kramer, A.E. (2015, October 3). "As Russia Returns to Middle East, a Look at Some of Its Weapons." *The New York Times*. https://www.nytimes.com/2015/10/03/world/middleeast/as-russia-returns-to-middle-east-a-look-at-some-of-its-weapons.html

56. Myers, S.L. (2015, October 4). "In Putin's Syria Intervention, Fear of a Weak Government Hand." *The New York Times*. https://www.nytimes.com/2015/10/04/world/europe/in-

putins-syria-intervention-fear-of-a-weak-government-hand.html

57. Hodge, C., & Myers, S.L. (2015, October 4). "What's Driving Putin into Syria." *The New York Times*. https://www.nytimes.com/video/world/middleeast/100000003956073/whats-driving-putin-into-syria.html

58. Schmitt, E., & Gordon, M.R. (2015, October 5). "U.S. Aims to Put More Pressure on ISIS in Syria." *The New York Times*. https://www.nytimes.com/2015/10/05/world/middleeast/us-aims-to-put-more-pressure-on-isis-in-syria.html

59. Kramer, A.E., & Barnard, A. (2015, October 6). "Russian Soldiers Join Syria Fight." *The New York Times*. https://www.nytimes.com/2015/10/06/world/middleeast/russian-soldiers-join-syria-fight.html

60. The Editorial Board. (2015, October 9). "An Incoherent Syria War Strategy." *The New York Times*. https://www.nytimes.com/2015/10/10/opinion/an-incoherent-syria-war-strategy.html

61. Kramer, A.E., Cooper, H., & Yeginsu, C. (2015, October 5). "Kremlin Says Russian 'Volunteer' Forces Will Fight in Syria." *The New York Times*. https://www.nytimes.com/2015/10/06/world/europe/nato-russia-warplane-turkey.html

62. The Editorial Board. (2015, October 6). "Mr. Putin's Motives in Syria." *The New York Times*. https://www.nytimes.com/2015/10/07/opinion/vladimir-putin-motives-in-syria.html

63. Reuters. (2015, October 7). "U.S. Says It Hasn't Agreed to Cooperate Militarily with Russia in Syria." *The New York Times*. https://www.nytimes.com/video/multimedia/100000003963127/us-says-it-hasnt-agreed-to-cooperate-militarily-with-russia-in-s.html

64. Reuters. (2015, October 13). "U.S., Russia Jets Came Within Visual Range Over Syria - U.S. Military." *The New York Times*. https://www.nytimes.com/video/multimedia/100000003974833/us-russia-jets-came-within-visual-range-over-syria-us-military.html

65. Macfarquhar, N. (2015, October 13). "Putin Says U.S. Fails to Cooperate in Syria." *The New York Times*. https://www.nytimes.com/2015/10/14/world/europe/putin-complains-about-us-cooperation-on-syria.html

66. Macfarquhar, N. (2015, October 20). "U.S. Agrees with Russia on Rules in Syrian Sky." *The New York Times*. https://www.nytimes.com/2015/10/21/world/middleeast/us-and-russia-agree-to-regulate-all-flights-over-syria.html

67. Reuters. (2015, October 20). "Pentagon: U.S., Russia Sign Memo to Air Conflict Over Syria." *The New York Times*. https://www.nytimes.com/video/multimedia/100000003988539/pentagon-us-russia-sign-memo-to-air-conflict-over-syria.html

68. The Associated Press. (2015, October 7). "Putin Meets with His Defense Minister." *The New York Times*. https://www.nytimes.com/video/world/100000003963919/putin-meets-with-his-defense-minister.html

69. Reuters. (2015, October 13). "Syrian Forces Gain After Russian Airstrikes." *The New York Times*. https://www.nytimes.com/video/multimedia/100000003973911/syrian-forces-gain-after-russian-airstrikes.html

70. Barnard, A., & Shoumali, K. (2015, October 12). "U.S. Weaponry is Turning Syria into Proxy War with Russia." *The New York Times*. https://www.nytimes.com/2015/10/13/world/middleeast/syria-russia-airstrikes.html

71. The Associated Press. (2015, October 5). "NATO Responds to Russian Plane in Turkey." *The New York Times*. https://www.

nytimes.com/video/world/middleeast/100000003958151/nato-responds-to-russian-plane-in-turkey.html

72. Reuters. (2015, October 5). "Russian Jets Head into War in Syria." *The New York Times.* https://www.nytimes.com/video/multimedia/100000003958341/russian-jets-head-into-war-in-syria.html

73. Goldman, R. (2015, October 6). "Russian Violations of Airspace Seen as Unwelcome Test by the West." *The New York Times.* https://www.nytimes.com/2015/10/07/world/europe/russian-violations-of-airspace-seen-as-unwelcome-test-by-the-west.html

74. Arango, T. (2015, October 6). "Russia Military's Actions in Syria Cause Rift with Turkey." *The New York Times.* https://www.nytimes.com/2015/10/07/world/middleeast/russia-turkey-tensions-rise-over-syria.html

75. Cooper, H., & Kanter, J. (2015, October 8). "NATO, Tested by Russia in Syria, Raises Its Guard and Its Tone." *The New York Times.* https://www.nytimes.com/2015/10/09/world/europe/russia-syria-intervention-nato.html

76. Yeginsu, C. (2015, October 16). "Turkish Jets Shoot Down Drone Near Syria." *The New York Times.* https://www.nytimes.com/2015/10/17/world/europe/turkey-drone-syria-border.html

77. Reuters. (2015, October 6). "White House: Putin Playing Checkers in Syria." *The New York Times.* https://www.nytimes.com/video/multimedia/100000003962034/white-house-putin-playing-checkers-in-syria.html

78. Fahim, K. (2015, October 17). "As Conflicts Flare Up, Leaders Fan Sectarian Flames in Middle East." *The New York Times.* https://www.nytimes.com/2015/10/18/world/middleeast/as-conflicts-flare-up-leaders-fan-sectarian-flames-in-middle-east.html

79. Gordon, M.R. (2015, October 11). "Shiites in Iraq Hailing Putin for Syria Push." *The New York Times*. https://www. nytimes.com/2015/10/12/world/middleeast/russian-intervention-in-syria-excites-iraqs-disillusioned-shiites. html

80. Reuters. (2015, October 11). "Russia's Foray into Syria Draws Concerns from Saudis." *The New York Times*. https:// www.nytimes.com/video/multimedia/100000003971448/ russias-foray-into-syria-draws-concerns-from-saudis.html

81. Peçanha, S., Almukhtar, S., & Rebecca, K.K. (2015, October 18). "Untangling the Overlapping Conflicts in the Syrian War." *The New York Times*. https://www.nytimes.com/ interactive/2015/10/16/world/middleeast/untangling-the-overlapping-conflicts-in-the-syrian-war.html

82. Fahim, K., & Barnard, A. (2015, October 21). "Russia Makes an Impact in Syrian Battle for Control of Aleppo." *The New York Times*. https://www.nytimes.com/2015/10/21/world/ middleeast/russia-makes-an-impact-in-syrian-battle-for-control-of-aleppo.html

83. Reuters. (2015, October 21). "Syria's Assad Makes Surprise Visit to Moscow." *The New York Times*. https://www. nytimes.com/video/multimedia/100000003989908/syrias-assad-makes-surprise-visit-to-moscow.html

84. Reuters. (2015, October 21). "Putin and Assad Hold Talks on Syria." *The New York Times*. https://www.nytimes.com/ video/world/europe/100000003990050/putin-and-assad-hold-talks-on-syria.html

85. Reuters. (2015, October 21). "Assad Flies to Moscow to Thank Putin for Syria Air Strikes." *The New York Times*. https:// www.nytimes.com/video/multimedia/100000003990610/ assad-flies-to-moscow-to-thank-putin-for-syria-air-strikes. html

86. Myers, S.L., & Barnard, A. (2015, October 22). "Bashar al-Assad Finds Chilly Embrace in Moscow Trip." *The New York Times.* https://www.nytimes.com/2015/10/22/us/politics/assad-finds-chilly-embrace-in-moscow-trip.html

87. Reuters. (2015, October 22). "Putin: Russia Close to Sharing Syria Data." *The New York Times.* https://www.nytimes.com/video/multimedia/100000003993413/putin-russia-close-to-sharing-syria-data.html

88. Reuters. (2015, October 15). "Russia Continues Bombing Syria: Iran Providing More Troops." *The New York Times.* https://www.nytimes.com/video/multimedia/100000003979571/russia-continues-bombing-syria-iran-providing-more-troops.html

89. Sengupta, S. (2015, October 23). "Calls Grow at U.N. for Security Council to Do Its Job: Keep the Peace." *The New York Times.* https://www.nytimes.com/2015/10/24/world/calls-grow-at-un-for-security-council-to-do-its-job-keep-the-peace.html

90. Fahim, K., & Samaan, M. (2015, October 26). "Violence in Syria Spurs a Huge Surge in Civilian Flight." *The New York Times.* https://www.nytimes.com/2015/10/27/world/middleeast/syria-russian-air-strike-refugees.html

91. Sanger, D.E. (2015, October 28). "Iran is Invited to Join U.S., Russia and Europe for Talks on Syria's Future." *The New York Times.* https://www.nytimes.com/2015/10/28/world/middleeast/iran-is-invited-to-join-us-russia-and-europe-for-talks-on-syrias-future.html

92. The Editorial Board. (2015, October 29). "Iran's Role in the Syrian Crisis." *The New York Times.* https://www.nytimes.com/2015/10/29/opinion/irans-role-in-the-syrian-crisis.html

93. The New York Times. (2015, September 30). "The U.S.-Russia Discord Over Syria." *The New York Times.* https://

www.nytimes.com/2015/09/30/opinion/the-us-russia-discord-over-syria.html

94. Gessen, M. (2015, September 30). "Vladimir Putin's Guide to World History." *The New York Times*. https://www.nytimes.com/2015/10/01/opinion/masha-gessen-vladimir-putins-guide-to-world-history.html

95. Friedman, T.L. (2015, September 30). "Syria, Obama and Putin." *The New York Times*. https://www.nytimes.com/2015/09/30/opinion/thomas-friedman-syria-obama-and-putin.html

96. Adams, G., & Walt, S.M. (2015, October 13). "A Road to Damascus, Via Moscow." *The New York Times*. https://www.nytimes.com/2015/10/13/opinion/a-road-to-damascus-via-moscow.html

97. Adams, G., & Walt, S.M. (2015, October 13). "A Road to Damascus, Via Moscow." *The New York Times*. https://www.nytimes.com/2015/10/13/opinion/a-road-to-damascus-via-moscow.html

98. Krastev, I. (2015, October 7). "Is Vladimir Putin Trying to Teach the West a Lesson in Syria?" *The New York Times*. https://www.nytimes.com/2015/10/08/opinion/ivan-krastev-is-putin-trying-to-teach-us-a-lesson.html

99. The New York Times. (2015, October 17). "Don't Align with Russia to Fight Isis." *The New York Times*. https://www.nytimes.com/2015/10/17/opinion/dont-align-with-russia-to-fight-isis.html

100. Montefiore, S.S. (2015, October 9). "Putin's Imperial Adventure in Syria." *The New York Times*. https://www.nytimes.com/2015/10/09/opinion/putins-imperial-adventure-in-syria.html

101. Ibish, H. (2015, October 19). "Putin's Partition Plan for Syria." *The New York Times*. https://www.nytimes.

com/2015/10/20/opinion/putins-partition-plan-for-syria.html

102. Trudolyubov, M. (2015, October 22). "Sheikh Putin of Syria." *The New York Times.* https://www.nytimes.com/2015/10/23/opinion/sheikh-putin-of-syria.html

103. McFaul, M.A. (2015, October 23). "The Myth of Putin's Strategic Genius." *The New York Times.* https://www.nytimes.com/2015/10/23/opinion/the-myth-of-putins-strategic-genius.html

104. Carter, J. (2015, October 24). "Jimmy Carter: A Five-Nation Plan to End the Syrian Crisis." *The New York Times.* https://www.nytimes.com/2015/10/26/opinion/jimmy-carter-a-five-nation-plan-to-end-the-syrian-crisis.html

105. Shapiro, J. (2015, October 8). "Putin's Boldness, Syria's Misery." *The New York Times.* https://www.nytimes.com/2015/10/09/opinion/vladimir-putin-russia-boldness-syria-misery.html

106. Mazzetti, M., & Kirkpatrick, D.D. (2015, March 25). "Saudi Arabia Leads Air Assault in Yemen." *The New York Times.* https://www.nytimes.com/2015/03/26/world/middleeast/al-anad-air-base-houthis-yemen.html

107. Mackey, R. (2015, March 27). "Yemenis Share Reports, Rumors and Wry Commentary Online as Bombs Drop." *The New York Times.* https://www.nytimes.com/2015/03/27/world/middleeast/yemenis-share-reports-rumors-and-wry-commentary-online-as-bombs-drop.html

108. Mackey, R. (2015, March 31). "Tired of War, Yemeni Bloggers Say, 'Enough.'" *The New York Times.* https://www.nytimes.com/2015/04/01/world/middleeast/tired-of-war-bloggers-in-yemen-say-enough.html

109. Mackey, R. (2015, April 17). "Under Bombardment in Yemen, Civilians Voice Terror and Despair Online." *The New York Times.* https://www.nytimes.com/2015/04/18/

world/middleeast/under-bombardment-in-yemen-civilians-voice-terror-and-despair-online.html

110. Mackey, R. (2015, April 20). "Vivid Accounts of War's Horror Stream from Yemen's Capital." *The New York Times.* https://www.nytimes.com/2015/04/21/world/middleeast/vivid-accounts-of-wars-horror-stream-from-yemens-capital.html

111. Reuters. (2015, March 27). "Tensions Simmer in Yemen After Airstrikes." *The New York Times.* https://www.nytimes.com/video/multimedia/100000003597428/tensions-simmer-in-yemen-after-airstrikes.html

112. Mazzetti, M., & Kirkpatrick, D.D. (2015, March 27). "A Policy Puzzle of U.S. Goals and Alliances in the Middle East." *The New York Times.* https://www.nytimes.com/2015/03/27/world/middleeast/a-policy-puzzle-of-us-goals-and-alliances-in-the-middle-east.html

113. Al-Batati, S., & Kirkpatrick, D.D. (2015, March 27). "Houthi Forces Move on Southern Yemen, Raising Specter of Regional Ground War." *The New York Times.* https://www.nytimes.com/2015/03/28/world/middleeast/houthi-forces-move-on-southern-yemen-raising-specter-of-regional-ground-war.html

114. Kirkpatrick, D.D. (2015, March 29). "Arab Nations to Form Military Force to Counter Iran and Islamist Extremists." *The New York Times.* https://www.nytimes.com/2015/03/30/world/middleeast/arab-leaders-agree-on-joint-military-force.html

115. Kirkpatrick, D.D. (2015, March 31). "As U.S. and Iran Seek Nuclear Deal, Saudi Arabia Makes Its Own Moves." *The New York Times.* https://www.nytimes.com/2015/03/31/world/middleeast/saudis-make-own-moves-as-us-and-iran-talk.html

116. Almukhtar, S., & Yourish, K. (2015, March 31). "Old, New and Unusual Alliances in the Middle East." *The New York Times.*

https://www.nytimes.com/interactive/2015/03/30/world/
middleeast/middle-east-alliances-saudi-arabia-iran.html
117. Kirkpatrick, D.D., & Al-Batati, S. (2015, March 28). "Ex-
Yemeni Leader Urges Truce and Successor's Ouster." *The
New York Times*. https://www.nytimes.com/2015/03/29/
world/middleeast/saudi-arabia-evacuates-diplomats-
from-yemeni-city-as-houthi-advance-continues.html
118. Reuters. (2015, March 29). "Saudi Arabia Has Not
Made Decision on Sending Ground Troops to Yemen."
The New York Times. https://www.nytimes.com/video/
multimedia/100000003600317/saudi-arabia-has-not-made-
decision-on-sending-ground-troops-to-y.html
119. Al-Batati, S., & Fahim, K. (2015, April 1). "Rebels in Yemen
Battle for Control of Strategic Port City." *The New York Times*.
https://www.nytimes.com/2015/04/02/world/middleeast/
dozens-of-civilians-die-in-yemen-as-factory-is-hit.html
120. Kirkpatrick, D.D., & Fahim, K. (2015, April 2). "Saudi
Leaders Have High Hopes for Yemen Airstrikes, But
Houthi Attacks Continue." *The New York Times*. https://
www.nytimes.com/2015/04/03/world/middleeast/yemen-
al-qaeda-attack.html
121. Bin-Lazrq, F., & Fahim, K. (2015, April 10). "Yemen's
Despair on Full Display in 'Ruined' City." *The New York
Times*. https://www.nytimes.com/2015/04/11/world/
middleeast/aden-yemen.html
122. Reuters. (2015, April 10). "'It's a Ghost Town' - Witness
in Suburban Yemen." *The New York Times*. https://www.
nytimes.com/video/multimedia/100000003622109/its-a-
ghost-town-witness-in-suburban-yemen.html
123. Reuters. (2015, April 13). "Saudi-Led Airstrikes Continue
in Yemen." *The New York Times*. https://www.nytimes.com/
video/multimedia/100000003625169/saudi-led-airstrikes-
continue-in-yemen.html

124. Reuters. (2015, April 3). "A Show of Support for Saleh in Sanaa." *The New York Times*. https://www.nytimes.com/video/multimedia/100000003610501/a-show-of-support-for-saleh-in-sanaa.html

125. Gordon, M.R., & Schmitt, E. (2015, April 15). "Tensions Flare between Iraq and Saudi Arabia in U.S. Coalition." *The New York Times*. https://www.nytimes.com/2015/04/16/world/middleeast/iraqi-prime-minister-criticizes-saudi-intervention-in-yemen.html

126. Gordon, M.R. (2015, April 17). "Iraqi Premier Softens Tone About Saudis." *The New York Times*. https://www.nytimes.com/2015/04/17/world/middleeast/iraqi-premier-softens-tone-about-saudis.html

127. Sengupta, S., & Gladstone, R. (2015, April 15). "U.N. Envoy in Yemen Conflict Says He Will Resign." *The New York Times*. https://www.nytimes.com/2015/04/16/world/middleeast/un-mediator-in-yemen-conflict-says-he-will-resign.html

128. Sengupta, S. (2015, April 14). "U.N. Security Council Bans Sales of Arms to Houthi Fighters in Yemen." *The New York Times*. https://www.nytimes.com/2015/04/15/world/middleeast/yemen-houthis-saudi-airstrikes-arms-embargo.html

129. Mazzetti, M., & Cooper, H. (2015, April 18). "Sale of U.S. Arms Fuels the Wars of Arab States." *The New York Times*. https://www.nytimes.com/2015/04/19/world/middleeast/sale-of-us-arms-fuels-the-wars-of-arab-states.html

130. Shear, M.D., & Rosenberg, M. (2015, April 21). "Warning Iran, U.S. Sends Two More Ships to Yemen." *The New York Times*. https://www.nytimes.com/2015/04/21/world/middleeast/warning-iran-us-sends-two-more-ships-to-yemen.html

131. Cooper, H. (2015, April 24). "American Naval Force Off Yemen Gets Credit After Iranian Convoy Turns Away." *The New York Times.* https://www.nytimes.com/2015/04/25/world/middleeast/american-naval-force-off-yemen-gets-credit-after-iranian-convoy-turns-away.html

132. Kalfood, M.A., & Fahim, K. (2015, April 20). "Yemen Houthi Leader is Defiant in Face of Saudi Airstrikes." *The New York Times.* https://www.nytimes.com/2015/04/20/world/middleeast/yemen-houthi-leader-is-defiant-in-face-of-saudi-airstrikes.html

133. Kalfood, M.A., & Fahim, K. (2015, April 20). "At Least 25 Die as Airstrike Sets Off Huge Blast in Yemen." *The New York Times.* https://www.nytimes.com/2015/04/21/world/middleeast/sana-yemen-explosion.html

134. Reuters. (2015, April 20). "Airstrike Hits Yemeni Capital." *The New York Times.* https://www.nytimes.com/video/world/middleeast/100000003638273/airstrike-hits-yemeni-capital-.html

135. Fahim, K., & Mazzetti, M. (2015, April 21). "Saudis Announce Halt to Yemen Bombing Campaign." *The New York Times.* https://www.nytimes.com/2015/04/22/world/middleeast/saudis-announce-halt-to-yemen-bombing-campaign.html

136. Reuters. (2015, April 22). "Saudi Arabia Announces End to Yemen Air Strikes." *The New York Times.* https://www.nytimes.com/video/multimedia/100000003642223/saudi-arabia-announces-end-to-yemen-air-strikes.html

137. Mackey, R. (2015, April 22). "Sighs of Relief from Yemen, Mixed with Fears of More Conflict." *The New York Times.* https://www.nytimes.com/2015/04/22/world/middleeast/sighs-of-relief-from-yemen-mixed-with-fears-of-more-conflict.html

138. Schmitt, E., & Gordon, M.R. (2015, April 22). "Saudi Resolve on Yemen Reflects Limits of U.S. Strategy." *The*

New York Times. https://www.nytimes.com/2015/04/23/world/middleeast/yemen-airstrikes.html

139. Al-Batati, S., & Fahim, K. (2015, April 26). "Saudi-Led Air Campaign Resumes in Yemeni Capital." *The New York Times.* https://www.nytimes.com/2015/04/27/world/middleeast/saudi-led-air-campaign-resumes-in-yemeni-capital.html

140. Mackey, R. (2015, April 23). "As War Grinds on, Yemenis Share Their Anguish Online." *The New York Times.* https://www.nytimes.com/2015/04/23/world/middleeast/as-war-grinds-on-yemenis-share-their-anguish-online.html

141. Reuters. (2015, April 27). "Yemen's Fighting Intensifies as Humanitarian Crisis Worsens." *The New York Times.* https://www.nytimes.com/video/multimedia/100000003651785/yemens-fighting-intensifies-as-humanitarian-crisis-worsens.html

142. Fahim, K. (2015, April 24). "Fighting Prompts an Exodus from Yemen, Often on Boats." *The New York Times.* https://www.nytimes.com/2015/04/24/world/middleeast/fighting-prompts-an-exodus-from-yemen-often-on-boats.html

143. Gordon, M.R., & Erdbrink, T. (2015, April 27). "Yemen Crisis Looms as Kerry Meets with Iranian Counterpart on Nuclear Deal." *The New York Times.* https://www.nytimes.com/2015/04/28/world/middleeast/iranian-general-says-saudia-arabia-will-soon-be-toppled.html

144. Gladstone, R. (2015, May 16). "Yemen: Aid Coordinator Asks Saudis to Simplify Restrictions." *The New York Times.* https://www.nytimes.com/2015/05/16/world/middleeast/yemen-aid-coordinator-asks-saudis-to-simplify-restrictions.html

145. Reuters. (2015, May 1). "Saudi-Led Air Strikes on Yemen Kill Civilians, Houthis Rally Against Riyadh." *The New York Times.* https://www.nytimes.com/video/multimedia/100000003661859/saudi-led-air-strikes-on-yemen-kill-civilians-houthis-rally-agai.html

146. Fahim, K. (2015, May 3). "Saudi-Led Group Said to Use Cluster Bombs in Yemen." *The New York Times*. https://www.nytimes.com/2015/05/03/world/middleeast/saudi-led-group-said-to-use-cluster-bombs-in-yemen.html

147. Al-Batati, S., & Fahim, K. (2015, May 4). "Yemeni Fighters Trained in Persian Gulf are Said to Join Saudi-Led Mission." *The New York Times*. https://www.nytimes.com/2015/05/04/world/middleeast/yemeni-fighters-trained-in-persian-gulf-are-said-to-join-saudi-led-mission.html

148. Hubbard, B. (2015, May 6). "Saudi Arabia: Yemeni Rebels Attack." *The New York Times*. https://www.nytimes.com/2015/05/06/world/middleeast/saudi-arabia-yemeni-rebels-attack.html

149. Reuters. (2015, May 13). "Obama Praises Saudi Leaders, Focus Now on Yemen." *The New York Times*. https://www.nytimes.com/video/multimedia/100000003681953/obama-praises-saudi-leaders-focus-now-on-yemen.html

150. Kalfood, M.A. (2015, May 22). "Yemen: 5 Migrants Killed by Shells." *The New York Times*. https://www.nytimes.com/2015/05/22/world/middleeast/yemen-5-migrants-killed-by-shells.html

151. Reuters. (2015, May 14). "Women and Children Rally for Houthis in Yemen." *The New York Times*. https://www.nytimes.com/video/multimedia/100000003684582/women-and-children-rally-for-houthis-in-yemen.html

152. Reuters. (2015, May 18). "Houthi Supporters Call for End to Saudi-Led Airstrikes in Yemen." *The New York Times*. https://www.nytimes.com/video/multimedia/100000003691020/houthi-supporters-call-for-end-to-saudi-led-airstrikes-in-yemen.html

153. Fahim, K. (2015, May 29). "Yemen: Amnesty Says Antiaircraft Fire by Houthis Has Killed Many Civilians." *The New York Times*. https://www.nytimes.com/2015/05/29/

world/middleeast/yemen-amnesty-says-antiaircraft-fire-
by-houthis-has-killed-many-civilians.html

154. Reuters. (2015, May 30). "Saudi-Led Air Strike Targets Home
of Houthi Leader in Sanaa." *The New York Times*. https://
www.nytimes.com/video/multimedia/100000003711755/
saudi-led-air-strike-targets-home-of-houthi-leader-in-
sanaa.html

155. Reuters. (2015, May 30). "Saudi-Led Airstrikes Target Sanaa
Air Base." *The New York Times*. https://www.nytimes.com/
video/multimedia/100000003711960/saudi-led-airstrikes-
target-sanaa-air-base.html

156. Reuters. (2015, May 31). "Yemen's Main Sports Complex
Destroyed by Air Strikes." *The New York Times*. https://www.
nytimes.com/video/multimedia/100000003713019/yemens-
main-sports-complex-destroyed-by-air-strikes.html

157. Fahim, K. (2015, June 1). "U.S. Citizens Held in Yemen
by Houthis." *The New York Times*. https://www.nytimes.
com/2015/06/01/world/middleeast/us-citizens-held-in-
yemen-by-houthis.html

158. Al-Batati, S., & Gladstone, R. (2015, March 30). "Dozens
are Reported Killed as Saudi-Led Strike Hits Camp for
Displaced Yemeni Civilians." *The New York Times*. https://
www.nytimes.com/2015/03/31/world/middleeast/yemen-
camp-air-raid.html

159. Fahim, K., & Cumming-Bruce, N. (2015, March 31). "Aid
for Yemen Dwindles as Need Rises Amid Chaos." *The New
York Times*. https://www.nytimes.com/2015/04/01/world/
middleeast/un-warns-of-total-collapse-in-yemen-as-
houthis-continue-offensive.html

160. Reuters. (2015, April 1). "Yemen Air Strikes Kill at Least 23
in Factory – Residents." *The New York Times*. https://www.
nytimes.com/video/multimedia/100000003606066/yemen-
air-strikes-kill-at-least-23-in-factory-residents.html

161. Kalfood, M.A., & Fahim, K. (2015, April 4). "Apparent Saudi Strike Kills at Least Nine in Yemeni Family." *The New York Times*. https://www.nytimes.com/2015/04/05/world/middleeast/apparent-saudi-strike-kills-at-least-nine-in-yemeni-family.html
162. Reuters. (2015, April 8). "Air Strike Hits Houthi Office in Yemeni Capital." *The New York Times*. https://www.nytimes.com/video/multimedia/100000003617379/air-strike-hits-houthi-office-in-yemeni-capital.html
163. Perlez, J. (2015, April 8). "Rescue Mission in Yemen Proves to Be Boon for Chinese Military's Image." *The New York Times*. https://archive.nytimes.com/sinosphere.blogs.nytimes.com/2015/04/08/rescue-mission-in-yemen-proves-to-be-boon-for-chinese-militarys-image/
164. Sengupta, S. (2015, May 2). "Russia Assails West Over Yemen." *The New York Times*. https://www.nytimes.com/2015/05/02/world/russia-assails-west-over-yemen.html
165. Fahim, K. (2015, May 7). "Aid Needs in Yemen are Dire, Kerry Says." *The New York Times*. https://www.nytimes.com/2015/05/07/world/middleeast/aid-needs-in-yemen-are-dire-john-kerry-says.html
166. Hubbard, B. (2015, May 11). "Despite Displeasure with U.S., Saudis Face Long Dependency." *The New York Times*. https://www.nytimes.com/2015/05/12/world/middleeast/persian-gulf-allies-confront-crisis-of-confidence-in-us.html
167. Hubbard, B., & Fahim, K. (2015, May 7). "Saudis Propose Truce for an Aid Effort in Yemen." *The New York Times*. https://www.nytimes.com/2015/05/08/world/middleeast/saudi-arabia-proposes-cease-fire-in-yemen.html
168. Reuters. (2015, May 7). "Kerry Welcomes Yemen Cease-Fire Proposal." *The New York Times*. https://www.nytimes.

com/video/world/middleeast/100000003671522/kerry-welcomes-yemen-cease-fire-proposal.html
169. Kalfood, M.A., & Fahim, K. (2015, May 10). "Houthi Rebels Agree to 5-Day Cease-Fire in Yemen." *The New York Times.* https://www.nytimes.com/2015/05/11/world/middleeast/houthi-rebels-agree-to-5-day-cease-fire-in-yemen.html
170. Kalfood, M.A., & Fahim, K. (2015, May 12). "A Cease-Fire in Yemen, But Fighting is Persistent." *The New York Times.* https://www.nytimes.com/2015/05/13/world/middleeast/iranian-cargo-ship-heads-toward-yemen-and-saudi-blockade.html
171. Kalfood, M.A., & Fahim, K. (2015, May 18). "Saudi-Led Airstrikes Resume in Yemen as Truce Ends." *The New York Times.* https://www.nytimes.com/2015/05/18/world/middleeast/saudi-led-airstrikes-resume-in-yemen-as-truce-ends.html
172. Fahim, K. (2015, May 21). "Yemen: Houthi Leader is Open to Talks." *The New York Times.* https://www.nytimes.com/2015/05/21/world/middleeast/yemen-houthi-leader-is-open-to-talks.html
173. Kalfood, M.A., & Fahim, K. (2015, May 28). "Medical Need Climbs Alongside Death Toll in Yemen." *The New York Times.* https://www.nytimes.com/2015/05/28/world/middleeast/medical-need-climbs-alongside-death-toll-in-yemen.html
174. The Editorial Board. (2015, March 31). "Saudi Arabia's Ominous Reach into Yemen." *The New York Times.* https://www.nytimes.com/2015/04/01/opinion/saudi-arabias-ominous-reach-into-yemen.html
175. Ashford, E. (2015, April 9). "Bombing Yemen Won't Help It." *The New York Times.* https://www.nytimes.com/2015/04/10/opinion/bombing-yemen-wont-help-it.html
176. Kirkpatrick, D.D. (2015, April 9). "Kerry Says U.S. Knew of Iran's Military Aid to Houthi Rebels." *The New York Times.*

https://www.nytimes.com/2015/04/10/world/middleeast/
kerry-us-iran-military-aid-houthi-yemen.html

177. Reuters. (2015, April 9). "Iran Calls Saudi Airstrikes on Yemen 'Genocide.'" *The New York Times.* https://www.nytimes.com/video/multimedia/100000003620178/iran-calls-saudi-airstrikes-on-yemen-genocide.html

178. Kirkpatrick, D.D. (2015, April 9). "Tensions Between Iran and Saudi Arabia Deepen Over Conflict in Yemen." *The New York Times.* https://www.nytimes.com/2015/04/10/world/middleeast/yemen-fighting.html

179. Fahim, K. (2015, April 13). "Saudi Spurns Call by Iran to Draw Back from Yemen." *The New York Times.* https://www.nytimes.com/2015/04/13/world/middleeast/saudi-spurns-call-by-iran-to-draw-back-from-yemen.html

180. Reuters. (2015, April 14). "Iran's Zarif Calls for Aid, Dialogue in Yemen." *The New York Times.* https://www.nytimes.com/video/multimedia/100000003627305/irans-zarif-calls-for-aid-dialogue-in-yemen.html

181. Reuters. (2015, April 14). "Iran Proposes Yemen Peace Plan as Houthis Dig in." *The New York Times.* https://www.nytimes.com/video/multimedia/100000003627937/iran-proposes-yemen-peace-plan-as-houthis-dig-in.html

182. Reuters. (2015, April 15). "Houthis in Yemen, 'Will Fail, We Will Make Sure of This' - Saudi Ambassador to U.S." *The New York Times.* https://www.nytimes.com/video/multimedia/100000003630700/houthis-in-yemen-will-fail-we-will-make-sure-of-this-saudi-ambas.html

183. Erdbrink, T. (2015, April 13). "Amid Tensions with Saudi Arabia, Iran Halts Minor Pilgrimages to Mecca." *The New York Times.* https://www.nytimes.com/2015/04/14/world/middleeast/amid-tensions-with-saudi-arabia-iran-halts-minor-pilgrimages-to-mecca.html

184. Kalfood, M.A., & Fahim, K. (2015, April 28). "Saudis Hit a Yemeni Airport, Possibly Closing Aid Route." *The New York Times*. https://www.nytimes.com/2015/04/29/world/middleeast/saudis-hit-a-yemeni-airport-possibly-closing-aid-route.html

185. Reuters. (2015, April 29). "Saudi-Led Planes Bomb Yemen Airport." *The New York Times*. https://www.nytimes.com/video/multimedia/100000003655739/saudi-led-planes-bomb-yemen-airport.html

186. Reuters. (2015, May 4). "Plane Burns on Runway at Sanaa Airport After Air Strike." *The New York Times*. https://www.nytimes.com/video/multimedia/100000003665448/plane-burns-on-runway-at-sanaa-airport-after-air-strike.html

187. Reuters. (2015, April 29). "Yemen Airport Bombed to Foil Iranian Plane." *The New York Times*. https://www.nytimes.com/video/multimedia/100000003656397/yemen-airport-bombed-to-foil-iranian-plane.html

188. Masood, S., & Fahim, K. (2015, April 6). "Saudis Ask Pakistan to Join the Fight in Yemen." *The New York Times*. https://www.nytimes.com/2015/04/07/world/middleeast/saudis-seek-pakistani-troops-for-yemen-campaign-official-says.html

189. Masood, S., & Gladstone, R. (2015, April 10). "Pakistani Lawmakers Urge Diplomacy in Yemen Conflict But Decline Combat Role." *The New York Times*. https://www.nytimes.com/2015/04/11/world/asia/pakistan-yemen-iran.html

190. Fahim, K., & Cumming-Bruce, N. (2015, April 7). "Expedited Weapons Deliveries to Saudi Arabia Signal Deepening U.S. Involvement." *The New York Times*. https://www.nytimes.com/2015/04/08/world/middleeast/yemen-houthis.html

191. Al-Batati, S., & Fahim, K. (2015, April 3). "Affiliate of Al Qaeda Seizes Major Yemeni City, Driving Out the Military."

The New York Times. https://www.nytimes.com/2015/04/04/world/middleeast/al-qaeda-al-mukalla-yemen.html

192. Cooper, H., & Schmitt, E. (2015, April 8). "Al Qaeda is Capitalizing on Yemen's Disorder, U.S. Warns." *The New York Times.* https://www.nytimes.com/2015/04/09/world/middleeast/ashton-carter-us-defense-secretary-warns-of-al-qaeda-gains-in-yemen.html

193. Al-Batati, S., & Fahim, K. (2015, April 16). "War in Yemen is Allowing Qaeda Group to Expand." *The New York Times.* https://www.nytimes.com/2015/04/17/world/middleeast/khaled-bahah-houthi-rebel-yemen-fighting.html

194. Reuters. (2015, April 14). "Iran Proposes Yemen Peace Plan as Houthis Dig in." *The New York Times.* https://www.nytimes.com/video/multimedia/100000003627937/iran-proposes-yemen-peace-plan-as-houthis-dig-in.html

195. Mazzetti, M., & Callimachi, R. (2015, May 8). "Top Qaeda Figure Dies in Yemen Drone Strike." *The New York Times.* https://www.nytimes.com/2015/05/08/world/middleeast/top-qaeda-figure-dies-in-yemen-drone-strike.html

196. Al-Batati, S., & Kirkpatrick, D.D. (2015, April 17). "Yemeni Army Tries to Safeguard Oil Fields as Qaeda Fighters Advance." *The New York Times.* https://www.nytimes.com/2015/04/18/world/middleeast/aid-agencies-increasingly-alarmed-by-yemen-crisis.html

197. Ferris, J. (2015, April 1). "Nasser's Ghost Hovers over Yemen." *The New York Times.* https://www.nytimes.com/2015/04/02/opinion/nassers-ghost-hovers-over-yemen-saudi-arabia-egypt.html

198. Mansour, A.R. (2015, April 12). "Yemen's President: The Houthis Must be Stopped." *The New York Times.* https://www.nytimes.com/2015/04/13/opinion/the-west-must-help-save-yemen.html

199. al-Maqtari, B. (2015, April 14). "Is There Any Hope Left for Yemen?" *The New York Times.* https://www.nytimes.

com/2015/04/15/opinion/is-there-any-hope-left-for-yemen.
html
200. The Editorial Board. (2015, April 24). "Catastrophe in Yemen." *The New York Times*. https://www.nytimes.com/2015/04/24/opinion/catastrophe-in-yemen.html
201. The New York Times. (2015, May 29). "The Voices of Students: And the Winners are…" *The New York Times*. https://www.nytimes.com/2015/05/31/opinion/the-voices-of-students-and-the-winners-are.html
202. Syrian Archive. (ND). "Russian Airstrikes Database." *Syrian Archive*. https://syrianarchive.org/en/datasets/russian-airstrikes
203. Yemen Data Project. (ND). "Yemen Data Project." https://yemendataproject.org/

Chapter 6. Worthy and Unworthy Disputes: the Chagos Islands, the South China Sea, and the East China Sea

1. "Declaration on the Conduct of Parties in the South China Sea." (2012, May 14). *ASEAN*. https://asean.org/declaration-on-the-conduct-of-parties-in-the-south-china-sea-2/
2. "Diplomatic Cable Signed by D.A. Greenhill, Dated August 24, 1966." (1966). *Wikimedia Commons*. https://commons.wikimedia.org/wiki/File:Diplomatic_Cable_signed_by_D.A._Greenhill,_dated_August_24,_1966.jpg
3. Doward, J. (2014, December 13). "Diego Garcia Guards Its Secrets Even as the Truth on CIA Torture Emerges." *Guardian*. https://www.theguardian.com/world/2014/dec/13/diego-garcia-cia-us-torture-rendition
4. Norton-Taylor, R., & Evans, R. (2010, December 21). "WikiLeaks Cables: Mauritius Sues UK for Control of Chagos Islands." *Guardian*. https://www.theguardian.com/world/2010/dec/21/mauritius-uk-chagos-islands
5. Foley Hoag. (2021, February 2). "Another UN Court Rules Chagos Archipelago Belongs to Mauritius." *Foley Hoag*

LLP. https://foleyhoag.com/news-and-insights/news/2021/february/another-un-court-rules-chagos-archipelago-belongs-to-mauritius/

6. Perlez, J. (2016, July 6). "Ruling on South China Sea Nears in a Case Beijing Has Tried to Ignore." *The New York Times.* https://www.nytimes.com/2016/07/07/world/asia/china-hague-philippines-spratlys.html

7. Perlez, J. (2016, July 10). "Philippines v. China: Q. and A. on South China Sea Case." *The New York Times.* https://www.nytimes.com/2016/07/11/world/asia/south-china-sea-philippines-hague.html

8. Hernández, J.C., & Ponomarev, S. (2016, July 11). "Our Boat was Intercepted by China." *The New York Times.* https://www.nytimes.com/interactive/2016/07/10/world/asia/south-china-sea-scarborough-shoal-philippines-hague.html

9. Perlez, J. (2016, July 12). "Tribunal Rejects Beijing's Claims in South China Sea." *The New York Times.* https://www.nytimes.com/2016/07/13/world/asia/south-china-sea-hague-ruling-philippines.html

10. The Associated Press. (2016, July 12). "Philippines and China React to Tribunal Decision." *The New York Times.* https://www.nytimes.com/video/world/asia/100000004525203/philippines-and-china-react-to-tribunal-decision.html

11. The New York Times. (2016, July 12). "Hague Announces Decision on South China Sea." *The New York Times.* https://www.nytimes.com/interactive/2016/07/12/world/asia/hague-south-china-sea.html

12. The Editorial Board. (2016, July 13). "Testing the Rule of Law in the South China Sea." *The New York Times.* https://www.nytimes.com/2016/07/13/opinion/testing-the-rule-of-law-in-the-south-china-sea.html

13. Ramzy, A. (2016, July 13). "Taiwan, After Rejecting South China Sea Decision, Sends Patrol Ship." *The New York*

Times. https://www.nytimes.com/2016/07/14/world/asia/south-china-sea-taiwan.html

14. Perlez, J. (2016, July 13). "Beijing Protests South China Sea Ruling with Modest Show of Strength." *The New York Times.* https://www.nytimes.com/2016/07/14/world/asia/beijing-south-china-sea-ruling-hague.html

15. The New York Times. (2016, July 13). "The South China Sea Dispute." *The New York Times.* https://www.nytimes.com/2016/07/14/opinion/the-south-china-sea-dispute.html

16. Fisher, M. (2016, July 14). "The South China Sea: Explaining the Dispute." *The New York Times.* https://www.nytimes.com/2016/07/15/world/asia/south-china-sea-dispute-arbitration-explained.html

17. Whaley, F. (2016, July 14). "After the Philippines Celebrates South China Sea Ruling, Reality Sets In." *The New York Times.* https://www.nytimes.com/2016/07/15/world/asia/philippines-south-china-sea.html

18. Heng. (2016, July 17). "Heng on the South China Sea Verdict." *The New York Times.* https://www.nytimes.com/2016/07/10/opinion/heng-on-the-south-china-sea-verdict.html

19. Ramzy, A. (2016, July 19). "KFC Targeted in Protests Over South China Sea." *The New York Times.* https://www.nytimes.com/2016/07/20/world/asia/south-china-sea-protests-kfc.html

20. Perlez, J. (2016, July 15). "Defending David Against the World's Goliaths in International Court." *The New York Times.* https://www.nytimes.com/2016/07/16/world/asia/south-china-sea-phillipines-hague.html

21. Forsythe, M. (2016, July 18). "China Begins Air Patrols Over Disputed Area of the South China Sea." *The New York Times.* https://www.nytimes.com/2016/07/19/world/asia/china-sea-air-patrols.html

22. Buckley, C. (2016, July 29). "Russia to Join China in Naval Exercise in Disputed South China Sea." *The New York Times.* https://www.nytimes.com/2016/07/29/world/asia/russia-china-south-china-sea-naval-exercise.html

23. Reuters. (2016, August 8). "Ex-Philippines Leader Travels to China." *The New York Times.* https://www.nytimes.com/video/world/asia/100000004575463/ex-philippines-leader-travels-to-china.html

24. Sanger, D.E., & Gladstone, R. (2016, August 8). "New Photos Cast Doubt on China's Vow Not to Militarize Disputed Islands." *The New York Times.* https://www.nytimes.com/2016/08/09/world/asia/china-spratly-islands-south-china-sea.html

25. The Editorial Board. (2016, August 13). "China's Defiance in the South China Sea." *The New York Times.* https://www.nytimes.com/2016/08/14/opinion/sunday/chinas-defiance-in-the-south-china-sea.html

26. Lyall, S. (2010, December 22). "Mauritius: British Actions Protested." *The New York Times.* https://www.nytimes.com/2010/12/22/world/africa/22briefs-MauritiusBrf.html

27. Sengupta, S. (2017, June 23). "U.N. Asks International Court to Weigh in on Britain-Mauritius Dispute." *The New York Times.* https://www.nytimes.com/2017/06/22/world/europe/uk-mauritius-chagos-islands.html

28. Simons, M. (2019, February 26). "U.N. Court Tells Britain to End Control of Chagos Islands, Home to U.S. Air Base." *The New York Times.* https://www.nytimes.com/2019/02/25/world/asia/britain-mauritius-chagos-islands.html

29. Bowcott, O., & Borger, J. (2019, May 22). "UK Suffers Crushing Defeat in UN Vote on Chagos Islands." *Guardian.* https://www.theguardian.com/world/2019/may/22/uk-suffers-crushing-defeat-un-vote-chagos-islands

30. Gladstone, R. (2019, May 22). "Britain Dealt Defeat at U.N. Over Its Control of Chagos Islands." *The New York Times*. https://www.nytimes.com/2019/05/22/world/africa/britain-chagos-mauritius.html

31. Horowitz, J. (2019, September 10). "Pope Francis: 'I Pray There are No Schisms.'" *The New York Times*. https://www.nytimes.com/2019/09/10/world/europe/pope-francis-schism.html

32. Sands, P. (2021, April 1). "Britain Holds On to a Colony in Africa, with America's Help." *The New York Times*. https://www.nytimes.com/2021/04/01/opinion/uk-mauritius-china-us.html

33. ChinaPower. (2021, January 25). "How Much Trade Transits the South China Sea?" *ChinaPower Project*. https://chinapower.csis.org/much-trade-transits-south-china-sea/

34. Davies, R. (2019, September 6). "A Game of Risk: The Indian Ocean's Most Strategically Important Ports." *Ship Technology*. https://web.archive.org/web/20221007213204/https://www.ship-technology.com/analysis/a-game-of-risk-the-indian-oceans-most-strategically-important-ports/

35. Johnson, W. (2016, May 11). "Everything You Need to Know About the South China Sea Conflict - in Under Five Minutes." *Reuters*. https://www.reuters.com/article/us-johnson-china-idUSKBN0OQ03620150610

36. Mahbubani, K. (2020). *Has China Won? The Chinese Challenge to American Primacy*. Hachette UK.

37. Doornbos, C. (2020, December 28). "Navy Challenges Vietnamese Claims to Seas Around Resort Island in South China Sea." *Stars and Stripes*. https://www.stripes.com/theaters/asia_pacific/navy-challenges-vietnamese-claims-to-seas-around-resort-island-in-south-china-sea-1.656609

38. Sanger, D.E., & Gladstone, R. (2015, April 8). "Piling Sand in a Disputed Sea, China Literally Gains Ground." *The New York Times*. https://www.nytimes.com/2015/04/09/world/asia/new-images-show-china-literally-gaining-ground-in-south-china-sea.html

39. Sanger, D.E., & Gladstone, R. (2015, April 8). "Piling Sand in a Disputed Sea, China Literally Gains Ground." *The New York Times*. https://www.nytimes.com/2015/04/09/world/asia/new-images-show-china-literally-gaining-ground-in-south-china-sea.html

40. Wong, E. (2015, April 9). "China Says Construction in Contested Waters is for Maritime Purposes." *The New York Times*. https://www.nytimes.com/2015/04/10/world/asia/china-south-china-sea-spratly-paracel-islands.html

41. The New York Times. (2015, April 10). "China's Statement on Its Construction in the South China Sea." *The New York Times*. https://archive.nytimes.com/sinosphere.blogs.nytimes.com/2015/04/10/chinas-statement-on-its-construction-in-the-south-china-sea/

42. Whaley, F. (2015, April 13). "China's Island-Building is Ruining Coral Reefs, Philippines Says." *The New York Times*. https://www.nytimes.com/2015/04/14/world/asia/chinas-island-building-is-ruining-coral-reefs-philippines-says.html

43. Perlez, J. (2015, April 16). "China Building Aircraft Runway in Disputed Spratly Islands." *The New York Times*. https://www.nytimes.com/2015/04/17/world/asia/china-building-airstrip-in-disputed-spratly-islands-satellite-images-show.html

44. Reuters. (2015, April 17). "'Chinese Construction' on Disputed Island." *The New York Times*. https://www.nytimes.com/video/multimedia/100000003634070/chinese-construction-on-disputed-island.html

45. Wong, E., & Perlez, J. (2015, June 16). "As Tensions with U.S. Grow, Beijing Says It Will Stop Building Artificial Islands in South China Sea." *The New York Times*. https://www.nytimes.com/2015/06/17/world/asia/china-to-halt-its-building-of-islands-but-not-its-projects-on-them.html

46. Perlez, J. (2015, September 15). "China Building Airstrip on 3rd Artificial Island, Images Show." *The New York Times*. https://www.nytimes.com/2015/09/16/world/asia/china-building-airstrip-on-3rd-artificial-island-images-show.html

47. Watkins, D. (2016, February 29). "What China Has Been Building in the South China Sea." *The New York Times*. https://www.nytimes.com/interactive/2015/07/30/world/asia/what-china-has-been-building-in-the-south-china-sea-2016.html

48. Forsythe, M., & Perlez, J. (2016, March 8). "South China Sea Buildup Brings Beijing Closer to Realizing Control." *The New York Times*. https://www.nytimes.com/2016/03/09/world/asia/south-china-sea-militarization.html

49. Buckley, C. (2016, December 16). "China Suggests It Has Placed Weapons on Disputed Spratly Islands in South China Sea." *The New York Times*. https://www.nytimes.com/2016/12/15/world/asia/china-spratly-islands.html

50. Forsythe, M. (2016, February 17). "Missiles Deployed on Disputed South China Sea Island, Officials Say." *The New York Times*. https://www.nytimes.com/2016/02/18/world/asia/china-missiles-south-china-sea.html

51. Landler, M., & Forsythe, M. (2016, February 18). "Chinese Missiles in South China Sea Underscore a Growing Conflict Risk." *The New York Times*. https://www.nytimes.com/2016/02/18/world/asia/chinese-missiles-underscore-a-growing-conflict-risk.html

52. Reuters and the Associated Press. (2016, February 17). "Officials on South China Sea Activity." *The*

New York Times. https://www.nytimes.com/video/world/asia/100000004215029/officials-on-south-china-sea-activity.html

53. The Editorial Board. (2016, February 18). "China's Missile Provocation." *The New York Times*. https://www.nytimes.com/2016/02/18/opinion/chinas-missile-provocation.html

54. Forsythe, M. (2016, February 23). "Possible Radar Suggests Beijing Wants 'Effective Control' in South China Sea." *The New York Times*. https://www.nytimes.com/2016/02/24/world/asia/china-south-china-sea-radar.html

55. Specia, M., & Takkunen, M. (2018, February 8). "South China Sea Photos Suggest a Military Building Spree by Beijing." *The New York Times*. https://www.nytimes.com/2018/02/08/world/asia/south-china-seas-photos.html

56. Villamor, F. (2017, April 8). "Philippines on Duterte's Order to Occupy Disputed Islands: Never Mind." *The New York Times*. https://www.nytimes.com/2017/04/08/world/asia/philippines-duterte-spratly-islands.html

57. Villamor, F. (2017, November 8). "Philippines Halts Work in South China Sea, in Bid to Appease Beijing." *The New York Times*. https://www.nytimes.com/2017/11/08/world/asia/philippines-south-china-sea.html

58. Myers, S.L. (2018, May 20). "Island or Rock? Taiwan Defends Its Claim in South China Sea." *The New York Times*. https://www.nytimes.com/2018/05/20/world/asia/china-taiwan-island-south-sea.html

59. Cochrane, J. (2016, March 21). "China's Coast Guard Rams Fishing Boat to Free It From Indonesian Authorities." *The New York Times*. https://www.nytimes.com/2016/03/22/world/asia/indonesia-south-china-sea-fishing-boat.html

60. Perlez, J., & Huang, Y. (2016, April 10). "Harrowing Trip for Chinese Trawler Before Bump in Territorial Tensions." *The New York Times*. https://www.nytimes.com/2016/04/10/

world/asia/harrowing-trip-for-chinese-trawler-before-bump-in-territorial-tensions.html

61. Cochrane, J. (2016, June 20). "Indonesia Confirms Seizing Fishing Boat in South China Sea, Defying Beijing." *The New York Times.* https://www.nytimes.com/2016/06/21/world/asia/indonesia-south-china-sea-fishing.html

62. The Associated Press. (2016, June 20). "China on Indonesia's Detention of Boat." *The New York Times.* https://www.nytimes.com/video/world/asia/100000004482032/china-on-indonesias-detention-of-boat.html

63. Cochrane, J. (2017, September 10). "Indonesia, Long on Sidelines, Starts to Confront China's Territorial Claims." *The New York Times.* https://www.nytimes.com/2017/09/10/world/asia/indonesia-south-china-sea-military-buildup.html

64. Gutierrez, J. (2019, June 12). "Philippines Accuses Chinese Vessel of Sinking Fishing Boat in Disputed Waters." *The New York Times.* https://www.nytimes.com/2019/06/12/world/asia/philippines-china-fishing-boat.html

65. Gutierrez, J., & Beech, H. (2019, June 13). "Sinking of Philippine Boat Puts South China Sea Back at Issue." *The New York Times.* https://www.nytimes.com/2019/06/13/world/asia/south-china-sea-philippines.html

66. Gutierrez, J. (2019, June 25). "Duterte Plays Down Chinese Ramming of Philippine Fishing Boat." *The New York Times.* https://www.nytimes.com/2019/06/25/world/asia/philippines-china-duterte-ships.html

67. Beech, H., Suhartono, M., & Dean, A. (2020, March 31). "China Chases Indonesia's Fishing Fleets, Staking Claim to Sea's Riches." *The New York Times.* https://www.nytimes.com/2020/03/31/world/asia/Indonesia-south-china-sea-fishing.html

68. Gutierrez, J., & Aznar, J. (2021, July 11). "Overwhelmed by Chinese Fleets, Filipino Fishermen 'Protest and Adapt.'"

The New York Times. https://www.nytimes.com/2021/07/11/world/asia/philippines-south-china-sea-fishermen.html

69. Villamor, F. (2017, September 25). "Philippines Promises Vietnam a Full Investigation into Fishermen's Deaths." *The New York Times.* https://www.nytimes.com/2017/09/25/world/asia/philippines-vietnamese-fishermen.html

70. Whaley, F. (2013, May 10). "Taiwan Demands Philippine Apology for Fisherman's Killing." *The New York Times.* https://www.nytimes.com/2013/05/11/world/asia/taiwan-demands-apology-from-philippines-for-fishermans-killing.html

71. Perlez, J. (2013, May 15). "Taiwan Recalls Its Envoy in Manila Over a Killing." *The New York Times.* https://www.nytimes.com/2013/05/16/world/asia/taiwan-recalls-representative-in-manila-over-killing.html

72. Tatlow, D.K. (2013, May 22). "Tensions Flare in Asian Seas, Now Involving Taiwan." *The New York Times.* https://archive.nytimes.com/rendezvous.blogs.nytimes.com/2013/05/22/tensions-flare-in-asian-seas-now-involving-taiwan/

73. Whaley, F. (2013, June 13). "Charges Urged in Filipino Raid on Taiwanese Boat." *The New York Times.* https://www.nytimes.com/2013/06/14/world/asia/charges-urged-in-filipino-raid-on-taiwanese-boat.html

74. Perlez, J. (2013, August 9). "Taiwan Ends Sanctions Against Philippines Over Shooting Death." *The New York Times.* https://www.nytimes.com/2013/08/10/world/asia/taiwan-drops-sanctions-against-philippines-over-fishermans-killing.html

75. Patag, K.J. (2019, September 18). "8 Coast Guard Personnel Convicted Over 2013 Killing of Taiwanese Fisherman." *Philstar.com.* https://www.philstar.com/headlines/2019/09/18/1952897/8-coast-guard-personnel-convicted-over-2013-killing-taiwanese-fisherman

76. Center for Strategic and International Studies. (2023). "Corporations: Our Donors." *Center for Strategic and International Studies.* https://www.csis.org/corporation-and-trade-association-donors

77. Asia Maritime Transparency Initiative. (2017, August 4). "Vietnam Builds Up Its Remote Outposts." *Asia Maritime Transparency Initiative.* https://amti.csis.org/vietnam-builds-remote-outposts/

78. Dang, V.H. (2020, March 11). "Malaysia Should Embrace Compliance on Its Overlapping Continental Shelf Claim." *Asia Maritime Transparency Initiative.* https://amti.csis.org/malaysia-should-embrace-compliance-on-its-overlapping-continental-shelf-claim/

79. Asia Maritime Transparency Initiative. (2016, May 11). "Vietnam's Island Building: Double-Standard or Drop in the Bucket?" *Asia Maritime Transparency Initiative.* https://amti.csis.org/vietnams-island-building/

80. Asia Maritime Transparency Initiative. (2015, July 29). "Airpower in the South China Sea." *Asia Maritime Transparency Initiative.* https://amti.csis.org/airstrips-scs/

81. Asia Maritime Transparency Initiative. (2018, May 25). "Philippines Launches Spratly Runway Repairs." *Asia Maritime Transparency Initiative.* https://amti.csis.org/philippines-launches-spratly-repairs/

82. Asia Maritime Transparency Initiative. (2019, February 6). "Under Pressure: Philippine Construction Provokes a Paramilitary Response." *Asia Maritime Transparency Initiative.* https://amti.csis.org/under-pressure-philippine-construction-paramilitary-response/

83. Nepomuceno, P. (2021, April 21). "WPS Security Assured With More Assets." *Philippine News Agency.* https://www.pna.gov.ph/articles/1137602

84. Johnson, W. (2016, May 11). "Everything You Need to Know About the South China Sea Conflict - in Under Five Minutes." *Reuters.* https://www.reuters.com/article/us-johnson-china-idUSKBN0OQ03620150610

85. Jatmiko, B.P. (2020, January 6). "Selama Jadi Menteri, Berapa Kapal China Ditenggelamkan Susi?" *KOMPAS.com.* https://money.kompas.com/read/2020/01/06/160600226/selama-jadi-menteri-berapa-kapal-china-ditenggelamkan-susi

86. Fackler, M. (2012, August 15). "Japan Holds 14 Chinese in Island Landing." *The New York Times.* https://www.nytimes.com/2012/08/16/world/asia/japanese-ministers-visit-tokyo-shrine.html

87. McDonald, M. (2012, August 16). "East Asia's Sea Disputes: Scar Tissue from War Wounds." *The New York Times.* https://archive.nytimes.com/rendezvous.blogs.nytimes.com/2012/08/16/east-asias-sea-disputes-scar-tissue-from-war-wounds/

88. Fackler, M. (2012, August 16). "China Urges Japan to Release Protesters Caught on Disputed Island." *The New York Times.* https://www.nytimes.com/2012/08/17/world/asia/china-urges-japan-to-release-protesters-caught-on-disputed-island.html

89. Fackler, M. (2012, August 17). "Japan Deports 14 Chinese Citizens in Island Dispute." *The New York Times.* https://www.nytimes.com/2012/08/18/world/asia/japan-plans-to-deport-chinese-on-island.html

90. Bradsher, K., Fackler, M., & Jacobs, A. (2012, August 19). "Anti-Japan Protests Erupt in China Over Disputed Island." *The New York Times.* https://www.nytimes.com/2012/08/20/world/asia/japanese-activists-display-flag-on-disputed-island.html

91. McDonald, M. (2012, August 20). "Simmering Chinese Anger at Japan is Now on the Boil." *The New York Times.*

https://archive.nytimes.com/rendezvous.blogs.nytimes.com/2012/08/20/simmering-chinese-anger-at-japan-is-now-on-the-boil/

92. Qin, A., & Wong, E. (2012, October 11). "Smashed Skull Serves as Grim Symbol of Seething Patriotism." *The New York Times*. https://www.nytimes.com/2012/10/11/world/asia/xian-beating-becomes-symbol-of-nationalism-gone-awry.html

93. Bradsher, K. (2012, August 20). "Activist Chinese Group Plans More Anti-Japan Protests." *The New York Times*. https://www.nytimes.com/2012/08/21/world/asia/activist-chinese-group-plans-more-anti-japan-protests.html

94. Fackler, M. (2012, August 22). "Dispute Over Islands Reflects Japanese Fear of China's Rise." *The New York Times*. https://www.nytimes.com/2012/08/22/world/asia/dispute-over-islands-reflect-japanese-fear-of-chinas-rise.html

95. Gries, P.H. (2012, August 24). "Why China Resents Japan, and US." *The New York Times*. https://www.nytimes.com/2012/08/24/opinion/why-china-resents-japan-and-us.html

96. The New York Times. (2012, August 27). "Resolving East Asia's Conflicts." *The New York Times*. https://www.nytimes.com/2012/08/28/opinion/resolving-east-asias-conflicts.html

97. McDonald, M. (2012, August 30). "Clinton to Visit China Amid Diplomatic Storms." *The New York Times*. https://archive.nytimes.com/rendezvous.blogs.nytimes.com/2012/08/30/clinton-to-visit-china-amid-diplomatic-storms/

98. Perlez, J., & Myers, S.L. (2012, September 3). "In Beijing, Clinton Will Push for Talks Over Disputed Islands." *The New York Times*. https://www.nytimes.com/2012/09/04/world/asia/in-beijing-clinton-to-discuss-island-disputes.html?searchResultPosition=17

99. Fackler, M. (2012, September 6). "Japan Said to Have Tentative Deal to Buy 3 Disputed Islands from Private Owners." *The New York Times.* https://www.nytimes. com/2012/09/07/world/asia/japan-agrees-to-buy-islands-at-center-of-dispute-with-china.html

100. Perlez, J. (2012, September 11). "China Accuses Japan of Stealing After Purchase of Group of Disputed Islands." *The New York Times.* https://www.nytimes.com/2012/09/12/ world/asia/china-accuses-japan-of-stealing-disputed-islands.html

101. Perlez, J. (2012, September 11). "China Accuses Japan of Stealing After Purchase of Group of Disputed Islands." *The New York Times.* https://www.nytimes.com/2012/09/12/ world/asia/china-accuses-japan-of-stealing-disputed-islands.html

102. Bradsher, K. (2012, September 12). "Hong Kong Impedes Trip to Islands, Activists Say." *The New York Times.* https:// www.nytimes.com/2012/09/13/world/asia/activists-face-barriers-in-return-to-disputed-islands.html

103. Fackler, M. (2012, September 14). "Chinese Ships Enter Japanese-Controlled Waters to Protest Sale of Islands." *The New York Times.* https://www.nytimes.com/2012/09/14/ world/asia/chinese-ships-enter-japanese-controlled-waters-to-protest-sale-of-islands.html

104. Tatlow, D.K. (2012, September 14). "Rising Tension – and Stakes – in Japan-China Island Dispute." *The New York Times.* https://archive.nytimes.com/rendezvous.blogs.nytimes. com/2012/09/14/rising-tension-and-stakes-in-japan-china-island-dispute/

105. Johnson, I., & Shanker, T. (2012, September 18). "More Protests in China Over Japan and Islands." *The New York Times.* https://www.nytimes.com/2012/09/19/world/asia/ china-warns-japan-over-island-dispute.html

106. Johnson, I., & Shanker, T. (2012, September 16). "Beijing Mixes Messages Over Anti-Japan Protests." *The New York Times*. https://www.nytimes.com/2012/09/17/world/asia/anti-japanese-protests-over-disputed-islands-continue-in-china.html

107. Tatlow, D.K. (2012, September 19). "The Meaning of the China-Japan Island Dispute." *The New York Times*. https://archive.nytimes.com/rendezvous.blogs.nytimes.com/2012/09/19/the-meaning-of-the-china-japan-island-dispute/

108. McDonald, M. (2012, September 26). "Even Panda Diplomacy Isn't Working." *The New York Times*. https://archive.nytimes.com/rendezvous.blogs.nytimes.com/2012/09/26/even-panda-diplomacy-isnt-working/

109. Bradsher, K. (2012, October 9). "In China Protests, Japanese Car Sales Suffer." *The New York Times*. https://www.nytimes.com/2012/10/10/business/global/japanese-car-sales-plummet-in-china.html

110. Fackler, M. (2012, October 10). "China Snubs Financial Meetings in Japan in Dispute Over Islands." *The New York Times*. https://www.nytimes.com/2012/10/11/world/asia/china-snubs-financial-meetings-in-japan-in-dispute-over-islands.html

111. Shaw, H. (2012, September 19). "The Inconvenient Truth Behind the Diaoyu/Senkaku Islands." *The New York Times*. https://archive.nytimes.com/kristof.blogs.nytimes.com/2012/09/19/the-inconvenient-truth-behind-the-diaoyusenkaku-islands/

112. Nishi, T. (2012, October 4). "The Diaoyu/Senkaku Islands: A Japanese Scholar Responds." *The New York Times*. https://archive.nytimes.com/kristof.blogs.nytimes.com/2012/10/04/the-diaoyusenkaku-islands-a-japanese-scholar-responds

113. McDonald, M. (2012, September 23). "How to Settle the Fight Over Some Guano-Covered Rocks." *The New York Times*. https://archive.nytimes.com/rendezvous.blogs.nytimes.com/2012/09/23/how-to-settle-the-fight-over-some-guano-covered-rocks

114. Fackler, M., & Johnson, I. (2012, September 21). "Sleepy Islands and a Smoldering Dispute." *The New York Times*. https://www.nytimes.com/2012/09/21/world/asia/japan-china-trade-ties-complicate-island-dispute.html

115. Fackler, M. (2012, September 22). "In Shark-Infested Waters, Resolve of Two Giants is Tested." *The New York Times*. https://www.nytimes.com/2012/09/23/world/asia/islands-dispute-tests-resolve-of-china-and-japan.html

116. Tabuchi, H. (2012, September 25). "Near Disputed Islands, Japan Confronts Boats from Taiwan." *The New York Times*. https://www.nytimes.com/2012/09/26/world/asia/near-disputed-isles-japan-confronts-boats-from-taiwan.html

117. Mackey, R. (2012, September 25). "Video Reports from Japan, Taiwan and China on Confrontation Off Disputed Islands." *The New York Times*. https://archive.nytimes.com/thelede.blogs.nytimes.com/2012/09/25/video-reports-from-japan-taiwan-and-china-on-confrontation-off-disputed-islands/

118. Perlez, J. (2012, September 28). "China Alters Its Strategy in Diplomatic Crisis with Japan." *The New York Times*. https://www.nytimes.com/2012/09/29/world/asia/china-alters-its-strategy-in-dispute-with-japan.html

119. Fackler, M. (2012, October 12). "China and Japan Say They Held Talks About Island Dispute That Has Frayed Relations." *The New York Times*. https://www.nytimes.com/2012/10/13/world/asia/china-and-japan-say-they-held-talks-over-islands-dispute.html

120. Gordon, M.R. (2012, October 20). "In Asia Trip, U.S. Group Will Tackle Islands Feud." *The New York Times*. https://www.nytimes.com/2012/10/20/world/asia/group-to-try-talks-on-islands-in-japan-china-trip.html

121. Fackler, M. (2012, October 17). "Japanese Politician's Visit to Shrine Raises Worries." *The New York Times*. https://www.nytimes.com/2012/10/18/world/asia/japan-opposition-leader-shinzo-abe-visits-war-shrine-a-possible-message-to-neighbors.html

122. McDonald, M. (2012, December 19). "To Japan-China Row, Add One Potential Provocateur." *The New York Times*. https://archive.nytimes.com/rendezvous.blogs.nytimes.com/2012/12/19/to-japan-china-row-add-one-potential-provocateur/

123. Perlez, J., & Bradsher, K. (2012, October 30). "Ex-Envoy Says U.S. Stirs China-Japan Tensions." *The New York Times*. https://www.nytimes.com/2012/10/31/world/asia/in-speech-organized-by-beijing-ex-diplomat-calls-islands-dispute-with-japan-a-time-bomb.html

124. Fackler, M. (2012, November 3). "Chinese Patrol Ships Pressuring Japan Over Islands." *The New York Times*. https://www.nytimes.com/2012/11/03/world/asia/china-keeps-up-pressure-on-japan-over-disputed-islands-with-patrols.html

125. Tabuchi, H. (2012, December 13). "Japan Scrambles Jets in Islands Dispute with China." *The New York Times*. https://www.nytimes.com/2012/12/14/world/asia/japan-scrambles-jets-in-island-dispute-with-china.html

126. Perlez, J. (2012, December 15). "China Steps Up Pressure on Japan in Island Dispute." *The New York Times*. https://www.nytimes.com/2012/12/16/world/asia/china-steps-up-pressure-on-japan-in-island-dispute.html

127. Sang-Hun, C. (2011, August 1). "Japanese Lawmakers Denied Entry in South Korea." *The New York Times*. https://www.nytimes.com/2011/08/02/world/asia/02korea.html

128. Sang-Hun, C. (2012, August 10). "South Korean's Visit to Disputed Islets Angers Japan." *The New York Times*. https://www.nytimes.com/2012/08/11/world/asia/south-koreans-visit-to-disputed-islets-angers-japan.html

129. Das, A. (2012, August 12). "South Korean Denied Medal Over Politics." *The New York Times*. https://www.nytimes.com/2012/08/12/sports/olympics/south-korean-soccer-player-park-jong-soo-denied-medal-over-politics.html

130. Sang-Hun, C. (2012, October 5). "Fight Over Rocky Islets Opens Old Wounds Between South Korea and Japan." *The New York Times*. https://www.nytimes.com/2012/10/05/world/asia/south-korea-and-japan-fight-over-rocky-islets.html

131. Sang-Hun, C. (2012, August 23). "South Korea Returns Letter on Islets From Japanese Leader." *The New York Times*. https://www.nytimes.com/2012/08/24/world/asia/south-korea-returns-letter-from-japanese-leader-or-tries-to.html

132. Fackler, M. (2012, August 24). "Japan Places Pressure on South Korea Amid Islets Dispute." *The New York Times*. https://www.nytimes.com/2012/08/25/world/asia/japan-vows-to-press-claims-over-disputed-islands.html

133. Cha, V., & Friedhoff, K. (2013, November 14). "Ending a Feud Between Allies." *The New York Times*. https://www.nytimes.com/2013/11/15/opinion/ending-a-feud-between-allies.html

134. The New York Times. (2014, October 25). "South Korean Protesters Rally Against Japan Over Disputed Islands." *The New York Times*. https://www.nytimes.com/video/multimedia/100000003197318/south-korean-protesters-rally-against-japan-over-disputed-island.html

135. Sang-Hun, C. (2019, July 23). "South Korean Jets Fire Warning Shots Toward Russian Military Plane." *The New York Times*. https://www.nytimes.com/2019/07/23/world/asia/south-korean-warning-shots-russia-planes.html

136. Sang-Hun, C. (2019, August 25). "South Korea Launches Military Exercise for Islets Also Claimed by Japan." *The New York Times*. https://www.nytimes.com/2019/08/25/world/asia/south-korea-japan-islands.html

137. Sang-Hun, C. (2019, August 31). "South Korean Lawmakers Visit Disputed Islets Claimed by Japan." *The New York Times*. https://www.nytimes.com/2019/08/31/world/asia/south-korea-dokdo-japan.html

138. Haberman, C. (1988, January 4). "Japanese Fight Invading Sea for Priceless Speck of Land." *The New York Times*. https://www.nytimes.com/1988/01/04/world/japanese-fight-invading-sea-for-priceless-speck-of-land.html

139. Van Dyke, J. (1988, January 21). "Speck in the Ocean Meets Law of the Sea." *The New York Times*. https://www.nytimes.com/1988/01/21/opinion/l-speck-in-the-ocean-meets-law-of-the-sea-406488.html

140. The New York Times. (2005, May 20). "Tokyo Governor Visits Disputed Islets." *The New York Times*. https://www.nytimes.com/2005/05/20/world/asia/tokyo-governor-visits-disputed-islets.html

141. The New York Times. (2007, June 15). "Japan Plants Coral Around Islets to Bolster Territorial Claim." *The New York Times*. https://www.nytimes.com/2007/06/15/world/asia/15iht-coral.1.6151693.html

142. Jacobs, F. (2012, May 29). "Ephemeral Islands." *The New York Times*. https://archive.nytimes.com/opinionator.blogs.nytimes.com/2012/05/29/ephemeral-islands/

143. Hana, L. (2019, October 25). "Events Nationwide Mark 20th Annual Dokdo Day." *Korea.net*. https://www.korea.net/NewsFocus/Culture/view?articleId=178479

144. Kyodo News. (2021, August 18). "Tokyo Protests to Seoul Over South Korean Lawmaker's Visit to Takeshima." *Kyodo News*. https://english.kyodonews.net/news/2021/08/b1b59e0e1cb5-tokyo-protests-to-seoul-over-s-korean-lawmakers-visit-to-takeshima.html

145. Sung-mi, A. (2021, November 18). "Japan Calls Off Joint News Conference Over Dokdo Dispute with S. Korea." *Korea Herald*. http://m.koreaherald.com/view.php?ud=20211118000736

146. Reuters. (2018, November 26). "South Korean Lawmakers Land on Disputed Isle, Prompting Japan Protest." *Reuters*. https://www.reuters.com/article/us-japan-southkorea-islands/south-korean-lawmakers-land-on-disputed-isle-prompting-japan-protest-idUSKCN1NV19M

147. Lendon, B. (2018, June 18). "Japan Protests South Korean Military Drills Near Contested Islands." *CNN*. https://www.cnn.com/2018/06/18/asia/south-korean-military-drills-disputed-islands-intl/index.html

148. Nikkei Asia. (2021, June 15). "South Korea Holds Drill Around Takeshima Islets Amid Japan Protest." *Nikkei Asia*. https://asia.nikkei.com/Spotlight/Japan-South-Korea-rift/South-Korea-holds-drill-around-Takeshima-islets-amid-Japan-protest

149. Hankyoreh. (2020, March 25). "Japan Continues to Authorize History Distorting Textbooks Saying Dokdo Has Always Been Japanese Territory." *Hani.Co.Kr*. https://english.hani.co.kr/arti/english_edition/e_international/934168.html

150. Kyodo. (2017, November 9). "South Korea Rebuffs Japan's Protest Over 'Dodko Shrimp' Served to Donald Trump for Dinner." *South China Morning Post*. https://www.scmp.

com/news/asia/diplomacy/article/2119189/south-korea-rebuffs-japans-protest-over-dokdo-shrimp-served
151. Clark, G. (2015, June 17). "Beijing is Getting a Bad Rap in South China Sea Disputes." *Japan Times*. https://web.archive. org/web/20210507005453/https://www.japantimes.co.jp/ opinion/2015/06/17/commentary/world-commentary/ beijing-getting-bad-rap-south-china-sea-disputes/
152. Jennings, R. (2016, April 29). "An Islet the Size of Your Bedroom Has Japan and Taiwan Fighting." *Los Angeles Times*. https://www.latimes.com/world/asia/la-fg-japan-taiwan-islet-dispute-20160429-story.html

Chapter 7. Worthy and Unworthy Around the World

1. Herszenhorn, D.M. (2013, November 22). "Ukraine Blames I.M.F. for Halt to Agreements with Europe." *The New York Times*. https://www.nytimes.com/2013/11/23/world/ europe/ukraine-blames-imf-for-collapse-of-accord-with-european-union.html
2. Herszenhorn, D.M. (2013, November 26). "Ukraine in Turmoil After Leaders Reject Major E.U. Deal." *The New York Times*. https://www.nytimes.com/2013/11/27/world/ europe/protests-continue-as-ukraine-leader-defends-stance-on-europe.html
3. Herszenhorn, D.M. (2013, November 26). "Ukraine in Turmoil After Leaders Reject Major E.U. Deal." *The New York Times*. https://www.nytimes.com/2013/11/27/world/ europe/protests-continue-as-ukraine-leader-defends-stance-on-europe.html
4. Wolczuk, R. (2013, November 27). "Ukraine on the Brink." *The New York Times*. https://www.nytimes.com/2013/11/28/ opinion/ukraine-on-the-brink.html
5. The Editorial Board. (2013, November 28). "Opinion: Ukraine Backs Down." *The New York Times*. https://web.

archive.org/web/20220616233105/https://www.nytimes.
com/2013/11/29/opinion/ukraine-backs-down.html

6. Gessen, M. (2013, December 2). "A Whiter Shade of Envy." *The New York Times.* https://archive.nytimes.com/latitude.blogs.nytimes.com/2013/12/02/a-whiter-shade-of-envy/?searchResultPosition=38

7. Interfax-Ukraine. (2013, February 25). "Yanukovych Happy with Results of Ukrainian-EU Summit." *KyivPost.* https://www.kyivpost.com/article/content/eu-ukraine-relations/yanukovych-happy-with-results-of-ukrainian-eu-summit-320915.html

8. BBC. (2013, April 8). "Ukraine President Viktor Yanukovych Pardons Yulia Tymoshenko Allies." *BBC News.* https://www.bbc.com/news/av/world-europe-22061269

9. Petro, N.N. (2013, December 3). "How the E.U. Pushed Ukraine East." *The New York Times.* https://www.nytimes.com/2013/12/04/opinion/how-the-eu-pushed-ukraine-east.html

10. Herszenhorn, D.M. (2013, November 24). "Thousands Protest Ukraine's Rejection of Trade Pacts." *The New York Times.* https://www.nytimes.com/2013/11/25/world/europe/thousands-of-ukrainians-protest-scrapping-of-trade-pact-with-eu.html

11. Herszenhorn, D.M. (2013e, November 29). "Ukraine Faces E.U.'s Dismay on Turnabout on Accords." *The New York Times.* https://www.nytimes.com/2013/11/30/world/europe/european-union-grapples-with-disappointment-over-ukraine.html

12. Herszenhorn, D.M. (2013e, November 29). "Ukraine Faces E.U.'s Dismay on Turnabout on Accords." *The New York Times.* https://www.nytimes.com/2013/11/30/world/europe/european-union-grapples-with-disappointment-over-ukraine.html

13. Kotsyuba, O. (2013, November 29). "Ukraine's Battle for Europe." *The New York Times*. https://www.nytimes.com/2013/11/30/opinion/ukraines-battle-for-europe.html

14. Interfax-Ukraine. (2013, November 26). "Poll: Ukrainian Public Split Over EU, Customs Union Options." *KyivPost*. https://www.kyivpost.com/article/content/ukraine-politics/poll-ukrainian-public-split-over-eu-customs-union-options-332470.html

15. Interfax-Ukraine. (2013, November 26). "Poll: Ukrainian Public Split Over EU, Customs Union Options." *KyivPost*. https://www.kyivpost.com/article/content/ukraine-politics/poll-ukrainian-public-split-over-eu-customs-union-options-332470.html

16. Ukrainian Pravda. (2013, October 16). "Over the Past Three Years, Ukrainians are Less and Less Willing to Go to Russia." *Pravda*. https://www.pravda.com.ua/news/2013/10/16/7000106/

17. Pifer, S., & Thoburn, H. (2013, November 18). "Viktor Yanukovych: Losing Europe ... and Losing the Ukrainian Public?" *Brookings*. https://www.brookings.edu/blog/up-front/2013/11/18/viktor-yanukovych-losing-europe-and-losing-the-ukrainian-public/

18. The Editorial Board. (2013, December 3). "A Moment of Peril in Kiev." *The New York Times*. https://www.nytimes.com/2013/12/03/opinion/a-moment-of-peril-in-kiev.html

19. Herszenhorn, D.M. (2013g, November 30). "Ukrainians Back in Street to Support E.U. Accord." *The New York Times*. https://www.nytimes.com/2013/12/01/world/europe/ukraine-protests.html

20. Reuters. (2013, December 1). "Violence at Protests in Ukraine." *The New York Times*. https://www.nytimes.com/video/world/europe/100000002579736/protests-turn-violent-in-ukraine.html

21. Mackey, R. (2013, December 2). "Video of Police Brutality in Kiev Fuels Rage." *The New York Times*. https://archive. nytimes.com/thelede.blogs.nytimes.com/2013/12/02/ video-of-police-brutality-in-kiev-fuels-rage/

22. Herszenhorn, D.M. (2013h, December 2). "Amid Unrest, Ukrainian President Defends Choice on Accords." *The New York Times*. https://www.nytimes.com/2013/12/03/world/ europe/ukraine-unrest.html

23. Herszenhorn, D.M. (2013i, December 4). "Kiev Protesters See Potent Ally Under a Spire." *The New York Times*. https:// www.nytimes.com/2013/12/05/world/europe/ukrainian-protesters-find-powerful-ally-in-orthodox-church.html

24. Kramer, A.E. (2013, December 6). "Pro-Government Ukrainians Take to Streets to Denounce European Social Values." *The New York Times*. https://www.nytimes. com/2013/12/07/world/europe/ukraine-protests.html

25. Herszenhorn, D.M. (2013j, December 9). "Ukraine's Forces Move Against Protesters, Dimming Hopes for Talks." *The New York Times*. https://www.nytimes.com/2013/12/10/ world/europe/ukraine-unrest.html

26. The New York Times. (2014, February 18). "Ukraine: 'Remove Riot Police' Plea." *The New York Times*. https:// www.nytimes.com/video/multimedia/100000002718261/ ukraine-remove-riot-police-plea.html

27. Halperin, C. (2014, February 18). "Scenes of Clashes in Ukraine." *The New York Times*. https://www.nytimes.com/ video/world/europe/100000002718456/scenes-of-clashes-in-ukraine.html?searchResultPosition=19

28. The New York Times. (2014, February 18). "Renewed Clashes in Ukraine Spark Worst Street Violence in More Than Three Weeks." *The New York Times*. https://www.nytimes.com/ video/multimedia/100000002718659/renewed-clashes-in-ukraine-spark-worst-street-violence-in-more-t.html

29. The New York Times. (2014, February 18). "Ukrainian Protesters and Police Light Up Kiev's Main Square with Petrol Bombs and Fireworks." *The New York Times*. https://www.nytimes.com/video/multimedia/100000002719331/ukrainian-protesters-and-police-light-up-kievs-main-square-with.html

30. The New York Times. (2014, February 19). "Satellite Images of the Protests in Kiev." *The New York Times*. https://www.nytimes.com/interactive/2014/02/18/world/europe/kiev-protests-satellite-imagery.html

31. The New York Times. (2014, February 18). "Ukrainian Protesters Attack Headquarters of President Yanukovich's Party." *The New York Times*. https://www.nytimes.com/video/multimedia/100000002718356/ukrainian-protesters-attack-headquarters-of-president-yanukovich.html

32. The New York Times. (2014, February 19). "Violent Clashes in Ukraine Kill at Least 14 People." *The New York Times*. https://www.nytimes.com/video/multimedia/100000002720199/violent-clashes-in-ukraine-kill-at-least-14-people.html

33. The New York Times. (2014, February 19). "At Least 25 Dead in Clashes." *The New York Times*. https://www.nytimes.com/video/multimedia/100000002720494/at-least-25-dead-in-clashes.html

34. The New York Times. (2014, February 19). "EU Calls for Dialogue as Russia Demands Ukrainian Opposition Stops Bloodshed." *The New York Times*. https://www.nytimes.com/video/multimedia/100000002721048/eu-calls-for-dialogue-as-russia-demands-ukrainian-opposition-sto.html

35. The New York Times. (2014, February 18). "White House Urges Yanukovich to 'Deescalate Immediately' Situation in Ukraine." *The New York Times*. https://www.nytimes.com/video/multimedia/100000002719646/white-house-urges-yanukovich-to-deescalate-immediately-situation.html

36. Higgins, A., & Kramer, A.E. (2014, February 19). "Ukraine Leader Strains for Grip as Chaos Spreads." *The New York Times*. https://www.nytimes.com/2014/02/20/world/europe/ukraine.html

37. Halperin, C. (2014, February 19). "Clashes Continue in Ukraine." *The New York Times*. https://www.nytimes.com/video/world/europe/100000002721017/scenes-as-clashes-continue-in-ukraine.html

38. The New York Times. (2014i, February 19). "Ukrainian Government Calls Protest 'Coup Attempt' as Sanctions Debate Emerges." *The New York Times*. https://www.nytimes.com/video/multimedia/100000002721328/ukrainian-government-calls-protest-coup-attempt-as-sanctions-deb.html

39. The New York Times. (2014k, February 19). "Woman Shot During Protests in Western Ukraine." *The New York Times*. https://www.nytimes.com/video/multimedia/100000002721511/woman-shot-during-protests-in-western-ukraine.html

40. Halperin, C. (2014, February 19). "Obama Reacts to Unrest in Ukraine." *The New York Times*. https://www.nytimes.com/video/world/europe/100000002722297/obama-reacts-to-unrest-in-ukraine.html

41. Kramer, A.E., & Higgins, A. (2014, February 20). "Ukraine's Forces Escalate Attacks Against Protesters." *The New York Times*. https://www.nytimes.com/2014/02/21/world/europe/ukraine.html

42. The New York Times. (2014l, February 20). "Gunfire, Violence in Kiev Despite 'Truce.'" *The New York Times*. https://www.nytimes.com/video/multimedia/100000002723463/gunfire-violence-in-kiev-despite-truce.html

43. The New York Times. (2014l, February 20). "Death Toll Mounts in Ukraine as Leaders Scramble for Peace."

The New York Times. https://www.nytimes.com/video/multimedia/100000002723698/death-toll-mounts-in-ukraine-as-leaders-scramble-for-peace.html

44. Perpetua, S., & El-Naggar, M. (2014, February 20). "The Ukraine Divide, Explained." *The New York Times.* https://www.nytimes.com/video/world/europe/100000002724416/the-ukraine-divide-explained.html

45. Higgins, A., & Kramer, A.E. (2014, February 21). "Ukraine Has Deal, But Both Russia and Protesters Appear Wary." *The New York Times.* https://www.nytimes.com/2014/02/22/world/europe/ukraine.html

46. The New York Times. (2014n, February 21). "Negotiators Reach Tentative Deal in Ukraine." *The New York Times.* https://www.nytimes.com/video/multimedia/100000002726300/negotiators-reach-tentative-deal-in-ukraine.html

47. Higgins, A. (2014, February 22). "With President's Departure, Ukraine Looks Toward a Murky Future." *The New York Times.* https://www.nytimes.com/2014/02/23/world/europe/with-presidents-departure-ukraine-looks-toward-a-murky-future.html

48. The New York Times. (2014o, February 22). "Ukraine's Yanukovich Says Not Resigning or Leaving Ukraine." *The New York Times.* https://www.nytimes.com/video/multimedia/100000002728886/ukraines-yanukovich-says-not-resigning-or-leaving-ukraine.html

49. The New York Times. (2014o, February 22). "As Ukrainian Parliament Celebrates, Yanukovich Denounces Coup." *The New York Times.* https://www.nytimes.com/video/multimedia/100000002729181/as-ukrainian-parliament-celebrates-yanukovich-denounces-coup.html

50. The New York Times. (2014q, February 22). "Ukrainian Parliament Votes to Oust President Yanukovich." *The New York Times.* https://www.nytimes.com/video/multimedia/

100000002728884/ukrainian-parliament-votes-to-oust-president-yanukovich.html

51. Perpetua, S. (2014, February 22). "Parliament Votes to Dismiss Yanukovych." *The New York Times*. https://www.nytimes.com/video/world/europe/100000002728851/parliament-votes-to-dismiss-yanukovych.html

52. Olsen, E. (2014, February 23). "Declaring Victory in Kiev." *The New York Times*. https://www.nytimes.com/video/world/europe/100000002729580/declaring-victory-in-kiev.html

53. Chivers, C.J., & Sneider, N. (2014, May 2). "Ukrainians Strike Rebel-Held City as Fighting Spreads." *The New York Times*. https://www.nytimes.com/2014/05/03/world/europe/ukraine.html

54. The New York Times. (2014r, May 2). "Rebels Shoot at Ukrainian Helicopters, Violence Erupts." *The New York Times*. https://www.nytimes.com/video/multimedia/100000002860052/rebels-shoot-at-ukrainian-helicopters-violence-erupts.html

55. The New York Times. (2014s, May 3). "Dozens Killed in Building Fire and Clashes in Ukraine's Odessa." *The New York Times*. https://www.nytimes.com/video/multimedia/100000002860284/dozens-killed-in-building-fire-and-clashes-in-ukraines-odessa.html

56. Smale, A., & Kramer, A.E. (2014, May 3). "Ukraine Presses Pro-Russia Militants After Fighting Spreads to a Port City." *The New York Times*. https://www.nytimes.com/2014/05/04/world/europe/ukraine.html

57. Kramer, A.E. (2014, May 5). "Ukraine's Reins Weaken as Chaos Spreads." *The New York Times*. https://www.nytimes.com/2014/05/05/world/europe/kievs-reins-weaken-as-chaos-spreads.html

58. The New York Times. (2014t, May 5). "Pro-Unity Ukrainians Claim Victory in Odessa Square." *The New York Times*. https://

www.nytimes.com/video/multimedia/100000002862107/
pro-unity-ukrainians-claim-victory-in-odessa-square.html

59. Cumming-Bruce, N. (2014, May 16). "U.N. Finds Rising Human Rights Violations in Ukraine." *The New York Times.* https://www.nytimes.com/2014/05/17/world/europe/united-nations-human-rights-ukraine.html

60. Reuters. (2020, August 9). "Protests Break Out in Belarus After Election That Critics Call Rigged." *The New York Times.* https://www.nytimes.com/video/world/europe/100000007280596/protests-belarus-election.html

61. Reuters. (2020, August 10). "Police Clash with Protesters in Belarus." *The New York Times.* https://www.nytimes.com/video/world/100000007281204/belarus-election-protests.html

62. The Associated Press. (2020, August 16). "Tens of Thousands Demonstrate Against the Government in Belarus." *The New York Times.* https://www.nytimes.com/video/world/europe/100000007291274/belarus-protest.html

63. Nechepurenko, I., & Higgins, A. (2020, August 10). "Belarus's Leader Vows to Crush Protests After Claiming Landslide Election Win." *The New York Times.* https://www.nytimes.com/2020/08/10/world/europe/belarus-election.html

64. Nechepurenko, I., & Troianovski, A. (2020, August 11). "After Vote That Many Called Rigged, Challenger to Belarus Leader Leaves." *The New York Times.* https://www.nytimes.com/2020/08/11/world/europe/belarus-election-Svetlana-Tikhanovskaya.html

65. Reuters. (2020, August 11). "'I Made a Very Difficult Decision,' Belarus Challenger Says." *The New York Times.* https://www.nytimes.com/video/world/100000007283284/belarus-elections.html

66. Specia, M. (2020, August 13). "Who is Svetlana Tikhanovskaya, Belarus's Unlikely Opposition Leader?" *The New York Times*. https://www.nytimes.com/2020/08/13/world/europe/belarus-opposition-svetlana-tikhanovskaya.html

67. Victor, D. (2020, August 13). "What's Happening in Belarus?" *The New York Times*. https://www.nytimes.com/2020/08/13/world/europe/belarus-protests-guide.html

68. Nechepurenko, I., & Troianovski, A. (2020, August 13). "Mass Beatings and Detentions in Belarus as President Clings to Power." *The New York Times*. https://www.nytimes.com/2020/08/13/world/europe/beatings-detentions-belarus-lukashenko.html

69. Nechepurenko, I., & Troianovski, A. (2020, August 14). "Workers Join Belarus Protests, as Leader's Base Turns Against Him." *The New York Times*. https://www.nytimes.com/2020/08/14/world/europe/Belarus-strike-Aleksandr-Lukashenko.html

70. The Associated Press and Reuters. (2020, August 14). "Belarus Workers Rally Against Government in Mass Demonstration." *The New York Times*. https://www.nytimes.com/video/world/europe/100000007289372/belarus-workers-demonstration.html

71. Nechepurenko, I. (2020, August 21). "Laying Down His Tools, Belarus Worker Takes Up Mantle of Protest Leader." *The New York Times*. https://www.nytimes.com/2020/08/21/world/europe/belarus-protest-election-Lukashenko.html

72. Mort, V. (2020, August 14). "My Country is Under Attack." *The New York Times*. https://www.nytimes.com/2020/08/14/opinion/belarus-protests-violence.html

73. Antusevich, S. (2020, August 20). "Impossible, Unthinkable Change is Happening in Belarus." *The New York Times*. https://www.nytimes.com/2020/08/20/opinion/belarus-strikes-workers.html

74. The Editorial Board. (2020, August 15). "A Dictatorship in Belarus is Shaken." *The New York Times*. https://www.nytimes.com/2020/08/14/opinion/belarus-protests.html

75. Erlanger, S. (2020, August 19). "E.U. Rejects Belarus Election, Without Demanding a New One." *The New York Times*. https://www.nytimes.com/2020/08/19/world/europe/eu-belarus-election.html

76. Higgins, A., & Nechepurenko, I. (2020, August 15). "Under Siege in Belarus, Lukashenko Turns to Putin." *The New York Times*. https://www.nytimes.com/2020/08/15/world/europe/belarus-russia-Lukashenko-Putin.html

77. Higgins, A. (2020, August 27). "Putin Warns Belarus Protesters: Don't Push Too Hard." *The New York Times*. https://www.nytimes.com/2020/08/27/world/europe/belarus-russia-putin.html

78. Triebert, C., Engelbrecht, C., Matsnev, O., & Chavar, A.J. (2020, August 17). "A Crackdown in Belarus Backfires. Here's What Videos Show." *The New York Times*. https://www.nytimes.com/2020/08/17/world/europe/belarus-crackdown-protests-minsk.html

79. Nechepurenko, I. (2020, August 18). "Belarus Leader Rejects Compromise and Pours Scorn on Opposition." *The New York Times*. https://www.nytimes.com/2020/08/18/world/europe/belarus-protests-lukashenko.html

80. Reuters. (2020, August 23). "Belarus President Carries Assault Rifle Outside Minsk Palace." *The New York Times*. https://www.nytimes.com/video/world/europe/100000007303359/belarus-president-rifle.html

81. Nechepurenko, I., & Troianovski, A. (2020, August 21). "In Belarus Town, People Tasted a Bite of Freedom. It Lasted 2 Days." *The New York Times*. https://www.nytimes.com/2020/08/21/world/europe/grodno-belarus-protests.html

82. Higgins, A. (2020, August 27). "Putin Warns Belarus Protesters: Don't Push Too Hard." *The New York Times.* https://www.nytimes.com/2020/08/27/world/europe/belarus-russia-putin.html

83. Troianovski, A., & Nechepurenko, I. (2021, May 23). "Belarus Forces Down Plane to Seize Dissident; Europe Sees 'State Hijacking.'" *The New York Times.* https://www.nytimes.com/2021/05/23/world/europe/ryanair-belarus.html

84. Vigdor, N., & Nechepurenko, I. (2021, May 24). "Who is Roman Protasevich, the Captive Journalist in Belarus?" *The New York Times.* https://www.nytimes.com/2021/05/23/world/europe/roman-protasevich.html

85. Stevis-Gridneff, M., & Pronczuk, M. (2021, May 24). "E.U. Leaders are Meeting Now to Consider New Sanctions Against Belarus." *The New York Times.* https://www.nytimes.com/2021/05/24/world/europe/eu-leaders-are-meeting-now-to-consider-new-sanctions-against-belarus.html

86. Chokshi, N., & Reed, S. (2021, May 24). "Airlines Start Skirting Belarus After It Forced Down a Plane." *The New York Times.* https://www.nytimes.com/2021/05/24/business/economy/belarus-ryanair.html

87. Troianovski, A. (2021, May 27). "Russia Rejects Some Flight Plans, as Belarus Grows More Isolated." *The New York Times.* https://www.nytimes.com/2021/05/27/world/europe/belarus-forced-landing-protasevich.html

88. Ives, M. (2021, May 29). "U.S. to Reimpose Sanctions on Belarus Over Forced Plane Landing." *The New York Times.* https://www.nytimes.com/2021/05/29/world/belarus-plane-sanctions.html

89. Troianovski, A. (2021, May 24). "Belarus is Isolated as Other Countries Move to Ban Flights." *The New York Times.*

https://www.nytimes.com/2021/05/24/world/europe/belarus-flight-ban.html

90. Nechepurenko, I. (2021, May 24). "Passengers Recall the Fear that Gripped the Dissident Journalist as Their Flight was Diverted." *The New York Times.* https://www.nytimes.com/2021/05/24/world/europe/passengers-recall-the-fear-that-gripped-the-dissident-journalist-as-their-flight-was-diverted.html

91. The Associated Press. (2021, May 25). "Belarus Perpetrated a 'State Hijacking,' European Union Says." *The New York Times.* https://www.nytimes.com/video/world/europe/100000007780891/european-union-belarus-flight-sanctions.html

92. The Editorial Board. (2021, May 24). "A State-Sponsored Skyjacking Can't Go Unanswered." *The New York Times.* https://www.nytimes.com/2021/05/24/opinion/belarus-plane-protasevich.html

93. Higgins, A., & Kramer, A.E. (2021, May 25). "Roman Protasevich: A Belarus Activist Who 'Refused to Live in Fear.'" *The New York Times.* https://www.nytimes.com/2021/05/25/world/europe/belarus-news-roman-protasevich.html

94. Troianovski, A., & Nechepurenko, I. (2021, June 4). "Putin Seeks Distance from Belarus Turmoil and Says Russia is 'Neutral.'" *The New York Times.* https://www.nytimes.com/2021/06/04/world/europe/belarus-activist-roman-protasevich.html

95. Kramer, A.E. (2021, June 11). "'It's All Ruined': Young Woman Caught Up in Belarus Clampdown." *The New York Times.* https://www.nytimes.com/2021/06/11/world/europe/belarus-roman-protasevich-friend-detained.html

96. Nechepurenko, I. (2021, June 14). "Jailed Belarusian Activist Praises President in Surprise Public Appearance."

The New York Times. https://www.nytimes.com/2021/06/14/world/europe/jailed-belarus-activist-protasevich.html

97. Robles, F. (2021, July 11). "Cubans Denounce 'Misery' in Biggest Protests in Decades." *The New York Times.* https://www.nytimes.com/2021/07/11/world/americas/cuba-crisis-protests.html

98. The Associated Press. (2021, July 12). "Cubans Take to the Streets to Protest Economic Crisis." *The New York Times.* https://www.nytimes.com/video/world/americas/100000007861939/cuba-protests.html

99. Lopez, O., & Londoño, E. (2021, July 12). "'Everyone Has a Tipping Point': Hunger Fuels Cuba's Protests." *The New York Times.* https://www.nytimes.com/2021/07/12/world/americas/cuba-protests-usa.html

100. Lopez, O., & Londoño, E. (2021, July 12). "'Everyone Has a Tipping Point': Hunger Fuels Cuba's Protests." *The New York Times.* https://www.nytimes.com/2021/07/12/world/americas/cuba-protests-usa.html

101. Janetsky, M. (2021, July 13). "'Patria y Vida' – Homeland and Life – Watchwords in Cuba's Protests." *The New York Times.* https://www.nytimes.com/2021/07/13/world/americas/cuba-protests-Patria-y-Vida.html

102. Londoño, E., & Robles, F. (2021, July 13). "'The Spark Has Been Lit': Cuban Dissidents Feel Emboldened Despite Crackdown." *The New York Times.* https://www.nytimes.com/2021/07/13/world/americas/cuba-protest-arrests.html

103. The New York Times. (2021, July 15). "Cubans Take to the Streets." *The New York Times.* https://www.nytimes.com/2021/07/15/podcasts/the-daily/cuba-protests.html

104. Sánchez, Y. (2021, July 19). "The New Generation of Cubans Who Won't Be Silenced." *The New York Times.* https://www.nytimes.com/2021/07/19/opinion/cuba-protest-freedom-youth.html

105. Corrales, J. (2021, July 14). "The Day Cubans Lost Their Fear." *The New York Times*. https://www.nytimes.com/2021/07/14/opinion/international-world/cuba-protests-freedom.html

106. Mazzei, P. (2021, July 17). "Miami Embraces Cuba Protests: 'I Never Thought That This Day Would Come.'" *The New York Times*. https://www.nytimes.com/2021/07/17/us/cuba-protests-miami-florida.html

107. Jakes, L. (2021, July 22). "New U.S. Sanctions Aim to Punish Cuban Forces for Crackdowns on Protesters." *The New York Times*. https://www.nytimes.com/2021/07/22/us/politics/sanctions-cuba-protesters.html

108. The Associated Press. (2021, July 23). "'We Will Stand with the Cuban People,' U.S. State Department Says." *The New York Times*. https://www.nytimes.com/video/us/politics/100000007882141/sanctions-cuba-ned-price-state-department.html

109. Londoño, E., & Politi, D. (2021, July 28). "'Terror': Crackdown After Protests in Cuba Sends a Chilling Message." *The New York Times*. https://www.nytimes.com/2021/07/28/world/americas/cuba-protests-crackdown-arrests.html

110. Amnesty International. (2019, August 31). "India: Uncertain Destiny for Millions in Assam Post NRC." *Amnesty International UK*. https://www.amnesty.org.uk/press-releases/india-uncertain-destiny-millions-assam-post-nrc

111. Ratcliffe, R., & Bhattacharya, K. (2019, August 31). "India: Almost 2M People Left Off Assam Register of Citizens." *Guardian*. https://www.theguardian.com/global-development/2019/aug/31/india-almost-2m-people-left-off-assam-register-of-citizens

112. Chatterji, A.P., Desai, M., Mander, H., & Azad, A.K. (2021, September 9). "Detention, Criminalisation, Statelessness: The Aftermath of Assam's NRC." *Wire*. https://thewire.

in/rights/detention-criminalisation-statelessness-the-
aftermath-of-assams-nrc

113. Purkayastha, B.K. (2022, March 29). "31 Declared Foreigners
Died in Detention Centres from 2016 to 2021: Assam Govt."
Hindustan Times. https://www.hindustantimes.com/india-
news/31-declared-foreigners-died-in-detention-centres-
from-2016-to-2021-assam-govt-101648551804550.html

114. Kalita, K. (2022, February 10). "Over 1.43 Lakh People
Were Declared Foreigners in Assam." *Times of India*.
https://timesofindia.indiatimes.com/city/guwahati/over-
1-43-lakh-people-were-declared-foreigners-in-assam/
articleshow/89464774.cms

115. Schultz, K. (2018, July 30). "As India Clamps Down on
Migration, Millions May Lose Citizenship." *The New York
Times*. https://www.nytimes.com/2018/07/30/world/asia/
india-citizenship-assam-muslim.html

116. Bal, H.S. (2018, August 10). "Is India Creating Its Own
Rohingya?" *The New York Times*. https://www.nytimes.
com/2018/08/10/opinion/india-citizenship-assam-modi-
rohingyas.html

117. Goel, V., & Nordland, R. (2019, June 20). "With Mandate
from India's Voters, Modi Promises Improved Economy
Again." *The New York Times*. https://www.nytimes.
com/2019/06/20/world/asia/india-modi-economy.html

118. Hamid, S. (2019, September 26). "Why I Resigned From
the Gates Foundation." *The New York Times*. https://www.
nytimes.com/2019/09/26/opinion/modi-gates-award.html

119. Gettleman, J., & Raj, S. (2019, December 9). "India Steps
Toward Making Naturalization Harder for Muslims." *The
New York Times*. https://www.nytimes.com/2019/12/09/
world/asia/india-muslims-citizenship-narendra-modi.html

120. Victor, D. (2019, December 17). "Why People are Protesting
in India." *The New York Times*. https://www.nytimes.

com/2019/12/17/world/asia/india-protests-citizenship-muslims.html

121. Surabhi, R.D. (2019, December 27). "We are Witnessing a Rediscovery of India's Republic." *The New York Times*. https://www.nytimes.com/2019/12/27/opinion/india-constitution-protests.html

122. Gettleman, J., & Kumar, H. (2019, August 17). "India Plans Big Detention Camps for Migrants. Muslims are Afraid." *The New York Times*. https://www.nytimes.com/2019/08/17/world/asia/india-muslims-narendra-modi.html

123. Raj, S., & Gettleman, J. (2019, August 31). "A Mass Citizenship Check in India Leaves 2 Million People in Limbo." *The New York Times*. https://www.nytimes.com/2019/08/31/world/asia/india-muslim-citizen-list.html

124. Ahmed, K.A. (2019, September 11). "Why is India Making Its Own People Stateless?" *The New York Times*. https://www.nytimes.com/2019/09/11/opinion/india-assam-stateless-bengalis-muslim.html

125. The Editorial Board. (2019, December 18). "Modi Makes His Bigotry Even Clearer." *The New York Times*. https://www.nytimes.com/2019/12/18/opinion/india-citizenship-bill-muslims.html

126. Schultz, K. (2019, December 22). "Modi Defends Indian Citizenship Law Amid Violent Protests." *The New York Times*. https://www.nytimes.com/2019/12/22/world/asia/modi-india-citizenship-law.html

127. Singh, K.D., & Raj, S. (2020, April 4). "'Muslims are Foreigners': Inside India's Campaign to Decide Who is a Citizen." *The New York Times*. https://www.nytimes.com/2020/04/04/world/asia/india-modi-citizenship-muslims-assam.html

128. Deb, S. (2021, September 15). "'They are Manufacturing Foreigners': How India Disenfranchises Muslims." *The*

New York Times. https://www.nytimes.com/2021/09/15/magazine/india-assam-muslims.html

129. Singh, K.D. (2020, September 8). "'The Lockdown Killed My Father': Farmer Suicides Add to India's Virus Misery." *The New York Times*. https://www.nytimes.com/2020/09/08/world/asia/india-coronavirus-farmer-suicides-lockdown.html

130. The Associated Press. (2020, November 30). "Farmers in India Protest New Agricultural Policies." *The New York Times*. https://www.nytimes.com/video/world/asia/100000007479323/india-farmers-protest.html

131. Schmall, E. (2020, December 4). "Indian Farmers' Protests Spread, in Challenge to Modi." *The New York Times*. https://www.nytimes.com/2020/12/04/world/asia/india-farmers-protest-pollution-coronavirus.html

132. Singh, K.D. (2020, December 8). "India's Police Detain Opposition Leaders as Farmers' Agitation Grows." *The New York Times*. https://www.nytimes.com/2020/12/08/world/asia/india-farmer-protests-police-detain.html

133. Mashal, M., Singh, K.D., & Khandelwal, S. (2021, January 9). "In the Cold and Rain, India's Farmers Press Their Stand Against Modi." *The New York Times*. https://www.nytimes.com/2021/01/09/world/asia/india-farmers-protest.html

134. Mashal, M., & Kumar, H. (2021, January 12). "Indian Farmers Vow to Continue Protest, Unappeased by Court Ruling." *The New York Times*. https://www.nytimes.com/2021/01/12/world/asia/india-farmers-protest-court-law.html

135. Bal, H.S. (2021, January 14). "Why are India's Farmers Angry?" *The New York Times*. https://www.nytimes.com/2021/01/14/opinion/india-farmers-protest.html

136. Mashal, M., Schmall, E., & Kumar, H. (2021, January 26). "As Angry Farmers Take to New Delhi's Streets, Protests Turn Violent." *The New York Times*. https://www.nytimes.

com/2021/01/25/world/asia/india-farmers-protests-delhi.
html

137. Schmall, E. (2021, October 4). "Eight Killed as Tensions Around India's Farm Protests Worsen." *The New York Times*. https://www.nytimes.com/2021/10/04/world/asia/india-farmer-protests.html

138. Singh, K.D. (2021, February 10). "Twitter Blocks Accounts in India as Modi Pressures Social Media." *The New York Times*. https://www.nytimes.com/2021/02/10/technology/india-twitter.html

139. Ovide, S. (2021, February 11). "Twitter vs. India." *The New York Times*. https://www.nytimes.com/2021/02/11/technology/twitter-vs-india.html

140. Mashal, M., & Yasir, S. (2021, February 3). "Modi's Response to Farmer Protests in India Stirs Fears of a Pattern." *The New York Times*. https://www.nytimes.com/2021/02/03/world/asia/india-modi-farmer-protest-censorship.html

141. Yasir, S., & Schmall, E. (2021, May 25). "Indian Police Visit Twitter Offices as Modi Goes on Pandemic Offense." *The New York Times*. https://www.nytimes.com/2021/05/25/technology/covid-india-twitter.html

142. Schmall, E., & Kumar, H. (2021, November 15). "Two Journalists Arrested as India Cracks Down on Media." *The New York Times*. https://www.nytimes.com/2021/11/15/world/asia/india-journalists-arrested-crackdown-tripura.html

143. Schmall, E. (2021, November 20). "How India's Farmers, Organized and Well Funded, Faced Down Modi." *The New York Times*. https://www.nytimes.com/2021/11/20/world/asia/india-modi-farmer-protests.html

144. Gladstone, R., & Neuman, W. (2013, July 2). "New Rumor of Snowden Flight Raises Tensions." *The New York Times*. https://www.nytimes.com/2013/07/03/world/europe/snowden.html

145. Neuman, W., & Smale, A. (2013, July 3). "Barring of Bolivian Plane Infuriates Latin America as Snowden Case Widens." *The New York Times*. https://www.nytimes.com/2013/07/04/world/snowden.html

146. Neuman, W., & Herszenhorn, D.M. (2013, July 5). "Venezuela Offers Asylum to Snowden." *The New York Times*. https://www.nytimes.com/2013/07/06/world/snowden.html

147. Herszenhorn, D.M., & Archibold, R.C. (2013, July 7). "Russian Official Says Venezuela is the 'Best Solution' for Snowden." *The New York Times*. https://www.nytimes.com/2013/07/07/world/europe/russian-official-says-venezuela-is-the-best-solution-for-snowden.html

148. Neuman, W., & Archibold, R.C. (2013, July 12). "U.S. is Pressing Latin Americans to Reject Snowden." *The New York Times*. https://www.nytimes.com/2013/07/12/world/americas/us-is-pressing-latin-americans-to-reject-snowden.html

149. Herszenhorn, D.M., & Roth, A. (2013, July 17). "Putin Does Not Expect Ties with U.S. to Be Harmed by Snowden Case." *The New York Times*. https://www.nytimes.com/2013/07/18/world/europe/putin-does-not-expect-ties-with-us-to-be-harmed-by-snowden-case.html

150. Neuman, W. (2013, September 21). "U.S. Denies Trying to Bar Venezuelan President from Airspace." *The New York Times*. https://www.nytimes.com/2013/09/21/world/americas/us-denies-trying-to-bar-venezuelan-president-from-airspace.html

Conclusion

1. Ahn, C. (2011, August 5). "Unwanted Missiles for a Korean Island." *The New York Times*. https://www.nytimes.com/2011/08/06/opinion/06iht-edahn06.html

2. Steinem, G. (2011, August 6). "The Arms Race Intrudes on Paradise." *The New York Times*. https://www.nytimes.com/2011/08/07/opinion/sunday/Steinem-the-arms-race-intrudes-on-a-south-korean-paradise.html

3. The New York Times. (2011, August 10). "U.S. Defenses in the Pacific." *The New York Times*. https://www.nytimes.com/2011/08/11/opinion/11iht-edlet11.html

4. Nam, J. (2011, August 15). "A Naval Base in South Korea." *The New York Times*. https://www.nytimes.com/2011/08/16/opinion/a-naval-base-in-south-korea.html

5. Hoey, M. (2011, August 18). "A Naval Base in South Korea (Continued)." *The New York Times*. https://www.nytimes.com/2011/08/18/opinion/a-naval-base-in-south-korea-continued.html

6. Steinem, G. (2011, August 6). "The Arms Race Intrudes on Paradise." *The New York Times*. https://www.nytimes.com/2011/08/07/opinion/sunday/Steinem-the-arms-race-intrudes-on-a-south-korean-paradise.html

7. Sang-Hun, C. (2011, September 2). "South Korean Police Detain Island Activists Opposed to Base." *The New York Times*. https://www.nytimes.com/2011/09/03/world/asia/03korea.html

8. Sang-Hun, C. (2015, February 26). "South Korean Island Grows Wary After Welcoming the Chinese." *The New York Times*. https://www.nytimes.com/2015/02/26/world/south-korean-island-grows-wary-after-welcoming-the-chinese.html

9. Sang-Hun, C. (2018, September 12). "Migrants Expected Warm Welcome on Korean Resort Island. They Were Wrong." *The New York Times*. https://www.nytimes.com/2018/09/12/world/asia/south-korea-jeju-yemen-refugees.html

10. Sang-Hun, C. (2018, October 17). "South Korea Denies Refugee Status to Hundreds of Fleeing Yemenis." *The New*

York Times. https://www.nytimes.com/2018/10/17/world/asia/south-korea-yemeni-refugees.html

11. Sang-Hun, C. (2019, May 28). "Memories of Massacres Were Long Suppressed Here. Tourists Now Retrace the Atrocities." *The New York Times*. https://www.nytimes.com/2019/05/28/world/asia/south-korea-jeju-massacres.html

12. Koleilat, L. (2019). "Spaces of Dissent: Everyday Resistance in Gangjeong Village, Jeju Island." *Cross-Currents: East Asian History and Culture Review, 1*(33).

13. Bielawa, L. (2011, June 15). "In Berlin, Moved by Music, Place and Memory." *The New York Times*. https://archive.nytimes.com/opinionator.blogs.nytimes.com/2011/06/15/in-berlin-moved-by-music-place-and-memory/?searchResultPosition=14

14. Olsen, E.L. (2011, September 1). "At Historic Berlin Airport, Picnics and Roller Skates." *The New York Times*. https://archive.nytimes.com/intransit.blogs.nytimes.com/2011/09/01/at-historic-berlin-airport-picnics-and-roller-skates/

15. Kim, L. (2012, December 6). "Up in the Air." *The New York Times*. https://archive.nytimes.com/latitude.blogs.nytimes.com/2012/12/06/up-in-the-air/

16. Kugel, S. (2013, May 28). "After the Thaw: Outdoor Fun in Berlin." *The New York Times*. https://archive.nytimes.com/frugaltraveler.blogs.nytimes.com/2013/05/28/after-the-thaw-outdoor-fun-in-berlin/

17. Huetteman, E. (2015, September 11). "Berlin Airport Used in Cold War Airlift Gets a New Humanitarian Mission." *The New York Times*. https://www.nytimes.com/2015/09/13/world/europe/berlin-tempelhof-airport-to-house-refugees.html

18. Hammer, J. (2016, May 12). "My Berlin: Reckoning with the Past." *The New York Times*. https://www.nytimes.com/2016/05/15/travel/berlin-germany.html

19. Rogers, T. (2017, September 12). "In Berlin, an Iconic Theater Gets a New Leader. Cue the Protests." *The New York Times*. https://www.nytimes.com/2017/09/12/arts/chris-dercon-volksbuehne-opening-tempelhof.html

20. McConnon, A. (2019, June 4). "The Largest Start-Up Ecosystem of the New Berlin." *The New York Times*. https://www.nytimes.com/2019/06/04/business/the-largest-start-up-ecosystem-of-the-new-berlin.html

21. Bennhold, K. (2020, October 24). "New Airport, Beleaguered Symbol of 'Irreverent' Berlin, is Opening at Long Last." *The New York Times*. https://www.nytimes.com/2020/10/24/world/europe/berlin-germany-new-airport.html

22. Bennhold, K. (2020, October 24). "New Airport, Beleaguered Symbol of 'Irreverent' Berlin, is Opening at Long Last." *The New York Times*. https://www.nytimes.com/2020/10/24/world/europe/berlin-germany-new-airport.html

23. Smale, A. (2015, February 9). "Crisis in Ukraine Underscores Opposing Lessons of Cold War." *The New York Times*. https://www.nytimes.com/2015/02/09/world/crisis-in-ukraine-underscores-opposing-lessons-of-cold-war.html

24. Rose, M., & Agarwal, S. (2020, April 4). "The Military Should Airlift New York City's Coronavirus Patients." *The New York Times*. https://www.nytimes.com/2020/04/04/opinion/coronavirus-new-york-hospitals-airlift.html

25. Schmitt, E. (2021, August 21). "U.S. Seeks to Compel Airlines to Provide Planes to Speed Evacuation of Afghans." *The New York Times*. https://www.nytimes.com/2021/08/21/world/asia/us-airline-pentagon-flight-evacuation.html

26. Hambouz, A., & Khan, J. (2008, May 21). "Where History Takes Off." *The New York Times*. https://archive.nytimes.com/learning.blogs.nytimes.com/2008/05/21/where-history-takes-off/

27. Kuhn, A. (2022, September 7). "Survivors of a Massacre in South Korea are Still Seeking an Apology from the U.S." *NPR*. https://www.npr.org/2022/09/07/1121427407/survivors-of-a-massacre-in-south-korea-are-still-seeking-an-apology-from-the-u-s

IFF
BOOKS

ACADEMIC AND SPECIALIST

Iff Books publishes non-fiction. It aims to work with authors and
titles that augment our understanding of the human condition,
society and civilisation, and the world or universe in which we live.
If you have enjoyed this book, why not tell other readers by
posting a review on your preferred book site.
Recent bestsellers from Iff Books are:

Why Materialism Is Baloney
How true skeptics know there is no death and fathom answers
to life, the universe, and everything
Bernardo Kastrup
A hard-nosed, logical, and skeptic non-materialist metaphysics,
according to which the body is in mind, not mind in the body.
Paperback: 978-1-78279-362-5 ebook: 978-1-78279-361-8

The Fall
Steve Taylor
The Fall discusses human achievement versus the issues of war,
patriarchy and social inequality.
Paperback: 978-1-78535-804-3 ebook: 978-1-78535-805-0

Brief Peeks Beyond
Critical essays on metaphysics, neuroscience, free will,
skepticism and culture
Bernardo Kastrup
An incisive, original, compelling alternative to current mainstream
cultural views and assumptions.
Paperback: 978-1-78535-018-4 ebook: 978-1-78535-019-1

Framespotting
Changing how you look at things changes how
you see them
Laurence & Alison Matthews
A punchy, upbeat guide to framespotting. Spot deceptions and
hidden assumptions; swap growth for growing up. See and be free.
Paperback: 978-1-78279-689-3 ebook: 978-1-78279-822-4

Is There an Afterlife?
David Fontana
Is there an Afterlife? If so what is it like? How do Western ideas
of the afterlife compare with Eastern? David Fontana presents the
historical and contemporary evidence for survival of
physical death.
Paperback: 978-1-90381-690-5

Nothing Matters
a book about nothing
Ronald Green
Thinking about Nothing opens the world to everything by
illuminating new angles to old problems and stimulating new
ways of thinking.
Paperback: 978-1-84694-707-0 ebook: 978-1-78099-016-3

Panpsychism
The Philosophy of the Sensuous Cosmos
Peter Ells
Are free will and mind chimeras? This book, anti-materialistic but
respecting science, answers: No! Mind is foundational
to all existence.
Paperback: 978-1-84694-505-2 ebook: 978-1-78099-018-7

Punk Science
Inside the Mind of God
Manjir Samanta-Laughton
Many have experienced unexplainable phenomena; God, psychic abilities, extraordinary healing and angelic encounters. Can cutting-edge science actually explain phenomena previously thought of as 'paranormal'?
Paperback: 978-1-90504-793-2

The Vagabond Spirit of Poetry
Edward Clarke
Spend time with the wisest poets of the modern age and of the past, and let Edward Clarke remind you of the importance of poetry in our industrialized world.
Paperback: 978-1-78279-370-0 ebook: 978-1-78279-369-4

Readers of ebooks can buy or view any of these bestsellers by clicking on the live link in the title. Most titles are published in paperback and as an ebook. Paperbacks are available in traditional bookshops. Both print and ebook formats are available online. Find more titles and sign up to our readers' newsletter at
www.collectiveinkbooks.com/non-fiction
Follow us on Facebook at
www.facebook.com/CINonFiction